English Diatonic Music
1887–1955

English Diatonic Music
1887–1955

MATTHEW RILEY

OXFORD
UNIVERSITY PRESS

Oxford University Press is a department of the University of Oxford.
It furthers the University's objective of excellence in research, scholarship,
and education by publishing worldwide. Oxford is a registered trade mark of
Oxford University Press in the UK and certain other countries.

Published in the United States of America by Oxford University Press
198 Madison Avenue, New York, NY 10016, United States of America.

© Oxford University Press 2025

All rights reserved. No part of this publication may be reproduced, stored in a retrieval system, transmitted, used for text and data mining, or used for training artificial intelligence, in any form or by any means, without the prior permission in writing of Oxford University Press, or as expressly permitted by law, by license or under terms agreed with the appropriate reprographics rights organization. Inquiries concerning reproduction outside the scope of the above should be sent to the Rights Department, Oxford University Press, at the address above.

You must not circulate this work in any other form
and you must impose this same condition on any acquirer

CIP data is on file at the Library of Congress

ISBN 978-0-19-768452-8

DOI: 10.1093/oso/9780197684528.001.0001

Printed by Marquis Book Printing, Canada

Contents

List of Music Examples and Tables	vii
Introduction: Re-mapping English Music	1
1. Processional Diatonicism I: Hubert Parry and *Blest Pair of Sirens*	11
Blest Pair of Sirens and Evolutionism: The Influences of Wesley and Wagner	18
Processional Diatonicism in *Blest Pair of Sirens*: Topic and Schemata	27
Public Processional Contexts	38
Parry, Processional Diatonicism, and Nationalism after *Blest Pair of Sirens*	40
2. Processional Diatonicism II: Elgar and Vaughan Williams to 1914	46
Elgar: Populism and Spectacle	47
Elgar: Nation and Spirituality	55
Elgar: Schemata, Transformation, and Apotheosis	64
Vaughan Williams's Words on Parry and Elgar	75
Diatonicism in Vaughan Williams's 'First Maturity' Choral Works	79
3. Diatonic Pastoral Music, 1914–1925: Vaughan Williams and Howells	90
Diatonic Pastoral as a Musical Topic	92
Form and Process	97
Mystical Pastoral: Vaughan Williams's 'Satellite Topics' and Visions of Eternity	104
Case Study: *The Lark Ascending*	116
Legacy: Competing Schools of English Pastoral Music	123
4. Songs of Pain and Beauty: On English Diatonic Song	127
Contexts	129
Style, Semantics, and Scope	131
New Paths around 1910, Taken and not Taken	132
Drawing-room Rapture and the Open ii^7	135
'Loveliest of Trees' as Musical Memorial	146
Gurney's Traditionalism: The Open ii^7 Sets the Georgians	149
Finzi's Traditionalism	156
Finzi's First 'English' Synthesis: Pastoral and Commemoration	162
Finzi's Later Hardy Cycles: Processional Diatonicism Revived	167

5. Tracts for the Times: English Diatonic Music at Peace and War,
   1937–1953   178
   Coronations, Festivals, and Commissions   180
   Orchestral Marches   183
   Vaughan Williams's Unison Hymns   188
   Cantatas   199
   Vaughan Williams's Symphony No. 5   212

6. The New Ecstasy: Howells and Tippett   226
   Howells's New Style   227
   Howells's English Traditions: Medievalism, Vaughan Williams,
      and Parry   234
   Tippett's Diatonicism   243
   Tippett and Vaughan Williams   250
   Concerto for Double String Orchestra   253
      The Midsummer Marriage   255
      Fantasia Concertante on a Theme of Corelli   261
   Conclusion and Legacy   263

Glossary of Conventions of English Diatonic Music   267
Appendix A: The Grail Knights' Communion Hymn 'Wein und Brot'
   from Parsifal *Act I as 'Begetter' of English Diatonic Music*   271
Appendix B: 'Regular Orders' of English Diatonic Conventions   273
Notes   275
Bibliography   291
Index   299

Music Examples and Tables

Ex. 1.1	Samuel Sebastian Wesley, 'Ascribe unto the Lord', bars 1–21 (reduction)	21
Ex. 1.2	Parry, *Blest Pair of Sirens*, bars 1–13[1] (reduction)	28
Ex. 1.3	Rising-fourth schema (outer voices) and typical first-level realization	30
Ex. 1.4	Stainer, 'God So Loved the World', *The Crucifixion*, bars 1–4 (reduction)	30
Ex. 1.5	Do–Re–Mi schema in first-level realizations	31
Ex. 1.6	'Meistersinger tetrachord' schemata	32
	(i) Meistersinger tetrachord and inversion	
	(ii) Wagner, *Die Meistersinger von Nürnberg*, Prelude, bars 1–4[1] (reduction)	
	(iii) Elgar, *Sea Pictures*, 'Sabbath Morning at Sea', bars 32–33 (reduction)	
Ex. 1.7	Parry, *Blest Pair of Sirens*, bars 1–12, schema analysis	34
Ex. 1.8	Walton, *Crown Imperial*, Coronation March, fig. 4, bars 1–8. 'Crown Imperial' by William Walton (1902–1983) © Oxford University Press 1937. All rights reserved.	36
Ex. 1.9	Parry, Symphony No. 3 'English', first movement, bars 22[2]–30	44
Ex. 2.1	Elgar, trio themes from orchestral marches	52
	(i) Pomp and Circumstance March No. 1, fig. I, bars 1–8 (reduction)	
	(ii) Pomp and Circumstance March No. 3, fig. G, bars 1–8 (reduction)	
	(iii) Pomp and Circumstance March No. 4, fig. G, bars 1–12 (reduction)	
	(iv) Empire March, fig. 8, bars 2–5 (reduction)	
	(v) Pomp and Circumstance March No. 5, fig. 9, bars 1–8 (reduction)	
Ex. 2.2	Elgar, 'trio style' in funeral marches	54
	(i) Funeral March, *Grania and Diarmid*, fig. H, bars 1–4 (reduction)	
	(ii) Symphony No. 2, second movement, fig. 68, bars 5[3]–9[2] (reduction)	
Ex. 2.3	Elgar, *Caractacus*, Scene 2, fig. 23, bars 1–4, 'Britain' theme (reduction)	56
Ex. 2.4	Elgar, 'Enigma' Variations, Variation IX ('Nimrod'), fig. 34, bar 5–fig. 35, bar 1[1] (reduction)	58
Ex. 2.5	Elgar, *The Dream of Gerontius*, Part I, fig. 37, bars 1–6 (orchestral parts in reduction)	59
Ex. 2.6	Elgar, *The Apostles*, Prelude, fig. 7, bar 2–fig. 8, 'Church' motive (reduction)	61
Ex. 2.7	Elgar, *The Apostles*, Part I, fig. 53, bars 1–6 (reduction)	62
Ex. 2.8	Elgar, *The Apostles*, Part II, fig. 236, bars 1–7 (reduction)	63

MUSIC EXAMPLES AND TABLES

Ex. 2.9	Elgar, Organ Sonata, third movement, bars 1–16	65
Ex. 2.10	'Plagal tritone' schema (C major version)	66
Ex. 2.11	Stainer, 'Cross of Jesus, Cross of Sorrow', *The Crucifixion*, bars 5–6 (without text)	67
Ex. 2.12	Elgar, *The Music Makers*, fig. 2, bar 1–fig. 3, bar 1, schema analysis	67
Ex. 2.13	Elgar, *Introduction and Allegro* Op. 47, fig. 2, bar 6–fig. 5, bar 1, schema analysis	69
Ex. 2.14	Elgar, Symphony No. 1, instances of Do–Re–Mi + plagal tritone	71
	(i) 'Motto theme', first movement, bar 3–fig. 1 bar 7 (reduction)	
	(ii) Third movement, fig. 104 bar 1–fig. 104 bar 5 (reduction)	
Ex. 2.15	Elgar, 'Enigma' Variations	73
	(i) Theme, bars 1–4 (reduction)	
	(ii) Variation XIV ('E.D.U.'), fig. 69 bar 1–fig. 69 bar 8 (reduction)	
	(iii) Variation XIV ('E.D.U.'), fig. 76 bar 5–fig. 76 bar 10 (reduction)	
	(iv) Variation XIV ('E.D.U.'), fig. 79 bar 1–fig. 80 bar 1 (reduction)	
Ex. 2.16	Vaughan Williams, 'Sine Nomine', *The English Hymnal*, bars 1–4. SINE NOMINE by Ralph Vaughan Williams (1872–1958) from The English Hymnal. Reproduced by permission of Oxford University Press. All rights reserved.	80
Ex. 2.17	Vaughan Williams, *Toward the Unknown Region*, 121–28 (reduction). © Copyright Stainer & Bell Ltd. Reproduced by permission. All rights reserved.	81
Ex. 2.18	Vaughan Williams, *A Sea Symphony*, first movement, 'A Song for All Seas, All Ships', bar 1–fig. A, bar 3, schema analysis	83
Ex. 2.19	Vaughan Williams, *A Sea Symphony*, fourth movement, 'The Explorers'	85
	(i) opening–fig. B, schema analysis	
	(ii) bars 1–7^3 (reduction). © Copyright Stainer & Bell Ltd. Reproduced by permission. All rights reserved.	
Ex. 2.20	Vaughan Williams, *Five Mystical Songs*, 'Easter'. © Copyright Stainer & Bell Ltd. Reproduced by permission. All rights reserved.	88
	(i) bars 1–6 (reduction)	
	(ii) bars 14–15 (reduction)	
Ex. 3.1	Howells, Fantasy String Quartet, bars 1–16 (reduction) Fantasy String Quartet. Music by Herbert Howells. Copyright © (Renewed) by Chester Music Limited trading as J. Curwen and Sons. International Copyright Secured. All Rights Reserved. *Reprinted by permission of Hal Leonard Europe Ltd.*	95
Ex. 3.2	Vaughan Williams *A Pastoral Symphony*, first movement fig. B, bar 8–fig. C, bar 5 (reduction). © 1990 by Joan Ursula Vaughan Williams All rights for the UK, Republic of Ireland, Canada, Australia, New Zealand, Israel, Jamaica and South Africa administered by Faber Music Ltd.	

MUSIC EXAMPLES AND TABLES   ix

Reproduced by kind permission of the publishers. *A Pastoral Symphony*. Music by Ralph Vaughan Williams. Copyright © (Renewed) by Ralph Vaughan Williams. International Copyright Secured. All Rights Reserved. *Reprinted by permission of Hal Leonard Europe Ltd.*   96

Ex. 3.3 Howells, Rhapsodic Quintet, bars 62–76 (reduction). © Copyright 1921 Stainer & Bell Ltd, 23 Gruneisen Road, London N3 1DZ, www.stainer.co.uk. Reproduced by permission. All rights reserved.   100

Ex. 3.4 Howells, Piano Quartet, first movement, bars 1–10. © Copyright 1918 Stainer & Bell Ltd, 23 Gruneisen Road, London N3 1DZ, www.stainer.co.uk. Reproduced by permission. All rights reserved.   102

Ex. 3.5 Howells, Piano Quartet, first movement. © Copyright 1918 Stainer & Bell Ltd, 23 Gruneisen Road, London N3 1DZ, www.stainer.co.uk. Reproduced by permission. All rights reserved.   103
(i)   fig. 1, bar 14–fig. 1, bar 15 (viola part)
(ii) fig. 1, bar 17–fig. 1, bar 19 (cello part)
(iii) fig. 2, bar 1–fig. 2, bar 5[1] (RH piano part)
(iv) fig. 5, bar 8–fig. 6, bar 8[1] (viola part)

Ex. 3.6 Vaughan Williams 'Linden Lea', bars 1–3. © Copyright 1912 by Boosey & Co Ltd. Reproduced by permission of Boosey & Hawkes Music Publishers Ltd.   106

Ex. 3.7 Vaughan Williams, 'Rhosymedre', *Three Preludes Founded on Welsh Hymn Tunes*, bars 8–12. © Copyright 1920 Stainer & Bell Ltd, 23 Gruneisen Road, London N3 1DZ, www.stainer.co.uk. Reproduced by permission. All rights reserved.   108

Ex. 3.8 Vaughan Williams, *Serenade to Music*, bars 1–6 (reduction). 'Serenade to Music' by Ralph Vaughan Williams © Oxford University Press 1938. All rights reserved.   110

Ex. 3.9 Vaughan Williams, *The Shepherds of the Delectable Mountains*, fig. 27, bar 1 to fig. 27, bar 11. 'The Shepherds of the Delectable Mountains', a Pastoral Episode founded upon Bunyan's 'Pilgrim's Progress' by Ralph Vaughan Williams © Oxford University Press 1925. All rights reserved.   112

Ex. 3.10 Vaughan Williams, *Flos Campi* 'Flos Campi' by Ralph Vaughan Williams. © Oxford University Press 1928. All rights reserved.   114
(i)   fig. 15, bar 5–fig. 15, bar 9 (reduction)
(ii) fig. 21, bar 15–fig. 21, bar 21 (solo viola part)
(iii) fig. 30, bar 11–fig. 30, bar 17 (solo viola part)

Ex. 3.11 Vaughan Williams, *The Lark Ascending*, introduction and coda cadenzas and accompaniment figures. 'The Lark Ascending' by Ralph Vaughan Williams © Oxford University Press 1925. All rights reserved.   118
(i)   Introduction, bars 1–3 (reduction)
(ii) Coda, fig. Y, bar 1–fig. Y, bar 6 (reduction)

MUSIC EXAMPLES AND TABLES

Ex. 3.12 Vaughan Williams, *The Lark Ascending*, A^1 module. 'The Lark Ascending' by Ralph Vaughan Williams © Oxford University Press 1925. All rights reserved.   119
   (i) Initial presentation (**A**), six bars before fig. A–fig. A, bar 3 (reduction)
   (ii) Final presentation (**A**): first 'round-singing' version, fig. E, bar 9–fig. F, bar 7 (reduction)
   (iii) Final presentation (**A'**): second 'round-singing' version, fig. X, bar 4–fig. X, bar 8 (reduction)

Ex. 3.13 Vaughan Williams, *The Lark Ascending*, generation of **B** section materials. 'The Lark Ascending' by Ralph Vaughan Williams © Oxford University Press 1925. All rights reserved.   121
   (i) Initial presentation of B^1 (**B**), two bars before fig. G–fig. G, bar 4 (reduction)
   (ii) Initial presentation of B^2 (**B**), fig. L, bar 1– fig. L, bar 5 (reduction)
   (iii) Heightened presentation of B^2 (**B'**), fig. S bar 1– fig. S, bar 6 (reduction)

Ex. 4.1 Elgar, *Chanson de Matin* Op. 15 No. 2   136
   (i) bars 5–8
   (ii) bars 21–3

Ex. 4.2 Elgar, 'Sabbath Morning at Sea' (*Sea Pictures*, Op. 39), bars 1–3^1 (reduction)   137

Ex. 4.3 Vaughan Williams, *The House of Life*. The House of Life. Words by Dante Gabriel Rossetti. Music by Ralph Vaughan Williams. Copyright © 1904 (Renewed) by Chester Music Limited trading as Edwin Ashdown. International Copyright Secured. All Rights Reserves. *Reprinted by permission of Hal Leonard Europe Ltd.*   138
   (i) 'Heart's Haven', bars 3–5
   (ii) 'Heart's Haven', bars 19–25^1
   (iii) 'Silent Noon', bars 67–73^1

Ex. 4.4 Quilter, 'My Life's Delight' Op. 12 No. 2   141
   (i) bars 15^4–21^2
   (ii) bars 40–44^2

Ex. 4.5 Ireland, 'Blow Out, You Bugles', bars 46–52. © Copyright 1918 by Winthrop Rogers Ltd. Reproduced by permission of Boosey & Hawkes Music Publishers Ltd.   143

Ex. 4.6 Ireland, 'If There Were Dreams to Sell', bars 1–15. © Copyright 1918 by Winthrop Rogers Ltd. Reproduced by permission of Boosey & Hawkes Music Publishers Ltd.   144

MUSIC EXAMPLES AND TABLES   xi

Ex. 4.7 Ireland, 'Ladslove', bars 2⁴–6. © Copyright 1921 Stainer & Bell Ltd, 23 Gruneisen Road, London N3 1DZ, www.stainer.co.uk. Reproduced by permission. All rights reserved. 146

Ex. 4.8 Butterworth, 'Loveliest of Trees' (*Six Songs from 'A Shropshire Lad'*) 148
  (i) bars 1–9¹
  (ii) bars 16–19

Ex. 4.9 Gurney, 'Black Stichel', bars 1–7. 'A first volume of ten songs' by Ivor Gurney © Oxford University Press 1938. All rights reserved. 151

Ex. 4.10 Gurney, 'The Boat Is Chafing', bars 1–4. 'A second volume of ten songs' by Ivor Gurney © Oxford University Press 1938. All rights reserved. 153

Ex. 4.11 Gurney, 'Severn Meadows', bars 1–5. 'Severn Meadows' by Ivor Gurney © Oxford University Press 1969. All rights reserved. 154

Ex. 4.12 Gurney, 'An Epitaph', bars 1–10. 'A second volume of ten songs' by Ivor Gurney © Oxford University Press 1938. All rights reserved. 156

Ex. 4.13 Gurney, 'The Scribe', bars 1–8. 'A second volume of ten songs' by Ivor Gurney © Oxford University Press 1938. All rights reserved. 157

Ex. 4.14 Finzi, 'Childhood among the Ferns' (*Before and After Summer*), bars 1–3². © Copyright 1949 by Boosey & Co. Ltd. Reproduced by permission of Boosey & Hawkes Music Publishers Ltd. 161

Ex. 4.15 Finzi, 'Only the Wanderer'. © Copyright 1966 by Boosey & Co. Ltd. Reproduced by permission of Boosey & Hawkes Music Publishers Ltd. 165
  (i) bars 1–5
  (ii) bars 14–20

Ex. 4.16 Finzi, 'Oh Fair to See', bars 1–12. © Copyright 1966 by Boosey & Co. Ltd. Reproduced by permission of Boosey & Hawkes Music Publishers Ltd. 166

Ex. 4.17 Finzi, 'When I Set out for Lyonesse' (*Earth and Air and Rain*). © Copyright 1936 by Boosey & Co. Ltd. Reproduced by permission of Boosey & Hawkes Music Publishers Ltd. 169
  (i) bars 5³–9
  (ii) bars 23–31

Ex. 4.18 Finzi, 'Channel Firing' (*Before and after Summer*), bars 42–7. © Copyright 1949 by Boosey & Co. Ltd. Reproduced by permission of Boosey & Hawkes Music Publishers Ltd. 172

Ex. 4.19 Finzi, 'The Too Short Time' (*Before and after Summer*). © Copyright 1949 by Boosey & Co. Ltd. Reproduced by permission of Boosey & Hawkes Music Publishers Ltd. 174
  (i) bars 14–17
  (ii) bars 29–32

xii   MUSIC EXAMPLES AND TABLES

Ex. 4.20 Finzi, 'Proud Songsters' (*Earth and Air and Rain*), bars 30–40.
© Copyright 1936 by Boosey & Co. Ltd. Reproduced by permission
of Boosey & Hawkes Music Publishers Ltd. 175

Ex. 5.1 Walton, *Spitfire Prelude and Fugue*, Prelude (reduction). 'Prelude
and Fugue ("The Spitfire")' by William Walton © Oxford University
Press 1961. All rights reserved. 185
  (i) bars 1–8
  (ii) fig. 1, bar 1–fig 1, bar 5[1]

Ex. 5.2 Ireland, *Epic March*, bar 95–102 (reduction). © Copyright 1942 by
Hawkes & Son (London) Ltd. Reproduced by permission of
Boosey & Hawkes Music Publishers Ltd. 187

Ex. 5.3 John Bacchus Dykes, hymns 192
  (i) 'Holy, Holy, Holy', bars 1–8
  (ii) 'Eternal Father, Strong to Save', bars 1–4[3]

Ex. 5.4 Vaughan Williams, 'The Airmen's Hymn', bars 4–11. 'The Airmen's
Hymn' words by 2nd Earl of Lytton, music by Ralph Vaughan
Williams © Oxford University Press 1942. All rights reserved. 193

Ex. 5.5 Vaughan Williams 'A Hymn of Freedom', bars 7–10. © Oxford
University Press. All rights reserved. 194

Ex. 5.6 Vaughan Williams, 'England, My England', bars 24–31. 'England,
My England' by Ralph Vaughan Williams, words by W. E. Henley
(1849–1903) © Oxford University Press 1941. All rights reserved. 195

Ex. 5.7 Vaughan Williams, 'A Song of Pity, Peace and Love' (*Six Songs to Be
Sung in Time of War*), bars. 42–49[1]. 'A Song of Pity, Peace and Love'
from 'Six Choral Songs to Be Sung in Time of War' by Ralph Vaughan
Williams © Oxford University Press 1940. All rights reserved. 197

Ex. 5.8 Vaughan Williams, *Dona Nobis Pacem* (reductions) Vocal score: 'Dona
Nobis Pacem' by Ralph Vaughan Williams © Oxford University
Press 1936. All rights reserved. Full score: 'Dona Nobis Pacem' by
Ralph Vaughan Williams © Oxford University Press 1936, 1971.
All rights reserved. 202
  (i) IV ('Dirge for Two Veterans') fig. 27 bar 1–fig. 28 bar 2
  (ii) VI, fig. 34 bar 11–fig. 34 bar 23

Ex. 5.9 Ireland, *These Things Shall Be*, bars 176–194 (reduction). © Copyright
1937 by Hawkes & Son (London) Ltd. Reproduced by permission
of Boosey & Hawkes Music Publishers Ltd. 206

Ex. 5.10 Finzi, *For St Cecilia: Ceremonial Ode*, bars 1–9 (reduction).
© Copyright 1948 by Boosey & Co. Ltd. Reproduced by permission
of Boosey & Hawkes Music Publishers Ltd. 208

Ex. 5.11 Finzi, *Intimations of Immortality*, fig. 4 bar 1–fig. 4 bar 11 (reductions).
© Copyright 1950 by Boosey & Co. Ltd. Reproduced by permission
of Boosey & Hawkes Music Publishers Ltd. 211

MUSIC EXAMPLES AND TABLES   xiii

Ex. 5.12 Vaughan Williams, Symphony No. 5, instances of imitation at the octave or unison. 'Symphony No. 5' by Ralph Vaughan Williams © Oxford University Press 1946. All rights reserved.   218
    (i) Preludio, fig. 1 bar 1–fig. 1 bar 6 (Violin, Viola, and Cello parts)
    (ii) Preludio, fig. 3 bar 8–fig. 3 bar 9 (Violin I and Violin II parts)
    (iii) Preludio, fig. 4 bar 1–fig. 4 bar 4 (Violin II and Viola parts)
    (iv) Preludio, fig. 6a bar 17–fig. 6a bar 18 (Violin and Viola parts)
    (v) Preludio, fig. 10 bars 5–fig. 10 bar 7 (Flute parts)
    (vi) Scherzo, fig. 2 bar 5–fig. 2 bar 7 (Clarinet and Bassoon parts)
    (vii) Romanza, fig. 4 bar 13–fig. 4 bar 16 (Oboe and Cor anglais parts)
    (viii) Passacaglia, fig. 4 bar 7–fig. 4 bar 13 (Clarinet and Trombone parts)

Ex. 5.13 Vaughan Williams, Symphony No. 5, Romanza, fig. 11, bar 16–fig. 11 bar 18 (reduction). 'Symphony No. 5' by Ralph Vaughan Williams © Oxford University Press 1946. All rights reserved.   220

Ex. 5.14 Vaughan Williams, harmonization of 'Lasst uns erfreuen' ('Ye Watchers and Ye Holy Ones'), *The English Hymnal*, 519, bars 4^3–6^2. LASST UNS ERFREUEN arr. Ralph Vaughan Williams (1872–1958) from The English Hymnal. Reproduced by permission of Oxford University Press. All rights reserved.   220

Ex. 5.15 Vaughan Williams, Symphony No. 5, Romanza, fig. 1, bar 1–fig. 1, bar 9 (Violin I part). 'Symphony No. 5' by Ralph Vaughan Williams © Oxford University Press 1946. All rights reserved.   221

Ex. 5.16 Vaughan Williams, Symphony No. 5, Passascaglia, contrapuntal ingredients. 'Symphony No. 5' by Ralph Vaughan Williams © Oxford University Press 1946. All rights reserved.   223
    (i) Passacaglia theme, bars 1–8^1 (Cello part)
    (ii) Countersubjects I and II, bars 8–21 (Violin I part)

Ex. 6.1 Howells, Te Deum (Collegium Regale), bars 190–203 (reduction). Te Deum (Collegium Regale) Liturgical Text and Music by Herbert Howells. Copyright © 1945 (Renewed) by Novello & Company Limited. International Copyright Secured. All Rights Reserved. *Reprinted by permission of Hal Leonard Europe Ltd.*   231

Ex. 6.2 Howells, Nunc Dimittis (Collegium Regale), bars 26–34. Collegium Regale 1945 Magnificat and Nunc Dimittis Liturgical Text and Music by Herbert Howells. Copyright © 1945 (Renewed) by Novello & Company Limited. International Copyright Secured. All Rights Reserved. *Reprinted by permission of Hal Leonard Europe Ltd.*   232

Ex. 6.3 Howells, *Hymnus Paradisi*, IV, 'Sanctus', fig. 36 + 5–fig 36 + 8. *Hymnus Paradisi*. Music by Herbert Howells. Copyright © 1938 (Renewed) by Novello & Company Limited. International Copyright Secured. All Rights Reserved. *Reprinted by permission of Hal Leonard Europe Ltd.*   233

xiv MUSIC EXAMPLES AND TABLES

Ex. 6.4   Howells, Nunc Dimittis (Collegium Regale), bars 1–15. Collegium Regale 1945 Magnificat and Nunc Dimittis Liturgical Text and Music by Herbert Howells. Copyright © 1945 (Renewed) by Novello & Company Limited. International Copyright Secured. All Rights Reserved. *Reprinted by permission of Hal Leonard Europe Ltd.*   236

Ex. 6.5   Parry, *Blest Pair of Sirens*, fig. H + 30–fig. H + 38   238

Ex. 6.6   Howells, *Hymnus Paradisi*, VI, 'Holy Is the True Light', fig. 71 + 4–fig. 72 + 1. *Hymnus Paradisi*. Music by Herbert Howells. Copyright © 1938 (Renewed) by Novello & Company Limited. International Copyright Secured. All Rights Reserved. *Reprinted by permission of Hal Leonard Europe Ltd.*   239

Ex. 6.7   Howells, *Hymnus Paradisi*, IV, 'Sanctus', fig. 42 + 3–fig. 42 + 5. *Hymnus Paradisi*. Music by Herbert Howells. Copyright © 1938 (Renewed) by Novello & Company Limited. International Copyright Secured. All Rights Reserved. *Reprinted by permission of Hal Leonard Europe Ltd.*   242

Ex. 6.8   Tippett, *Concerto for Double String Orchestra*, first movement, fig. 3 + 10–fig. 4. Reproduced by permission of Schott Music Ltd. All rights reserved.   246

Ex. 6.9   Tippett, *The Midsummer Marriage*, 'Transformation' (*Ritual Dances*), fig. 152–fig. 152 + 6. Reproduced by permission of Schott Music Ltd. All rights reserved.   247

Ex. 6.10 Tippett, Piano Concerto, first movement, bars 1–5. Reproduced by permission of Schott Music Ltd. All rights reserved.   249

Ex. 6.11 The topic 'deep call' in English diatonic music   251
   (i) Elgar, *The Dream of Gerontius*, Part II, bars 1–4
   (ii) Vaughan Williams, *A London Symphony*, first movement, bars 1–3 (reduction). © Copyright Stainer & Bell Ltd, 23 Gruneisen Road, London N3 1DZ, www.stainer.co.uk. Reproduced by permission. All rights reserved.
   (iii) Vaughan Williams, *A Pastoral Symphony*, second movement, fig. G + 3–fig. G + 6, E flat natural trumpet part. © 1990 by Joan Ursula Vaughan Williams All rights for the UK, Republic of Ireland, Canada, Australia, New Zealand, Israel, Jamaica, and South Africa administered by Faber Music Ltd. Reproduced by kind permission of the publishers. *A Pastoral Symphony*. Music by Ralph Vaughan Williams. Copyright © (Renewed) by Ralph Vaughan Williams. International Copyright Secured. All Rights Reserved. *Reprinted by permission of Hal Leonard Europe Ltd.*
   (iv) Tippett, *The Midsummer Marriage*, Act III, Scene 9, fig. 484 + 1–fig. 485 + 4. Reproduced by permission of Schott Music Ltd. All rights reserved.

MUSIC EXAMPLES AND TABLES XV

Ex. 6.12 Tippett, *Concerto for Double String Orchestra*, third movement, fig. 45 + 3–fig. 45 + 7. Reproduced by permission of Schott Music Ltd. All rights reserved. 255

Ex. 6.13 Tippett, *The Midsummer Marriage*, Act III, Scene 9, fig. 498–fig. 498 + 9. Reproduced by permission of Schott Music Ltd. All rights reserved. 259

Ex. 5.14 Tippett, *The Midsummer Marriage*, Act III, Scene 9, fig. 501 + 2–fig. 504 + 2 (flute and solo voice parts only). Reproduced by permission of Schott Music Ltd. All rights reserved. 260

Ex. 6.15 Tippett, *Fantasia Concertante on a Theme of Corelli*, fig. 79–fig. 79 + 3. Reproduced by permission of Schott Music Ltd. All rights reserved. 263

Table 3.1 Vaughan Williams, *The Lark Ascending*, formal analysis 117

Introduction

Re-mapping English Music

This book proposes a new understanding of English art–music repertory from the late nineteenth to the mid-twentieth centuries, from Hubert Parry's *Blest Pair of Sirens* (1887) to Michael Tippett's *The Midsummer Marriage* (1955). It aims for an historical 'remapping' of the field by means of technically informed criticism that treats music as a semiotic medium. The book interprets music in relation to historical ideas and contexts but with an awareness of how music signifies in the first place. Much of its inspiration lies in revolutionary developments in music theory of recent years that have revived the pedagogical methods of 'partimento' of the old Italian conservatoires and that developed systems of newly named conventions termed 'schemata'.[1] The somewhat earlier musicological concept of 'topic'—also originating in eighteenth-century studies—is another guiding principle.[2] These concepts cannot be applied as rigorously as they are for eighteenth-century music, not least because there was no pedagogy in English educational institutions to support them. Instead, the aim is to draw on the principles of convention-based analysis to arrive at a new historical overview of the repertory that starts with the musical experience of a literate listener and works 'out'. In this way, musicological concepts and practice are brought into relationship with informed, sense-making musical experience.

This book's central theme of diatonicism gives much English music of this time its recognizable tone.[3] This is a semiotically 'marked' feature of the repertory. Although, in Western 'tonal music', chromatic harmony is often understood as an embellishment of diatonic harmony, for several centuries the default tonality for art music could be described as a chromatically inflected diatonicism. Much English music of the era from the 1890s through the 1950s stands out for its intensive diatonicism, meaning a studied avoidance of chromaticism and an elaboration of the expressive possibilities of purely diatonic writing and its conventionally established semantics. Intensive diatonicism does not characterize all English music of this period, of course, but the concept of English diatonic music as used here is supposed to capture a strong and distinctive trend in the repertory and can be regarded as an outcome of a coherent late-Victorian musical reform movement. Intensive diatonicism is heard especially in canonical compositions that are frequently performed and recorded, but its scope is much wider than that and reflects long-standing performance traditions, tastes, intellectual concepts, and aesthetic values.

Relative to musicology and its intellectual movements, the approach developed in this book stands out for its interest in conventions and tradition, which it views positively. Compositional activity is treated as a craft and not an object of mystique. The book offers an alternative to intellectually idealist and post-idealist approaches, which tend to view tradition and convention negatively. There is limited interest here in grand conceptions of tonality, which tends to be where idealism and music analysis meet. The discussion concerns a more local level, the level of musical gestures and the melodic/harmonic patterning that lies just 'beneath' them, not 'deeply'. Tonality does not provide the ground for interpretation, nor does it guide the first steps in analysis or criticism. These benignant sentiments towards musical conventions are not to be taken to imply that 'cliché' in the negative sense cannot exist, Instead, the implication is that the perception of cliché is a matter of fastidious taste and connoisseurship rather than a recognition of music's 'failure' at any historical moment to capture 'truth' in relation to grand historical currents flowing along the 'depths'.

The composers who produced English diatonic music were a fairly diverse group by the standards of the society of their day. Elgar, Gurney, Howells, and Walton were hardly to the manor born. Quilter, Ireland, and Tippett were gay. Finzi was Jewish. Elgar was Catholic. Wesley was born out of wedlock. Gurney suffered from profound mental ill health and often slept rough, sometimes on the streets of east London. He was confined in psychiatric hospitals for the last fifteen years of his life. No women composers appear in the pages of this book; they chose alternative compositional paths, including Elizabeth Maconchy and Grace Williams who were taught by Ralph Vaughan Williams, but whether that is significant is hard to say.[4]

The conventions studied in this book can be grouped broadly into two types: topics and schemata. *Topics* are conceived as multidimensional musical conventions with some combination of rhythmic, melodic, textural, harmonic, registral, and dynamic aspects. A topic amounts to a discrete unit of significance: in semiotic terms, a musical sign. Eighteenth-century topics include dances such as the minuet, sarabande, and contradance, along with other standardized gestures such as fanfare, singing style, or learned style. *Schemata* are more abstract models of multi-voice contrapuntal patterns, with minimal, if any, rhythmic or textural definition. Schemata may also function as musical signs, as may the standardized concatenation of schemata. Schemata, though, must be 'realized' in a musical context. Their acquisition of rhythmic and textural shape and the melodic elaboration of the bare models are treated here as compositional decisions or acts. Eighteenth-century schemata are usually two-part contrapuntal models; in this book they occasionally fall into three parts, or possess a textural dimension, or they may even amount to a melodic pattern with certain harmonic tendencies. Often the term 'schema' is used as shorthand for a realization, although strictly the schema is the model or, perhaps better, the wide family of realizations of an implicit model in the repertory as a whole. Since a schema is really a set of family resemblances, in analysis the definitions of schemata are treated pragmatically.

Not every aspect of the inferred model needs to be present on every occasion in order for the convention and its musical significance to be relevant. In the compositional practices discussed in this book, certain schemata may be associated with certain topics, although that is not always the case. Beyond topic and schemata, a few additional conventions are relevant to English diatonic music, such as keys strongly associated with certain topics and melodic motives adopted by composers for the purpose of intertextual allusion. The glossary at the end of the book describes the main conventions in this repertory. Appendix B provides a summary of 'regular orders' of conventions, that is, standard ways of concatenating pairs of schemata, usually as primary and secondary elements of an opening thematic statement.

Much of the book has the character of a survey of the repertory with commentary, undertaking the large-scale 'remapping' of the terrain from 'inside out' that is the book's ultimate purpose. In practice, a fair amount of historical discussion precedes or follows analysis and interpretation. The analytical moves are, first, the naming of conventions and second, the examination of passages of compositions—seldom complete compositions—in terms of topics and schemata. The naming of previously unnamed things is now a familiar practice in schema theory; names often do not survive from historical sources or were never given by musicians or pedagogues. It is a paradox arising from the split of theory and practice in Western music that neologisms are needed to counter the division, which at first may result only in the reader's alienation. Much of the analysis has an element of 'description' in the sense of taxonomy and labelling. Description in music analysis is another concept viewed positively here; adequate description is by no means straightforward or to be taken for granted. Description, naming, and taxonomy may not sound like the most exciting scholarly activities, but, on the view taken here, traditional Western musical education does not guarantee that they can be achieved, even for mainstream Western art music. The exceptions to the general methodological rules of the book lie in its extended interpretations of two major—and familiar—compositions by Vaughan Williams: *The Lark Ascending* and Symphony No. 5. The aim here is to apply the new perspectives and insights developed in the book to shed new light on these pieces and shake up outworn response patterns.

One of the neologisms found in this book, 'processional diatonicism', embodies a strong claim: that much of the repertory of English music of this period should be understood relative to a category that has never before been identified or named. Processional diatonicism was the most prevalent musical topic in English diatonic music for seven decades and more. The first two chapters of this book follow it through Parry's occasional choral works, the whole of Elgar's output in his most productive years, and Vaughan Williams's music up to World War I. It recurred in diatonic English song after the war, which, as shown in Chapter 4, amounted to something of a Parry revival, and it enjoyed a major resurgence in the celebratory, occasional, and functional music in the era of the coronations and World War II from the mid-1930s to the mid-1950s, as shown in Chapter 5.

The reform movement that laid the groundwork for English diatonic music proposed two metaphors for its mission: renaissance and evolution. This book follows the Durham school of research in this area by underlining evolution.[5] English diatonic music was essentially a post-Victorian cultural modernity that stood in a relationship of continuity with the recent past, despite extensive critique and reform of the Victorian musical legacy. The terms on which the music communicates are largely those set by sacred choral music as heard in performance and composed in nineteenth-century England. Handel and Mendelssohn were significant for their prestige, although the reform movement sought to change what came to be perceived as idolatry around those favourites, turning instead to Wagner and Bach. Still, even the early twentieth-century English Bach revival was in a sense a post-Victorian movement, as most of the hymns set by composers as chorale-preludes were Victorian or followed Victorian models. For these reasons, the historical field covered by this book straddles World War I, which, although a landmark, is not regarded here as a moment of cultural rupture. The experience of World War I was processed by means of cultural resources—and often, musical conventions—inherited from the nineteenth century.[6] Musical styles may have been adapted, but the terms of communication, the codes, remained in place.

Given these priorities, Hubert Parry is naturally a central figure for this study. Parry was pivotal in mediating Victorian radical thinking, including evolutionism and ethical concepts, to musicians and applying them in his own compositional practice.[7] Parry did not invent the diatonic conventions, but he brought together idioms from Victorian music and from Bach and Wagner in a powerful synthesis that was taken to convey the values for which he stood as Director of the Royal College of Music and *de facto* musical leader in England before World War I. In particular, his much-admired *Blest Pair of Sirens* (1887), a celebratory choral setting of Milton's 'Ode: At a Solemn Musick', was a model for later musicians at many levels. *Blest Pair of Sirens* became doubly important because, in hindsight, Parry was seen to have been unable to follow up on it. Parry laid out an intellectual and ethical vision for English music and hinted at its realization in musical composition, but in the end he left his vision unfulfilled. This fact, along with Parry's charisma and inspirational personality—the 'marked kindling quality' that Herbert Howells noted in Parry[8]—helps to account for the extraordinary energy and endurance of English diatonic music, which lasted in art music alone at least until the 1950s.

Parry is also key to understanding the semantics of English diatonic music. For the most part, intensive diatonicism signified an ethical concept of music and the musician, transcendent values, and a metaphysical, sometimes mystical, vision of eternity, in line with the elevated neo-Platonism of Milton's 'Ode'. English diatonic music is not primarily 'about' coronations, patriotic community singing, pastoral idylls, and so on, although it may serve those functions in practice. At moments of clearest articulation—sometimes also moments of reductiveness—there is a tendency to capitalize abstract nouns in the texts that were set: 'Love', 'Light', 'Heart', 'Liberty', 'Peace', 'Nobleness', 'Honour'. A good illustration can be found in Vaughan Williams's *Six Choral Songs to Be Sung in Time of War* (1940), a cycle of unison choral songs for amateur performance, the titles of each of which carry abstract nouns of this kind. The fifth song and the expressive climax of the cycle, 'A Song of Pity, Peace and Love', has three abstract nouns in its title alone and many more in its text. This piece (discussed further in Chapter 5) is an expansive exercise in processional diatonicism in E flat major, the key of *Blest Pair of Sirens*, which in the meantime had become by far the most commonly selected key for the topic. More specifically, it adopts a 'subtopic', here designated 'unison hymn'; thus, it continues the manner of pieces such as Elgar's 'Land of Hope and Glory' and Parry's 'Jerusalem' in a more extended and complex compositional realization. Its bass moves almost entirely by stepwise motion, in accordance with the topic of processional diatonicism, although there are many tied notes and the bass does not regularly articulate the pulse, so that the piece is not just a march. The 'Song' employs melodic patterns commonly found in Victorian hymns, but it initially presents them loosely, drawing them together for a grandiose, structurally 'regularized' version only in its climactic final bars. If this convergence of English diatonic convention and the imagery of transcendence were not enough, with its subtopic, key, and triplet-chord accompaniment, the 'Song' evokes a central source of conventions for the whole of English diatonic music: the Grail Knights' communion hymn 'Wein und Brot' from Wagner's *Parsifal* (see Appendix A). Not everything in the repertory is this straightforward, perhaps thankfully—Vaughan Williams laid on the allusions and conventions here with a trowel—but the code Parry established in 1887, its techniques, and its meanings, were largely intact over half a century later. Vaughan Williams applied them in 1940 in an effort to address a new national crisis on musical terms.

The choice of this piece by Vaughan Williams to illustrate the tradition of English diatonic music is a deliberate attempt to counter at the very outset of the book the widely held assumption that pastoralism defines English music of this era and diatonic music in particular. A recurrent concern, especially in Chapters 3 and 4, is to define and clarify the pastoral dimensions of this repertory. In the account developed here, the predominant topic of English diatonic music was processional diatonicism, canonized in *Blest Pair of Sirens* and persisting until the 1950s. Pastoral themes, texts, and paratexts were common, but their musical realization was often by means of some kind of processional diatonicism, as in the songs of Ivor Gurney and Gerald Finzi, or else by means of idioms that were not intensively diatonic, thus lying outside the scope of this study. The latter usually involved the music or style of Frederick Delius. A Delian school of English pastoral music emerged rather earlier than the modal-diatonicism associated with Vaughan Williams and, in the view taken here, outlasted it. To be sure, Vaughan Williams and Herbert Howells vigorously pursued a new diatonic pastoral style for about a decade—in the case of Vaughan Williams mainly for a period of about five years after World War I. In those years and for those two composers, pastoral ideas and texts came together with an updated, modern, and yet still intensively diatonic, pastoral topic. The convergence did not last, however, and by 1925 the main phase in this diatonic pastoral music had run its course. In any case, Vaughan Williams's interests in pastoral composition were ultimately religious and mystical, and, as shown in Chapter 3, the diatonic pastoral topic in his compositions of this time usually gave way to 'satellite topics' drawn from sacred music that revealed mystical visions of eternity.

These perspectives on pastoralism inevitably lead to a critique of the nationalist school of thought articulated most clearly by Frank Howes in his book *The English Musical Renaissance* (1966), which is still influential in its interpretations and priorities, even among writers who do not share Howes's tastes or values. Although his phrase 'Parry the instigator' is sound, Howes's concept of a revolutionary act by Vaughan Williams and Gustav Holst to emancipate English music from 'German bondage' is less convincing.[9] According to Howes, Vaughan Williams set about to create a 'substantial corpus of English music' based on folksong and Tudor counterpoint. To be sure, the folksong movement and the Tudor revival were real phenomena of the musical culture, especially in research, performance, and criticism, as opposed to composition. These movements amounted to a form of cultural nationalism and were supposed to contribute to musical 'renaissance' through reinvigoration of a past golden age of English music. The publication of a selection of Vaughan Williams's writings on music after his death, first in 1963 and again in 1987, under the title *National Music and Other Essays*, in effect identified him with these movements.[10] But a hearing of English diatonic music from the 'inside', attuned to its language and conventions, does not support Howes's wholesale interpretation of Vaughan Williams's compositional practice in terms of folk music and Tudor music. Aside from harmonic progressions that suggest false relations, it is unclear why the archaic idioms of Holst, Vaughan Williams, and later composers should be regarded as specifically English, and it should be recalled that French modernism was a major influence on music of this kind as well. Vaughan Williams certainly shaped some of his melodic language around models that he selected from English folksongs. As will become clear in Chapter 5, however, in many of his singable tunes—often heard in his major compositions at moments redolent of transcendence and redemption—he followed the melodic patterns of Victorian hymns, patterns that replicated the model of the Lutheran chorale

'Wachet auf' far more closely than anything English, either folksong or Tudor. This book attempts to hear Vaughan Williams's music anew, in particular by paying attention to his preference for nontranspositional counterpoint (contrapuntal repetition at the unison or octave). This strong preference for nonfugal contrapuntal structures throws up some of his most favoured musical topics, such as round singing and chorale-prelude, which have attracted little comment in the literature on Vaughan Williams, probably because of the story recounted by Howes and his ilk.

Today a far wider range of Vaughan Williams's writings on music is available than those published in *National Music and Other Essays*, and hundreds of his letters have been published too.[11] These documents clearly show that his interests within music and beyond were far wider than a preoccupation with folksong and the Tudor revival. Vaughan Williams declared Bach his favourite composer—a preference that applied to Parry and to Ivor Gurney as well, and probably others discussed in this book too—and put the Bach revival into practice in his everyday community music-making through the direction of amateur choirs. Bach epitomized Parry's understanding of the 'great' composer as a product of the everyday environment. As a working musician from a large family of German town musicians, Bach was in touch with the hymn-singing of the people around him in their music and worship. Vaughan Williams took up this vision and tried to put it into practice in musical life and composition. (Had the title of the original volume of his published writings been *Bach the Great Bourgeois and Other Essays*, a truer picture of his life's work in music might have emerged from them.) His aim was to make English musical composition an expression of English everyday life and to establish dialogue between trained and untutored musicians. To realize this vision, it was all but inevitable that Vaughan Williams would have to draw heavily on Victorian musical sources. Folksong could never suffice, as it was remembered only by a few elderly people in far-flung rural places, while Tudor music was an object of academic scholarship, not of everyday practice. Thus, Vaughan Williams wrote Bachian chorale-preludes on Victorian hymn tunes, as did Parry, Howells, and Gurney. As far as Howes's idea of 'German bondage' is concerned, English musicians of intensively diatonic inclinations seemed to welcome it. After a phase in the 1910s and 1920s during which French modernism was influential, composers soon reverted in whole or in part to the legacy of Parry, and the allusions to Bach and Wagner poured back in, as the analyses of topic and schemata in the following pages abundantly demonstrate. Vaughan Williams's Symphony No.

5, a centrepiece of the English diatonic repertory, illustrates this principle most clearly of all, for its celestial conclusion undertakes the absorption of elements of Victorian sacred semi-vernacular melody into topics and forms associated with Beethoven and Bach.

It is already clear that Vaughan Williams is a recurrent preoccupation of and subject for dispute in research in this area, and something of a test case. He is certainly a provocation for the most recent broad study of the field, which, however, is now thirty years old: Meirion Hughes and Robert Stradling's *The English Musical Renaissance 1840–1940* (1993, 2001). This book is difficult to evaluate because it is inconsistent in both content and quality. It was written by two different authors, and it often reads as such. Although the authors deny music the power to signify anything on its own and provide no musical extracts or any formal discussion of musical syntax or rhetoric, the flashes of musical insight that occasionally appear indicate that at least one member of the team was a musical connoisseur, even if the book keeps this quiet. The authors are at their best when they are engaged in nuanced argument rather than polemics and are strong on the ambivalence of the English musical revival towards Germany. At other times, their knockabout rhetoric runs away with them, especially in the first half of the book, where they posit a monolithic English musical establishment. The slogans aimed at the alleged hegemony keep shifting—'historical-pastoral', 'English Folk-Music Revival', 'Pastoral School', 'Folksong School'—so it is difficult to know what the real claim is.[12] Taking Howes at his word, and with only *National Music and Other Essays* at their disposal as regards Vaughan Williams's published writings, the authors believe that after 1910 Vaughan Williams pursued 'twin obsessions': folksong and Tudor revival.[13] Vaughan Williams's pastoral music in particular makes the authors see red. Factual errors and distortions—always unflattering to Vaughan Williams—creep into the book and cluster around him.[14] The impression left from parts of the book is that the Royal College was a factory for turning out pastoral compositions manufactured to Vaughan Williams's prescription. Elsewhere it is clear that this is not the whole story, but the inconsistencies of tone, register, and intellectual content are not resolved.

As indicated above, the scope of the present study stretches roughly from Queen Victoria's Golden Jubilee of 1887, the year of *Blest Pair of Sirens*, to 1955, the year of the premiere of Michael Tippett's opera *The Midsummer Marriage*. The mid-1950s were not the absolute end of the tradition of English diatonic music. But what was to prove the last British coronation of the twentieth century, and thus the final English musical tradition-building occasion of its kind, had taken place in 1953, while the major new compositional projects in diatonicism of the mid-twentieth century—those of Tippett and Howells—were drawing to a close. Later allusions to the conventions of English diatonic music were more intermittent, although they might well reward future study.

1
Processional Diatonicism I

Hubert Parry and *Blest Pair of Sirens*

'Processional diatonicism', as it is dubbed in this book, is an instantly recognizable musical idiom that emerged in English composition in the 1880s, flourished in choral and orchestral music until World War I, and endured in these and other genres well beyond World War II. It is heard clearly first in the work of Hubert Parry (1848–1918), especially in his choral-orchestral ode *Blest Pair of Sirens* (1887), setting Milton's 'Ode: At a Solemn Musick'. The elevated mood of that piece encapsulates Parry's high-minded musical ethics as laid out in his writings and displayed in his personality and his leadership as Director of the Royal College of Music from 1895. The lofty, metaphysical tone of Milton's verses was definitive for English diatonic music at least until 1914 and in many cases well beyond. Parry's intensively diatonic language appealed to the listener's 'high-raised phantasie', which might thereby discern a vision of eternity, hear the celestial choirs about the throne of God and recall the 'undisturbèd song of pure concent' that human beings once sang and that they might hope soon to renew. After his Milton 'Ode', Parry himself pursued the idiom only intermittently, reserving it mainly for occasional pieces such as the coronation anthem 'I Was Glad' (1902) and the patriotic hymn 'Jerusalem'. Edward Elgar (1857–1934), however, took it up and made it the centrepiece of his personal style with many variants. He and Parry influenced one another in their development of this manner, which was in many ways a collaborative effort between them. Ralph Vaughan Williams (1872–1958) was initially attracted to processional diatonicism too, although by the time of World War I, his style was moving in other directions. In the interwar period, Gerald Finzi (1901–1956) built another personal style around processional diatonicism, with his own peculiar spectrum of variants. Ivor Gurney (1890–1937), John Ireland (1879–1962), and William Walton (1902–1983) switched in and out of the idiom as occasion demanded, confident of its meaning and prestige and of their audience's ability to recognize it. After a fallow period beginning around the start of

World War I, processional diatonicism enjoyed a resurgence in the late 1930s in a series of occasional works and official commissions that addressed the crises faced by the society at that time. The story of English processional diatonicism tells of a sustained investment by musicians in a sense of tradition and meaning grounded in musical syntax and semantics.

Despite the remarkable scope and endurance of this idiom and the evident consensus around its meanings, it was never named, described, called for, or discussed in print. No English style of composition was specified by the intellectuals of the late Victorian period who advanced a regenerative programme for English music, founded institutions, and assumed positions of influence. Sir George Grove (1820–1900) and his associates sought to improve the quality of music in England by cultivating and professionalizing performance, teaching and composition and by raising English musical taste, not by creating a dialect within European musical speech of the kind pursued by Balakirev, Borodin, and Rimsky-Korsakov in Russia, Smetana and Dvořák in Bohemia, and Grieg in Norway. There was no nationalist compositional pedagogy at the Royal College of Music. The professors who taught composition, Charles Villiers Stanford (1852–1924) and Hubert Parry, were at one with Grove in favouring a German canon of master composers culminating in Wagner and Brahms. It appears that composers who adopted the style of processional diatonicism simply listened carefully to one another's music and understood its meanings with reference to Parry's teachings about musical values and music history.

As a musical topic, processional diatonicism is typified by stepwise bass motion within a conspicuously diatonic, major-mode harmonic context—the diatonicism exaggerated relative to late-nineteenth-century defaults—along with certain characteristic textures and melodic/harmonic schemata. Processional diatonicism is a 'topic' in the sense first used by music historians for standard eighteenth-century musical gestures: a conventionalized unit of vocabulary that any composer could evoke to activate certain associations before perhaps switching freely to other available idioms or conventional gestures.[1] Intensive application of diatonic dissonances such as 7–6 or 9–8 suspensions or multiple, overlapping appoggiaturas are often prominent. More or less concrete, physical realizations of processional diatonicism were possible, for the processional aspect could be encoded in two different ways: the regular, march-like articulation of pulse, usually by the bass, and the stepwise nature of the bass motion. Both rely on well-established metaphors in musical discourse that shape the intuitions of listeners to Western classical music: 'walking' bass and 'stepwise' motion. It is the second, less literal, sense that is generally definitive of the topic, the meaning of which is broader than 'march'. At least two 'subtopics' may be discerned, although categorization at this level is not always feasible. 'Choral ode' describes a contrapuntal choral texture of an elevated, even ecstatic, mood with grand, rising melodic figures and a text of praise or expansive sentiments, usually on a metaphysical subject. 'Unison hymn' refers to a serene melody with a vocal compass and character if not actually sung by voices, with a march-like accompaniment. The realization of schemata in the former tends to be more complex and indirect than in the latter, the musical language more 'figurative'.

The topic of processional diatonicism can be regarded as specifically English for at least four reasons. First, it is grounded in indigenous traditions of choral music of the cathedrals, provincial festivals, and amateur societies. Strong participative choral traditions had grown up across the Protestant regions of Europe during the nineteenth century, but in England they held a special place. Handel's oratorios had been composed in and for England and at times embodied a distinct sense of national 'chosenness': a 'Covenantal nationalism'.[2] These works, which feature the chorus prominently, had been performed regularly and grandly over many generations, including at royal and state occasions such as the Handel Commemoration Festival of 1784 at Westminster Abbey and its subsequent iterations. Later oratorios by Haydn and Mendelssohn showed the greatest composers of their eras responding to Handel's legacy and developing it into a living tradition, which was continued by the Victorian provincial music festivals, such as those of Birmingham, Leeds, and Norwich, which repeated these works, especially Mendelssohn's *Elijah* (premiered at Birmingham in 1846), in ritual manner. Second, processional diatonicism was a development of certain currents in Victorian cathedral music, given its debts to the style of Samuel Sebastian Wesley, the most skilful and artistic of Victorian Cathedral musicians. Parry and his associates accorded Wesley special prestige as a mediator of old ways to the present and sometimes regarded his style as characteristically English. Third, the idiom came to be connected with national themes in compositions such as Parry's 'English' Symphony (1889) and Elgar's *Caractacus* (1898; the 'Britain' theme). It figures again at prominent moments in compositions for patriotic celebration such as Elgar's Pomp and Circumstance marches and in occasional works for royal ceremonial such as Parry's 'I Was Glad' (1902), Elgar's *Coronation Ode* (1902), and Walton's marches *Crown Imperial* (1937) and *Orb and Sceptre* (1953). Finally, processional diatonicism came to be associated with the celebration of the music profession in England. *Blest Pair of Sirens*, for instance, was performed at the laying of the foundation stone of a new Royal College of Music building by the Prince of Wales in 1890.[3] Twentieth-century British coronation services, at which the idiom featured prominently, became elaborate festivals of newly commissioned and traditional ceremonial music of indigenous composers. All that said, on purely musical terms, as will shortly become clear, the most significant musical models for processional diatonicism were found, ironically, in the music of Wagner, especially *Die Meistersinger von Nürnberg* and *Parsifal*.

It would have been possible—if not altogether straightforward—for the English musical revival of the late nineteenth century to have rejected the provincial choral tradition outright. It offered commissions, to be sure, but in other ways it was stultifying, locked in a Mendelssohnian aesthetic and a distrustful, Puritanical outlook on music shared by the Anglican clergy and the Nonconformist families on the city corporations. The revival might instead have sought precursors in metropolitan and cosmopolitan traditions of instrumental music and opera, centred on the Royal Academy of Music, limited though these were in the nineteenth century. But English composers, and Hubert Parry above all with *Blest Pair of Sirens*, found a way to set the choral tradition resounding anew. With eight-part choral writing of a kind that reflected the priorities of Victorian musical pedagogy and patrons, Parry applied familiar conventions of Victorian choral music—the intensive application of diatonic dissonance, characteristic voicings of certain chords, standard cadential evasions, a closing fugue with a long dominant pedal—in a novel fashion that proved enormously fertile.

Later composers sensed the possibilities of this style and responded. At the same time, the opening of Parry's *Blest Pair of Sirens* evoked the beginning of the Prelude to Wagner's *Die Meistersinger von Nürnberg*, a clear precedent for the style of processional diatonicism, which itself celebrated the art and profession of music. This was, in fact, something of an anti-Mendelssohn insurgency within the English choral tradition, a symbolic gesture of reform. It followed the more obvious revolutionary compositional deed of Parry's *Prometheus Unbound* (1880), a radical, antidoctrinal statement with Wagnerian stylistic allusions, premiered at the Three Choirs Festival within the sacred space of Gloucester Cathedral.[4] But *Blest Pair of Sirens* was far more musically compelling and influential.

By no means, then, was the new English style an exotic historical confection, without a living connection to musical experience, charges that might plausibly be levelled against the slightly later movement that drew on English folksong. As well as reform, it foregrounded continuity with the recent Victorian musical past, especially the choral and organist traditions, in values, style, and practice. Organists had many of Parry's idioms beneath their fingers, the anthems of Wesley were well known to some at least, and amateur singers were familiar with the elevated tone, massive choral effects, and multi-part counterpoint. But the relationship to that recent past was very sensitive—a love–hate affair—and a strong filter was applied to the idioms of the Victorian sacred repertory with an eye to chromaticism and morality. In particular, some of the hymns of John Bacchus Dykes, with their (intermittently) chromatic harmonic palette, and possibly those of Joseph Barnby, incurred the censure of the musicians of the English revival. Charles Stanford, its most influential composition teacher, as well as an important composer of Anglican church music, said that such hymns 'degrade religion and its services with slimy and sticky appeals to the senses'.[5] Ralph Vaughan Williams complained that English organists relied on 'the sickly harmonies of Spohr, overlaid with the operatic sensationalism of Gounod', and that 'church hymns had followed suit'.[6]

Here distaste for the wrong kind of harmony and Parry-like disdain for insincerity and theatricalism go hand in hand. In his editor's preface to a landmark publication in the reform of choral music, the *English Hymnal* (1906), aimed at the English grassroots, Vaughan Williams explained the exclusion of certain tunes that he and his committee deemed 'unsuitable' on 'moral rather than ... musical' grounds. 'No doubt it requires a certain effort to tune oneself to the moral atmosphere implied by a fine melody; and it is far easier to dwell in the miasma of the languishing and sentimental hymn tunes which so often disfigure our services'.[7] In speaking of this moral 'tuning', he echoed Milton's 'Ode', which foresaw that humanity would soon again 'keep in tune with heaven'. Still, Vaughn Williams and his committee valued continuity of practice too. They retained 118 tunes by Victorian composers because they had become part of everyday English musical life. Their editorial practice was selective, and not a purge.[8]

Moreover, the very idea that music should be judged on moral terms had been advocated by Victorian intellectuals: the musicians at the end of the century merely applied it in a new way. The rapturous mid-Victorian reception of Mendelssohn, touched by the evangelical revival, is exemplary. Mendelssohn's veritably redemptive status for the English relied at first on a conflation of the composer and his music. When the subject was given more reflective treatments by H. R. Haweis in his widely read *Music and Morals* (1871) and, more briefly, by John Ruskin in *The Queen of the Air* (1869), the focus turned to musical style, society, and institutions in ways that informed the campaign by the founders and patrons of the later Royal College of Music. Haweis called for the healthy development of the individual and society through music and for the establishment of a national school for music, though he still favoured the style of Mendelssohn.[9] Haweis viewed music as the expression of emotional states or atmospheres, and judged musicians and national schools accordingly. He insisted on the emotional regulation of the individual and warned against indulgence in emotional excesses, above all sentimentality.[10] Musicians such as Parry and Stanford were less censorious than mid-Victorian critics and advocated progressive music such as Wagner's. Beyond this more liberal taste and less pronounced religiosity, Parry, under the influence of Ruskin and probably Haweis, reconceived the subject of music and morals in a less biographical, more stylistic and cultural, fashion, arguing that a composer's work inevitably reflected the surrounding cultural environment. These musicians rejected sentimentality—a form of emotional dysregulation according to Haweis—rather than sensuality, a quality often associated with Wagner's chromatic idioms. Many years later, Herbert Howells, echoing Vaughan Williams in 1906, complained that 'Many of our hymn tunes . . . are ruined by false and very beastly harmony, chromaticism which is not that of *Tristan und Isolde* by any means, but something that is quite cheap. [It is] what I call . . . sentimental chromaticism. . . .'[11]

The reform movement was typically Victorian in yet another way: It was underpinned by the concept of social evolution, which Parry elaborately applied to music in *The Evolution of the Art of Music* (1893/1896).[12] For instance, fifteen years after Parry's death, in his lecture series 'National Music' given at Bryn Mawr College, Bryn Mawr, Pennsylvania, Vaughan Williams drew deeply on Parry's contextualist thinking. In a lecture entitled 'Tradition', Vaughan Williams explained that while creative originality was necessary when tradition threatened to harden into convention, outside a tradition it could not thrive at all. Nevertheless, according to Vaughan Williams, there are good and bad traditions—and in making this point he was surely thinking of the directions that English music had taken in the nineteenth century. The heirs of bad traditions cannot escape them. But 'it is up to us to see that the sins of one generation turn into the virtue of the next': a programme of reform after the fashion of Parry himself.[13] In this way, with their characteristically Victorian concepts of aesthetic morality and evolutionism, the musicians of the reform movement established an environment for development of an English musical style as the outcome and refinement of a musical tradition and even a way of life. They did not call openly for processional diatonicism—or any kind of English style—but when it came, they were ready for it with concepts and principles.

The evolutionary contexts and the intensity of the movement's engagement with musical pasts—recent and distant, English and German—mean that a music-analytical approach to processional diatonicism makes sense. The process of canonization, shared reference points, intertextual allusions, and the everyday activities of musicians such as Parry, Vaughan Williams, and Finzi, aimed, as they were, at creating and sustaining an English tradition, invite an investigation of musical syntax and rhetoric. Convention-orientated music analysis can reasonably claim to model the perceptions of listeners literate in and interested in the tradition. Certain full-texture realizations of diatonic stepwise bass motion became so deeply embedded in English musical practice that the analyst may inductively infer a collection of schemata akin to those of the eighteenth-century 'galant style' and even an English 'rule of the octave', at least in fragments. Although there was no pedagogical concept of this kind, such a theoretical approach captures the almost improvisatory quality and the apparent ease and spontaneity with which musicians seem to have generated this kind of music. Finally, analysis can clarify the uses and meanings of processional diatonicism as a musical topic in individual compositions, which may be elaborately developed. In substantial compositions, long stretches of pure diatonic writing and stepwise bass motion are sometimes found, while at other times a few schemata may appear as diatonic islands amidst unstable tonality and an unfolding fabric of Wagner-style leitmotivs.

The rest of the present chapter examines Hubert Parry's *Blest Pair of Sirens* as a deliberate act of tradition building under the influence of Victorian evolutionist thought and as a repository of what would become established musical conventions (topics and schemata). The chapter initiates an analytical approach to the repertory of English diatonic music based on diatonic conventions. It includes a broad-brush account of English public processional culture and ends with a summary of Parry's later efforts in processional diatonicism. For a full understanding of this topic in English music of the years before World War I, the chapter must be taken as one of a pair along with Chapter 2, which examines the music of Elgar and Vaughan Williams up to 1914 and introduces further schemata. The three musicians worked concurrently. Elgar and Parry appear to have influenced one another, while Vaughan Williams's music of this time develops an intertextual network of allusions that encompasses both of the others. The two chapters together demonstrate that the English musical tradition was built in the years before World War I in at least five interrelated ways: compositional development and use of the topic of processional diatonicism (the simplest and most common); consolidation of certain gestures into schemata and the use of these and other conventions of style and tonality; cultivation of choral music and of the genre of the orchestral march; allusions to canonical pieces or passages, leading to a sometimes elaborate intertextual network; writings that point out connections between composers, styles, and pieces, especially in terms of historical evolution; and choices of repertory for programmes in performance, especially at festivals and coronations.

Blest Pair of Sirens and Evolutionism: The Influences of Wesley and Wagner

Insofar as there was a single founding moment of the English tradition, it was the premiere in May 1887 of Parry's choral-orchestral setting of Milton's 'Ode: At a Solemn Music', known by its first line, 'Blest Pair of Sirens'. Composed for the Bach Choir, which was conducted by Parry's colleague, Charles Stanford, the work had no ceremonial function, although its general sentiment was deemed appropriate for the year of Queen Victoria's Golden Jubilee, a revival of Parry's *The Glories of Our Blood and State* (1883) having been rejected as too sombre. Milton's 'Ode' celebrates sacred vocal music in Christianized neo-Platonist terms, disclosing a vision of eternity to the 'highraised phantasy' of its auditors in the original image of spiritual elevation of the English diatonic tradition. Parry's response was an ecstatic outpouring of intensively dissonant diatonicism in eight-part choral counterpoint, much of it in processional style. With hindsight it is clear that Parry anticipated the idiom in earlier compositions such as *Glories* and the Bridal March from his incidental music for a Cambridge University production of Aristophanes' *The Birds* (1883), but he had never before applied it in such a sustained or intensive way. *Blest Pair of Sirens* achieved immediate popularity with choral societies and set off a series of provincial festival commissions for more choral works from Parry. After Parry was promoted to Director of the Royal College of Music in 1895 (but at the same time was seen, by critics and by the musicians whom he mentored, to have failed, in his oratorios *Judith* (1888), *Job* (1892), and *King Saul* (1894), to build on his initial choral success), *Blest Pair of Sirens* came to be viewed retrospectively as still more important. The Ode's assured vision in its closing bars of an 'endless morn of light' was now associated with Hubert Parry himself: his genial and inspirational personality, his extraordinary energy, his ethical conception of music and the musician, and the impression he left on students that their art was not just entertainment or even a profession but a calling. Elgar, who had played Parry's music as an orchestral violinist, told the composer that *Blest Pair of Sirens* was 'among the noblest works of man', and in his professorial lectures at the University of Birmingham Elgar called it an 'English masterpiece'. As late as the 1950s, Vaughan Williams maintained with only a touch of irony that, even with Byrd, Purcell, and Elgar in mind, it was his 'favourite piece of music written by an Englishman' and 'the finest musical work that has come out of these islands'.[14] For Finzi, it was 'acknowledged as one of the supreme fusions of voice and verse'. For Herbert Howells, it 'brought a new note into choralism'.[15] Parry 'was on fire', Howells said, 'to span the frightening syntax and structures [of Milton's poetry] with music shiningly clear and of untroubled control'.[16] None of Parry's other compositions attracted anything like this kind of praise or consensus of opinion.

In his youth, Hubert Parry was steeped in the English choral tradition and the Victorian attitudes and tastes that underpinned it. His father, Thomas Gambier Parry, a Gloucester magistrate and on occasion High Sheriff of the county and Deputy Lieutenant, was closely involved in Gloucester Three Choirs Festivals, where he approved the diet of oratorios by Handel, Haydn, Mendelssohn, and Louis Spohr. Hubert made the acquaintance of Samuel Sebastian Wesley during his early schooldays at Twyford, who allowed him to sit in the organ loft during services at the nearby Winchester cathedral, where he was organist.[17] From 1863 to 1866, during his time at Eton, Parry studied composition with Sir George Elvey, organist at St George's Chapel, Windsor, receiving the orthodox education of a Victorian musician in counterpoint and the composition of anthems and cantatas, with Handel and Mendelssohn as models. Parry came to know Wesley again in 1865 when Wesley took up the organist position at Gloucester and led the Three Choirs Festival there. Wesley often visited Parry's father's nearby country estate, Highnam Court. Much Mendelssohn, whom Parry at that time admired, was performed at Gloucester.[18] In 1866, at the age of eighteen, Parry composed a cantata for the Oxford B.Mus. examination, including a bass solo that, according to the *Eton College Chronicle*, revealed 'a flowing and original melody in the Mendelssohnian style'.[19] Parry's composition submission and his written paper on counterpoint impressed the Oxford professor, Sir Frederick Ouseley, who had reformed the Oxford syllabus to emphasize traditional technical facility.[20]

As Jeremy Dibble has shown, some of Wesley's best known and most frequently performed anthems in the nineteenth century as now, such as 'Cast Me not away from Thy Presence' (1847), 'Thou Wilt Keep Him in Perfect Peace' (1853), and 'Wash Me Throughly' (1853) foreground passages of intensive diatonic dissonance.[21] Wesley evidently relished the clashes thrown up by freely unfolding contrapuntal lines. His multiple appoggiaturas and suspensions, chords of the seventh, ninth, and eleventh, diatonic sequences, and long pedal points anticipate Parry's elevated diatonic idiom.[22] Moreover, Wesley's diatonically dissonance passages often unfold above extensive unidirectional stepwise bass motions, which may span an octave and a half, especially in grand or solemn passages. The anthem 'O God, Whose Nature and Property' (1831), for instance, has a bass line that moves almost uniformly by step except at cadences. One of Wesley's grandest anthems, 'Ascribe unto the Lord' (1851), begins, after a short recitative, with a bass that descends stepwise from degree 8 down to 3 (Ex. 1.1). The texture is crammed with suspended sevenths, ninths, and elevenths. A semitone and a tone are stacked above each other (bars 17^3) and are directly followed by parallel ninths (bar 18^1–18^2). Wesley may have inherited his love of stepwise bass motion from the organ style of his father, Samuel Wesley, the greatest organist of his day in England.[23]

Parry retained a fondness for his teacher's music throughout his life. After exploring progressive contemporary Continental music in his twenties under the influence of his new mentor Edward Dannreuther, an affiliate of the New German School, and becoming more critical of Mendelssohn,[24] in the 1880s, he returned to his roots in Victorian choralism with broader, more enlightened attitudes, replacing conventional Anglicanism with the radical thought of John Ruskin. Vaughan Williams's later remark that 'Hubert Parry derived largely from S. S. Wesley' may have been an exaggeration to serve his own arguments about the grounding of great art in everyday national life (thereby illustrating Parry's own theories), but it contained a grain of truth.[25]

Although Parry's voluminous writings and diaries never directly account for his return to the language of diatonic dissonance on these—or indeed on any—terms, his compositional choices are consistent with a story of English

Ex. 1.1 Samuel Sebastian Wesley, 'Ascribe unto the Lord', bars 1–21 (reduction)

musical survival and revival being developed by others at the time. In the face of foreign musical dominance in nineteenth-century England, it was argued that the flame of indigenous art had been kept alive principally in the Cathedral tradition, along with glee clubs and ballad operas. Sir George Grove himself had put this argument into the mouth of the Duke of Albany for his scripted speech at a fund-raising meeting on 12 December 1881 in Manchester to support the creation of a new national college of music, which would become the Royal College of Music.[26] Ouseley, still Professor at Oxford, made the same points in the writings he published around the time of the premiere of *Blest Pair of Sirens*. In this work, he maintained that England was a genuinely musical country with a proud musical history, sustained during its lowest ebb in the early nineteenth century by the glee and by Anglican church music, the latter growing from a 'national style' with its origins in Tallis. Ouseley singled out Samuel Sebastian Wesley and John Goss for creating a repertory that would 'preserve and hand down the true old English cathedral style' while creating a 'modern phase of English Church Music'.[27] J. A. Fuller Maitland, Grove's successor as editor of the *Dictionary of Music and Musicians* and chief music critic of the *Times*, argued in his programmatic development of the 'musical renaissance' idea in *English Music in the XIXth Century* (1902) that organists were the only class of musicians that had preserved an independent tradition of English music through the nineteenth century, above all in the anthem. Moreover, he believed that 'It is through [Samuel Sebastian] Wesley rather than through any other single composer that the pure tradition of English church music has descended.' From Wesley, Hubert Parry in turn 'imbibed the pure traditions of the English Cathedral school'.[28] A staunch supporter of Parry's music, Maitland compared his choral works favourably with Mendelssohn's.[29] Wesley was largely exempt from the critique of his Victorian successors and of Mendelssohn by the writers and composers of the English revival; even Dannreuther was a warm admirer.[30] In 1880 Parry confessed that he found *The Wilderness*, one of Wesley's biggest anthems with much diatonic dissonance, 'essentially an English work'. 'Its home is an English Cathedral and it speaks the best language and the best thoughts people who frequent such places of worship are in a state to comprehend.'[31] Although broadly a compliment, this verdict also contains an offhand dismissal of conventional Victorian taste and organized religion and allows for a future evolution of Wesley's style within a more favourable environment, in effect paving the way for a compositional response.

By the time he made that remark, Parry had become a passionate Wagnerian, and his new interest opened a second evolutionary context for *Blest Pair of Sirens* with much broader scope. For Parry as a music historian at this time, as Bennett Zon points out, 'it is Wagner, rather than Beethoven or Mozart, who represents the apogee of musical mastery and survival'.[32] As Parry put it in *The Evolution of the Art of Music*, Wagner's approach to music drama was 'the logical outcome of the efforts of the long line of previous composers, and the most elaborately organised system for the purposes of dramatic musical expression that the world has ever yet seen.'[33] He cited Mozart, Beethoven, and Schubert as Wagner's precursors, each representing a stage of development towards the 'ultimate method' of the Master. Aside from a final summary, the discussion of Wagner ends the book, which traced the evolution of music from its primitive origins. In this respect, Parry was of a mind with a group of Victorian musical intellectuals without any affiliation to English choralism, including Francis Huneker and Richard Wallaschek, who placed Wagner at the climax of their evolutionary schemes too.

Parry's Wagnerism grew from direct experiences in his relationship with Edward Dannreuther, the leading advocate of Wagner in Victorian Britain, whose home in Orme Square, Bayswater, was a centre of progressive musical thought and practice in London in the 1870s. In 1873 Parry began piano lessons with Dannreuther.[34] Dannreuther was a leading figure in the London Wagner Society, for which Parry too soon served on the committee. Dannreuther planned and organized a Wagner festival in London in 1877 and hosted Wagner at his home for its duration, where Parry heard Wagner read the libretto of *Parsifal*. Parry became an ardent Wagner enthusiast and for a time did not establish any critical distance from the Master's works. From 1875 he attended many performances of complete Wagner operas, including the complete *Ring* cycle in Bayreuth at its premiere run in 1876; he returned to Bayreuth in 1882 for the first season of *Parsifal*. His diary is full of superlatives in response to these experiences, which he felt were beyond description. 'I give up all attempts to describe my own feelings' he wrote after hearing the *Ring* cycle for the first time. An extract from *Götterdämmerung* was 'the greatest thing in the world and made me quite cold with ecstasy'.[35]

At first sight, it might appear odd for Wagner to be the model for a new diatonic style, as for the Victorians Wagner was notorious for his chromatic harmony. As models for composition, what Parry and his successors in English diatonic music appear to have valued in Wagner was above all the purely orchestral music for the onstage processions in *Die Meistersinger* and *Parsifal*: the entry of the mastersingers in the Festival Meadow scene in Act III of *Die Meistersinger*, elaborated in purely orchestral form in the Prelude; the 'transformation music' of Act I of *Parsifal*; the Grail Knights' processions into and out of the Grail Castle; and their communion hymn during the Grail service. These passages together amount to a consistent style of processional diatonicism in Wagner, defined by firm, broad textures, march rhythms and elaborate interweaving of contrapuntal lines with rich diatonic dissonance indicating an elevated tone rising to ecstasy. This tone and style were echoed time and again in English diatonic music.

Parry said nothing specifically about Wagner's diatonicism. Nevertheless, something of his reaction to Wagner's processional passages might be discerned in his praise for 'The wide sweeps of his sequences, the long and intricate growth towards some supreme climax, the width and clearness of the main contrasts, the immense sweep of his basses, the true grandeur of many of his poetic conceptions . . .',[36] although these sentiments were meant to apply generally to Wagner's music-dramatic art too. His colleague Stanford was more specific, however, and his reactions probably overlap with Parry's to some extent:

> It is curious to note how Wagner, apparently so consistently chromatic, always became diatonic at his greatest moments; even accentuating those 'high lights' by a quantity of preceding chromatic passages. The greatness and nobility of these broad diatonics are evident at once. The treatments of the depths of the Rhine, the Walhalla themes, or rather phrases, for they cover pages and not bars, the sword theme, the Siegmund and Siegfried tragedy, the forest music, the Rhine-daughters' song, the death-march of Siegfried are all conspicuous for their persistent diatonics, and that Wagner's theory was always to rely upon these for his great moments is obvious to any student of 'Tristan' (otherwise so crushingly chromatic) or of the 'Meistersinger' or of 'Parsifal'.[37]

Stanford's phrase 'greatness and nobility' as a reaction to these diatonic passages, and his evident relish for those qualities, seem directly in line with the compositional practices of Parry and many later English composers, especially Elgar, when writing processional diatonicism. The phrase 'broad diatonics' echoes Parry's terms 'wide sweeps' and 'width'. Moreover, for Stanford this diatonicism is a non-default mode of writing in Wagner, which the composer reserves only for special, elevated moments that are highly memorable. That point too could sometimes apply to English compositional practice, especially before World War I. In Elgar's oratorios and symphonies, for instance, intensive diatonicism often emerges as a transformation of its opposite, intensive chromaticism, for a redemptive, elevated climax, just as Stanford observed in Wagner. In his book *Musical Composition* (1911), Stanford expressed similar sentiments, adding that in *Die Meistersinger* 'diatonics are written large upon every page'.[38] He noted that Wagner did not immediately master chromaticism, at first labouring under the influence of Spohr, whose impact was 'surprisingly far-reaching in the early part of the nineteenth century'.[39] For these English musicians, it was Spohr rather than (the mature) Wagner who was the perpetrator of 'bad' chromaticism. The fact that, today, Spohr's oratorios have fallen out of the choral repertory and are no longer 'in the ears' of literate musicians probably works to obscure the originally Wagnerian tone and intentions of English diatonic music.[40]

Nevertheless, Parry and Stanford differed in their reactions to Wagner in ways that reflect the musical landscape of late Victorian Britain and probably vestiges of the Bayreuth / Leipzig division in German musical life of the time. Diatonicism in itself was common in English music of the late Victorian age and can be found in the works of Parry's contemporaries such as Arthur Sullivan (1842–1900), John Stainer (1840–1901), Charles Wood (1866–1926), and Stanford himself. None of these composers, however, conducted the purge of Mendelssohnian phraseology that Parry did in his Wagnerian phase. Stanford in particular, who attended the conservatoire in Leipzig as a student, never wholly abandoned its ethos of Classicism, inherited from Mendelssohn as its founder, or, in his compositions, melodic touches reminiscent of that composer. He described the chromaticism of *Tristan* as 'crushing', after all, and preferred, he said, the Wagner of the *Siegfried Idyll*, *Die Meistersinger,* and *Parsifal* to 'the Wagner of unbridled excitement and sensuality'.[41] The notion that Wagner's music needed 'bridling' was not consistent with an evolutionary conception of Wagner as a 'survivor' and as the logical outcome of a historical process. For Parry, 'the perfect balance of expression and design'—one of the chapter headings in *The Evolution of the Art of Music*—was exemplified by Beethoven, not Wagner, and that was not to Wagner's detriment. In composition too, Parry's new diatonicism was different from that of his British contemporaries. For Parry, as for most of his later followers and admirers, diatonicism conveyed ideas of elevated, spiritual thoughts, and even ecstasy, with no need for bridling. In compositions such as *Blest Pair of Sirens*, diatonicism flows in abundance, bubbling over unconstrained, just like Parry's enthusiasm for Wagner's music. This ecstatic tendency, along with sprawling construction and avoidance of Mendelssohnian idioms, remained in place in English diatonic music long after Parry.

Parry put nothing into words about how Wagner might be a model for English music or how the separate evolutionary lines—indigenous and universal—might be connected in compositional practice. In the 1880s, he evidently felt that English music could be regenerated through a response to Wagner, but his first efforts were not in choral music. He set about to achieve this goal with his unfinished Arthurian opera *Guenever*, which he worked on from 1884 to 1886.[42] He completed the opera in short score but never scored it for orchestra, as, by 1886, it was clear that the opera would not be performed. Parry in fact did not apply Wagnerian operatic principles very thoroughly, and it seems that his compositional gifts did not lie in that area— something that had become evident ever since *Prometheus Unbound*—even though he could appreciate Wagner's achievements. Parry's very next artistic endeavour was *Blest Pair of Sirens*, which effected a synthesis of his Wagnerism and his background in English choralism. This composition was far better suited to performance in England than *Guenever*, as well as to Parry's own abilities, as evidenced by its swift rise to popularity with choral societies and festivals. Once Parry returned to choral music he effected a synthesis of diatonic dissonance and Wagnerian allusion, and even, it might be argued, of the thinking of musicians like Ouseley and Dannreuther. The opening of Parry's setting of Milton's 'Ode' echoes the opening of the Prelude to *Die Meistersinger* in its melodic contour, massive texture, heavy tread, and descending bass from scale degree 8 to degree 5 beneath a sustained tonic chord in the upper parts. Even the second-beat minim on the bass's degree 7 is recalled, creating a characteristic syncopation. The closing bars of *Blest Pair of Sirens*, with its plagal close IV–I, slow, rising melodic figure Do– Re–Mi, and equally massive texture allude no less directly to the end of the *Meistersinger* Prelude and the end of Wagner's opera as a whole. As soon as choral voices enter, the melody recalls the Grail Knights' communion hymn 'Wein und Brot' from Act I of *Parsifal*, in the same key, E flat major. This was the first, but by no means the last, reference to 'Wein und Brot' in English diatonic music (see Appendix A), which became the favoured model for the subtopic 'unison hymn'.

Die Meistersinger was a favourite of Parry's: during London's Wagner glut in the summer of 1882, he attended a rehearsal and six performances within a month, describing the first of them as one of the musical highlights of his life.[43] He attended nine other London performances of Wagner operas in May and June, before moving on to Bayreuth later in the summer. The Prelude provides not only a model for the opening bars of *Blest Pair of Sirens*, but a strong precedent for Parry's compositional decisions and the twist he put on Milton's poem. Through its representation of the procession of the Mastersingers' Guild, Wagner's Prelude celebrates the art and profession of music, and it does so through exuberant processional diatonicism, abundant diatonic dissonance, and intensive counterpoint. By contrast, Milton's text celebrates the aesthetic and spiritual effect of the 'mixed power' of 'voice' and 'verse' specifically in sacred vocal music and contains no reference to processional activity. Both Wagner's and Parry's openings are orchestral, but, just as the chorus enters later in the *Ode*, so the music of the Prelude is eventually realized as a chorus during the Festival Meadow scene in Act III of Wagner's opera—a staging of the nineteenth-century German festival movement with its craft displays, pretend guilds, historical revivals, and competitive song contests, an elaborately processional culture.[44] The pompous staged procession of the mastersingers guild in Act III is comical, but ultimately, as Hans Sachs explains, the mastersingers are to be respected, and the music of the Prelude overall surely conveys this. *Blest Pair of Sirens* in turn came to be associated with the new musical institutions of England and with the musical profession; it was performed, for instance, by the Royal College of Music chorus and orchestra at the laying of a foundation stone by the Prince of Wales for a new College building in 1890.[45] It celebrates music as an elevating spiritual force, in line with Parry's own nondoctrinal humanist spirituality and with his aim, as College Director, of cultivating musical citizenship.

Processional Diatonicism in *Blest Pair of Sirens*: Topic and Schemata

Along with the elevated processional idiom, the stepwise bass motion, and the diatonic dissonance, certain characteristic traits of *Blest Pair of Sirens* stimulated an English tradition in composition. Melodic figures such as falling sevenths, upward leaps, and bounding dotted rhythms in combination with even quavers later became hallmarks of Elgar's style, especially for his royal or chivalrous rhetoric.[46] Herbert Howells spoke of 'Parry-cum-Elgar leaping sevenths' (acknowledging that he borrowed them in his own music).[47] The essentially three-part contrapuntal texture of much of the orchestral introduction to *Blest Pair of Sirens* reappears time and again at elevated moments in English music. The melodic figure and the wide spacing of the chord at 'O may we soon again renew that song' resounds through Elgar's oratorios, as Jeremy Dibble has shown.[48] The key of *Blest Pair of Sirens*, E flat major, was strongly favoured for the topic of processional diatonicism by almost all English composers after Parry who chose to use it. Had Parry's

Guenever ever been produced, its audience would have heard the leitmotiv representing King Arthur—as it happens, an allusion to the 'Grail' motive in *Parsifal*—sounding in a diatonic E flat major, an effect that Parry then transferred directly to his Milton setting.[49] Finally, just below the musical 'surface', Parry's particular 'styling' of the diatonic idiom was influential and led to characteristic realizations of certain stepwise bass progressions. In this regard Parry's functional transformation of conventions of sacred music was significant.

A closer look at the opening bars of *Blest Pair of Sirens* up to the dominant pedal that begins at bar 13 reveals a predominance of stepwise bass motion (Ex. 1.2). When registral adjustments are discounted and the bass C in bar 6 is treated as a local prolongation of the Fs sounded before and after it, there are only four leaps, and they are mainly clustered in the middle (bar 3^1 to bar 5^1). Descent is the primary direction of this stepwise motion: after two phases of descent (bars 1^1 to 3^1 and 5^1 to 9^1), a stepwise ascent follows (bars 9^1 to 13^1), and a more disguised stepwise ascent can be inferred roughly between

Ex. 1.2 Parry, *Blest Pair of Sirens*, bars 1–13^1 (reduction)

the two phases of descent (bars 3^3 to 5^3). This motion supports an upper-part texture composed primarily of sixth chords, over which is laid a wash of diatonic dissonance, in this passage represented mainly by sevenths that resolve to their respective sixths. From bar 5^1 the upper parts unfold a series of sequences over the space of twenty-one bars, first over a dominant pedal in the bass, then over an inverted tonic pedal that tonicizes the subdominant key but with minimal local chromaticism. Although the stately tread is unmistakable, the articulation of pulse—either crotchet or minim—does not correspond to the changing diatonic steps of the bass, for the durations, or, more properly, prolongations, of those notes vary considerably.

This approach typifies processional diatonicism. Most later instances feature mainly stepwise bass motion, with descent primary and parallel sixth chords the default harmonization. Sometimes long passages or even entire sections rely on descending stepwise bass motion, with the bass occasionally leaping up by a seventh instead of descending by step in order to remain within a manageable compass. Parry's sequences are also characteristic. Especially at the 'choral ode' end of the subtopic spectrum, the structures of this kind of music tend to be sprawling in form, shaped by imitative entries in free counterpoint rather than the functional units of Classical instrumental music such as idea, phrase, period, or sentence. Finally, bass notes do not necessarily articulate a regular pulse. To be sure, a sense of steady motion, appropriate to a ritual public occasion, is often prominent, but the processional quality is registered in the bass primarily through the nature of its motion, that is, step*wise*, rather than through a correspondence of its attacks with the footfall of imagined processional participants.[50]

With chromaticism at a minimum, expressive significance at the opening of *Blest Pair of Sirens* centres on the melodic and textural realization of the stepwise bass part through, for instance, melodic leaps of a fourth within the flow of sixth chords and 'open sonorities' on first-inversion or seventh chords, where the parts above the bass are laid out in wide intervals, especially on scale degrees 2 and 3 (ii^7, vii^6, and I^6). The 4–3 step in the bass accumulated several conventionalized realizations in English diatonic music. Bar 2 of *Blest Pair of Sirens* in particular resonated down the decades, especially its melodic rising fourth from degree 2 to degree 5, a leap into a higher voice within a compound melodic structure. Parry has a pair of 7–6 suspensions in the lower voice, so the overall melodic pattern is 3–2–5, with the 3 and 2 suspended (Ex. 1.3). The 'rising-fourth' schema probably derives from a conventional cadential evasion in nineteenth-century sacred music,

Ex. 1.3 Rising-fourth schema (outer voices) and typical first-level realization with 'Blest Pair' suspensions

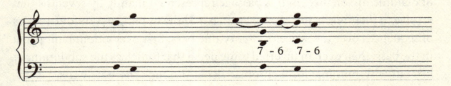

Ex. 1.4 Stainer, 'God So Loved the World', *The Crucifixion*, bars 1–4 (reduction)

sometimes found in Mendelssohn, the bass leaving 5 by slipping down through 4 to 3, the melody avoiding the descent to 1 by rising to 5. A stage in its functional transformation from a cadential evasion can already be found at the opening of 'God So Loved the World' from Stainer's *The Crucifixion* (also 1887), a work aimed at, and swiftly beloved of, small church choirs (Ex. 1.4). At the end of the number, this figure is folded back into its conventional function as an evasion before an altered version completes the piece with a melodic descent to degree 1. Parry's transformation has no cadential function at all, and in *Blest Pair of Sirens* it never acquires one; instead, its leaping profile conveys surging energy within a long, ecstatic, melodic line. The rising-fourth schema with its initial 7–6 resolution is found in Elgar's 'Nimrod' (its potential cadential implication realized on this occasion, at the end of the consequent phrase of the main theme; see Ex. 2.4); twice, in grand 'choral ode' guise, near the opening of Vaughan Williams's *A Sea Symphony* (1910; see Ex. 2.18; the schema dominates the elevated moments in the rest of the movement); at the start of the grand trio tune in Walton's coronation march, *Crown Imperial* (1937; see Ex. 1.8); throughout the redemptive, processional theme in Ireland's coronation cantata, *These Things Shall Be* (1937;

see Ex. 5.9); and in many other pieces: the list could go on. If melodic inversion of the rising fourth as a descending fifth is counted, the 3–2–5 figure is found even more abundantly.

The most familiar of all stepwise bass motions in tonal music is the succession 1–2–3, one of the versions of the schema that Robert O. Gjerdingen has termed 'Do–Re–Mi' for eighteenth-century styles, here with the 1–2–3 in the bass.[51] *Blest Pair of Sirens* has such a Do–Re–Mi in bars 9 to 11, extended later so that the bass reaches degree 5, and an even earlier one, rather disguised by interpolated notes, in bars 3^3 to 5^3. According to the rule of the octave and in line with general practice in tonal music, this progression would typically be realized harmonically with 5/3 6/3 6/3 (tonic in root position, leading-note triad in first inversion, tonic in first inversion). The English version of the rule typically preserves this realization but may touch on an open sonority above degree 2 or 3, either on the (minor) secondary seventh that then resolves to a vii^6, or on the sixth chord itself with the diatonic augmented fourth / diminished fifth conspicuous in the upper parts, possibly with another open sonority on the I^6 (Ex. 1.5). Elgar was especially fond of open sonorities above degree 2: as noted above, in his oratorios he especially remembered Parry's use at 'O may we soon again renew that song'. Unlike the rising fourth, the Do–Re–Mi can be used as an opening gesture in a theme or section. It is heard in Elgar at the start of the unison-hymn-style trio of Pomp and Circumstance No. 1 (for the very words 'Land of hope and glory' in the later vocal setting); at the start of the 'Enigma' theme; at the start of the motto theme of his Symphony No. 1 (1908); and at climactic moments of *The Music Makers* (1912). It was a favourite of Ireland's too in his passages of heightened diatonicism.

Parry's initial descending bass figure from 8 to 5 is a version of another familiar formula in tonal music;[52] here it is labelled the 'Meistersinger tetrachord' for its characteristic bass passing notes on 7 and 6 beneath a sustained

Ex. 1.5 Do–Re–Mi schema in first-level realizations

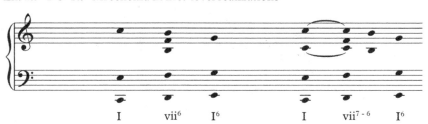

tonic chord in the upper parts, the 7 suspended through a strong beat, as in the first two bars of the *Meistersinger* Prelude (Ex. 1.6 (i) and (ii)). This pattern is usually found as an opening gesture, and for this function it was even more popular than the Do–Re–Mi, reflecting the primacy of descending stepwise bass motion in the idiom. In the rest of this book the term 'Meistersinger tetrachord' is also applied to any passage with stepwise descending bass from 8 to 5 that has a grand, processional rhythm and thick texture in the upper parts, even when the harmony changes in those upper parts, as this in itself amounts to an allusion to the opening of the *Meistersinger* Prelude. Sometimes the Meistersinger tetrachord is combined with an 'inverted 'tetrachord'. This melodic figure overlaps with or closely follows an allusion to

Ex. 1.6 'Meistersinger tetrachord' schemata
(i) Meistersinger tetrachord and inversion

(ii) Wagner, *Die Meistersinger von Nürnberg*, Prelude, bars 1–4[1] (reduction)

(iii) Elgar, *Sea Pictures*, 'Sabbath Morning at Sea', bars 32–33 (reduction)

the tonic opening chords of the *Meistersinger* Prelude or at least the tetrachord schema; it consists of a rising 3-4-5-6 in the melody line that recalls the final three quavers of bar 2 and the first beat of bar 3 of Wagner's Prelude. Often in the English repertory the first three notes of the inverted tetrachord are triplets, as found, for instance, in 'Sabbath Morning at Sea' from Elgar's *Sea Pictures* (Ex. 1.6 (iii)).[53]

A schema-based analysis of the opening 12 bars of *Blest Pair of Sirens* shows Parry's dense deployment of these formulae (Ex. 1.7). The bass line is presented without rhythmic values to emphasize its stepwise motion. The bottom layer of annotation demonstrates the primacy of descent in that stepwise motion. Ascent is present but appears only as a secondary phase of motion. The next layer of annotation shows the conventionalized successions of stepwise bass motions. The figures above the staff line show the predominance of harmonization by means of 6/3 chords, mostly with 7-6 suspensions or appoggiaturas. (The rising-fourth schema with its pair of 7-6 suspensions appears when the bass reaches the 4-3 step, but the principle of the 7-6 applies elsewhere too.) The exceptions to the rule occur once the pedal is reached at the end of the extract analysed here, and at the very beginning, where the initial descending tetrachord is given a Meistersinger-tetrachord realization instead, tonic harmony held in upper parts while the bass descends. Open sonorities are used at almost every opportunity when the bass reaches degree 2 or 6 and secondary seventh harmonies are thereby available.

This way of thinking takes inspiration from the schemata of the eighteenth-century 'galant style' as explained by Gjerdingen and other writers who have revived the partimento-based pedagogy of the old Italian conservatoires. It is now fundamental to music theorists' understanding of eighteenth-century musical syntax and rhetoric, and it is relevant to some nineteenth-century styles as well.[54] Training in the application of such rules of thumb was taught in conservatories and handed down through oral pedagogy and hundreds of written exercises, enabling composers to speak a common language fluently and to turn out music in the fashionable galant style speedily, almost in an improvised fashion. Even S. S. Wesley's 'Ascribe unto the Lord' is still grounded in these routines, with its 'descending tetrachord', 'Prinner' and 'Romanesca' schemata (Ex. 1.1, bars 6-8, 9-15, and 16-17). The 'rule of the octave' was essential to this conception of the musician's task and role, teaching how to realize stepwise bass motion in formulaic ways.[55] The notional English version presents the descending tetrachord (8-7-6-5) of the rule of the octave;

Ex. 1.7 Parry, *Blest Pair of Sirens*, bars 1–12, schema analysis a bass motion akin to the 'Passo indietro' (cadential evasion through the bass motion 5–4–3);[56] and the 'ascending pentachord' (1–2–3–4–5) or at least a part of it (1–2–3), each of which is given a characteristic accent arising from harmonization, melodic shapes, and textures. Each of these fragments of the complete octave descent or ascent can be seen in the analysis of the bass steps in Ex. 1.7. Moreover, even the typical functions of 'gambit' (first thing, tonic based) and 'riposte' (second, answering thing) in the galant style have their analogy in the Meistersinger tetrachord and the rising-fourth schemata.[57] Many subsequent compositions of English diatonic music echo *Blest Pair of Sirens* by beginning with the former and moving to the latter, in effect following a script established by Parry. (For a summary of 'regular orders' of schemata, see Appendix B.)

To be sure, the analogy with the rule of the octave cannot be pressed too far. There is no evidence of the actual teaching of schemata in English musical institutions, after all. In general, it is not possible to account for every note of a diatonic passage of this repertory by means of schemata, as it often is for music of the galant style. Some schemata are better defined than others: the rising fourth and the Do–Re–Mi, for instance, have clearer textural, contrapuntal, and metrical traits than the Meistersinger tetrachord, which is more nebulous and requires latitude in its analytical identification. The impression of schematic composition in English diatonic music reflects the swift canonization of *Blest Pair of Sirens* and the abundant intertextual interplay found throughout the repertory. The rising-fourth schema, the Meistersinger tetrachord, and the application of open sonorities on secondary seventh chords and first-inversion tonics were habituated procedures for many composers when they slipped into processional style.

In the analyses and annotated music examples presented here, schemata are often indicated above the staff lines, and the relevant stepwise bass progressions are shown below them. That should not be taken to mean that the schemata consist of upper-voice harmonizations alone: the bass motions are an integral part of each schema. The identification of bass motions is supposed to draw attention to a notional complete stepwise bass octave ascending or descending, of which only fragments usually appear in musical reality. Occasionally, as at the outset of the trio from Walton's coronation march *Crown Imperial*, the complete descending octave does appear (here with just a single interpolation of degree 4) along with the 'correctly' scripted schema realizations in their regular order (Ex. 1.8). From the conceptual 'rule of the octave' perspective, this passage takes on the character

Ex. 1.8 Walton, *Crown Imperial*, Coronation March, fig. 4, bars 1–8. 'Crown Imperial' by William Walton (1902–1983) © Oxford University Press 1937. All rights reserved.

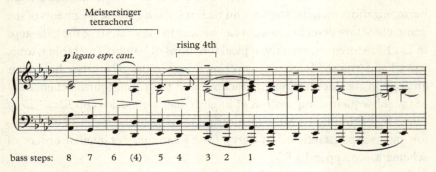

of a well-realized student exercise. It should be understood also that the criteria for identifying schemata are not hard-and-fast; schemata are family resemblances, after all, and as such their definitions may be applied a little loosely. Thus, the rising fourth schema, for instance, will not always have a pair of 7–6 suspensions, while the characteristic rising-fourth interval will sometimes be hidden within the texture or inverted.

A practical origin of Parry's intensive stepwise bass motion may lie in organ playing. Parry learned to play the organ under Elvey during his schooldays at Eton, mainly at St George's Chapel, Windsor, where they frequented the organ loft. He studied Wesley's playing at close quarters.[58] As Brian Newbould points out with reference to Elgar's stepwise bases, for the inexpert player, which Elgar at least probably was when he succeeded his father as organist at St George's, Worcester, stepwise pedalling is attractive, as the foot can pivot on the pedal at the heel or the toe and feel its way to an adjacent pedal rather than searching for a leap.[59] Stepwise bass motion is thus one way to generate serviceable processional music in improvisation. The skilled organist, by contrast, might regard excessively stepwise pedal parts as unidiomatic. As it happens, Vaughan Williams admitted to being a mediocre organist during his time at St Barnabus, Lambeth,[60] even though he believed in the value of good music in parish worship. Gustav Holst (1874–1934), Herbert Howells, Ivor Gurney (1890–1937), John Ireland, and Gerald Finzi were more accomplished organists. From this perspective, the overall picture that emerges from the English repertory of this era is mixed, even though some kind of improvisatory origin seems plausible. The Organ Voluntaries of Samuel Wesley (father of Samuel Sebastian), which may have started the whole tradition of stepwise bass motion, are at least conceptually improvisatory and might record an actual improvisatory practice. However, it is music for expert players by an expert player, and it is notated on only two staves, probably for organs without pedals, with the stepwise bass parts almost invariably marked 'Diapasions'. The organ pedal part near the end of the finale of Elgar's 'Enigma' Variations (see Ex. 2.15(iv)) moves stepwise for long stretches, as does that of the third movement of his Organ Sonata (see Ex. 2.9), and that of much of his very processional anthem with organ accompaniment 'Great Is the Lord' (1912). All these bass parts are notated on a third staff, pointing to pedals. On the other hand, the extensively stepwise bass part in 'Procession to Calvary' from Stainer's *Crucifixion*, a piece for church choirs and church organists, is marked alternately 'con Ped.' and 'senza Ped.', the organ part being notated on two staves only, thus blocking any exact correspondence of stepwise bass and organ pedal part. The pedal parts of Parry's solo organ music such as the *Chorale Preludes* (1912, 1915) and the *Chorale Fantasias* (1915), are challenging and do not rely on stepwise motion. The opening of *Blest Pair of Sirens* looks and sounds like an orchestral version of an organ texture, with a pedal part doubled in octaves beneath a thick upper-part texture (playable by two hands on manuals), while 'Jerusalem' begins in a way that invites realization with the pedals beneath the massive chords above, even though the organ part in the original version was notated on just two staves. When the introduction to *Blest Pair of Sirens* moves to descending thirds in the bass (bars 17–20 and 23–24)—still stepwise motion in a sense, as the descending leaps move downwards sequentially—it imitates an idiomatic organ pedal part that could easily be executed by a reasonably skilled player.

At a concrete level, the influence of *Blest Pair of Sirens* on later English diatonic music took two main forms. First, processional diatonicism as a topic was soon in widespread use, especially in connection with the key of E flat major. It was fundamental to Elgar's musical 'voice', and before 1914 it was important to Vaughan Williams too, as shown in Chapter 2. After World War I, processional diatonicism in a new form was taken up by Gerald Finzi (Chapter 4), again as a carefully crafted personal style, and it was used more intermittently but tellingly by composers such as John Ireland and William Walton, almost invariably in a context of grand, idealistic sentiments (Chapter 5). Second, the very opening of *Blest Pair of Sirens*, and often specifically the schematic succession Meistersinger tetrachord / rising fourth, became a favourite for grand diatonic openings and climaxes in English music. It is found, for instance, in grand choral guise near the opening of the first movement of Vaughan Williams's *A Sea Symphony* (1910; see the discussion in Chapter 2) and at the first great climax of Holst's *The Cloud Messenger* (premiered 1913), both passages clearly referencing the opening of Parry's 'Ode' at several levels. The organ introduction to Elgar's anthem 'Great Is the Lord' (1913), a piece saturated with stepwise bass motion in processional style, likewise refers to the two elements from the opening of Parry's ode. From the late 1930s, one or both of these schemata, often in direct succession, was favoured for the opening of celebratory or occasional pieces or sections of pieces—not always choral—by composers such as Walton, Bax, Arthur Bliss (1891–1975), Ireland, Finzi, and Vaughan Williams (detailed in Chapter 5). A few other features of *Blest Pair of Sirens* were taken up too: Vaughan Williams favoured G major as a secondary key within E flat major diatonic passages or pieces, just as in Parry's 'Ode', while Howells in his later choral music sometimes elaborated on Parry's Meistersinger-like concluding bars (explained in Chapter 6), again for climactic passages.

Public Processional Contexts

English processional diatonicism was first and foremost a musical, aesthetic, and intellectual phenomenon rather than a sonic accompaniment to live ceremony. Its musical origins lie in the onstage processions in Wagner's music dramas. Nevertheless, it cannot be irrelevant that processional behaviour was central to Victorian public life. During the 1850s and 1860s, the industrial city corporations organized spectacular ceremonies to celebrate the inauguration of civic buildings, the unveiling of statues and monuments, royal visits, the opening of the Assizes Commissions, and the funerals of civic worthies. The historian Simon Gunn has written of a 'public processional culture' of the industrial towns and cities of Victorian Britain. In this way, the corporations displayed themselves, asserted their authority, and celebrated their cities and their communities.[61] In medium-sized towns such as those of the Three Choirs Festival, these ceremonies flourished, in less lavish fashion, up to World War I. This was a world with which musicians such as Hubert Parry and Edward Elgar were deeply familiar and in which they participated. The Three Choirs Festival in particular was not just a musical event but a traditional local society gathering in September coordinated with the county

Assizes. At the start of the 1905 festival in his hometown of Worcester, the title of Honorary Freeman of the City was conferred upon Elgar in a ceremony at the Guildhall. The composer, dressed in his Yale doctoral robes, was photographed leaving the building with his childhood friend Hubert Leicester, who at that time was mayor of the city. They, the high sheriff, and the aldermen in their civic robes then processed down High Street past the Elgar family music shop, where the composer saluted his elderly father, and on to the cathedral for a performance of his oratorio *The Dream of Gerontius*. This work, most significantly in light of the English musical revival and its priorities, displaced Mendelssohn's *Elijah* from its traditional place at the start of the festival.[62] If the aldermen had been paying close attention to the performance, they might have noticed two choruses in Part I in processional style: 'Be merciful' (from fig. 35) and the final section from 'Go, in the Name of God' (from fig. 70). In the latter, the priest and the supplicants dispatch the soul of the dying man in a grand hymn that fades into ethereal echoes and a sonic image of the soul's departure from the body and ascent to heaven. The occasion encapsulates Elgar's civic patriotism (his affection for his hometown), the canonization of his choral compositions, and the intertwining of civic and religious ceremony.

Victorian processional culture extended well beyond civic ceremony, encompassing political party rallies, royal jubilees, coronations, and, in the years before World War I, trade-union demonstrations and Suffragette marches. At the same time, religious ceremony was revived in Victorian England under the influence of the Oxford movement and the Catholic Church, in part as an appeal to working-class worshippers. The social and institutional contexts for English processional diatonicism are rather wide, encompassing more than just royal and state ceremony and hierarchical spectacle. By the late nineteenth century, the terms of civic ceremonies were usually negotiated with participants such as guilds and trade societies and with popular opinion via the press.[63] Civic processions needed to adapt to compete with popular entertainment; if they did not, the events did not attract an audience. Planning documents indicate that account was taken of public opinion, and the events became a blend of ceremony and recreation with participation by the public rather than just observation.[64] At the 1897 Diamond Jubilee, hierarchical display was replaced by popular processions and impromptu celebrations that anticipated the street parties that marked royal weddings and coronations in the twentieth century.[65]

This was also the moment that Elgar brought together processional diatonicism and patriotic celebration with his *Imperial March* (1897). In his occasional, patriotic compositions, Elgar developed a blend of the popular and the elevated that corresponds with the negotiated ceremony of its era. Along with idioms redolent of the circus or the music hall, he favoured the 'unison hymn' subtopic in the trios of his orchestral marches. Both Elgar and Parry wrote music for coronation ceremonies, at which real grand processions took place, and Parry belatedly produced the patriotic unison hymns 'Jerusalem' (1916) and 'England' (1919). Later occasional music in Elgarian manner by Walton and Arnold Bax (1883–1953) was commissioned for coronation ceremonies. But processional diatonicism was much more than the correlate of state ceremony, and composers did not always cooperate with the authorities. Parry declined an invitation from the conductor Hans Richter to write a 'Jubilee Overture' in 1897 because of what he regarded as commercialization of the anniversary occasion.[66] Elgar refused to attend the 1911 coronation, thus missing the premiere of his *Coronation March*, apparently because he regarded George V and his court as philistines. And while Parry originally composed 'Jerusalem' for the ultrapatriotic 'Fight for Right' movement, he withdrew his support from that organization in 1917 and found a new purpose for the song, conducting it at a women's demonstration meeting on March 17, 1917. After it was sung at a Suffrage demonstration concert in March 1918, he and women's Suffrage advocate Milicent Fawcett agreed that the song should become the Women Voters' Hymn.[67]

Parry, Processional Diatonicism, and Nationalism after *Blest Pair of Sirens*

It is at times all too easy to conflate the styles of Parry and Elgar. The two composers almost merge in the patriotic atmosphere of the Last Night of the Proms, where 'Land of Hope and Glory', as part of Elgar's Pomp and Circumstance March No. 1 and 'Jerusalem', as orchestrated by Elgar in a glittering style (somewhat at odds with Parry's own taste and his own orchestral version), are sung alongside one another. But although processional diatonicism marks what are today Parry's three most famous pieces—*Blest Pair of Sirens*, *I Was Glad*, and 'Jerusalem', in most of his output Parry used the idiom sparingly. Intensive diatonicism appears in pieces for similar choral forces to the Milton 'Ode', such as *De Profundis* (1891) for 12-part chorus, solo soprano, and orchestra (Parry exaggerated the stepwise bass motion in parts of this piece to the point of parody); the double-choir anthem *God Is Our Hope* (1913); and the a capella *Songs of Farewell* (1916-1917).[68] Parry's symphonies have grand, diatonic themes at certain moments, many of which echo the main theme of the finale of Brahms's First Symphony, not least in their key, usually C major, and the low violin scoring for their melodies.[69] Another instrumental realization—perhaps Parry's first and an anticipation of the orchestral marches of Elgar—is the 'Bridal March' from his incidental music to a Cambridge production of Aristophanes' *The Birds* (1883).[70]

When it came to patriotism and populism, Elgar, to whom these things came much more naturally, led the way and was far more prolific. Parry followed Elgar's music closely from *Caractacus* (1898) onwards, hearing all the major works in early performances and recording his reactions in his diaries.[71] By 1902, the year of 'I Was Glad', he would therefore have known Elgar's patriotic and redemptive treatment of processional diatonicism in *Caractacus*, along with Variations IX ('Nimrod') and XIV (the finale) of the 'Enigma' Variations, the chorus 'Be merciful', and the finale of Part I of *Gerontius*, the *Imperial March*, and the Pomp and Circumstance March No. 1. His private reactions to Elgar's music were mixed—he took exception to the doctrinal religion of *Gerontius* in particular—and he seems not to have warmed to Elgar's at-times exasperating personality.[72] His excursions down parallel paths may have been rare, but the results have kept his name alive more effectively than his lengthy oratorios, numerous songs, or even his orchestral works.

With 'I Was Glad' Parry adapted the idiom of processional diatonicism to actual ceremony: in fact, a processional entrance. The work's premiere occurred within a programme of deliberate tradition-building in English music by Sir Frederick Bridge, organist of Westminster Abbey, organizer of the 1902 coronation programme, and a member of the Royal College of Music network.[73] The text of Psalm 122 had been a fixture at English coronations since 1626, but Parry's new setting, the main choral commission for the 1902 event, was monumental in form, exploiting the 430 singers and 75 instrumentalists Bridge had assembled. Bridge chose to restrict the selection of choral music—the programme of the service itself—to works by native composers, and he provided an historical survey of, as he put it, 'five centuries of English Church music' up to the present day, including Tallis, Gibbons, Handel (counted as English), Samuel Sebastian Wesley, Sullivan, Stanford, and Stainer.[74] By contrast, the orchestral programme played during the assembly of the invited international congregation and their later dispersal was a mixture of British and Continental pieces, with Elgar, Frederick Cowen, Alexander Mackenzie, and Percy Godfrey alongside Wagner (three pieces), Gounod (two), Saint-Saëns, and Tchaikovsky.[75] This was a practical application of the principle advanced by Frederick Ouseley and Fuller Maitland that it was specifically in choral music that a continuous English musical tradition across the centuries was to be found. And by commissioning Parry's anthem, Bridge demonstrated that the tradition was alive and well. (There were also shorter new anthems by himself and Sir Walter Parratt.) In terms of recent ceremonial tradition, 'I Was Glad' revisited the triple association established at the Royal College of Music foundation-stone laying of 1890: celebration of English music, processional diatonicism and Albert, Prince of Wales, first as president of the college and then as King Edward VII. Ironically, the premiere of 'I Was Glad' was something of a debacle. 'Bridge made a sad mistake in the processional music and seemed to lose his head', as Parry related. He finished the anthem before the king had even entered the building, and, embarrassingly, he had to repeat the *vivat* cries and the whole of the second half of the piece.[76] Thus, potentially the greatest moment of convergence of English processional diatonicism and processional ceremony fell flat. By contrast, Bridge's promotion of a conception of musical tradition was much more successful. Later coronations preserved his all-English choral service, along with most of the pieces on the 1902 programme, including 'I Was Glad' for the processional entry of the monarch. At both the 1937 and 1953, coronations the stylistic connections with the Victorian past could have been picked up by an experienced listener from Wesley's anthem 'Thou Wilt Keep Him in Perfect Peace', one of his most richly diatonic compositions.[77]

In 'Jerusalem' (1916), Parry composed a unison hymn that evokes the subtopic of that name, although the intensive diatonic dissonance and thick accompaniment textures are characteristic of his full choral writing. His key, D major, is the same as that of Elgar's Pomp and Circumstance March No. 1, and patriotism is for once conspicuous in the text Parry chose to set. There is no connection with royalty or with a real ceremonial occasion, however; the hymn returns to the high spiritual aspirations of *Blest Pair of Sirens* (both it and 'I Was Glad' refer in different ways to the New Jerusalem). 'Jerusalem' was intended for community singing, although the questions of which community and for what purpose were, as noted above, negotiable. If there is a musical precedent for 'Jerusalem', it is probably the communion song 'Wein und Brot' from Act I of Wagner's *Parsifal*, sung in unison by several offstage voices while the elements of communion are distributed to the grail knights. This episode anticipates English diatonic music in numerous ways (see Appendix A): the key is E flat major; the melodic syncopations anticipate the trio of Elgar's Pomp and Circumstance March No. 1 ('Land of Hope and Glory'); and the tonicization of the mediant key along with a 'fifth drop' from degree 7 to 4 anticipates 'Jerusalem'. Vaughan Williams's unison hymns composed during World War II also echo 'Wein und Brot' at times (see Chapter 6).

Parry's Symphony No. 3 ('The English') in its various versions is a study in Elgar's influence and the two composers' gradual convergence. Parry probably began working on it in 1887, shortly after the premiere of *Blest Pair of Sirens*. It eventually fulfilled a commission from the Philharmonic Society for an orchestral work smaller than a full symphony. Parry said it could be called a 'short symphony' in what he described as the 'plain' key of C major. That version was premiered in 1889 and acquired its nickname 'English' from the programme note of the music critic Joseph Bennett—which must have been approved by Parry—on account of its thematic material. The name was then used in the title of the published score of 1907. In the 1890s, the 'English' Symphony enjoyed many more performances than most native symphonies of the time, although that was due as much to its dimensions and limited scoring, which appealed to amateur orchestras, as to its title.[78] Much of its thematic material is dance-like in a somewhat archaic, seventeenth- or eighteenth-century style: the cheerful opening theme of the first movement, the minuet-like scherzo, and some of the finale's variations. Parts of the symphony are thus cut from the same cloth as Parry's *Suite Moderne* (1886) and *Lady Radnor Suite* (1894) for string orchestra, the latter being a set of ancient–modern dance movements laid out in the manner of a Baroque suite. Processional diatonicism appears most prominently in the second tonic-key theme of the first movement, marked 'largamente' (Ex. 1.9). Each phrase begins with a stepwise bass descent in steady crotchets. Some of these ingredients are also present in the finale's theme, although the stepwise bass is less evident there. The model of the main theme of the finale of Brahms's First Symphony is everywhere apparent. In this work, processional diatonicism inhabits a wider 'English' world of historical dances, a blending of topics that Elgar, despite his interest in ballet-style writing and old-fashioned dance idioms,[79] never attempted. Especially in its original, concise format, the vigorous dance rhythms and frank-and-forthright tone of

Ex. 1.9 Parry, Symphony No. 3 'English', first movement, bars 22²–30

Parry's 'English' Symphony not only resuscitated eighteenth-century styles but also preserved something of an eighteenth-century patriotic mode of anti-aristocratic, anti-French reformist moralism.[80] Parry shared the ethos of that movement; his moralizing tone and interest in 'sincerity' reveal its legacy in his writings.

Over a period of twenty years Parry revised the 'English' Symphony several times. As he did so, it grew longer, grander, and, it must be said, more Elgarian. The first revision was for the subscription concerts at Leeds in 1895. The first movement was rescored, three trombone parts were added, and new variations were written for the finale. In 1902, the first movement was revised again for a performance at Bournemouth, and then Parry worked on the piece for the last time in 1905 in advance of its publication. Thus, the published version—and the one that is available to us today on a recording—is less like a chamber symphony or dance suite than was the 1889 original. The structural alterations in the 1902 version are the most important. By this time, Parry knew Elgar's contributions to the processional style and was himself developing a more grandiose approach in 'I Was Glad'.

In the first movement, it is precisely the 'largamente' processional theme in its two appearances and the passages preparing them that Parry altered,[81] adding and subtracting certain passages, and changing the scoring, the dynamics, and the function of the theme within the sonata-form scheme. Parry made no other structural alterations in the movement, restricting the changes elsewhere to scoring, dynamics, phrase markings, and tinkering with inner parts. On its first appearance the 'largamente' theme is rescored with extra wind instruments: one clarinet, two bassoons, and two horns double the string parts. The new scoring, especially the doubling of the melody on horn and clarinet, gives it a distinctly Elgarian, and rather less Brahmsian, sound.[82] The theme is prepared more deliberately, with extra bars of transition and preparation in advance of both its appearances. Originally, the recapitulation began with the fifth bar of the movement's jaunty opening theme, which continued in parallel with the exposition until the *largamente* processional theme, which was marked *mf*.[83] In the 1902 version, the moment of reprise is also a transformation of the work's opening. It is given a grand preparation with a longer dominant pedal and a timpani roll. The movement's opening theme does not reappear in the recapitulation at all; instead, the processional theme appears resplendent at *f* dynamic as the goal of the development section's energy at the moment of reprise and the recapturing of stable tonic harmony. The original merry dance is thus replaced by processional diatonicism at the head of the movement's array of thematic materials. If the 1889 conception of the 'English' Symphony is a rare instance of processional diatonicism as the expression of the well-established concept of English national character as hale and hearty rather than elevated and ceremonial, then the lure of the latter proved stronger in the long term, as Parry moved towards a more Elgarian approach in his revisions.

Hubert Parry had unfolded a vision and pointed a way forward for English composers. He was intellectually up to date; his generous and inspiring personality as leader of the English musical profession matched the ethical values that he espoused in art; and he had composed *Blest Pair of Sirens* in a distinctive diatonic style, which seemed to translate those values into music. Yet, most discerning musicians were aware that the rest of his compositional output was of mixed quality. For ten glorious minutes his music seemed to fulfil the lofty vision of Milton's 'Ode', disclosing eternity to the listener's imagination through its diatonic language. Thereafter, however, as a composer Parry had stumbled. But precisely because he had opened a rich field but left his project incomplete, his work seemed to invite continuation in whatever way others saw fit, and and that is what two of them—Edward Elgar and Ralph Vaughan Williams—now set out to achieve.

2

Processional Diatonicism II

Elgar and Vaughan Williams to 1914

In the years of Hubert Parry's prestige as a composer, musical thinker, and leader, it was Edward Elgar and Ralph Vaughan Williams who adopted the topic of processional diatonicism most frequently, applied it most resourcefully, and, in their different ways, took steps to fulfil Parry's unfinished project. For Elgar the topic was definitive for his mature style—in fact, his musical 'persona'—whereas for Vaughan Williams it was central only for a while before he developed a distinctive diatonic idiom of his own with a different aesthetic. Elgar knew Parry's major compositions well.[1] In his inaugural lecture as Professor of Music at the University of Birmingham, he called Parry 'the head of our art in this country'.[2] But he left little by way of verbal commentary on Parry's style or ideas, aside from his ubiquitous score marking 'nobilmente'—otherwise very rare in Western classical music—which, however, does not always correspond with the topic of processional diatonicism. Vaughan Williams, by contrast, was much more prolific as a public commentator on musical matters and pursued a broad cultural programme of musical reform that encompassed the ethos of singing and singers; the collection and promotion of English folksong; the improvement of English church music; the revival of Tudor music; the organization of a local festival at Leith Hill in Surrey; the rehearsal and direction of amateur choirs; and the delivery or publication of public essays, lectures and broadcasts. In the 1900s, he studied the music of both Parry and Elgar, and in his own music he developed a complex web of intertextual allusions to diatonic passages in their scores in what appears to have been an act of deliberate tradition-building in musical composition. This was a specifically modern musical tradition without reference to a Tudor 'golden age' or to folksong. And even when Vaughan Williams had left processional diatonicism behind in his compositional work, he still kept hold of Parry's ideas about musical evolution and about the relationship of music to its cultural environment; he cited Parry's writings liberally in his lectures at Bryn Mawr College in 1932.[3]

Beyond Elgar and Vaughan Williams, along with a few of Parry's own works, instances of processional diatonicism were rarer in the years before World War I. John Ireland's Passiontide anthem 'Greater Love Hath No Man' (1912) stands out as an impressive essay in the style, building especially on passages from Elgar's *The Apostles*. The climactic setting of the words 'O glorious cloud I welcome thee' in Gustav Holst's *The Cloud Messenger* (premiere 1913) is nothing less than a fulsome tribute to Parry's *Blest Pair of Sirens*, with Meistersinger-tetrachord and rising-fourth schemata in the standard order within a massive choral-orchestral texture. George Butterworth's (1885–1916) Orchestral Rhapsody *A Shropshire Lad* (premiere 1913) has its grand diatonic climaxes in E flat major, despite being tonally distant from that key at other times, and it again draws on the Meistersinger tetrachord in those passages. Charles Wood echoed both Parry and Elgar in his anthem 'O Thou, the Central Orb' (1915), without entirely relinquishing his ties to the Mendelssohn legacy. One quality united the efforts of all six composers: feelings of elevation, whether through doctrinal religion and its liturgy, mysticism, populism and patriotism, or transcendent humanism. Until the onset of World War I, at least, these composers continued to appeal with their processional diatonicism to the listener's 'high-raised phantasie', which, according to Milton, might disclose a vision of the 'sapphire-coloured throne' and the everlasting music of the seraphim and cherubim.

Elgar: Populism and Spectacle

From the late 1890s, Elgar returned to processional diatonicism time and again for elevated and thematically referential passages. Elgar gave the topic fresh impetus, adapting and applying it imaginatively. He was less suspicious than Parry of sensational effects and arresting timbre—the older composer might have deemed this aspect of Elgar's work 'materialistic'—and was readier to explore subjective religious experiences. The first tendency can be instantly gauged by a comparison of Elgar's extravagant orchestration of Parry's 'Jerusalem' with the composer's more self-effacing one. But as well as extrovert, populist applications, Elgar also pursued Parry's more inward kind of nobility in a succession of major choral and orchestral works in the 15 years from *Caractacus* (1898) to *Falstaff* (1913). Here the significance of the idiom was regal, spiritual, and at times mystical, and it became strongly linked with the key of E flat major even in compositions set in other, distantly related keys: an inter-opus association with *Blest Pair of Sirens* that Parry himself did not pursue. Elgar applied the idiom flexibly and built it into compositions of larger scale than Parry's occasional choral works, alternating intensively diatonic and chromatic passages in sprawling, post-Wagnerian designs. He sometimes combined multiple processional idioms, as though in a grand pageant, exploring spatial effects through 'fade ins' and 'fade outs', as though musicians were approaching and receding from the listener. Elgar developed his own preferences amongst diatonic schemata, including some sense of an opening 'regular order' that followed a different script from the one established by the opening of *Blest Pair of Sirens*. The manipulation of diatonic conventions contributed quite subtly to Elgar's post-Lisztian practices of thematic transformation and apotheosis.

In Elgar's music, processional diatonicism accompanied processional practices, literal or implied, and became a vehicle for popular unison singing, patriotism, and monarchism. He initiated these applications and pursued them more explicitly and more consistently than Parry, at first in a few sections of the *Imperial March* (1897) and then systematically in *Caractacus* (1898). With his later orchestral marches Elgar brought the atmosphere of popular celebration into the concert hall, a participative tradition continued today in the party atmosphere of the Last Night of the Proms. Audience participation was conspicuous already at the London premiere of Pomp and Circumstance March No. 1 at the Queen's Hall on 21 October 1901, when the audience demanded an unprecedented second encore of the entire piece. Pomp and Circumstance No. 1 recalls nineteenth-century brass band repertory and even the circus ring: its chromatic quick march and hymn-like melody are precisely the ingredients of Julius Fučík's recent march, *Entry of the Gladiators* (1897). The trio melody is one of the first instances of the 'unison hymn' subtopic of processional diatonicism in English music. Its two grand apotheoses thus suggested popular singing even before the addition of the words of the song 'Land of Hope and Glory' by A. C. Benson when Elgar incorporated the tune into his *Coronation Ode* (1902). The *Empire March* (1924) has trombone antics again redolent of the circus, and in Pomp and Circumstance No. 5 (1930) Elgar widened the popular references to the idioms of the music hall, using a bouncing 6/8 metre for the quick march. As these examples indicate, Elgar's processional writing was wide-ranging; the diatonic version, though central, does not exhaust it.

Elgar embraced spectacle and concrete processional applications beyond military marches and royal ceremonial, including the craze for historical pageantry that began in Britain in the mid-1900s, which would hardly have appealed to Parry. Elgar was drawn to these events for financial reasons that did not trouble Parry, but he also genuinely believed in their value. Ernest Newman wrote of Elgar in his *Sunday Times* obituary that 'He saw the outer world as a magnificent pageant, every line and colour of which thrilled him'.[4] The historical pageant was a phenomenon of mass entertainment, officially sanctioned education, and outdoor spectacle, depicting episodes from a community's history through the participation of large numbers of local people.[5] More than 40 such pageants were staged in Britain in the decade before 1914. They first flourished in the provincial urban centres, mingling local and national patriotism and often ending with an empire-themed finale.[6] Three major pageants followed in London: the English Church Pageant (1909), the Army Pageant (1910), and the Pageant of London at the Festival of Empire (1911). The Pageant of London was organized by the prolific pageant master Frank Lascelles, who had a distinctive, spectacular style that minimized dialogue and mobilized very large casts in mass processions and dances, their costumes forming blocks of colour. The journalist Arthur Mee, echoing Newman on Elgar, observed that 'Frank Lascelles must think of life as one stupendous spectacle; he must see it down the avenues of time like a vast unfolding of picture after picture'.[7] The Pageant of London included in its final part a 'Masque Imperial' that presented episodes in the history of England and its empire up to the proclamation of Queen Victoria as Empress of India in 1877. It ended with an 'Allegory of the Advantages of Empire' that personified ideas such as 'Britannia' and 'Genius of the World'. In the following year, 1912, Elgar wrote, rehearsed, and conducted music for a pageant-like theatrical 'masque' entitled *The Crown of India*, which followed Lascelles' model in more than just its generic title. The masque was staged at the London Coliseum as part of a music hall programme. Like the recent Dehli Durbar, which it partly mimicked, it celebrated the coronation of George V as Emperor of India. Lavish stage sets, pantomimes, processions, songs, spoken text, and choruses depicted scenes from Indian life and history and showed India's cities, personified, gathering with 'John Company' (the East India Company) and St. George.[8] The masque was part of a variety show, sharing a programme with a comedian, a ventriloquist, tightrope walkers, a pantomime, and musical and dramatic extracts.[9]

Elgar again engaged this blend of spectacular ceremony, entertainment and imperialism in his *Empire March* and his songs for the British Empire Exhibition held at the Empire Stadium (later Wembley Stadium) in 1924.

Elgar conducted the music at the opening ceremony on St George's Day, which included his *Imperial March* and 'Land of Hope and Glory', Parry's 'Jerusalem', and the National Anthem (although not, in the end, the *Empire March* itself). By this time, audio amplification was available, and Elgar conducted massed London choirs of at least 1000 voices in the open air, the sound transmitted to the rest of the stadium by loudspeakers.[10] Later that year, the Exhibition continued with a monumental 'Pageant of Empire', again organized by Lascelles, at which Elgar's new songs introduced processions representing South Africa, India, New Zealand, and Australia. Again he conducted the opening performance, which included 'With Proud Thanksgiving', an outdoor adaptation of the finale of his wartime cantata *The Spirit of England* in a more sombre—and harmonically chromatic—processional style. The pageant was a spectacular outdoor event to match the scale of the stadium, involving a cast of 15,000 people and thousands of animals, including horses, donkeys, camels, monkeys, doves, and elephants. The exhibition blended entertainment and education, Elgar's music competing for attention with attractions that included an amusement park, an operational colliery, a dance hall, a miniature railway, and a life-size sculpture of the Prince of Wales and his horse in Canadian butter.[11] In this way Elgar participated as composer and performer in spectacular events based around mass processions that were partly entertainment, partly officially approved propaganda, telling sweeping stories of the British Empire. The music he composed for these events is relatively uninspired, admittedly, but his participation forms the everyday context for the idealized processions that fill his finest scores as well.

Although 'pageant fever' did not fully break out in Britain until 1905, the title page of the published score of Elgar's overture *Cockaigne (In London Town)* (1901) by Boosey & Hawkes captures its spirit, with assorted images of London past and present, including St Paul's Cathedral, medieval lancers at a tournament, Big Ben, archers in Renaissance-era costume, a modern golfer, Piccadilly, Tudor-style shop fronts, and modern soldiers marching behind their bandsmen. Elgar's overture invites this visual framing with its abundant and contrasted processional rhythms, representations of the 'citizen' and the 'cockney' (or 'young citizens'), a military march that has a band approaching and marching away, an idyllic scene with a pair of lovers, a Salvation Army band, and a scene in a church. The overture presents a picturesque overview of city life imagined in its teeming diversity and realized through spatial effects that recall a staged urban procession: the military band marches 'towards' the listener and fades away again into the distance; the Salvation Army band is 'heard' in the 'distance' playing out of tune; the cockney and the lovers 'enter' the church.[12] Elgar linked this portrayal of popular spectacle with civic values and an ethos of nobility, creating another blend in the manner of the negotiated ceremony of the era. The 'citizen' theme, marked *nobilmente*, full of descending stepwise bass motion and leaping melodic figures, which returns in apotheosis to end the overture, came to Elgar, he related, 'one dark day in the Guildhall: looking at the memorials of the city's great past & knowing well the history of its unending charity, I seemed to hear far away in the dim roof a theme, an echo of some noble melody'.[13] These sentiments could stand for English processional diatonicism in general: the imagination uplifted to the roof of the building (the 'high-raised phantasie'), the associations of transcendent values and eternity in 'unending charity' (eternal Love) and the distant echo of noble melody, not so far, perhaps, from the 'undisturbèd Song of pure concent' that humans can strain to discern once again only in imagination. In the processional diatonicism of the citizen theme, Elgar endeavoured to 'renew that song' in a noble but populist musical idiom.

No less than in Parry's *Blest Pair of Sirens*, the Prelude to Wagner's *Die Meistersinger* is a strong point of reference for the music of *Cockaigne*, first through the tonal scheme—the C major tonic with E flat major as a prominent secondary key—and the diminution of the 'citizen' theme for the 'young Londoners', which parallels Wagner's portrayal of the procession of apprentices.[14] Just as Wagner staged the historical festival movement in Act III of *Die Meistersinger*, Elgar brought into his overture a London pageant. (Arnold Bax evidently recognized this when he alluded directly to the climactic approach to and apotheosis of the citizen theme near the end of his own coronation-year showpiece *London Pageant* (1937)).[15] Twenty-five years after receiving the honorary freedom of the city of Worcester, in his *Severn Suite* (1930) for brass band, Elgar returned for the last time to the practice of historical pageantry, which in the meantime had become a recreational craze in British provincial towns, gaining momentum especially in the late 1920s.[16] The suite's movements have subtitles that refer to historic places in Worcester, all of them consistent with the historical coverage of such pageants, which usually stopped before the English Civil War: 'Worcester Castle' (in processional style), 'Tournament', 'The Cathedral', and 'Commandery'.

Elgar wrote several types of orchestral march. One could be called the 'Pomp and Circumstance' type, in scherzo format with a quick march and trio; the *Imperial March* and the *Empire March* fall into this category.

Processional diatonicism appears mainly in the trios (Ex. 2.1). The melodies are broad and serene, while the bass marches softly, usually stepwise, with detached notes clearly articulating the pulse. The texture is uncluttered—sometimes with only two parts—and diatonic dissonance is inconspicuous in comparison with, say, Parry's multi-part choral textures (the manner of

Ex. 2.1 Elgar, trio themes from orchestral marches
(i) Pomp and Circumstance March No. 1, fig. I, bars 1–8 (reduction)

(ii) Pomp and Circumstance March No. 3, fig. G, bars 1–8 (reduction)

(iii) Pomp and Circumstance March No. 4, fig. G, bars 1–12 (reduction)

Ex. 2.1 Continued

(iv) Empire March, fig. 8, bars 2–5 (reduction)

(v) Pomp and Circumstance March No. 5, fig. 9, bars 1–8 (reduction)

'choral ode'). Sometimes the subtopic is clearly 'unison hymn' (Ex. 2.1(i), (iii) and (v)), sometimes the tunes are 'chivalrous' with leaps and flourishes (Ex. 2.1(ii) and (iv)); the latter tend to evoke intensive diatonicism briefly before shifting between keys. The melodies are usually given to violins in their low register, sometimes doubled by woodwind instruments (clarinets, bassoons or horns). An apotheosis version occurs near the end of the march, and sometimes a preliminary apotheosis as well within the trio itself. Pomp and Circumstance March No. 2 is the exception to the rule, as it has no processional diatonicism and no apotheosis for its trio melody. In the *Imperial March* and Pomp and Circumstance March No. 3, fully realized processional diatonicism appears only in the middle of the trios, while the outer sections of the trios have delicate melodies in dotted rhythms that recall ballet music. Elgar's 'trio manner' is found at slower tempi in the major-key sections of his funeral marches: the one for the incidental music to George Moore and W. B. Yeats's play *Grania and Diarmid* (1901) and the second movement of Symphony No. 2 (1911) (Ex. 2.2). The latter is one of the many instances of three-part diatonic counterpoint in the Symphony and in Elgar's works in general, often in E flat major, with an active inner part.

Elgar's second type of orchestral march is loosely organized and episodic: a rather literal translation into music of the panoramic experience of beholding a spectacular grand procession. The very title of the 'Triumphal March' from *Caractacus* recalls the spectacle of Verdi's *Aida*, where the march accompanies a procession on the operatic stage, something that, of

Ex. 2.2 Elgar, 'trio style' in funeral marches
(i) Funeral March, *Grania and Diarmid*, fig. H, bars 1–4 (reduction)

(ii) Symphony No. 2, second movement, fig. 68, bars 5^3–9^2 (reduction)

course, the Leeds Festival could not provide at the cantata's premiere. The Roman legions, returned from Britain, hold a victory procession in the heart of their imperial city, with the defeated British leaders trailing behind them. Elgar's march includes a brassy opening in C major; passages of fast string figuration in C minor; a style that approaches processional diatonicism in E flat major (although with a faster-moving bass than usual); and a subdued, trudging theme for the British captives. The *Coronation March* (1911), composed as the recessional music for the coronation service of George V, is another sprawling affair that moves through two leisurely presentations of a sequence of independent thematic sections, each with its own character. Elgar reverses the usual order of topics, holding back the quick march for the middle of the piece. The G-minor, triple-metre opening is a Bach-like conception with one contrapuntal line after another added over a repeated descending ground bass: a novel merging of the processional topic with that of the Baroque chaconne. The march proper begins with a series of interlinked themes with leaping melodies and largely stepwise basses, which modulate more than usual for Elgar. The march as a whole begins in G minor but ends grandly in B flat major, a rare rejection on Elgar's part of tonal unity for a piece on this scale that reinforces its sense of diffuseness. The *Crown of India March* (1912) is similarly episodic, and it too accompanied an actual procession, on this occasion on stage. All three of these marches have moments when themes fade in or out, some sections being audibly curtailed and denied completion by a quick transition, as though next the part of the procession were pushing into view.

Elgar: Nation and Spirituality

From 1898 Elgar brought processional diatonicism into his artistically ambitious choral and orchestral works. Beyond the level at which this topic became simply a personal style, certain patterns in its application are evident, representing significant compositional decisions. The most notable of these patterns is a loose cluster of associations surrounding the key of E flat major, themes of nation, spirituality, and redemption, and the usual musical characteristics of nobility and elevation.[17] In the oratorios, passages of this type sometimes transform the rhythms of physical footfall into an ethereal vision, turning an earthly procession into a heavenly ascent. There is no clearer example of the creation of a musical tradition than these passages taken together, all of them in the key of *Blest Pair of Sirens*.

In Elgar's cantata *Caractacus*, composed for the Leeds Festival of 1898 and dedicated to Queen Victoria, the association of processional diatonicism and national identity emerges for the first time. The style is worked into a scenario that evokes central themes of nineteenth-century cultural nationalism: ancient legends, exemplary heroes, their sacrifices, an attractive local landscape that represents the national homeland, a people dwelling in the landscape, and a sense of the glorious destiny of that people.[18] Processional diatonicism now enters a work of 'national music' that in its ideological commitment reaches beyond a sense of indigenous choral tradition or popular patriotic celebration. The idiom appears for the first time as a topic and a leitmotiv within a post-Wagnerian conception of the provincial festival commission executed in an advanced and flexible tonal language. Its key is almost invariably E flat major.

Processional rhythms of diverse kinds are found throughout the cantata: in the opening chorus 'Watchmen, alert!', a menacing military march; the sinister ritual of the Druids in Scene 2 ('Tread the mystic circle round'); the lament 'Oh my warriors', a set piece of processional diatonicism, although, ironically, in septuple metre; the 'Triumphal March' in all its variety; the final chorus, which returns to the military idioms of the work's opening in more celebratory mood with a closing hymn; and, throughout the work, the many recurrences of the 'Britain' theme.[19] The latter, associated with native nobility and sovereignty, appears almost always in E flat major in Scenes 1 and 2, although at that stage only in fragmentary form, as a leitmotiv (for instance, Scene 1, fig. 32 and fig. 35 + 7; Scene II, fig. 23). The snatches of its broad melody thus point to an ideal that stands above the people's cares and fighting. This is the time when Caractacus's Britons are still free, although they are raw and uncivilized. There is a pervasive association of diatonicism and the key of E flat major, apparent already in Caractacus's first solo (Scene 1, fig. 18) and in his aria 'The air is sweet' (fig. 21). At the end of the ensuing trio, the big E flat major climax has a largely stepwise bass (fig. 52). The Arch-Druid's pronouncement about the outcome of the forthcoming battle (even though inaccurate) is in E flat, grand and magisterial (Scene 2, fig. 22 + 5), and leads into the 'Britain' theme in the same key (fig. 23), its most extended presentation to that point (Ex. 2.3). The 'Britain' theme is absent from Scenes 3, 4 and 5, which describe respectively a pastoral idyll, preparation for the battle, and news of the battle and its aftermath. It returns in Scene 6 for Caractacus's noble plea for clemency in C minor and E flat major, with regal melodic flourishes and open sonorities at

Ex. 2.3 Elgar, *Caractacus*, Scene 2, fig. 23, bars 1–4, 'Britain' theme (reduction)

climaxes. In the choral epilogue, which stands outside the story of Caractacus, it appears first in C major and then, as though corrected, in E flat major for a hymn-like, apotheosis version. This version is not only the final musical event of the cantata, but, by 'completing' the fragments of the theme presented hitherto, forming them into a complete, regular, multi-phrase unit that ends with a complete cadence, it stands as the musical goal of the cantata.[20] It thereby reinforces the epilogue's jingoistic text, which celebrates Britain's contemporary sovereignty and imperial dominance as a new, improved Roman Empire, resolving the conflicts of the work and transforming tragedy into redemption. The emergence of the E flat major complete version is a musical symbol of the nation as a higher synthesis produced by the historical struggles and sacrifices described in the rest of the cantata.

Soon after the premier of *Caractacus*, Elgar returned to noble E flat major diatonicism in 'Nimrod', Variation IX from the 'Enigma' Variations (1899). 'Nimrod' stands out from its surroundings, being the only variation of the fourteen not to have a G tonic, and it is exceptional also in its very slow tempo, hymn-like texture, and elevated mood. The first six melody notes of the variation parallel the beginning of the work's theme almost exactly in melodic contour and rhythmic values, but with its major key, serene mood, and eschewal of the rests that fragment the melody of the theme, it is a positive, indeed redemptive, inversion of the melancholy theme. The fact that the opening of 'Nimrod' is quoted in the finale, which overall represents the composer himself, confirms once again its special status. In writing it, Elgar had in mind his friend A. J. Jaeger's inspiring discourse on the slow movements of Beethoven, which may have raised his mood after a period of depression, as well as, presumably, Jaeger's sympathetic personality and insightful responses to Elgar's music.[21] In *The Music Makers* (1912) the variation is quoted at length, initially again in E flat major, with a text that refers to the inspirational effect of one person's words on another. The processional topic emerges only gradually in 'Nimrod'; at its outset, the primary topic is hymn and the articulation of the pulse is light. Much of 'Nimrod' is metrically ambiguous: it is the first of Elgar's triple-metre processional pieces, although it often breaks into the more normative duple groupings. Stepwise descending bass motion and recognizable schemata appear only in the continuation of the consequent phrase, where the bass descends through an octave and a half beneath sequences that rely on chords of the sixth (Ex. 2.4). This is another instance of Elgar's three-part counterpoint in E flat major with an active, leaping inner part (compare Ex. 2.2(ii)).

Ex. 2.4 Elgar, 'Enigma' Variations, Variation IX ('Nimrod'), fig. 34, bar 5–fig. 35, bar 1¹ (reduction)

The procession is highly idealized rather than concrete, an impression heightened by the slow tempi of modern performances, which are closer to adagio or even lento than the score's moderato marking. (The composer began this trend in his 1926 recording.[22]) The Variation has no direct national associations, although it echoes the theme that appears near the end of *Caractacus* that Elgar called 'Modern Britain. A March' (figs. 54, 55, and 60; in E flat major on its final appearance).[23] The function of 'Nimrod' as music of national commemoration emerged only in its reception and with its arrangement for brass band for the purpose of outdoor performance. This appropriation is not musical inapposite, for with its redemptive transformation of the character of the 'Enigma' theme and the closing apotheosis of its initial motive it invites thoughts of suffering and transcendence. At British Remembrance Day ceremonies, it is played at a solemn moment when the processing veterans and worthies are standing still, an appropriate external correlate to its oblique realization of the processional topic.

Elgar took forward the association of processional diatonicism with spirituality and E flat major in his three oratorios for the Birmingham Triennial Festival: *The Dream of Gerontius* (1900), *The Apostles* (1903), and *The Kingdom* (1906). The ingredients included layered contrapuntal combinations, resulting in free diatonic dissonance and a recurrent set of leitmotivs, each of which is cross-referenced in several of the oratorios. Processional diatonicism appears at moments of elevation, climax, and transcendence that touch on themes of Christian apostleship and redemption. Several of the longer passages undertake transitions from physical and concrete realizations of processional rhythms to spiritual and mystical ones, creating the spatial effect of heavenly ascent as an earthly procession dissolves into a mystical vision. In Part I of *Gerontius*, soft but urgent steps are first heard in the bass on the word 'trod' as the dying Gerontius searches for the energy to face death: 'Rouse thee, my fainting soul, and play the man;/ And thro' such waning span/ Of life and thought as still has to be trod,/ Prepare to meet they God'. The processional tread becomes the basis for the ensuing chorus 'Be merciful', which opens in A flat major but finds its way to E flat major for a section of elevated, purely diatonic, three-part invertible counterpoint shaped around the melodic figure that A. J. Jaeger in his 'analysis' of the oratorio identified as a 'Christ idea' (fig. 37; Ex. 2.5).[24] The textual theme of 'rising' here is reflected in all three contrapuntal parts. The basic contrapuntal block is repeated twice, realizing three of its possible permutations, the first two with the largely stepwise part in the bass. This repetitive and tonally stable passage is the uplifting centrepiece of the otherwise gloomy and tonally unanchored chorus. The 'Christ' motive and the diatonic counterpoint return only at the end of the chorus as a fade-out effect as the procession recedes, as it were: the two contrapuntal iterations are marked ***pp*** for

Ex. 2.5 Elgar, *The Dream of Gerontius*, Part I, fig. 37, bars 1–6 (orchestral parts in reduction)

the chorus, *ppp* and *pppp*, respectively, for the orchestral parts. This same motive and counterpoint return peacefully once again at the end of Part I of the oratorio to crown a grand processional chorus after the Priest's administration of the last sacrament ('through the same, through Christ our Lord'). Here it begins a coda that transforms the representation of a physical procession into a mystical vision as the soul of Gerontius departs the body and 'rises' to heaven (fig. 76). The outer parts of the chorus, in D major, are almost purely diatonic, contrasting with the vigorous, march-like central section ('Go forth'), which is highly chromatic. These were critical moments in the emerging tradition of English processional diatonicism: Elgar's 'Christ' theme reappears in *The Apostles* and, in only slightly modified form, in 'The Explorers' from Vaughan Williams's *A Sea Symphony* and 'Easter' from his *Five Mystical Songs*, in all cases in E flat major.

The Apostles has three substantial choral sections that foreground E flat major diatonicism, either in long spans or at a succession of referential formal junctures leading to a stable close in the same key. In the Prologue, which is in A flat major overall, Elgar places the 'Church' theme, as it was named by A. J. Jaeger ('For as the Earth bringeth forth her bud'; fig. 7 + 1), in E flat major. Again the texture is three-part counterpoint; the outer parts move largely by parallel tenths, while the doubled middle part is more active. (Ex. 2.6; this is a largely diatonic E flat major despite the key signature).[25] The metre is triple, without even duple tendencies, but the stepwise bass and diatonic dissonance define the topic plainly. The climactic final part of Section I of the oratorio ('The Calling of the Apostles') is a chorus in E flat major, 'The Lord hath chosen them': a grand design for the central theme of Elgar's entire multi-opus 'Apostles' concept. The chorus begins with an incomplete version of the 'Apostles' motive in E flat major, which is presented in full, *grandioso*, again in E flat, half-way through. It is followed by a string of open sonorities on secondary sevenths resolving to open tritone intervals in upper parts on 'He hath chosen', and a succession of diatonic leitmotivs almost crammed together at E flat major moments, including 'Church' and 'Gospel'. In the 'Apostles' motive, melodic quavers and triplets mix in a way that recalls the 'Christ' theme from *Gerontius*, and, just as in the *Gerontius* choruses, the Apostles' procession eventually fades out, to be replaced by atmospheric spatial effects (fig. 51 + 2).[26] The chorus ends with a richly scored, leisurely paced section that alternates elevated, purely diatonic passages with more disturbed, chromatic ones, ending with a grand climax on the 'Apostles' motive and a diminuendo, in Wagnerian fashion, on the final E flat major chord.

Ex. 2.6 Elgar, *The Apostles*, Prelude, fig. 7, bar 2–fig. 8, 'Church' motive (reduction)

Serene statements of the 'Apostles' motive (figs. 53 and 54) are worked into three-part diatonic counterpoint in E flat major, the second iteration partly inverted just as in 'Be merciful'. At the first of these, in a further complexity of counterpoint, the Angel sings the 'Church' motive in triple metre against the quadruple metre of the other parts (Ex. 2.7), resulting in still more free diatonic dissonance. As in *Caractacus*, these diatonic themes develop strong tonal associations with E flat major in the rest of *The Apostles* and in *The Kingdom*, along with the equally central 'Gospel' motive.[27]

The final section of the oratorio, 'The Ascension', is a grand canvas that heightens many of these tendencies: counterpoint, diatonic dissonance, a wide range of processional effects, swiftly changing leitmotivs, and chromatic harmonic progressions alternating with stable thematic references in E flat major. The idea of Ascension is conveyed by the choral scoring: the main chorus parts are headed 'On Earth' and the semi-chorus

Ex. 2.7 Elgar, *The Apostles*, Part I, fig. 53, bars 1–6 (reduction)

parts 'In Heaven'. A stable E flat major is reached for the semi-chorus's diatonic reiterations of 'Alleluia' (fig. 220). Thereafter Elgar alternates chromatic progressions for mystical effect with a series of significant thematic statements in, or beginning in, E flat, including a new theme that Jaeger called 'Christ's Glory' (fig. 229), along with 'The Spirit of the Lord', the opening theme of the work, normally heard in A flat major but now transposed into E flat major (figs. 231 and 234). The second statement of 'The Spirit of the Lord', marked 'nobilmente', is the climax of the Ascension section and of the oratorio as a whole, the bass descending stepwise through the interval of an eleventh to the tonic. Thereafter the music settles into a largely diatonic E flat major for ethereal 'Alleluias' from the semi-chorus and musical images of ascent (fig. 235 + 4). Finally, the 'Christ' motive from *Gerontius* is recalled in E flat ('In His love and in His pity He redeemed them') in totally diatonic and freely dissonant counterpoint with the 'Alleluia' reiterations (Ex. 2.8). Any sense of physical tread dissolves in these closing bars. The oratorio ends, like Section I, with a grand swell and a diminuendo on a final E flat major chord.

Ex. 2.8 Elgar, *The Apostles*, Part II, fig. 236, bars 1–7 (reduction)

The Kingdom begins and ends in E flat, and much of the score is notated with a three-flat key signature. The serene E flat major swell and diminuendo, now familiar from *The Apostles*, is used for the end of Part I and the end of the work as a whole. The Prelude presents a succession of processional themes, including 'New Faith', replete with diatonic dissonance, the chromatic 'Penitence', and the serene 'Prayer', mainly in E flat major, again diatonically dissonant with, initially, a rising stepwise bass. 'Prayer' combines with 'New Faith' in a peaceful diatonic passage to conclude the Prelude (fig. 13). Later returns of 'New Faith' for the conversion scene in Part III and in the 'Prayers' music near the end of the oratorio are usually in E flat major, and the work ends with 'Prayer' in E flat major. The contralto *scena* 'The Sun goeth Down' leads from darkness and despair to glowing, visionary climaxes in E flat major with the diatonic motives 'Beatitudes' (marked 'Nobilmente') and 'Church' (figs. 161 and 163–65).

In instrumental music Elgar pursued the E flat major complex still further. *Cockaigne* is a striking example because the apotheosis of the processional 'citizen' theme at the end of this C major overture occurs in E flat major. Having appeared first in the tonic near the start of the exposition, its recapitulatory return is deferred, and the work seems about to close stably in C before a sudden switch to E flat. After the apotheosis (with organ), the overture ends abruptly with a five-bar flourish in C. The E flat major 'citizen' apotheosis is therefore interpolated within a C major tonic recapitulation, the key of the theme following the logic of its inter-opus topical associations, not that of the composition to which it belongs, a compositional decision that speaks of the almost archetypal power that *Blest Pair of Sirens* appears to have assumed for Elgar.[28] In the *Introduction and Allegro* for string orchestra (1905), the lyrical theme that he dubbed the 'Welsh tune' is placed initially in E flat major in an overall G minor context, much like 'Nimrod' in the Enigma Variations. In *The Music Makers* (1912), a series of expressive climaxes within the orchestral introduction occur in E flat major despite the beginning and ending of the introduction being in F minor, while, as noted earlier, the quotation of 'Nimrod' in that work is initially in E flat major too (fig. 51). In Elgar's 'symphonic study' *Falstaff* (1913), which begins and ends in C minor, the regal 'Prince Hal' theme, with its marching stepwise bass and leaping and dipping melodic line, begins in the tonic key's relative major, E flat major, for each of its complete appearances. Elgar's Symphony No. 2 is in the key of E flat overall and is the most substantial of all Elgar's orchestral pieces to explore the complex, especially in the Larghetto second movement and in the finale; both present a long series of processional episodes, the finale even approaching the pageant style of some of Elgar's marches. In a way that parallels the oratorios, the serene coda dissolves the steady physical tread, and the symphony ends with the fourth and final grand E flat major swell and diminuendo of Elgar's musical career. The Second Symphony and *Falstaff* return the E flat processional complex to the national framework established in *Caractacus*, the symphony through its dedication to the memory of King Edward VII and the symphonic study through the thematic characterizations of a future English monarch and of the eponymous English anti-hero.

Elgar: Schemata, Transformation, and Apotheosis

As regards the details of processional diatonic technique, Elgar and Parry shared stepwise basses and regal or chivalrous melodic flourishes with leaping sixths and sevenths. But Elgar at times tolerated more chromaticism within the processional idiom. In the 1890s he developed his own post-Mendelssohnian 'churchy' style, apparently independently of Parry's influence and somewhat less 'reformed' in manner in relation to Victorian defaults. This style is much in evidence in works such as *The Black Knight* (1893), the Organ Sonata (1895), and *The Banner of St George* (1897), often in the lengthy passages in G major and triple metre that Elgar wrote in those pieces. The third movement of the Organ Sonata opens with an almost totally stepwise pedal part for thirty-two bars (octave leaps occurring for convenience to keep the part within a restricted range) and has Parry-like melodic features: dotted figures on rising and falling sixths and sevenths and melodic quaver/semi-quaver syncopations (Ex. 2.9 gives only a sample of this lengthy passage). Less reminiscent of Parry, however, are the applied diminished sevenths seamlessly integrated within a conventional language of melody, phrase, theme, and cadence. Elgar himself later tended to eschew this particular harmonic style for processional music in his major compositions, but local chromaticism is still found, including in stepwise basses such as those of the 'citizen' theme in *Cockaigne*, the 'Prince Hal' theme from *Falstaff*, and even 'Nimrod' (see also Ex. 2.1(ii)). The finale of the Second

Ex. 2.9 Elgar, Organ Sonata, third movement, bars 1–16

Symphony alternates diatonic stepwise bass motion with chromatic motion in its 'Nobilmente' theme and in the final theme of the exposition (fig. 142, fig. 143 + 5).

Elgar added a further schema to the English diatonic language and used it intensively. This is another realization of the 4–3 bass step. In contrast to the rising-fourth schema, though, this 'plagal tritone' schema is a subdominant realization of the step, which probably derives from plagal 'Amen' progressions with rising inner-part motion in four-part chorale harmony. This type of figure was widespread enough to become a quick code for 'churchy' harmonization (Ex. 2.10).[29] The version with bass 4-3 (as opposed to the fully 'plagal' 4-1) was a commonplace of Victorian hymns such as Wesley's 'Hereford', 'Colchester', and 'Gweedore'. Elgar exploited the dissonance of the plagal tritone in the passing half-diminished-seventh harmony in many ways, often situating it at the expressive climax of a phrase or theme. The parallel tenths between the outer parts of the plagal tritone schema, with 6–5 in the treble, are familiar from a ubiquitous schema of the eighteenth-century galant style that Gjerdingen calls the 'Prinner riposte'.[30] As with the Prinner, in Elgar and elsewhere in the English repertory this pattern never appears as the 'opening gambit' of a theme or phrase, but as a later, contrasting event within a thematic unit. Parry seldom used the plagal-tritone schema, though it does appear in the 'largamente' theme of the 'English' Symphony (see Ex. 1.9, bars 24–25). Elgar especially favoured a sighing 4–3 suspension on the second chord, a version also to be found in 'Cross of Jesus, Cross of Sorrow' from Stainer's *The Crucixion*, which Parry would probably have found cloying (Ex. 2.11). (Stainer's use here anticipates Elgar's in positioning the schema at the melodic and expressive climax of the hymn.) In his writings, Parry warned contemporary musicians against the careless melodic use of the tritone, citing a popular song not dissimilar to some of Elgar's tunes.[31]

A good example of expressive climax at the plagal tritone schema, as well as its position as a second, contrasting event in a theme, is found in the main

Ex. 2.10 'Plagal tritone' schema (C major version)

Ex. 2.11 Stainer, 'Cross of Jesus, Cross of Sorrow', *The Crucifixion*, bars 5–6 (without text)

Ex. 2.12 Elgar, *The Music Makers*, fig. 2, bar 1–fig. 3, bar 1, schema analysis

theme of *The Music Makers*. The theme begins in a four-flat region (F minor / A flat major) but modulates via a stepwise descending bass to E flat major to climax with the sighing 4–3 suspension (Ex. 2.12). In later iterations of the passage, the expressive articulation of the schema is elaborately developed by means of accents, dynamic swells, reduction in tempo, pauses, expression markings and, on one occasion, a ***ppp*** direction on the passing half-diminished seventh chord, leading to complete silence before the resolution.[32] A cliché of Victorian four-part writing has been transformed and absorbed into Elgar's code for his Romantic-mystical vision of the art of music and the creative artist. It is worth noting that Elgar touches on this schema while still in the four-flat region (the earlier D flat to C motion in the bass is already a '4–3' step relative to A flat major). The rule-of-the-octave analogy again seems relevant here, the same stepwise bass progression relative to different keys receiving the same treatment as the bass moves downward steadily by step. As often occurs in Elgar, there is an almost improvisatory sense of the spontaneous generation of the full texture through rules of thumb.

In the 'Welsh tune' from the *Introduction and Allegro*, the expressive importance of the plagal-tritone schema is even more marked, positioned as it is within an overwhelmingly diatonic context. The tune is presented in three iterations, the first two in the Introduction, the third in the coda of the Allegro. The first is 'distant': a realization of the composer's memory of a song drifting into his ears on a cliff in Cardiganshire. The hushed, near-static accompaniment builds an atmospheric sense of landscape and space, through which the viola solo emerges gradually with the tune. In the second iteration the tune is 'present': louder, more fully scored, with greater rhythmic and harmonic motion and shape.[33] Both iterations present the plagal-tritone schema as a 'second thing' that functions as their expressive climaxes, marked by slowing of harmonic pace and a change of scoring to solo string quartet. The first iteration has a 'first attempt' that does not fully realize the schema, slipping away to iii instead of I^6 (fig. 2 + 10), with an unusual minor 5/3 triad as the second harmony; this is the 'distant' version of the tune, after all. For the 'second attempt' (fig. 3), with the introduction of the solo quartet, the resolution changes to the conventional I^6, albeit here somewhat obscured by part motion. This is the moment of expressive climax, and also a turn to a more personal, subjective mode of experience. The second, 'present' iteration of the tune (beginning at fig. 3 + 3) draws closer to processional topic as the harmonic pace picks up. The overwhelmingly descending stepwise bass motion (upward leaps by sevenths or ninths can be regarded as stepwise motion with registral 'correction') and the harmonization almost exclusively with diatonic sixth chords are exemplary for the topic (illustrated in the analysis in Ex. 2.13). They are coordinated with regular, march-like pulse attacks, although pastoral indicators remain in the 'rustling' or 'babbling' of the second-violin triplets.[34] The harmonic pace slows again for the plagal-tritone realization, again scored for solo quartet, and an even more marked expressive disjunction in this second iteration. The 'Welsh tune' never cadences; its second iteration moves straight into a transition back to the opening G minor music of the introduction. Its two iterations heard in the Introduction thus represent a cyclical mode of musical time and an idealized

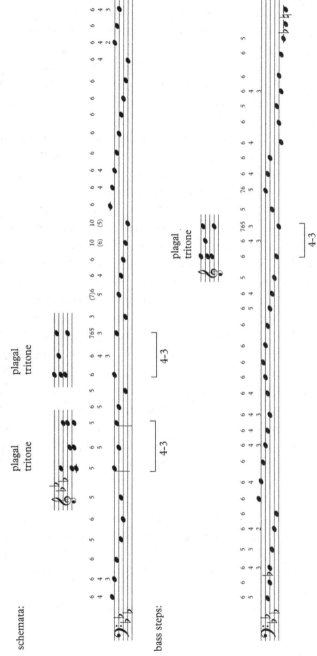

Ex. 2.13 Elgar, *Introduction and Allegro* Op. 47, fig. 2, bar 6–fig. 5, bar 1, schema analysis

Romantic vision. The processional dimension of the 'Welsh tune' is directly realized in the opening phrases of its grand apotheosis version in the coda of the *Introduction and Allegro* (fig. 30). The tune begins here with the Introduction's second iteration, the processional pulse fully underlined and the pastoral dimension overridden by the fortissimo dynamic, full-string texture and heavy, regular attacks. As Brian Newbould puts it, the bass 'positively march[es] down, where previously it flowed'.[35] However the plagal tritone schema interrupts this march. It is now sounded three times, first in the 'second attempt' version and twice in the 'first attempt' version, after which the 'Welsh tune', still in its non-cadencing, cyclical temporality, fades out again, and the piece concludes with fast 'Allegro' music. The processional aspect of the 'Welsh tune' remains partially latent, conveyed by bass motion and schemata but only intermittently by the articulation of pulse.

As noted in Chapter 1, Elgar favoured the 'Do–Re–Mi' schema, the stepwise rising pattern being placed in the bass, with a secondary-seventh 'open sonority' above degree 2 and usually a melodic contour that falls from degree 8. He opted for simple, straightforward realizations of the schema, usually functioning as an initial statement or 'first thing' within a phrase or lengthier passage (Ex. 2.1(i), for instance). Elgar linked up realizations of Do–Re–Mi and plagal-tritone schemata in a 'gambit–riposte' fashion often enough to establish an alternative script to the Meistersinger-tetrachord / rising-fourth pair of the opening bars of *Blest Pair of Sirens*.[36] The opening motto theme of his Symphony No. 1 (which Elgar described as an 'ideal call') takes this form (Ex. 2.14(i)), as does its transformation in the coda of the Adagio third movement (Ex. 2.14(ii)), a passage that preserves the motto theme's schematic structure and order, along with a dominant arrival between the two schemata, while altering almost all other musical parameters. Both versions contain score markings such as hairpin crescendo swells to give expressive emphasis to the plagal-tritone schema, just as in *The Music Makers* and *Introduction and Allegro*.

The motto theme makes an excellent study in Elgar's position within the emerging English tradition. It packs diatonic conventions and allusions into a tight space (see the analytical annotations in Ex. 2.14(i)). It is initially in Elgar's 'unison hymn' style, mainly in two parts, occasionally three, with a regular bass tread; as in his march trios, the first, soft, iteration is followed immediately by a strong tutti ('chorus') version. The key, A flat major, is the

Ex. 2.14 Elgar, Symphony No. 1, instances of Do–Re–Mi + plagal tritone
(i) 'Motto theme', first movement, bar 3–fig. 1 bar 7 (reduction)

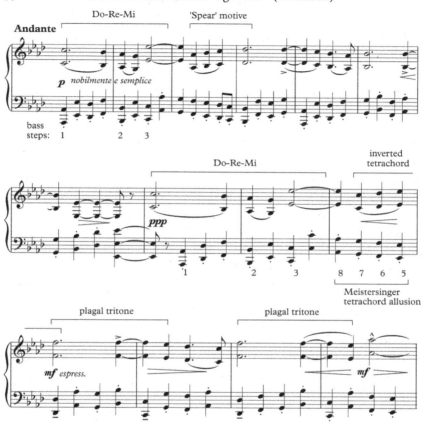

(ii) Third movement, fig. 104 bar 1–fig. 104 bar 5 (reduction)

same as that of *The Apostles* and of the Prelude to Wagner's *Parsifal* and the music for celebration of the communion in Act I. The motto theme quotes the 'Spear' motive from *Parsifal* in its third and fourth bars. Finally, it gestures to a Meistersinger-tetrachord pair in its tenth and eleventh bars, although the customary thick textures for those schemata are not realized in this instance and the allusions could easily pass unnoticed. The Symphony overall is redemptive in its rhetoric. Serene diatonic oases and visionary glimpses of spiritual 'higher things' and the 'eternity' of the unison hymn emerge briefly from amidst swirling, fragmentary orchestral textures, aggressive climaxes and unstable chromatic harmony, all of which presumably stands for the 'worldly', the 'material' or the 'temporal'. Elgar here stands out as a former provincial organist with Victorian church-music and marching-band idioms under his fingers but with grand aspirations both populist and Wagnerian. His conventional language has a different 'accent' from Parry's, being less rooted in the austere, Wesleyan strand of the Victorian tradition, more populist in tone, and in tune with the cross-denominational evangelicalism of the era.[37]

Further light is cast on Elgar's handling of schemata by the finale of the 'Enigma' Variations, another piece of redemptive diatonic apotheoses, thematic transformations, and sharp mood swings. The 'Enigma' theme itself anticipates the motto theme of Symphony No. 1 by pairing a Do–Re–Mi with a plagal-tritone schema. In this case, the initial mode is minor, and the melody rises rather than making the more customary fall from 8, while the plagal tritone (bar 3) must be heard in relation to the relative major key and is left incomplete (Ex. 2.15(i)). English diatonic schemata of this time are very rarely set in the minor mode.[38] The first phase of transformation and apotheosis occurs in Variation IX ('Nimrod'), as discussed above, but the finale contains three further instances, each of which effects regularization relative to voice-leading and schematic conventions, including very steady and unidirectional stepwise bass motion in even minims or semibreves and topical transformation into major-mode hymn and march. Elgar adapted the second instance and added the third on the advice of his friend A. J. Jaeger and the conductor Hans Richter after the first performance.[39]

In the first instance, the melody of 'Nimrod' returns in lively, celebratory guise with a much more consistently stepwise bass than in Variation IX, initially in fast dotted rhythms, then later, in the rather heady passage marked 'stringendo' (Ex. 2.15(ii)), in regular minims rising stepwise for two octaves. This passage, like the 'Enigma' theme itself, begins with a Do–Re–Mi, converted to major mode and realized by means of a broad, homophonic, diatonic, hymn-like texture.

Ex. 2.15 Elgar, 'Enigma' Variations
(i) Theme, bars 1–4 (reduction)

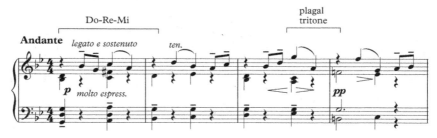

(ii) Variation XIV ('E.D.U.'), fig. 69 bar 1–fig. 69 bar 8 (reduction)

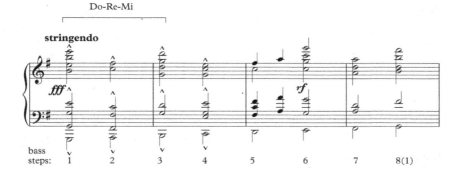

(iii) Variation XIV ('E.D.U.'), fig. 76 bar 5–fig. 76 bar 10 (reduction)

Ex. 2.15 Continued

(iv) Variation XIV ('E.D.U.'), fig. 79 bar 1–fig. 80 bar 1 (reduction)

The original bass motion for the descending seventh in 'Nimrod' was stepwise descending; the direction is here reversed in a 'positive' upward direction for a headlong surge quite typical of the dynamics of the finale variation as a whole. The second instance of diatonic apotheosis and transformation (Ex. 2.15(iii)) brings back the 'Enigma' theme and its Do–Re–Mi schema, now in the major mode and with the customary open sonority to harmonize the bass's degree 2 (the bass 1 is missing on account of the 'dovetailing' of this passage with the preceding orchestral climax, but the presence of the schema is clear from the continuation). The bass now moves stepwise for 11 bars of perfectly even semibreves, resembling the 'cantus firmus' in a counterpoint exercise. The orchestral bass instruments are doubled by the pedals of an organ part, which enters for the first time in the work at this point. The topical allusions to both march and hymn represent a third level of regularization. In the third and final instance (Ex. 2.15(iv)), these processes of regularization and transformation are taken to an extreme. The bass now begins a stepwise descent that is almost uninterrupted in even semibreves for three-and-a-half octaves over the course of 34 bars ('corrections' for register via ascending sevenths disregarded). The organ enters here for a second time; the subtopic can now be called unison hymn. The texture is low, homophonic and thick, with violins playing on the G string only—it would be 'organ-like' even if the organ itself were not playing. The passage renounces individuality in several respects. The scoring involves much doubling and little idiomatic writing for orchestral instruments; it is no longer clear whether the melody represents the 'Enigma'-theme version or the 'Nimrod' version; and recognizable diatonic schemata are no longer in evidence. All that is left is the general impression of a grand hymn. Elgar even has an 'upper octave' repetition like one of the 'all together', chorus-like repetitions of the melodies in his march trios. In his revised and extended finale, Elgar continued the processes of redemptive transformation and regularization that he had initiated in the first version.

Vaughan Williams's Words on Parry and Elgar

There was something of a cult of Parry at the Royal College of Music when Vaughan Williams first arrived there in September 1890 at the age of 17. He was, he recalled, 'quite prepared to join with the other young students of the R.C.M. in worshipping at that shrine'.[40] The metaphor of a religious cult was echoed by Herbert Howells, who described himself when a student at the College—rather later than Vaughan Williams—as a 'Parry devotee'.[41] Near the end of his life Vaughan Williams confessed that as a young man he fell 'under his spell . . . completely'.[42] He remembered with special fondness the Parry of 'the earlier days, when *The Glories of our Blood and State* and *Blest Pair of Sirens* were new'.[43] 'Walt Whitman says: "Why are there men and women that while they are nigh me sunlight expands my blood." Parry was one of these'.[44] Parry, moreover, showed the young Vaughan Williams 'the greatness of Bach and Beethoven as compared with Handel and Mendelssohn', and in this respect was 'an out-and-out radical both in art and life'.[45] Vaughan Williams remembered most fondly the Parry of the years before he became Director of the Royal College of Music and before his later, books, lectures, and cares. Those who knew him then best understood what he stood for: intellectual radicalism, rejection of standard Victorian musical tastes (Handel and Mendelssohn), acceptance of Wagner, and the inseparability of art and life.

When Vaughan Williams returned to the Royal College of Music in 1895 after his time at Cambridge University, Parry had just taken on the position of Director, and so he studied composition instead with Stanford. But he had not forgotten Parry's values and outlook. In the 1900s their compositional paths ran parallel at times. Parry was working on his 'ethical cantatas', which mainly set texts of his own written in something of the style of Walt Whitman, whose verse Parry admired.[46] Vaughan Williams, meanwhile, set Whitman's own words twice in major choral works for commissions from the Leeds Festival: *Toward the Unknown Region* (1907) and *A Sea Symphony* (1910). These works put Parry's vision into practice, and not only by echoing passages from the ethical cantatas on occasion.[47]

Vaughan Williams twice recounted in prose Parry's instruction to him: 'Write choral music as befits an Englishman and a democrat'. Although ringing in tone, Parry's remark—if Vaughan Williams quoted it accurately—is ambiguous. It could mean 'continue the English choral tradition because choral music is a peculiarly English national genre'. This would certainly be in harmony with ideas of the time amongst Parry's circle, as shown in Chapter 1. In 'A Musical Autobiography' (1950), that seems to be the way Vaughan Williams took it, given that he continued:

> We pupils of Parry have, if we have been wise, inherited from Parry the great English choral tradition which Tallis passed on to Byrd, Byrd to Gibbons, Gibbons to Purcell, Purcell to Battishill and Greene, and they in their turn through the Wesleys to Parry. He has passed on the torch to us, and it is our duty to keep it alight.[48]

There is something of the tone of a public-school Founder's Day speech in this comment, but with a touch of irony. The full evolutionary history of English choral music that Vaughan Williams attempts here is fanciful, after all, not least because many readers might have scratched their heads at the names of Battishill and Greene, at least when invoked in such resounding tones. Moreover, it is not clear why Vaughan Williams's choral tradition going back to Byrd is 'democratic'. On the other hand, Parry's instruction could mean, 'write only that type of choral music that befits an Englishman and a democrat'. That could mean the avoidance of certain types of choral music: perhaps sentimental hymns or oratorios in the manner of Spohr or Gounod, or the avoidance of 'aristocratic' attitudes such as a hedonistic or consumption-oriented understanding of art. In a BBC broadcast talk entitled 'The Teaching of Parry and Stanford' (1956), Vaughan Williams seems to have taken Parry's remark in this sense by citing it immediately after explaining that Parry 'never tried to divorce art from life' and that he disliked 'mere luscious sound', ideas that derived from Parry's ethical conception of music and art in general.[49] The instruction then would be that one should bring choral music into line—perhaps back into line—with English life, by writing in a grand, spiritual-humanist mode, rather than relying either on the doctrines of religious organizations or on sensational effects. Read in this way, Parry's remark is almost a prescription for the choral works that Vaughan Williams did indeed write in the 1900s, which also draw substantially on Parry's elevated diatonic manner.

If this is true, then Vaughan Williams's devotion to the cult did not last forever. Speaking of the 'shrine' in 1950, he said: 'I think I can truly say that I have never been disloyal to it',[50] but the fact that this needed to be said at all, and in such ironic terms, indicated that he had moved on. Looking back, he became more circumspect about Parry, noting that at the age of 17 he 'naturally absorbed him wholesale'.[51] With the 'weakening digestion of old age' he could no longer 'swallow Parry's music whole as I did then'.[52] He nevertheless added, in a tone of mock back-straightening, 'I hereby solemnly declare, keeping steadily in view the works of Byrd, Purcell and Elgar, that "Blest Pair of Sirens" is my favourite piece of music written by an Englishman'. This oath of allegiance really amounts to a tender tribute to his own youthful enthusiasm. In a broadcast BBC talk in 1956 he gave a variant:

> What about Parry as a composer? Personally, I believe, he was among the greatest. But something stood in the way of complete realization. There is however one outstanding exception. I fully believe—and keeping the achievements of Byrd, Purcell and Elgar firmly before my eyes,— Blest Pair of Sirens is the finest musical work that has come out of these islands.[53]

Did Vaughan Williams—whose often dry and self-deprecatingly gruff delivery cannot be recorded on paper—really expect his listeners to believe, or even to believe that he believed, that Parry was 'among the greatest' and that *Blest Pair of Sirens* trumps every other piece of music ever composed in the British Isles? These dutiful avowals of devotion conceal a more plausible thought: that for Vaughan Williams Parry's work was somehow inhibited and incomplete. In this sense, Parry was an English musical Moses dying within sight of the Promised Land. He pointed the way and inspired others, and they were to complete and realize the vision. Again, that appears to have been exactly what Vaughan Williams set about to do in the 1900s.

Elgar, by contrast, was not a 'shrine' for Vaughan Williams, and his reactions to the music were mixed. He admitted to 'cribbing' from Elgar and in a commemorative essay, 'What Have We Learned from Elgar?', following the elder composer's death in 1934 said that he was astonished to discover how much he had done it.[54] Vaughan Williams admitted that in the 1900s he spent hours in the British Museum studying the full scores of the 'Enigma' Variations and

Gerontius. 'The results are obvious in the opening pages of the finale of my Sea Symphony'.[55] He said that the single phrase from Elgar that most influenced him was what he called 'Thou art calling me' from *Gerontius*, not in its initial form, when it sets those words, but when it appears later in the chorus 'Be Merciful'. With a musical extract, he quoted a passage of intensively dissonant diatonic counterpoint from near the climax of the opening section of 'The Explorers' (the finale of the *Sea Symphony*), which illustrates the use of this motive.[56] As will become clear, this was absolutely to the point, as that section of that movement records Vaughan Williams's deepest debts to Elgar—as well as some to Parry—in his early choral works, and possibly in any of his works. Vaughan Williams did not name this motive 'Christ', although the way he treated it suggests that he must have been alert to that association.

Vaughan Williams singled out certain pieces by Elgar for praise over others, the dividing line corresponding closely—although by no means exactly—with diatonic and chromatic idioms. In 1932 Vaughan Williams expressed a preference for the chorus 'Be Merciful' from *Gerontius* over the oratorio's Prelude, which contained evidence of 'influences not so germane to me', influences that surely included chromatic harmony of a kind that he associated with Spohr.[57] Judging by his other remarks, the passage from the chorus that most appealed to him was the one in E flat major in which the 'Christ' motive is presented in intensively diatonic, three-part invertible counterpoint (Ex. 2.5). Elsewhere he also mentioned 'Nimrod' and 'W.N.' from the 'Enigma' Variations, both of them highly diatonic, as well as the final section of *Gerontius* ('Softly and Gently'), which at least begins in a diatonic style.[58] He felt a sense of 'familiarity' in these pieces, and regarded them as somehow beyond criticism and essentially English.[59] He expressed a strong preference for the quiet Elgar, preferring the pieces listed above to 'deliberately popular' ones such as *Cockaigne* and Pomp and Circumstance March No. 1, pieces which, as it happens, share with the ones he liked a good deal of diatonicism.[60] This taste reflected a broader movement in the reception of Elgar at the time, which defined Elgar's 'Englishness' in terms of the private and the pastoral, and rejected his more extroverted side, which was associated with pre-war overconfidence.[61] By contrast, in Vaughan Williams's compositions of the 1900s, the assertive Elgar is clearly recollected, including grand passages from 'Sabbath Morning at Sea' from *Sea Pictures* and possibly even Pomp and Circumstance March No. 1.

Vaughan Williams regarded both Elgar and Parry as 'English' in musical substance and both as mediators of tradition. He recalled his brother telling him as a boy that 'there was something, to his mind, peculiarly English about [Parry's] music'.[62] As for Elgar, he had established a rare 'bond of unity' with his compatriots. 'When hearing such music as this we are no longer critical or analytical, but passively receptive.'[63] He placed the pieces by Elgar that he liked alongside older tunes such as Purcell's 'Fairest Isle' and the hymns 'Lazarus' and 'St Anne'. There were nevertheless distinctions between the composers' respective versions of English tradition. Whereas Parry 'derived largely from S. S. Wesley', that influence, according to Vaughan Williams, 'seems to have passed Elgar by'. Instead, he suggested, perhaps with deliberate tendentiousness, that Elgar's immediate precursors were the 'little group of organists who were writing small but rather charming music when Elgar was a young man, such as Henry Smart and John Goss'.[64] Whether or not he was right about Smart and Goss, Vaughan Williams's basic points were sound. Elgar was less directly indebted to Wesley's 'pure' diatonic dissonance than Parry was and was open to wider influences in Victorian sacred music. He was less an ideological reformer than either Parry or Vaughan Williams, even if his music participated in the definition of a new, reformed English style. Vaughan Williams was evidently familiar with the idioms of Victorian sacred music, alert to stylistic differences within it and what they might mean, and swift to interpret the music of Parry and Elgar in relation to that background.

Diatonicism in Vaughan Williams's 'First Maturity' Choral Works

Vaughan Williams explored a wide variety of diatonic effects in his compositions of the 1900s. The song cycles *The House of Life* (1903) and *Songs of Travel* (1903-1905) at times strike a note of 'drawing-room rapture' (explored in Chapter 4). On occasion they anticipate the harmonic stasis, modal melodic lines, and parallel root-position triads that would later become hallmarks of his larger compositions (explained in Chapter 3). 'The Infinite Shining Heavens' from *Songs of Travel*, for instance, is an atypical application of the principles of the stepwise bass and intensive diatonic dissonance, creating a soft, atmospheric piece for which there is little parallel elsewhere in English music of this time. The orchestral tone poem *In the Fen Country* (various versions completed between 1904 and 1907) has two big diatonic climaxes. Vaughan Williams's first published essay in fully fledged English processional diatonicism is 'Sine Nomine' (Ex. 2.16) from

Ex. 2.16 Vaughan Williams, 'Sine Nomine', *The English Hymnal*, bars 1–4. SINE NOMINE by Ralph Vaughan Williams (1872–1958) from The English Hymnal. Reproduced by permission of Oxford University Press. All rights reserved.

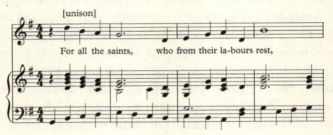

The English Hymnal (1906), a tune of the 'processional-hymn' subtopic. It maintains a stepwise bass almost throughout, which articulates the pulse in even crotchets. Vaughan Williams never forgot this tune, which is echoed in some of his later works.[65] But processional diatonicism found its fullest flowering in three choral works he composed for the Leeds Festivals of 1907 and 1910 (*Toward the Unknown Region* and *A Sea Symphony*) and for the Worcester Three Choirs Festival of 1911 (*Five Mystical Songs*). Here he took his diatonic coordinates primarily from Parry, at times from Elgar, and possibly occasionally even from Wesley in what must be interpreted as a deliberate act of tradition building in musical composition.

Toward the Unknown Region (1907) establishes processional references from the outset, in response to the text 'walk out with me'. A soft bass tread dominates the settings of the first, third, and fourth stanzas. There are no accidentals in the score until bar 17, and the opening has much diatonic dissonance, mainly seventh chords and their inversions, although it is in minor (D minor without a raised seventh) rather than the customary major for the topic of processional diatonicism. A processional breakthrough comes at the start of the fifth stanza, 'Then we burst forth', a grand diatonic march that recalls the opening of 'Sine Nomine', with heavy, unambiguous articulation of pulse by the largely stepwise bass, and a pair of Meistersinger tetrachords in their standard descending bass / treble inversion order (Ex. 2.17).[66] The harmonic vocabulary is still reliant on seventh chords and their inversions, but the style here is much more reminiscent of *Blest Pair of Sirens*, as Jeremy Dibble has pointed out.[67] The allusions to Elgar are no less telling: 'Be Merciful' in the soft processional music near the beginning, 'The Ascension'

Ex. 2.17 Vaughan Williams, *Toward the Unknown Region*, 121–28 (reduction).
© Copyright Stainer & Bell Ltd. Reproduced by permission. All rights reserved.

from *The Apostles* in the repeated triplet chords at 'Oh joy!', and above all the inverted tetrachord from 'Sabbath Morning at Sea' (see Ex. 1.6 (iii)), which at the beginning of the piece provides the setting for the very words 'unknown region'. This phrase, especially in the chromaticized ascending sequence in which Elgar uses it, comes to dominate the settings of Stanzas 4 and 5. From the perspective of schemata, the redemptive setting of 'Then we burst forth' is notable not just for its transformation of chromaticism into diatonicism, but for its regularization of the presentation of the schemata, the inverted tetrachord now fulfilling its conventional role in following a descending bass tetrachord, just as in 'Sabbath Morning at Sea' and indeed as at the outset of the Prelude to *Die Meistersinger* itself. It is as though this melodic figure has been searching for its 'correct' function and finally discovers it as the music returns to an established script.

Vaughan Williams's great diatonic climax might seem at first sight to present paradoxes in the choice of topic. The text ('Darest thou now O soul / Walk out with me toward the unknown region, / Where neither ground is for the feet nor any path to follow?') appears to invite a setting something like the transformation from physical steps to heavenly ascent found in Elgar's oratorios, including in 'Be Merciful'. Vaughan Williams largely rejects this option in *Toward the Unknown Region*, which at its climax becomes more physically concrete in its rhythms, not less. The ecstatic words 'we float, in time and space' (Ex. 2.17) are ironically given a firm grounding in the rhythms of regular footfall and the most harmonically stable writing of the work. Moreover, Vaughan Williams meets Whitman's advance into the unknown with a turn from chromaticism to diatonicism and with allusions to the music of his senior English forebears. In fact, from within his intellectual framework these compositional decisions make sense in two respects. First, the logic of the topical transformation into processional diatonicism has to do with the elevated tone of the topic and the 'high-raised phantasie' that it invites: in this respect, it is a coherent response to the text, regardless of the differences between floating and pacing. Second, for Vaughan Williams artistic innovation had to emerge from a tradition for it to make sense. In his lecture 'Tradition' at Bryn Mawr College, alluding to Whitman's text, he explained that the 'young adventurer branch[es] out into all known and unknown directions', yet remains always standing firmly on the foundations of the past. To illustrate his point he quoted further words by Whitman about the necessity of perennial struggle. For Vaughan Williams, tradition meant the course of musical evolution as it could be seen in the past; its future continues in the same path, even though in the present that path may be as yet 'unknown'.

The apparent paradoxes of Vaughan Williams's approach in *Toward the Unknown Region* are only exacerbated in the musical language of *A Sea Symphony* (1910, genesis from 1903), which, except in places in its scherzo, avoids the representation of waves or wind, let alone 'floating' on water, in favour of processional rhythms. The activity of organized walking or marching is not an obvious association for the seamen that Whitman's text celebrates or the seascapes he describes. The link, as before, lies in the transcendent vision, for which, since Parry's setting of Milton's verses, processional diatonicism could stand as the musical code. That code might also explain why Vaughan Williams selected lines from Whitman's poetry that emphasize universal humanism, international friendship and spiritual transcendence,[68] only to set them in an idiom now recognized as 'English'. Presumably there was something here of the 'democratic' side of Parry's instruction. Processional diatonicism features at the openings of the outer movements and at climactic moments throughout the four movements of this vast work: the subtopic 'choral ode' serves for the ecstatic opening; 'unison hymn' later in the first movement for 'Token of all brave captains', recalling 'Wein und Brot', the communion song from *Parsifal*; a diatonic ostinato in E flat major for the mystical sentiments at 'A vast similitude interlocks all'; a triple-metre rewriting of 'Sine Nomine' at 'Where the great vessel sailing'; and rising-fourth schemata throughout the elevated passages of the first movement, which even ends on a melodic degree 5 over the harmony I⁶.

Vaughan Williams's debts to Parry in *A Sea Symphony* have, unsurprisingly, often been pointed out. His biographer Michael Kennedy called *A Sea Symphony* 'perhaps English music's highest tribute' to Parry.[69] An awareness of diatonic conventions only confirms this view, revealing that the opening pages pay homage to *Blest Pair of Sirens*, unfolding a grand elaboration of the schemata of Parry's first two bars in the standard order: first a Meistersinger tetrachord and then, somewhat later, two realizations of the rising-fourth schema, with its characteristic 3–2–5 melodic pattern and suspended sevenths (Ex. 2.18). The passage is not diatonic overall but works its way flatwards around the circle of fifths from D major through G major to C major, realizing the locally diatonic schemata in each of these keys in turn. A Parry-orientated hearing of this passage is encouraged by the very opening

Ex. 2.18 Vaughan Williams, *A Sea Symphony*, first movement, 'A Song for All Seas, All Ships', bar 1–fig. A, bar 3, schema analysis

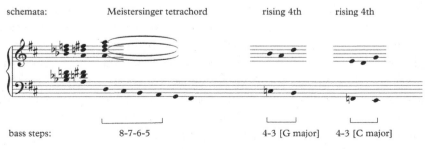

of the Symphony, a thrilling harmonic shift from a chord of B flat minor to a chord of D major,[70] which recalls the equally massive chromatic triadic progression of B flat major to G major at the first choral entry of Parry's 'I was Glad'.

The slow introduction to the finale ('The Explorers') is probably the most extravagant passage of processional diatonicism in the English repertory (Ex. 2.19(i)). The text picks up the themes of *Toward the Unknown Region*, and the mood of Vaughan Williams's music is mystical and aspirational. The section comprises two long passages of intensive diatonic dissonance in a stable E flat major enclosing a middle section based on diatonic passages in G major. There is not a touch of chromaticism for the whole 43 bars aside from the tonal shifts between E flat and G and a quick turn to E flat minor ('teeming spiritual darkness'). The bass traces Whitman's 'Unspeakable high processions of sun and moon' with descending stepwise motion almost throughout, occasionally rising by a seventh to make a registral correction. Although in quadruple metre, until the closing orchestral ritornello, it could hardly be further from march topic: its tempo is molto adagio, the opening bars are very soft, the texture is contrapuntal, and there is much flexibility in the duration of the bass notes with many syncopations. The non-coordination of stepwise motion and articulation of pulse matches the transcendental intuitions of the text ('unspeakable'); on this occasion Vaughan Williams takes the option he had rejected in *Toward the Unknown Region*, perhaps because of the much wider range of processional idioms already established in the Symphony. In the second half of the closing orchestral ritornello, however, the topic becomes more ceremonial, the scoring grandiose, and the pulse articulation more directly coordinated with the bass steps. The application of diatonic schemata is notably denser here too. The introduction thus ends finally with clarity: 'Now first it seems my thoughts begin to span thee'.

It is tempting to hypothesize an improvisatory origin for this introduction. There are five instances of a complete octave descent in the bass from 8 to 1, each with quite different activity in the upper parts. Three of these instances are referential moments that mark formal junctures: the very beginning; the return to E flat for the second stable section in that key (A' in the ternary form); and the start of the climactic orchestral passage near the end of the section. They are not thematically connected in any conventional sense: what happens above the formulaic bass is free. A single template— the stepwise descending octave—for generating an elevated style yields

Ex. 2.19 Vaughan Williams, *A Sea Symphony*, fourth movement, 'The Explorers'
(i) opening–fig. B, schema analysis

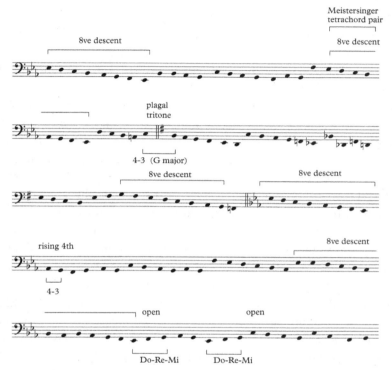

(ii) bars 1–7³ (reduction). © Copyright Stainer & Bell Ltd. Reproduced by permission. All rights reserved.

five contrasted realizations. The improvisatory quality is underlined by the free counterpoint: in effect any note from the diatonic collection can sound against any other note.

The very opening of 'The Explorers' (Ex. 2.19(ii)), with its E flat major key, mixture of melodic duplets and triplets, conjunct melodic motion with changes in direction, and rising fifth 1–5, recalls the 'Christ' motive from *Gerontius*. In his essay on Elgar, Vaughan Williams referred to the motive as 'Thou art calling me', the text it sets at its initial presentation near the start of Elgar's oratorio, but he noted that his passage owes even more to the motive's contrapuntal presentation in 'Be merciful', an elevated moment of processional diatonicism in E flat major (see Ex. 2.5).[71] He could equally have cited the elevated and climactic contrapuntal setting of the same motive at the E flat major conclusion of *The Apostles* (see Ex. 2.8). There are further Elgarian touches, such as the plagal tritone at the sudden modulation to G major and the final orchestral passage with its two Do–Re–Mi schemata and its open sonorities, which leave a ceremonial impression. The melody at this point even recalls that of 'Land of Hope and Glory'—a tune that likewise begins with a Do–Re–Mi (see Ex. 2.1(i)). If the opening of the Symphony's first movement shows what Vaughan Williams had gleaned from Parry, then the opening of 'The Explorers' reveals his debt to Elgar. The distinction is not hard-and-fast: the Christ motive is echoed at the start of the first movement too, while, on the other hand, the finale's E flat–G–E flat tonal scheme (a favourite of Vaughan Williams's) follows that of *Blest Pair of Sirens*.[72]

Although Vaughan Williams did not refer to the Elgar motive as the Christ motive, it cannot be coincidence that it returns later in the finale at a grand, 'largamente' climax on the words 'The true son of God shall come' (fig. H + 14). This is yet another case of freely dissonant, contrapuntal diatonicism, here arising from intensive imitation of the Christ motive, taking Elgar's own treatment of the motive in both *Gerontius* and *The Apostles* to an extreme. The organ enters the finale at this point with a largely stepwise pedal part. For Vaughan Williams, this motivic association is perhaps a surprisingly concrete religious response to Whitman's words, another respect in which Elgar's influence is more relevant in the finale than that of Parry. (The passage is preceded by allusions to the semi-chorus 'Alleluias' from the *Apostles* and the accompaniment of 'Sea Slumber-Song' from *Sea Pictures*.) Vaughan Williams, after all, shared with Parry a spiritual humanism without doctrinal commitment, but with Elgar a mystical temperament.

The rest of this long movement, although it shows some further signs of the influence of Parry and Elgar,[73] does not develop processional diatonicism much further. After the introduction comes a steady march in a faster tempo (Andante con moto; 'Wandering, yearning with restless explorations'), but not an especially diatonic one. There are two further phases of E flat major diatonicism, at 'O we can wait no longer' (fig. L + 19), and, based on the same theme, the final section, 'O my brave soul! O farther sail!' (fig. Aa). The freely dissonant counterpoint is missing here, though. In the second half of the movement, hymn takes over from procession as the primary topical reference, at moments such as 'O thou transcendent' (fig. R), for instance. As in Elgar's oratorios and symphonic music, processional diatonicism functions as a topic that may be evoked selectively at elevated or redemptive phases within the larger design.

Vaughan Williams returned to the E flat major diatonic complex one last time in the pre-war years in 'Easter', the first of his *Five Mystical Songs* (1911), which sets religious poems by the seventeenth-century priest George Herbert. 'Easter' begins with an ecstatic melodic leap to a ii^7 sonority and a stepwise melodic descent: a combination that recalls 'O may we soon again renew that song' from *Blest Pair of Sirens* and its successors in Elgar's oratorios. (This is in effect a Do–Re–Mi schema with the bass Do missing, similar to the one in Variation XIV of the 'Enigma' Variations.) The melodic profile is very similar to the opening of Elgar's Christ motive, an initial rising leap (here a fourth) being followed by a mixture of triplet (descending) and duplet (ascending) quavers in the melody (Ex. 2.20(i); compare Ex. 2.5). The text ('Rise heart; thy Lord is risen') echoes Cardinal Newman's words that Elgar sets at the E flat major entrance of the Christ motive in the chorus 'Be Merciful' ('By Thy rising from the tomb'). The opening lines are set in a texture of intensive diatonic dissonance, while the bass descends stepwise almost without exception for the first 20 bars. This is not a directly march-like procession, for the metre is triple and the rhythmic surface is dominated by throbbing repeated triplet chords akin to those near the end of *The Apostles* and *Toward the Unknown Region* and ultimately those of 'Wein und Brot', which by now has become a marker of mystical experience in this tradition. However, memories of the opening bars of the *Meistersinger* Prelude creep in even here, for instance, in the inverted tetrachord 3–4–5–6 over the descending tetrachord in bars 14–15 (Ex. 2.20(ii)), where for two bars the metre turns quadruple and the triplet accompaniment abates.

Ex. 2.20 Vaughan Williams, *Five Mystical Songs*, 'Easter'. © Copyright Stainer & Bell Ltd. Reproduced by permission. All rights reserved.

(i) bars 1–6 (reduction)

(ii) bars 14–15 (reduction)

The closing lines of Herbert's text turn to musical metaphysics, comparing three-part harmony with the Holy Trinity. An allusion to *Blest Pair of Sirens* would be the most obvious move to make here by the composer. Vaughan Williams is already in E flat major and in an intensively diatonic, processional style, so he has little room for manoeuvre, but he does introduce two instances of the rising-fourth schema at this stage (for 'Consort both heart and lute' and 'Or since all music'), which bestow a further touch of Parry on the reprise of the opening music.

'Easter' was Vaughan Williams's final essay in processional diatonicism for many years. His devotion to the Parry cult was wearing off. Elsewhere in the *Five Mystical Songs*—including the episodes within 'Easter'—can be found the parallel root-position triads, chromatic mediant shifts, modality, and melismatic vocal writing that he was developing into a personal style. He soon moved more decisively in the direction anticipated there and in his early song cycles. Nevertheless, much later, during World War II, Vaughan Williams, in line with several of his colleagues, returned to processional diatonicism, and he never abandoned Parry's ideas about musical ethics and evolution.

By the end of the long Victorian peace, the visions of English musical tradition outlined by Frederick Ouseley, Hubert Parry, J. A. Fuller Maitland, Frederick Bridge, and Ralph Vaughan Williams himself had been realized in musical compositions, not perhaps in a way they could all have envisaged in the late nineteenth century, but, on account of precise topical definition and recurrent schemata, in a manner that was at the time distinctive and instantly recognizable and remains so to this day. Hubert Parry's compositional proposal in 1887 about what should constitute the elevated style of a new English music had been agreed to by major artistic figures, who had realized their spiritual visions on his terms.

3

Diatonic Pastoral Music, 1914–1925

Vaughan Williams and Howells

In the 1910s, a new kind of intensively diatonic writing arose among English composers that broke with processional diatonicism. It drew on an updated version of pastoral as a musical topic, a new approach to musical form, and a contemplative, at times mystical, sensibility. As a topic, the pastoral was nothing new in Western music, as shown by the finale of Corelli's 'Christmas Concerto', 'Pifa' from Handel's *Messiah*, Beethoven's Symphony No. 6 ('Pastoral'), and many other compositions. Diatonicism was already a defining feature of this traditional topic. The new English approach modified it, drawing on the techniques and aesthetics of French modernism—harmonic stasis, parallel root-position triads, modality, and a taste for harmonic sonority over harmonic function—and something of the aesthetic and the melodic contours of plainchant or organum. Unlike processional diatonicism, then, this type of writing did not represent the taking of a position within a wider post-Wagnerian field, but a thorough clearing out of the 'leading-note tensions' of modern Western harmonic practice in general, epitomized by, even if much broader than, nineteenth-century chromaticism. These composers conducted a 'war on the leading note' of a kind that held no interest for Parry or Elgar. In fact, their approach was typified by rather strict patterns of avoidance of an almost religious kind. The new diatonic pastoral style amounted to an attempt to make musical experience anew within deliberately imposed restraints, resulting in meditative states that sometimes led to musical ecstasy. The composition of this type of music was led by Vaughan Williams in works such as *The Lark Ascending* (first composed 1914, revised 1920, premiered 1921), *A Pastoral Symphony* (1922), *The Shepherds of the Delectable Mountains* (1922), and *Flos Campi* (1925) and by Herbert Howells in his early chamber and orchestral music between 1916 and 1925. Other composers of the interwar period such as E. J. Moeran and Gerald Finzi adopted the style intermittently or blended it with other pastoral idioms.

On this understanding, intensively diatonic pastoral music was a phenomenon of a rather brief period of little more than a decade, which for Vaughan Williams included the interruption for World War I and ended by 1925. Indeed, given that the revisions to the *Tallis Fantasia* and *The Lark Ascending* took place just after World War I, Vaughan Williams's strongly pastoral phase may have been even shorter. This is a remarkable fact given the centrality of this idiom to the popular reception of his music and his popular image and the centrality of pastoralism in the reception of British music of this period. It is important to recognize, then, not only that not all English diatonic music was pastoral—a point already abundantly demonstrated in Chapters 1 and 2—but also, crucially, that not all English 'diatonic pastoral music' of this time—music with pastoral texts, contexts or paratexts—relied on pastoral as a musical topic, either new or old. As Chapter 4 will show, the songs of Ivor Gurney and Gerald Finzi, which set texts concerned with nature and landscape, instead represent a revival of prewar idioms, especially processional diatonicism, along with a keen awareness of Parry as a musical forebear. In the mid-1920s, Finzi largely reversed his early attraction to the new diatonic pastoral style of Vaughan Williams in what appears to have been a deliberate compositional choice, though he never relinquished pastoral texts in his vocal music. In the long run, moreover, as Chapter 5 demonstrates, processional diatonicism enjoyed a strong revival from the late 1930s through the 1950s in music for official occasions and for grand public performance. Only Howells made a concerted effort to build on the new pastoral style in his new approach to sacred choral music of the 1940s and 1950s.

This chapter traces a path through these complexities. It defines the new diatonic pastoral style partly as a topic, partly as an aesthetic and a self-imposed discipline, first describing it and then explaining what Vaughan Williams and Howells were trying to accomplish with it as they remade English diatonic music in a new guise for a new generation. It discusses the subtle dynamic processes that underlie the apparently static surface of this music and explores Vaughan Williams's practice of topical transformation in his pastoral compositions, which turn religious and mystical in their search for the experience of eternity. Attention is drawn to the religious 'satellite topics' that appear in Vaughan Williams's practice and the musical plots associated with their appearance. A case study of *The Lark Ascending* examines his first, and most elusive, execution of this kind of pastoral transformation. Finally, the chapter sketches an alternative school of English pastoral music led by Frederick Delius that Vaughan Williams and Howells at first rejected but that arguably outlived their approach.[1]

The last point indicates that diatonic pastoral music was by no means the single dominant force in English composition of the era—as is sometimes assumed—or even in English pastoralism. In this way and in others, this chapter works against clichéd views of English pastoral music that both its unreflective admirers and its unreflective critics still hold. It draws boundaries around the new diatonic pastoral style and undertakes a careful hearing that attends closely to musical topics and their signals, working against a too-sweeping conception of 'English pastoral music' in which pastoralism, diatonicism, modality, folksong, and the Tudor revival are allowed to merge, whether the writer loves or hates the outcome. CD covers of English music of this time often show a single green landscape that stands for a diverse range of composers and styles on the recorded tracks, some of which evoke pastoral as a musical topic, while others do not. Unfortunately, academic scholarship has not always taken the distinctions much further, and the results endure in everyday assumptions and associations.

Diatonic Pastoral as a Musical Topic

Vaughan Williams pointed the way to the new approach in passages from his early song cycles and in 'Bredon Hill' from *On Wenlock Edge* (1909), 'Love Bade Me Welcome' from *Five Mystical Songs* (1911), the 'Prelude' of the *Phantasy Quartet* (1912), and 'Come Love, Come Lord', from *Four Hymns* (1914). He then moved decisively to the new pastoral approach for sizeable complete compositions in *The Lark Ascending* (1914/1920), *A Pastoral Symphony* (1922), *The Shepherds of the Delectable Mountains* (1922), and *Flos Campi* (1925). Howells took a similar course in his Piano Quartet (1916), Fantasy String Quartet (1917), Violin Sonatas Nos. 1 and 2 (both 1917, both revised 1919), Rhapsodic Quintet (1917), *Elegy* for solo viola, string quartet, and string orchestra (1917), and String Quartet ('In Gloucestershire') (1923), and then in orchestral compositions such as *Sine Nomine* (1922), *Pastoral Rhapsody* (1923), and *Paradise Rondel* (1925). In terms of genre, these compositions were mainly orchestral, but there was a chamber dimension as well. Voices are often present: solo in 'Love Bade Me Welcome', 'Come, Love, Come Lord', and the *Pastoral Symphony*, choral in 'Love Bade Me Welcome' and *Flos Campi*, and both in *Shepherds* and *Sine Nomine*. Howells noted that he and Vaughan Williams 'reacted to things musically in a very similar way' because of an 'intuitive affinity'. Both were attracted to 'Tudor music, plainsong and the modes', and both felt they 'needed to write in these modes and in the pentatonic scale'.[2] Despite stylistic similarities, the pastoral compositions of the two composers met with contrasted fortunes. Vaughan Williams became a leading figure in English composition after World War I. His *Pastoral Symphony* influenced English composers of the 1920s and even acquired notoriety in its reception, while to this day *The Lark Ascending* regularly tops UK classical music 'charts'. By contrast, even though Howells's Piano Quartet won a competition for funding by the Carnegie United Kingdom Trust, his instrumental compositions of this period were little known until recordings were issued in the late twentieth century. His orchestral pieces failed to find publishers either because Howells neglected to promote the works or even because he withdrew them. These contrasting fortunes can obscure the fact that Vaughan Williams and Howells were closely allied in their approach to diatonic music in these years, far more so than either was with anyone else.

The updated pastoral topic is marked by a free-flowing melodic style, often with an improvisatory quality, sometimes unmeasured or with frequent changes in the notated metre that may obscure the perception of metrical organization. Melodies are often pentatonic or at least based on a 'gapped scale' of some kind, and they usually feature a mixture of duplet- and triplet-quaver figures. Florid melodic lines are sometimes given to a wordless solo voice and sometimes to solo orchestral instruments, especially woodwind and solo strings. Vocal and/or instrumental lines of this kind may intertwine, resulting in chamber music textures even in those compositions that are scored for full orchestra. Sometimes melodies appear to imitate cow calls (alphorn tunes), idealized shepherds' piping, or stylized folksong (as these musicians understood English folksong to be). This stylization is more common than literal folksong quotation; indeed, the regular, measured structures of folksongs are often avoided. Another 'zone of avoidance' is conventional part-writing, counterpoint usually arising instead from the free intertwining of solo melodic lines. Functional harmonic progressions are either absent or extremely slow in pace, whereas modal diatonic pitch collections are used freely, sometimes even leading to 'bimodality' when two such collections appear in different parts. Juxtaposition of chords or collections related as though by chromatic mediant keys result in 'false relation' effects. It is common to find consecutive fifths, parallel root-position triads, or harmonic stasis, a modern updating of the bagpipe-style drones of eighteenth-century pastoral topic. The texture may suggest slow 'rustling' or 'murmuring', but the surface rhythm is usually slower than that of a typical late-nineteenth-century 'sound sheet'. Dance rhythms are relatively inconspicuous; compound duple metre is by no means the default that it is with eighteenth-century pastoral topic. Likewise, the doubling of melodies in thirds, once a definitive feature of musical pastoral, is not typical.[3]

Howells's Fantasy String Quartet (Ex. 3.1) opens with the presentation of a florid pentatonic melody, with a mixture of duplet and triplet quavers that suggests stylized folksong, but including wide leaps and an overall compass much greater than would be comfortable for a folk singer. There is minimal harmonic motion, aside from the occasional punctuation by a sustained chord drawn from the same four-note collection as the opening of the melody (a diatonic 'minor seventh'). The melody is marked 'espress', and indeed this opening is highly expressive, even rather spicy, given its dissonant opening chords marked *sff* but played with mutes. The notes of the first 15 bars are drawn entirely from a four-flat diatonic collection. There are no leading notes or dominant harmonic function. The first change of harmony is a move to another seventh chord with roughly subdominant function (bar 13), so the overall harmonic progression, if read in F minor, is roughly i^7—iv^7—i^7 (disregarding inversions). The notated metre changes frequently and there is little sense of audible metre. The secondary theme of the first movement of Vaughan Williams's *Pastoral Symphony* (Ex. 3.2) opens with a pentatonic melody for cor anglais that mixes semiquavers and triplet quavers. Further instrumental 'voices' are added in turn—solo viola, solo violin, clarinet, flute and oboe—gradually overlapping and intertwining in a chamber music texture. As Howells noted in his review of the *Pastoral Symphony*, the solo instruments here seem 'gradually to dismiss the orchestral thought and substitute chamber-music'.[4] As in the Howells extract, the notated metre fluctuates, and there is little audible sense of metre.

The new pastoral style stands in contrast to processional diatonicism in several ways. It avoids a public manner, pointing instead to subjective moods, contemplative states of mind, and private experience. The schemata typically found in the processional idiom seldom appear, and the key of E flat major is not favoured. The collection-based writing, avoidance of raised leading notes, interest in harmonic sonority, and lack of harmonic function aligns with the radical syntactic innovations of Debussy and Ravel. By contrast, the densely applied diatonic dissonances of Parry's occasional choral music ultimately resolve conventionally. Consecutive fifths are avoided,

DIATONIC PASTORAL MUSIC 95

Ex. 3.1 Howells, Fantasy String Quartet, bars 1–16 (reduction) Fantasy String Quartet. Music by Herbert Howells. Copyright © (Renewed) by Chester Music Limited trading as J. Curwen and Sons. International Copyright Secured. All Rights Reserved. *Reprinted by permission of Hal Leonard Europe Ltd.*

and conventional harmonic functions are upheld.[5] Although the bass of Ex. 3.2 moves stepwise, it often does so beneath parallel 5/3 sonorities, and thus there are consecutive fifths rather than the 6/3 chords typical of processional diatonicism and acceptable under traditional contrapuntal regulations.

Ex. 3.2 Vaughan Williams *A Pastoral Symphony*, first movement fig. B, bar 8–fig. C, bar 5 (reduction). © 1990 by Joan Ursula Vaughan Williams All rights for the UK, Republic of Ireland, Canada, Australia, New Zealand, Israel, Jamaica and South Africa administered by Faber Music Ltd. Reproduced by kind permission of the publishers. *A Pastoral Symphony*. Music by Ralph Vaughan Williams. Copyright © (Renewed) by Ralph Vaughan Williams. International Copyright Secured. All Rights Reserved. *Reprinted by permission of Hal Leonard Europe Ltd.*

In a major historical study of the musical topics of hunt, military, and pastoral in Western art music, Raymond Monelle argues that the pastoral as conceived by Vaughan Williams 'is a *style*, not a topic' because 'he is never out of it'. Vaughan Williams 'does not *cite* the pastoral style; it is his very soul'.[6]

It is better, according to Monelle, to say that Vaughan Williams was a 'pastoral artist' because he believed that modern musicians should return to a point of musical origin in the simplicity of country people.[7] Monelle's view gives clear articulation to assumptions about Vaughan Williams that are probably quite widespread. But the new pastoral idiom described above does amount to a musical topic—even if it was more than that too—and one that Vaughan Williams did not always employ, especially in major works after 1925. In earlier compositions, he sometimes used it for long stretches, to be sure, although, as will become clear later in this chapter, even then he usually changed eventually, if discretely, to an alternative topic. Monelle's claim that 'every measure of his music recalls the modal and gapped scales of English folksong'[8] is clearly an exaggeration, aside from its unwise acceptance of Vaughan Williams's own taste for 'modal and gapped scales' as representative of English folksong as such. Moreover, to describe Vaughan Williams simply as a 'pastoral artist' ignores his evolutionist ideology, which meant that no straightforward 'return' could ever be possible or even make sense. In short, something of Frank Howes's sweeping treatment of Vaughan Williams's artistic activities, later derided but not contested by Robert Stradling and Meirion Hughes as 'twin obsessions' with folksong and Tudor music,[9] still hangs over Monelle's account.

Form and Process

Form in this style is elusive. In many ways, Vaughan Williams and Howells made a virtue of indefiniteness, leaving an impression of stasis and contemplation rather than a thread of musical 'thought' or a sense of 'plot', at least on a first impression. The distinction of 'thematic presentation' and 'development' familiar from traditional formal conceptions—'development' meaning varied repetition and usually fragmentation of material earlier presented in complete and stable guise—is neglected in favour of the unfolding of variants and alternative versions of a complete melody. As a result, varied strophic form is often in the background. In Ex. 3.1, for instance, a varied second strophe begins at bar 10, while in Ex. 3.2 each solo instrument introduces a new variant of the melody with its own gapped scale. As Howells put it, again in relation to the *Pastoral Symphony*, '"Tune" never ceases. One after another come tributary themes, short in themselves, and so fashioned as to throw one into doubting their being new'.[10] A generative process of 'reverse fragmentation' is sometimes used, whereby a musical figure is introduced in fragmentary form and is built up only gradually, acquiring a melodic continuation in its later iterations. Again, in Ex. 3.2, the initial motive of the melody creeps in while the previous section is still in the process of ending and its texture is still in place: the motive is thus repeated twice before unfolding a complete phrase with its 'own' accompaniment. In his review, Howells noted the 'growth in significance of seemingly unimportant details' here and elsewhere in the work. Likewise, this style avoids the rhetoric of thematic 'antithesis' in the sense of strong local contrast or juxtaposition. Changes of motivic shapes are subtle and are made by degree. The preference is for gradual evolution of thematic materials as well as of mood. Harmonic and tonal processes are elusive too. Changes in modal diatonic collections, as in Ex. 3.2, are at least as important as changes of tonal centre, insofar as the latter still make sense.[11] The avoidance of leading-note function and tritone-driven harmonic progressions blocks dominant–tonic progressions, including local applied dominants and, crucially, authentic cadences. For this reason, musical sections and movements often end with fade-out effects; one of these in fact reaches its conclusion at the beginning of Ex. 3.2.

In short, the diatonic pastoral style shows organizational tendencies that elsewhere in musicology have been termed 'paratactic'.[12] The rhetoric of the 'teleological' process, meaning a sense of the discharge and resolution of tension and a sense that the end of a section or movement functions as the goal of a musical process, is abandoned. Such 'hypotactic' modes of organization, which are so central to the symphonic aesthetics of the nineteenth century and are fully present in English diatonic music up to 1914 in Parry, Elgar, and Vaughan Williams himself, are replaced by the paratactic organization of thematic variants and varied strophic forms. Atmospheric introductions are often answered by framing atmospheric codas, and, even when a climax has occurred late in a movement, these codas create fade-out effects that diminish any sense of a goal achieved or at least impose distance from it. Vaughan Williams's lifelong predilection for *al niente* conclusions is much in evidence.

The harmonic stasis of the new pastoral topic can be broken by a switch between diatonic pitch collections. This procedure is again reminiscent of Debussy and Ravel, although the nondiatonic collections—whole-tone and octatonic—on which they also drew are avoided. The switch, when coordinated with alterations in texture and scoring, may underpin a change of or a transition in mood. Howells's *Rhapsodic Quintet* for clarinet and string quartet presents its opening materials in complete form in a series of changing diatonic contexts. The first phrase, reminiscent of that of Debussy's String Quartet (a work often recalled in the chamber music of Vaughan Williams and Howells), has a pentatonic melody and overall is based on a white-note diatonic collection. A contrasted second phrase over static harmony draws on a one-flat diatonic collection before these elements are repeated, in varied strophic fashion, in three-sharp and one-sharp diatonic collections, respectively. A little later (Ex. 3.3) a slightly more dramatic approach emerges. The pentatonic melody is presented in a three-sharp diatonic context (second violin, bar 62) and in a three- or four-sharp diatonic context, before there is a sudden, complete change of texture, register, dynamics, and melodic material for a rapt, harmonically static passage marked *pp* and 'tranquillo' (bar 70). A pentatonic melody marked 'assai espressivo' is unfolded around a three-flat diatonic collection. The whole phrase later shifts up a semitone to a four-sharp collection. This example illustrates not just the changing moods associated with shifts in diatonic collections, but also their gradation, some being more expressively heightened than others.

In writing of his own Violin Sonata No. 1, Howells made sense of the elusive and indefinite aspects of the formal process in the pastoral style by linking form and mood. In particular, during this time he was interested in developing a 'mixed mood' by drawing together materials from different sections of a composition. The purpose of the composition was:

> to experiment in a new form of sonata; a form which, though without break from beginning to end, should establish three definite moods; and attain unity from a use of themes common to all three movements in varied rhythms and keys, and diversity from the careful metamorphosis of the themes to suit contrasted moods. I conceive the value of such a form to be in this: that while it ensures a logical growth as a whole; and while it preserves in itself the contrast of line and of colour which is provided by the sequence of three separate movements as commonly adopted in the Sonata or Symphony; it at the same time draws all three moods under a closer, unified spell. It becomes a triple mood.[13]

Howells explored these possibilities further in his Piano Quartet, Fantasy Quartet, and Rhapsodic Quintet.[14] He recognized much of his own interest in sustaining and developing mood also in the *Pastoral Symphony*: Vaughan Williams 'builds up a great mood', which is comparable to a 'frame of mind'[15].

Ex. 3.3 Howells, Rhapsodic Quintet, bars 62–76 (reduction). © Copyright 1921 Stainer & Bell Ltd, 23 Gruneisen Road, London N3 1DZ, www.stainer.co.uk. Reproduced by permission. All rights reserved.

If this 'frame of mind' is similar to the 'mixed mood', then movements or complete compositions in this style can be said to have their own kind of goal, albeit one defined subjectively. The first and last movements of the Symphony certainly reach climactic passages that might be heard on these terms before their fade-out endings.

The first movement of Howells's Piano Quartet is a substantial and energetic sonata allegro movement that adapts the traditional form with a strong awareness of mood and its variations. The unfolding of this movement relies mainly, if not exclusively, on the presentation and juxtaposition of diatonic and/or pentatonic collections. Harmonically functional progressions within a single key are not absent but are limited in scope. The movement begins with soft, 'white-note' pentatonic murmuring in the string instruments, mixing duplet and triplet quavers over bass pedal notes in the piano (Ex. 3.4). The tonal context gradually emerges as A minor with a modally Aeolian flavour; the tonic-like referential sonority is an A minor seventh chord, the notes of the C major triad being prominent. This passage is closely in line with traditional musical representations of sunrise, confirmed by Marion Scott's published comments on the Quartet, which she claimed were based on Howells's remarks. At the opening of the composition, she says, it is dawn, while the wind blows across Chosen Hill in Gloucestershire, and the half-light turns to 'full radiance'.[16] In terms of thematic process, this opening 'generates' the eventual melody heard in the piano right hand from bar 8, which has some similarities with the original, undifferentiated pentatonic rusting.

A second phase of motivic generation occurs at approximately the location of a sonata-form secondary theme: a dotted-note motive (x) is introduced obliquely at first (Ex. 3.5(i)) half-way through a melodic unit, in the middle of the texture (on the viola), and within a phase of harmonic 'process' rather than stability. Only the marcato accents suggest that is it for attention. While the murmuring from the opening is heard in another pentatonic context, the motive appears with a single-crotchet anacrusis (x') on a local subdominant-substitute harmony (Ex. 3.5(ii)). The motive next appears with a two-crotchet anacrusis (x")—which it then retains for the rest of the composition—in a more stable, 'presentational' context, at the head of a four-bar phrase that is the best candidate for the secondary theme proper, being followed, conventionally enough at last, by an answering phrase (Ex. 3.5(iii)). The motive receives another theme-like realization at the outset of the development, this one being akin to a folksong over harp-like rippling accompaniment

Ex. 3.4 Howells, Piano Quartet, first movement, bars 1–10. © Copyright 1918 Stainer & Bell Ltd, 23 Gruneisen Road, London N3 1DZ, www.stainer.co.uk. Reproduced by permission. All rights reserved.

DIATONIC PASTORAL MUSIC 103

Ex. 3.5 Howells, Piano Quartet, first movement. © Copyright 1918 Stainer & Bell Ltd, 23 Gruneisen Road, London N3 1DZ, www.stainer.co.uk. Reproduced by permission. All rights reserved.

(i) fig. 1, bar 14–fig. 1, bar 15 (viola part)

(ii) fig. 1, bar 17–fig. 1, bar 19 (cello part)

(iii) fig. 2, bar 1–fig. 2, bar 5^1 (RH piano part)

(iv) fig. 5, bar 8–fig. 6, bar 8^1 (viola part)

figuration in the piano (Ex. 3.5(iv)). The three-flat diatonic collection here lasts for twenty-three bars of idyllic, lyrical outpouring, the full realization of the generated motive being in two varied strophes. The recapitulation has two further treatments of the motive, one in G minor (with F sharps) and one in a three-sharp, A-Mixolydian diatonic context. Still more versions appear in the Quartet's second movement and in the finale, where the motive finally appears in the tonic key, affording symbolic resolution of a traditional, recapitulatory kind.

The first movement of the Piano Quartet adapts conventional musical forms to accommodate the new pastoral style. It gradually builds an idyll or 'second naivety' (Ex. 3.5(iv)) out of complexity and fragmentary materials. The conventional order of thematic process—statement of a theme followed by its fragmentation and development—is avoided in favour of the piecing together of variant versions to generate a complete product. Changes of diatonic collections often define formal sections and contribute to the constantly changing moods. There is certainly drama in the movement, but it ends as softly as it began, its energy dwindling in the closing bars. The Piano Quartet is dedicated 'To the hill at Chosen and Ivor Gurney who knows it', thus being perhaps the only composition in Western art music to be dedicated to a topographical feature. According to Scott's notes, the three movements offer different perspectives on the hill at different times of day and in different seasons, although Howells appears to have discouraged the reproduction of this information. The Piano Quartet is evidently an attempt to integrate a contemplative aesthetic within a genre and forms handed down by musical tradition.

Mystical Pastoral: Vaughan Williams's 'Satellite Topics' and Visions of Eternity

Whatever the technical innovations of the new pastoral style, the metaphysical leanings of English diatonic music ever since *Blest Pair of Sirens* were by no means rejected. Composers continued to reach for visions of eternity in mystical and ecstatic experience. The visionary religious dimension is clear from the texts Vaughan Williams chose to set in 'Love Bade me Welcome' from *Five Mystical Songs* (George Herbert), 'Come Love, Come Lord' from *Four Hymns* (Richard Crashaw), *The Shepherds of the Delectable Mountains* (John Bunyan), and *Flos Campi* (Song of Solomon) and in the epigraph to *The Lark Ascending* (George Meredith). The rapt central section of Howells's Fantasy String Quartet (fig. 9) is marked 'molto tranquillo e mistico' (also *con sord.*, ***ppp***, thus a special sonority) and the Rhapsodic Quintet concludes in a similar mood. Vaughan Williams's blend of the pastoral musical style and mystical religious sentiments is unmistakable in *Sancta Civitas* (1926; text from Revelation), as is Howells's in his somewhat later *Hymnus Paradisi* (completed 1938). Vaughan Williams evidently associated the pastoral style with divine love, but the tone is languorous and sensuous too, and at times it appears that, just as in the early Rossetti song cycle *The House of Life* (1903), divine and earthly love are intertwined, or that the latter provides an intimation of the former or even a path to it.

Vaughan Williams was evidently interested in shaping paths to the experience of eternity in his pastoral compositions. That usually meant topical transformation to a field of satellite topics that replace pastoral for a while with musical imagery of apocalypse and heavenly hosts. The new topics were well worn in Vaughan Williams's general compositional practice and were still diatonic: the imitation of round-singing, chorale-prelude idioms, hymn-like textures, distant fanfares, bell-ringing effects, and wordless singing voices. Processional effects are in evidence too, although not processional diatonicism of the kind that Vaughan Williams practised in his choral works of the 1900s. The result is a kind of topical antithesis. Vaughan Williams's pastoral compositions are in this respect surprisingly unstable and composite, the pastoral default tending to yield, after sustained contemplation, to the mystical vision. This affiliation of topics is also found in pieces that are ostensibly religious in theme but that draw on the new pastoral style as well, such as 'Love Bade Me Welcome', 'Come Love, Come Lord', and *Sancta Civitas*.

Compositions that work themselves out of the pastoral topic into one or more new diatonic topics also tend to move out of their shifting subjective moods and oblique ways of presentation to a mode of expression that is definite, 'public', and 'revealed' in the religious sense, even if physically or aurally distant. The representation of community singing, for instance, is present and complete, with repetitions of a single version of a melody rather than variants. Although trumpet calls may be heard from afar, as it were, as 'calls' they are unambiguous. Still, in these pieces the definite vision cannot be held, and it fades as the pastoral idiom returns. This fading of the vision, along with the never-ending loop of the round-singing imitations, which can only end by the voices dropping out one by one, conveys a sense of eternity within the temporally finite musical experience. The same applies to the sounds of chiming bells, processions, and hymns, which in the end give only glimpses of the heavenly city. In this sense, the pastoral meditation is a mystical one that gradually leads to a revelation of an ultimate reality that cannot be sustained in everyday, lived time.

Topics associated with community singing usually rely on the characteristic nontranspositional counterpoint that Vaughan Williams favoured, in which melodic repetition takes place at the unison or octave. Either a melody is reiterated at the unison or octave by different overlapping voices, essentially in canon, or it is reiterated or pursued in a single voice while contrapuntal embellishments are gradually added in other voices. Repetition at the unison or octave blocks fugato procedure—the staple texture of English choralism—with its 'dux-comes' pattern of entries at tonic and dominant levels and gives rise to contrapuntal genres such as ground bass, ostinato, passacaglia, chorale prelude, variation, and round singing. Vaughan Williams moved easily into such counterpoint. Victorian music intellectuals had identified round singing as a distinctively English national genre of early origin and historical persistence. Edward Francis Rimbault in *The Rounds, Catches, and Canons of England* (1879?) claimed that rounds, catches, and glees are 'of English origin' and are the only musical genres with a 'distinctive national feature'.[17] In the *Grove Dictionary* article 'Round', William Barclay Squire deemed rounds and catches 'the most characteristic forms of English music' and noted their popularity in England down to the present.[18] W. S. Rockstro in the *Grove* article 'Sumer is icumen in' thought that the tune was a folksong but that it emerged from the minds of English people who were used to hearing the church modes.[19] This way of thinking was in harmony with Vaughan Williams's understanding of early English musical 'evolution', which he regarded as an exchange between rural people and the English church. Local motivic imitation at the octave is already crammed into the short opening piano introduction to 'Linden Lea' (1902), a piece presented on the title page as 'a Dorset song', although the tune was composed by Vaughan Williams. It is as though, in the background, behind the published song with piano accompaniment, there is an eternal English community round in spontaneous, untutored vocal counterpoint, only a fragment of which can be heard (Ex. 3.6; see bracketed motives). Howells felt that the melodies of the third movement of the *Pastoral Symphony* came closer than the others to being 'on speaking terms with ordinary man', who would not mind the contrapuntal imitation of the first two motives presented in the movement—the first at the octave, the second at the unison (bars

Ex. 3.6 Vaughan Williams 'Linden Lea', bars 1–3. © Copyright 1912 by Boosey & Co Ltd. Reproduced by permission of Boosey & Hawkes Music Publishers Ltd.

1–19)—because 'by constitution his type loves a tune that plays the cat trying to catch up with its own tail'.[20]

When a melody is repeated at the same pitch level in a single voice while other voices gradually weave contrapuntal lines around it, the resulting chorale-prelude-like texture represents, from an evolutionary perspective, a notional move indoors from the English field into the English church. Chorale-prelude writing was by no means a widespread practice in English music history. Rather, it was a phenomenon of the English Bach revival, led by Hubert Parry with his book *Johann Sebastian Bach* (1909), his two volumes of *Chorale Preludes* (1912, 1916), and his *Three Chorale Fantasias* (1915). Parry placed the Bach of the church music—the choral preludes, chorale partitas, cantatas, and passion settings—above the Bach of formal fugues and instrumental suites. For Vaughan Williams, who as noted above (Introduction) considered Bach his favourite composer, Bach provided a model for the engaged community musician that Vaughan Williams himself wished to be, one whose music would elaborate the everyday tunes of the people around him. By shifting Handel from the centre stage that he occupied in the Victorian era and by writing Bach-inspired chorale preludes on nineteenth-century hymns, Parry and Vaughan Williams furthered their visions of the English music revival, maintaining contact with Victorian community musical practices but guiding them in a new direction. Vaughan Williams's 'Rhosymedre' from *Three Preludes Founded on Welsh Hymn Tunes* (1920)—all three of the hymns Victorian—gives a typical instance of diatonic counterpoint freely interweaving around a slower hymn melody that eventually is reiterated in full one octave higher. In imitation of Bach, the added parts are introduced first, the hymn melody creeping in slowly against them only later (Ex. 3.7; see LH part). In Vaughan Williams's compositional practice, chorale-prelude writing is interconnected with folksong, in line with his understanding of an evolutionary exchange between hymn singing inside the church and folksong outside it. His setting of 'The Saviour's Love' from *Twelve Traditional Carols from Herefordshire* (1920) resembles the style of a chorale prelude, while the opening Adagio from *Five Variants of Dives and Lazarus* (1939), based on another folksong, concludes with similar interweaving contrapuntal voices over a slower main melody in chorale-prelude style (from score letter B). The faster figures in the latter are very close to the figures that Vaughan Williams added to the melody in his hymn prelude on 'Dominus regit me' (1936), one of a pair of chorale preludes on Victorian hymns, this one by John Bacchus Dykes and the other, 'Eventide', by William Henry Monk.

Ex. 3.7 Vaughan Williams, 'Rhosymedre', *Three Preludes Founded on Welsh Hymn Tunes*, bars 8–12. © Copyright 1920 Stainer & Bell Ltd, 23 Gruneisen Road, London N3 1DZ, www.stainer.co.uk. Reproduced by permission. All rights reserved.

From about 1914, in large-scale compositions Vaughan Williams began to introduce passages of diatonic counterpoint at the octave or unison as the harmonically stable, expressively heightened climax of a movement or composition. The 'subject' of the overlapping contrapuntal entries is usually shaped in a smooth curve of mainly stepwise motions or small leaps, rising to a peak and sometimes falling away again. The entries usually begin with the lowest available voice or part and rise through the texture. The 'Epilogue' of the finale of the *London Symphony* in its original 1914 version has a phase of this type of counterpoint, suggestive of round singing, part of an extended and evidently redemptive passage of intensive diatonicism that was unheard for many decades, as the composer expunged it from his revised version. Similar effects appear in 'Job's Dream'—a vision of eternity—from *Job: A Masque for Dancing* (1931), and in Movement VI of *Dona Nobis Pacem* (1936) immediately after the very word 'peace', the moment of transformation and redemption in the composition, and, once again, a vision of eternity (see Ex. 5.7(ii)). Imitation at the octave and unison is evident throughout Symphony No. 5 (see Ex. 5.10 and discussion in Chapter 5). At the end of the finale ('Passacaglia'), two countersubjects appear repeatedly, always at tonic pitch level, with various contrapuntal elaborations in other voices, in the manner of a chorale prelude. This coda shares its mood, tone, melodic shapes, and formal processes with Vaughan Williams's hymn prelude on 'Eventide', as well as with Section VI of *Flos Campi*, in the same key (D major). As regards his explicitly pastoral-themed compositions of the 1910s and 1920s, aside from *Flos Campi* Vaughan Williams used these techniques in *The Shepherds of the Delectable Mountains* and, more obliquely, in *The Lark Ascending*.

Another diatonic convention that Vaughan Williams favoured is a grand plagal harmonic progression, typically with 7–6 and/or 9–8 appoggiatura or suspension for the IV chord. This 'big IV', as it is termed here, is admittedly more a schema than a topic. The harmonic progression is either the 'straight' plagal IV–I, with a 'churchy' or 'Amen' quality, or sometimes the more ambivalent IV–vi, in which vi substitutes for I. The big IV takes Vaughan Williams back to intensive diatonic dissonance within 'correct' part writing, but of a direct and often luxuriant kind that Parry and even Elgar avoided. It functions as a climax or heightened moment that sounds rich, ecstatic, or rapt, and the moment is usually extended by repetition, with the progression milked for all it is worth. A soft, atmospheric type of big IV is found in *A Sea Symphony*, second movement ('On the Beach Alone at Night'), *A London Symphony*, second movement, and at the opening of *Serenade to Music* (Ex. 3.8). In *Serenade to Music*, the enriched subdominant harmony is reiterated in several guises. The solo violin line, soaring above the rich string texture, matches the work's text for 'sweetness'.[21] The big IV in its harmonically ambivalent form appears at significant structural moments in *The Lark Ascending* and *Flos Campi* (opening of Section V). Symphony No. 5 relies on reiterated big IV progressions for its heightened diatonic climaxes in the first movement (fig. 5 to fig. 6) and the third movement (fig. 1 to fig. 2; fig. 3 to fig. 4). The 'Ballad' from *Suite for Viola and Orchestra* (1934) resumes the *Lark Ascending* version in a more direct form. The lush opening theme from the film score for *49th Parallel* (1941) begins with a big IV that holds nothing back.

In Vaughan Williams's pastoral compositions, satellite topics usually cluster around the theme of apocalypse in text and music. The topical domain includes trumpet or bugle calls, possibly offstage; singing voices, perhaps wordless, usually female, suggesting angelic choirs, again possibly offstage; cries of agony; and bell-chiming and processional effects, the

Ex. 3.8 Vaughan Williams, *Serenade to Music*, bars 1–6 (reduction). 'Serenade to Music' by Ralph Vaughan Williams © Oxford University Press 1938. All rights reserved.

sounds of celebration in the holy city. Apocalypse as such was a familiar theme of English choral music, which often dealt with 'last things', death and judgement, the direct experience of divine love, or simply a mystical frame of mind, usually drawing on some or all of the topical field described here. In Vaughan Williams's works alone, this obviously applies to *The Shepherds of the Delectable Mountains* (later absorbed by the opera *The Pilgrim's Progress*) and *Sancta Civitas*. Other works that invoke the apocalyptic mode include Elgar's *The Dream of Gerontius* (1900), the unrealized concept of his projected *The Last Judgement*, Eugene Goossens's *The Apocalypse* (1954), and Edmund Rubbra's Symphony No. 9 (*Sinfonia Sacra*; 1973). The musical language of such pieces can also be discerned in a wider repertory of choral compositions of a mystical temperament that includes Elgar's *The Apostles* (1903), Holst's *The Hymn of Jesus* (1920), Howells's *Hymnus Paradisi* (first performance 1950) and *Missa Sabrinensis* (1954), and Finzi's *Intimations of Immortality* (1950). The holy city is a theme of Parry's diatonic choral music, including 'I Was Glad' and 'Jerusalem', and apocalypse is the theme of 'At the Round Earth's Imagined Corners' (from the *a cappella Songs of Farewell*).

Vaughan Williams's pastoral compositions borrow something of the atmosphere and musical vocabulary of this choral tradition.

The transformation from pastoral topic to satellite topics and the apocalyptic mode can be discerned most clearly in *Shepherds* on account of the dramatic action and the text. The 'Scene' begins with Pilgrim's meeting with the shepherds on the mountains and ends with his death and resurrection. The default musical idiom is the new pastoral style. The very opening is a viola solo marked 'senza misura', giving a melody of moderate, smooth contours based on stepwise motion and small leaps around a gapped scale with a mixture of duplet and triplet quavers and of course no overall metrical organization. The ensuing vocal parts are in a similar style, and there are alternating chords and consecutive fifths in the accompaniment, chamber-music textures and changing metre.

Half-way through the scene, a 'Celestial Messenger' appears to call Pilgrim to the Celestial City but also to tell him that he must plunge into a deep river to reach it. After Pilgrim enters the waters, there is a long pause before distant offstage trumpet calls sound: an image of apocalypse and judgement established famously in Verdi's *Requiem*. Pilgrim is greeted in the Celestial City with offstage voices (female double chorus) singing 'Alleluia' accompanied by processional music for offstage harp and deep bells (Ex. 3.9). Here, whether deliberate or not, is a direct musical representation, of a kind not attempted even by Hubert Parry, of the 'immortal harps of golden wires', the 'hymns devout and holy psalms' and the 'cherubic host', which, according to Milton, sacred vocal music could disclose to the receptive imagination. Both trumpet calls and 'alleluia' figures are presented in round-singing style: close imitation at the unison over static diatonic harmony. The voices and instruments give the impression of approaching and receding, the music finally dying away 'al niente'. The default pastoral topic is transformed into a new field of conventions that presents an image of eternity glimpsed. The 'Scene' ends with the solo viola playing its original tune, unmeasured, also fading 'al niente', but reasserting the world and time frame of the still-living Shepherds in the mountains.

Although the music of the celestial vision is a transformation, the opposition of topics is not absolute. The pastoral and the religious are blended throughout *Shepherds*: with references to sheep in the text; moods of pain and melancholy in the pastoral music with flatward descending sequential steps that anticipate Pilgrim's longing for God and his submerging in the waters; short phases of triple-metre processional music that anticipate the

Ex. 3.9 Vaughan Williams, *The Shepherds of the Delectable Mountains*, fig. 27, bar 1 to fig. 27, bar 11. 'The Shepherds of the Delectable Mountains', a Pastoral Episode founded upon Bunyan's 'Pilgrim's Progress' by Ralph Vaughan Williams © Oxford University Press 1925. All rights reserved.

welcome in the Celestial City; and brief phases of counterpoint with octave-level imitation that anticipate the eternity of the round singing. The 'Alleluia' call at the processional climax itself presents a new version of the opening viola solo. Nevertheless, there is a strong sense of Pilgrim's journey from life to death and beyond in the transition from one topical vocabulary to another, the second one characterized by directness of expression and formal completeness but distance and detachment.

The *Pastoral Symphony*, composed at the same time as *Shepherds*, shares much of its musical language, as Daniel M. Grimley has pointed out.[22] It also shares something of the same trajectory of topical transformation from pastoral to apocalypse, as well as an aesthetic of distancing. The climax of the first movement occurs when the opening motive of the movement is presented in the coda in a repetitive, processional passage with bell-chiming effects similar to those of the celestial procession in *Shepherds* and melodic motives in octave and unison repetitions that closely recall the trumpet fanfares that immediately precede that procession (R + 3).[23] This climax is, however, even more elusive than the one in *Shepherds*, and it soon fades before the pastoral default is reasserted to close the movement. In the famous 'bugle call' of the second movement (on E flat natural trumpet), the topical field of musical apocalypse again pushes through the pastoral surface, but it remains a distant call without issue, as the pastoral idiom is resumed, and no synthesis ensues. The third and fourth movements do not continue the pattern of the first two in this regard, but their topical plots are still relevant. The third begins with a vigorous dance with unison and octave imitation in round-singing style, as noted by Howells; the pastoral topic appears as a contrast (fig. B + 6); it is followed by a rumbustious folk dance (fig. D + 6), while the trio is a 'fantastic scherzo' ('Presto'; fig. S + 3).[24] The finale begins and ends with a long, unmeasured, wordless solo for offstage soprano over a soft timpani roll, consistent in idiom with pastoral topic (gapped scale, mixture of duplet and triplet quavers), although here so unearthly that it could be heard as coming from the same place as the processional music and the bugle call.

Flos Campi is not apocalyptic in its text—each of its six labelled sections is prefaced by a quotation in Latin from the Song of Solomon—but it draws on a similar musical vocabulary as *Shepherds* and the *Pastoral Symphony*, and it effects another topical transformation, in this case leading from languishing lovesickness to the peace of divine love. The new pastoral topic is the starting point, dominating the first three sections of the piece. As in *Shepherds*, the very opening features an unmeasured solo viola melody, this time in duet with a solo oboe. In Sections I and III, the pastoral style is less overtly diatonic than usual in Vaughan Williams; conflicting pitch collections introduce acute dissonance, bimodality, and some chromaticism. The sighing figures for the wordless female chorus underline the pain that is presented more obliquely in *Shepherds* and the *Pastoral Symphony*. The rest of *Flos Campi* can be considered as a quest to find various 'ways out' of this state.

The first step is Section II. This music does not present a new topic, but it is highly contrasted relative to Section I: lushly sensuous, diatonic, harmonically stable, rhythmically measured, lyrical, with a literally 'murmuring' accompaniment. A second attempt at transformation occurs with the ecstasy of a big IV, at the start of Section V (Ex. 3.10(i)). This gesture follows a repetitive, ostinato march in Section IV and functions as a cathartic release after the building of tension. The final—and successful—attempt at transformation is the lengthy phase of vocal-style counterpoint—first instrumental, then literally, though wordlessly, vocal—in Section VI, shaped around octave and/or unison imitation. This is one of the most intensively diatonic passages in all of Vaughan Williams's music, lacking a single accidental aside from a brief move from D major to an equally diatonic G major. There are fifteen entries at the octave or unison of a rising and falling melody of mainly

Ex. 3.10 Vaughan Williams, *Flos Campi* 'Flos Campi' by Ralph Vaughan Williams. © Oxford University Press 1928. All rights reserved.
(i) fig. 15, bar 5–fig. 15, bar 9 (reduction)

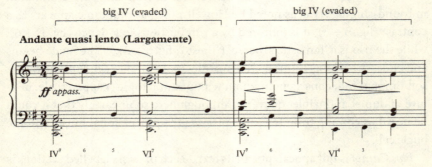

(ii) fig. 21, bar 15–fig. 21, bar 21 (solo viola part)

(iii) fig. 30, bar 11–fig. 30, bar 17 (solo viola part)

stepwise motion (Ex. 3.10(ii)), most of them complete, before ten similar entries of a related melody that initially descends from the tonic rather than rising. These are the two phrase components of the melodic schema 'Victorian hymn' (described in Chapter 5). At each stage, the entries are initially presented successively, with little overlap, like the reiterations of a chorale-prelude melody, but later they are compressed in a texture that is more akin to round-singing. As in 'The Explorers' from *A Sea Symphony* (discussed in Chapter 2; see Ex. 2.19(ii)), the counterpoint is free: the rules of dissonance resolution are not observed, and the music simply inhabits a diatonic collection. When a bass note is present at all, it is a tonic pedal; no harmonic process is implied. This is a transformation to clarity and definiteness: simple rising and falling diatonic melodic shapes dominate along with grand dynamic waves. The accompaniment of harp and celesta means that the imagery of heavenly peace could hardly be mistaken.

One further element of the alternative topical domain is subtly presented at the very end of *Flos Campi*. When the final contrapuntal wave is complete and the vocal parts die away (half-closed lips, 'niente') on Ds in all parts, the viola/oboe duet from the work's opening returns. Unlike in *Shepherds*, eternity does not remain entirely distant this time, as the music of the contrapuntal 'round' returns softly, though it soon dies away yet again, like a distant recollection. Solo flute and solo viola play a new version of the round melody with a rising fourth figure (dominant and tonic notes) at the end like a distant bugle call (Ex. 3.10(iii)), a topical gesture now familiar from *Shepherds* and the *Pastoral Symphony*. In context, the melodic leap stands in clear relief from the otherwise stepwise motion that dominates all parts in the texture. The call is echoed in the accompanying vocal parts. *Flos Campi* therefore ends ambivalently, the eternity of the heavenly round singing held in recollection even though distanced.

Sancta Civitas, which Vaughan Williams composed almost concurrently with *Flos Campi*, is not such an overtly pastoral composition, but it sustains the association of the pastoral topic with its apocalyptic satellite topics while reversing the transformational plot. The text is from Revelation, and unsurprisingly the work opens with the full range of apocalyptical topical elements and spatial effects. The text describes a mystical state of mind ('I was in the spirit'). The 'many people praising God and saying "Alleluia"' is illustrated with the chorus loud and 'present', before a 'distant chorus' is heard along with fanfare calls from a 'distant trumpet' with a rising fifth figure. Such spatial effects continue through the work as the mystical vision approaches and fades.[25] Full revelation is reached with a vision of the holy city ('And I saw a new heaven and a new earth'). At this moment the music, at first sight paradoxically, switches out of its apocalyptical vocabulary to the new pastoral topic, with sinuous pentatonic solo melodies for cor anglais, solo violin, and oboe, a mixture of duplet and triplet quavers and crotchets, rustling textures, uneven metre, and parallel triads. The significance of the pastoral topic here may be spiritual/erotic, as the city is 'prepared as a bride adorned for her husband', or it may arise from the image of the 'new earth'. In line with Vaughan Williams's practice, the vision then fades, and at the end of the work the mystical sounds of the opening return but without the definiteness of the vision. Eternity is once again glimpsed but not held.

Case Study: *The Lark Ascending*

The Lark Ascending took a long time to reach its current warhorse status. In Vaughan Williams's lifetime it was overshadowed by the *Pastoral Symphony*, which had a much greater audible influence on contemporary English composers. The *Lark* has attracted relatively little attention from academic musicologists, perhaps because it is perceived as hackneyed.[26] In fact, though, it is a rather subtle piece, and with its understated but real transformational process, it belies its own idyllic and contemplative surface. There is an overall 'plagal' drift in diatonic collections, from a two-sharp to one-sharp collection. The opening and closing cadenzas exemplify this drift: even though the notes of the solo violin are very similar, the diatonic contexts given by the soft accompanying chords change from two-sharp to one-sharp. As Wilfrid Mellers observed, 'it is, for all its quietude, a "symphonic" piece which evolves, even develops.'[27] Intensive diatonic writing lies at the heart of the piece, and the choices between diatonic collections and the subcollections within them determine the subdued process of change that spans the work.

The *Lark* is the first of Vaughan Williams's compositions to effect a transformation from pastoral style to a religious musical vocabulary, although it does so in such a discrete fashion that without the benefit of hindsight, informed by the later compositions of the 1920s, the appearance of the satellite topics could easily pass unnoticed. Vaughan Williams had recently tested intensive modal diatonicism in the mystical visions of 'Love Bade me Welcome' and 'Come Love, Come Lord', but he had not undertaken a process of topical transformation in the fashion of an unfolding plot. He prefaced the *Lark* with stanzas selected from George Meredith's poem of the same title, which in its complete version contains lines surprisingly convergent with Milton's 'Ode: At a Solemn Musick',[28] and the composition itself retains tenuous but telling links to the Victorian musical idioms that guided Parry, Elgar, and Vaughan Williams himself before 1914.

The *Lark* leaves an overall impression of indefiniteness on account of its formal fluidity:[29] its dynamic processes cut across its outward formal boundaries. The outward form can be described as palindromic (**ABCB'A'**), with a solo violin cadenza as introduction and coda furthering the symmetry (Table. 3.1). Within each main section the order of presentation of materials does not follow the palindromic scheme, but rather a broadly 'rotational' principle,[30] the module A² following A¹ in both **A** and **A'** sections, for instance, and likewise the B modules in the **B** sections. The solo violin's cadenza represents the lark (the freely unfolding melodic line imitates the bird's intermittently but progressively ascending song-flight as much as its

Table 3.1 Vaughan Williams, *The Lark Ascending*, formal analysis

Section	Module	Diatonic coll.	Metre	Score
Intro (cadenza)		2♯	6/8 then none	
A	A¹	2♯	6/8	A-6
	A²	2♯/1♭/1♯		B-1
	A¹	2♯		F
Cadenza		2♯	none	
B	B¹	2♯ (mainly)	2/4	G-2
	B²	2♯		L
Cadenza-like			2/4 then 6/8	
C		White-note	6/8	M
Cadenza-like			6/8 'senza misura'	
B'	B¹	1♯	2/4	R
	B²	1♯		S
A'	A¹	2♯	6/8	U-1
	A²	1♯/1♭/1♯		Y-3
	A¹	1♯		X+3
Coda (cadenza)		1♯	6/8 then none	

118 ENGLISH DIATONIC MUSIC

song as such). Further, shorter, cadenzas appear between most of the main sections (**A**, **B**, **C**, **B'**) and cadenza-like passages are sometimes partially integrated with other, measured, music as an accompaniment.

Characteristic aspects of the new pastoral topic are spread between the cadenza and the A materials (compare Ex. 3.11(i) and Ex. 3.12(i)). Both have pentatonic melodic patterns and prominent consecutive fifths in their accompaniment patterns, but only the former is unmeasured, while the latter has alternating harmonies over a bass pedal. A^2 is really a group of motives and introduces contrapuntal exchanges in chamber-music style. The high register of the violin in the A^1 and A^2 modules—atypical for pastoral topic,

Ex. 3.11 Vaughan Williams, *The Lark Ascending*, introduction and coda cadenzas and accompaniment figures. 'The Lark Ascending' by Ralph Vaughan Williams © Oxford University Press 1925. All rights reserved.

(i)   Introduction, bars 1–3 (reduction)

(ii)   Coda, fig. Y, bar 1–fig. Y, bar 6 (reduction)

DIATONIC PASTORAL MUSIC 119

Ex. 3.12 Vaughan Williams, *The Lark Ascending*, A^1 module. 'The Lark Ascending' by Ralph Vaughan Williams © Oxford University Press 1925. All rights reserved.

(i) Initial presentation (**A**), six bars before fig. A–fig. A, bar 3 (reduction)

(ii) Final presentation (**A**): first 'round-singing' version, fig. E, bar 9–fig. F, bar 7 (reduction)

(iii) Final presentation (**A'**): second 'round-singing' version, fig. X, bar 4–fig. X, bar 8 (reduction)

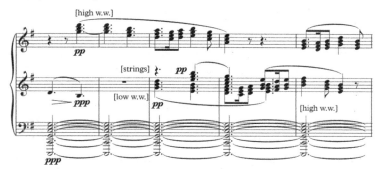

new or old—is carried over from the cadenza: an instance of the integration of sections across formal boundaries. The A materials are set in the default 'old' pastoral 6/8 metre with dotted rhythms that later are usually missing from Vaughan Williams's major pastoral compositions, and at times the music approaches pastoral cliché. A^1 returns in a round-singing version (Ex. 3.12(ii)), with fourfold overlapping imitation at the octave and unison, the topic thus already partially transformed, a step in the material's musical 'evolution'.

The **B** materials present a sharper contrast in topic, rhythm, and texture. The metre is now simple duple (2/4). B^1 (Ex. 3.13(i)) is a folksong stylization presented in three varied strophes, the melody lying at a more human pitch level than that of the A modules, although violin figuration continues at times in the accompaniment. The brief B^2 (Ex. 3.13(ii)) suggests a 'churchy' big IV with elements of the schema 'plagal tritone' in the ascending inner part, even though its resolution is evaded to iii. C for the first time is dance-like, in a fast 6/8 metre. In terms of topic, then, the *Lark* evolves from nature (cadenza), though conventional pastoral (6/8 pentatonic), through the round singing of the human dwellers of the countryside to fully developed English folksong, followed by hints of religious community singing and finally, in the central section of the work's palindromic scheme, a grounded, physical way of being (dance).

On the interpretation advanced here, however, the churchy B^2 module, rather than the dance-like **C**, is the crux of the composition. Its significance is fully realized in the **B'** section; in the earlier **B** section it is only 'planted', as might be said in the terminology of the rotational theory of musical form,[31] awaiting full realization. The generative process begins with B^1, as B^2 is audibly derived from the opening motive of the folksong-like tune, recalling once again Vaughan Williams's view that English folksong and the music of the English church were interconnected in their historical evolution. **B'** shifts the emphasis to the B^2 module: there is now only one iteration of B^1 rather than three, and instead B^2 is strengthened and reiterated. On its first two presentations the big IV, which increasingly implies a plagal resolution to I in G major, 'dissolves' into the iii harmony (relative to G major) while the solo violin adds double-stopped figuration in the *Lark*'s most atmospheric moments (Ex. 3.13(iii)). This, rather than the central **C** section of the scheme, is the expressive core of the composition, and the antithetical point of furthest remove from the pastoral idioms of the cadenza and **A**. A sense of striving or searching is conveyed by the crescendos on the reiterated IV harmonies, followed each time by evasion of full harmonic resolution. These

Ex. 3.13 Vaughan Williams, *The Lark Ascending*, generation of **B** section materials. 'The Lark Ascending' by Ralph Vaughan Williams © Oxford University Press 1925. All rights reserved.

(i)   Initial presentation of B¹ (**B**), two bars before fig. G–fig. G, bar 4 (reduction)

(ii) Initial presentation of B² (**B**), fig. L, bar 1– fig. L, bar 5 (reduction)

(iii) Heightened presentation of B² (B'), fig. S bar 1– fig. S, bar 6 (reduction)

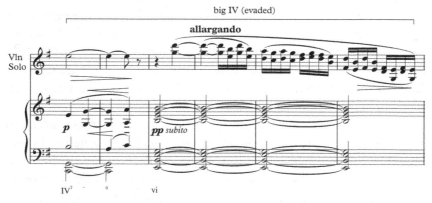

effects suggest a reflective and self-conscious state of mind in contrast to the idyllic states of the bird, the folksong, and the folk dance. There is even a somatic sense of drawing breath or sighing that is found nowhere else in the composition. And despite the indefiniteness—the fragmentation, the lack of resolution to the tonic for a full 'plagal' progression—an alternative, non-pastoral vein of English diatonic music is evoked by the big IV, stretching back through Victorian hymn writing and plagal 'Amen' figures.

The choices between alternative diatonic pitch collections reinforce this elusive but recognizable plot. From Table 3.1 it is evident that the *Lark* tends to venture 'flatwards'—to borrow the metaphor of the circle of fifths in traditional tonal music—but never 'sharpwards' from the initial two-sharp diatonic collection. In particular, the gradual replacement of the two-sharp collection by the one-sharp collection implied by the key signature in the score—sometimes to support identical melodic materials—is crucial for the transformation process. **A** accomplishes this to some degree; **A'** does so much more thoroughly. The very opening accompaniment figures in the strings outline a two-sharp diatonic collection that includes C sharps. The E natural in the bass suggests an E Dorian interpretation of that collection. The solo violin cadenza that follows, however, relies largely on only four pitch classes of the collection (D, E, A, B). This initial, undetermined 'nature' finds a more definite realization in the pentatonicism of A^1, outlined by the violin already near the end of the cadenza. The first stage of the flatward drift occurs already in **A**, with a decisive (*ff* 'Largamente') move to a one-flat diatonic collection at the climactic version of A^2. A^2 material is then presented in a one-sharp diatonic context. When A^1 returns in its round-singing version (Ex. 3.12(ii)), however, the diatonic collection is ambiguous, neither C sharp nor C natural being sounded. A return to the two-sharp collection for the end of **A** is signalled by the reiteration of the opening string accompaniment to the cadenza with its C sharps. **B** makes a more decisive move to a one-sharp collection more with its immediate subdominant harmony (C major) relative to a putative G major tonic. **C** takes a further step around the circle, relying entirely on a white-note diatonic collection (either as D Dorian or A Aeolian).

Although **A'** ostensibly presents the same materials as **A** at unchanged overall pitch levels, it does so in a new way, clinching the flatward move from the two-sharp to the one-sharp diatonic collection that was hinted at in **A** but undertaken more decisively in the intervening sections of the work. The initial, two-sharp presentation of A^1 is condensed; A^2 begins already in a one-sharp rather than two-sharp context; while the round-singing version of A^1—ambiguous as to diatonic collection in its A presentation—unfolds entirely within a one-sharp diatonic context with a transformed texture. The latter (Ex. 3.12(iii)) even has a C major triad triple pedal in the lower parts in an unusually low, thick texture, recalling other significant 'C-plagal' moments earlier in the composition, such as the big IV of B^2. Finally, and perhaps most importantly, the accompaniment chords that preface the final solo violin cadenza foreground C naturals within a one-flat collection (Ex. 3.11(ii)) and even recall the C major to E minor harmonic progression of the crucial B^2. The concluding bars thus amount to a kind of synthesis, the antithetical pole of the elaborated B^2 being in a sense incorporated into the pastoral A materials, which are in turn partly transformed. This transformation re-frames the solo violin cadenza that follows, which, although not identical in content with the work's opening cadenza, begins with the same four-pitch-class subcollection as before (D, E, A, B). Thus the *Lark*'s outwardly palindromic form and idyllic character in fact conceals a subtle overall process of change, achieved not suddenly but progressively over the course of the work, leading to the final presentation of the solo violin cadenza in a one-sharp rather than a two-sharp diatonic context.[32] The alternation of diatonic collections, topical transformation, and texture is coordinated in this process of change, which cuts across the outward formal boundaries in a dynamic fashion.

Wilfrid Mellers felt that the *Lark* 'takes us to the heart of the composer's religious sensibility'.[33] The observation is sound, although there is a little more to it than the 'English Nature-mysticism' of W. H. Hudson and Richard Jeffries, to which Mellers linked the piece. Consistent with his Parry-inspired evolutionary perspective on English music history, Vaughan Williams transformed the lark's cadenza first into human song and dance and then into allusions to sacred-music idioms, even if only indirectly and fleetingly. It is now clear that the *Lark* initiates the practice of topical transformation and the partial disclosure of religious vision that typifies Vaughan Williams's pastoral compositions of the decade to 1925. The transformation is less obvious than in *Shepherds* or *Flos Campi*, as the developmental process is fluid and overrides sectional boundaries. But the fragments of round-singing, the incomplete big IVs, and the violin cadenzas and harmonic stasis already offer their glimpses of eternity.

Legacy: Competing Schools of English Pastoral Music

On a casual impression, one might conclude that the new pastoral style and approach of Vaughan Williams and Howells can stand for a wider 'English pastoral music' that dominated compositional style in the first half of the twentieth century. On closer inspection, however, it is clear that this was far from the case. The popular image of Vaughan Williams as a pastoral composer rests on folksong arrangements and transcriptions and on a few famous orchestral pieces in intensively diatonic styles such as the *Fantasia on a Theme by Thomas Tallis*, *The Lark Ascending*, the *Pastoral Symphony*, and the Fifth Symphony. All of these orchestral pieces rely to some degree on the new pastoral style, but only the Fifth Symphony was not crammed into the short period 1919–1925, if the *Tallis Fantasia* and *The Lark Ascending* are considered in the revised versions performed today. After 1925, Vaughan Williams's large-scale compositions moved in a wide, almost bewildering, range of directions that make his work difficult to pin down. (This may well be a reason why the easier, reductive associations with folksong, Tudor music, and pastoralism have endured.) Mostly, the tone was more extroverted, and the genres included liturgical music, abstract symphonic forms, and opera. The Violin Concerto, *Te Deum* in G, Piano Concerto, *Magnificat*, Fourth Symphony, *Riders to the Sea*, and *Five Tudor Portraits* share little with the aims of his major pastoral compositions and seldom adopt the pastoral approach of the early 1920s. Howells, meanwhile, suffered a crisis of confidence, and his compositional activity faltered; when he later resumed, he remade himself as a composer of choral music.

Eric Saylor has argued convincingly that although pastoral was a consistent interest of English composers in the years before World War I, there was a striking stylistic diversity of approach until a phase of consolidation began in the early 1920s.[34] With an eye to diatonic idioms, a further distinction can be made. By the early 1920s, there were two distinct, alternative versions of English musical pastoral. The earliest, perhaps the most vigorous, and certainly the longest lasting of these versions derived from the short orchestral pieces of Frederick Delius. The very first orchestral piece of English pastoral music was Delius's *Brigg Fair: An English Rhapsody* (1907), a set of variations on a Lincolnshire folksong collected by Percy Grainger. Delius followed it up with a series of idyllic tone pictures: *In a Summer Garden* (1908), *On Hearing the First Cuckoo in Spring* (1912), *Summer Night on the River* (1912), *A Song before Sunrise* (1918), and *Song of Summer* (1929–1930). The four movements of *North Country Sketches* (1914) directly portray landscapes of northern England. In some ways, these pieces are more conventionally pastoral than those of Vaughan Williams and Howells, relying heavily on compound duple metre, dance rhythms, and bird call effects. They sometimes burst into ecstatic melodic pentatonicism, but such passages are often accompanied or surrounded by harmonic chromaticism, especially descending chromatic lines, in a way that recalls Delius's mentor, Grieg. Delius's aesthetic was not one of 'intensive' diatonicism and was not grounded in patterns of avoidance, especially not avoidance of leading-note-based harmony. His approach had no religious dimension. Delius relished kaleidoscopic changes of colours, rich orchestral harmony, scoring influenced by Wagner and Debussy, and a languid, melancholy tone.

Despite Delius's voluntary expatriation and his explicit disavowal of English culture and values, some of his short orchestral pieces were probably composed with English taste and performance in England in mind, in contrast with his earlier operas, songs, and choral works.[35] By the 1900s, he was attracting the interest of orchestral conductors in Britain, while, a little later, critics such as Philip Heseltine, Cecil Gray, Eric Fenby, and Arthur Hutchings had no hesitation in calling Delius's music English and associating it with the English countryside. But composers such as Frank Bridge, Percy Grainger, Peter Warlock (Heseltine), C. W. Orr, E. J. Moeran, and Arnold Bax responded swiftly too, assimilating Delius's style and executing pastoral-themed compositions and passages in a way reminiscent of him. Bridge's *Summer* (1915), which predates the premieres of any of Vaughan Williams's major pastoral compositions, has Delius-like moments of ecstatic diatonicism within a chromatic harmonic context. The many pastoral episodes in the six symphonies of Bax and in his orchestral tone poems of the interwar period invariably recall Delius. In the 1920s, Moeran appears to have effected a synthesis of Delius and Vaughan Williams in his orchestral *Rhapsodies* (1922, 1924), and Howells took similar steps in the 1930s.[36] The 1929 London Delius festival, the later disinterment of Delius's remains in France after his death in 1934, and his literal repatriation through re-burial in Surrey[37] were only the culmination of a movement already well underway in musical composition.

Vaughan Williams was not attracted to either Delius's musical personality or his world view, and the intensively diatonic pastoral idiom he and Howells developed can be viewed as a reaction to Delius's growing stature and as an attempt to reclaim and redefine English pastoral music. If so, then, in the long run it does not appear to have been successful, the pastoral legacy of Delius proving rather more tenacious. It had a legacy of sorts, to be sure. Vaughan Williams returned to the style in parts of his Symphony No. 5 and in *An Oxford Elegy* (1949), although the latter is not one of his artistically significant compositions of the time, but a throwback to the interests of his youth. Howells's *Hymnus Paradisi* (premiere 1950) at times alludes to the language of the *Pastoral Symphony*, although it shapes its shattering climaxes in the manner of Delius. The second movement of Bax's Symphony No. 3 (1929) also points to the *Pastoral Symphony* and possibly to *Flos Campi*, yet it swiftly reverts to a Delius-influenced idiom. Likewise, Moeran's Symphony in G (1937) gives glimpses of the approach of Vaughan Williams and Howells in the secondary theme of its first movement, but by the end, the movement has again reverted to the Delius manner for its lyrical utterances. Beyond pastoral as a topic, one might hear Vaughan Williams's visionary breakthroughs parodied by Holst in his bleak *Egdon Heath* (1927), in which the trumpet call in the concluding bars sounds like a failed apocalypse, and even by Vaughan Williams himself with the organ entry in the 'Landscape' movement of *Sinfonia Antartica* (1952), a moment of sublime horror that begins with a chromatic two-part canon that suggests eternally petrified round singers in a frozen hell.[38] In this light it is important to recognize that the style and approach that Vaughan Williams and Howells developed in the 1910s did not 'win' or establish a hegemony in English music.[39] Given the later revivals of processional diatonicism, especially in music for public broadcast and official occasions, it was not even the dominant style of intensively diatonic English music.

It is possible that a Delius-orientated clique in London affected Howells's confidence in his own work after the premiere of his Piano Concerto No. 2 (1925)—a piece that he called 'a diatonic affair'[40]—and helped to bring on his period of artistic silence. The work was a prestigious Royal Philharmonic Society commission, and its premiere, at which it shared the programme with Vaughan Williams's *Pastoral Symphony*, was well attended. One of the supporters of Peter Warlock shouted an insulting remark after the Concerto was finished, and in response Vaughan Williams and Howells's friends stood up and applauded strongly. Still, if Howells was right and the Warlock group thought that Moeran should have received the commission in the first place, then they were simply asking for pastoral music with a different accent.[41] Whatever the case, this episode reveals some of the divisions within English pastoral aesthetics and marks an endpoint for the new pastoral style as the main diatonic topic in English composition. When Howells returned to ambitious compositional projects in the 1930s, as Chapter 6 will show, he had adopted a good deal of the Delius idiom himself.

4

Songs of Pain and Beauty

On English Diatonic Song

In English solo art songs with the accompaniment of piano and/or string ensemble composed between 1900 and the end of World War II, intensive diatonicism was a consistent musical response to the contemporary pastoral poetry that musicians favoured. The literary themes that appealed to them were landscape and nature; longing for western regions of the British Isles; and feelings of wonder at life and beauty but regret for their transience. Composers forged a tradition of English song around codes that were both textual and musical, encompassing the poets' words and the available diatonic conventions. Ironically, they drew on the new diatonic pastoral style only occasionally, preferring the processional diatonicism inherited from the orchestral and choral works of Parry and Elgar, which were now adapted for piano accompaniment, along with hymn and chorale-prelude topics. The schemata of processional diatonicism described in Chapters 1 and 2 became a vital expressive resource in the art-song repertory and provided an opportunity for subtle compositional strategies. The work of Ivor Gurney and Gerald Finzi after World War I amounted to something of a Parry revival. Finzi's songs of the interwar period present the strongest single case in English music of a self-conscious programme of tradition building and amount to the richest synthesis of schemata and processional idioms in English diatonic song. This strand of English song offers striking evidence of continuity, tradition, and the resilience of the pre-war musical language in the post-war world.

However, in contrast to English choral and orchestral music, intensively diatonic art songs turned away from grand public statements to a mainly private realm of tender thoughts and melancholy reflections. The far-reaching, almost compulsive melancholy of Gurney and Finzi's projects arose from the diatonic paradoxes of English song. The central literary image for this repertory was A. E. Housman's cherry tree, especially as remembered from

George Butterworth's setting of 'Loveliest of Trees', a point of frequent musical allusion. The cherry tree was an image of transience. As such, its significance was reinforced by the loss of Butterworth in the war, who was seen to have lived out the destiny of Housman's Shropshire Lad by dying overseas while fighting for the British Empire. But the diatonic language-to-hand for these organists-turned-song-composers represented eternity, the 'immortal harps', everlasting singing and 'eternal morn of light' that Hubert Parry had portrayed with it. With Parry dead too and Elgar lapsed into compositional silence, their music everywhere sought the vision but captured it only in fleeting glimpses and subjective intuitions.

This chapter examines the codes of English diatonic art song, sketching lines of influence and their branches; identifying phases of innovation and consolidation; differentiating levels of taste; and exploring compositional applications of the topics and schemata at some length in the works of Gurney and Finzi. It sometimes considers literary and topographical contexts (poetic themes and modes, regions, locations, associations), but the perspective is primarily musical and aesthetic. Although the compositional strategies for setting a text are of interest, no particular value is placed on the 'marriage' of poetry and music as a grounding principle of art song—despite Milton's injunction to the pair of sirens ('voice' and 'verse') to 'wed your divine sounds, and mixt power employ'. Indeed, the perspective adopted here recognizes a productive tension between texts and musical idioms. The diatonic music speaks first through its own system of signs, and understanding that system is the first and most important step in understanding the repertory, including composers' strategies for the musical interpretation of the texts. The diatonic conventions in themselves are autonomous relative to the texts, belonging to their own musical tradition which extends well beyond the art-song genre.

Although many musicians were born in or moved to the regions of western England referred to in the texts, experienced the landscape immediately, and even longed for it when they were absent, just as do the poetic subjects of some of the texts, it is no less true that some places mentioned in songs were never visited by the musicians who celebrated them, just as A. E. Housman himself—the central poetic figure of the tradition—never visited the eponymous county of his *A Shropshire Lad* (1896). By contrast, the diatonic conventions remained consistent regardless of whether the composer had personal experience of the places mentioned in the texts. Ivor Gurney walked and worked in the landscape of his native

Gloucestershire, and, when absent, he recorded his feelings of homesickness in his poetry. But his musical realizations of those experiences relied on schemata found in the occasional choral compositions of Parry, the Director of the Royal College of Music where Gurney studied. They even relied on procedures found in the popular drawing-room ballad, which he was able to absorb and apply in imaginative ways. For these reasons, the approach to English song taken here does not adopt the phenomenological perspective that has been tested in some recent scholarship on English music and landscape.[1] The repertory may well appear to speak of the experience of landscape, direct, personal, physical or embodied, and some of the reception of the music may adopt those terms, but the system of conventions revealed in the following discussion was a musical rhetoric effected through the response to literary tropes with musical topics and schemata.

Contexts

Of the composers discussed in this chapter, Vaughan Williams, Butterworth, Gurney, and Ireland taught or studied at the Royal College of Music. Elgar, Roger Quilter (1877–1953), and Finzi did not, although Finzi studied privately with R. O. Morris (1886–1948), who taught at the College. Parry, the College Director, and the leading figure in a close network of reformist musicians, in some ways laid the ground for the repertory that later emerged, conducting a campaign to raise the quality and quantity of English art song and to stimulate the growth of a compositional tradition. Parry and his colleagues were especially concerned about good taste. They distrusted conventional Victorian taste in song, in particular the taste represented by the 'drawing-room ballad' or 'royalty ballad'. In a typically reformist article entitled 'The Present Condition of English Song-Writing' (1888), Parry complained that English song was commercialized and vulgar and inhabited a 'Slough of Musical Despond'. In his extensive published writings, Parry's son-in-law Harry Plunket Greene (1865–1936), an accomplished baritone, treated singing as an art of 'interpretation', recording a shift in the conception of the singer from virtuoso to interpreter. Greene, who acquired a leadership role amongst vocalists akin to that of his father-in-law in English music in general, called for a uniquely English style of singing akin to English speech to replace imitation *bel canto*.[2] The repertory that emerged, with its characteristically intimate, confidential tone and relative avoidance of dramatic effect and vocal display, was consistent with these attitudes and priorities.

But the relationship between institutions and their intellectual programmes and the eventual compositional practices was indirect. Neither Parry nor Plunket Greene—nor anyone else for that matter—ever called for intensive diatonicism in English song. And, as noted in Chapter 1, there is no evidence that the idioms of the English diatonic tradition were taught within the Royal College curriculum. As a composition teacher, Stanford may have communicated his discreet approach to folksong arrangement and the principle of composing in the diatonic modes, but apparently he went no further. Neither was there any stated preference at the Royal College for the poetry that was most often chosen for setting in diatonic styles: Housman, the poets of the Georgian Anthologies, and Thomas Hardy. Hubert Parry's own quarter-century-long project of English song composition, the twelve sets of *English Lyrics*, did not offer a model in either respect. His poets were Elizabethan, Jacobean, and Victorian, while his influence on the tradition's stylistic code came through his occasional choral works, not through his songs.[3] Moreover, the principles of elevating musical taste and shunning vocal display and the commercial ballad did not consistently guide composers. The repertory remained only partially 'emancipated', 'top notes' being permitted on certain characteristic diatonic sonorities. So, although a theoretical notion of English song may have been promoted by a loose network connected with the Royal College and the journal *Music & Letters*, the core aesthetic of English diatonic song as it was actually composed must have developed in the student generations of the 1900s and 1910s mainly through listening, shared interests, and ways of responding to favourite texts and poets. After World War I, the consolidation of the tradition was accomplished by a handful of musicians with minimal public profile, whose works were published and recorded only much later. A deeper connection between these composers may lie in the fact that most—Elgar, Vaughan Williams, Ireland, Gurney, and Finzi—were at some stage of their lives, like Parry, practising organists.

The repertory of English song that emerged during and after the campaigns of Parry and his cohort was closely associated with a few singers and their voices, which may have encouraged a range of intimate moods. Greene appears to have offered a vocal model.[4] Some contemporary reactions suggest that his baritone voice was a light one, and he certainly placed sincerity and subtlety of interpretation over virtuosity or technical prowess. Greene championed contemporary English song composition and was the dedicatee of Vaughan Williams's *Songs of Travel*, which he regularly performed, as well as songs by Parry and Stanford. Gervase Elwes (1866–1921) premiered Vaughan Williams's *On Wenlock Edge*, received its dedication and sang on its first recording, and premiered many songs by Roger Quilter. Vaughan Williams thought that the character of Quilter's music was shaped by Elwes's vocal style.[5] Elwes and John Coates (1865–1941) maintained international careers while also advocating contemporary English vocal music and receiving dedications of new works. In modern performance and recording, the type of English song that relies on an intensively diatonic language is mainly realized by male singers, especially those with light voices.

By identifying Parry as a key musical influence on English diatonic song, the interpretation advanced here underlines continuity across generations and departs from several alternative accounts of the repertory and its development. Although a generational shift took place around 1910, with settings of Housman by Vaughan Williams and Butterworth influenced by English folksong and French modernism, the schemata found in Parry's diatonic idiom and the predilection for stepwise bass motion never abated in English song and resurfaced strongly in the 1920s and 1930s in the songs of Gurney and Finzi. For this repertory, it is misleading to claim that English music came into its own with the generation of Vaughan Williams, Butterworth, and Holst by sloughing off the remnants of a Germanic musical language that had clung to Parry, Stanford, and Elgar.[6] The claim that the movement succeeded in transcending the Victorian ballad tradition and in developing a higher quality 'art song' likewise should not be pushed too far, as certain idioms of the ballad were never wholly abandoned and even contributed to intensively diatonic climaxes.[7] In short, English art song owed a good deal to Victorian music, of both lofty and sentimental-commercial varieties. Like English diatonic music as a whole, this was a modern tradition with Victorian roots.

Style, Semantics, and Scope

The expressive core of English diatonic song is tender and melancholic, dwelling on the experience of beauty, especially in nature, but also on the pain of its loss. Gurney's poem 'Song of Pain and Beauty', published in the Royal College of

Music magazine in 1917, captures this mood in its title alone.[8] The singer's terrible cry of pain on a sudden dissonant chord at the words 'splendour and glory' in 'Rhapsody' from Finzi's *Dies Natalis* is an irony altogether unprompted by Thomas Traherne's text. Songs that inhabit this expressive world are predominantly in a moderate or slow tempo, and for the most part they avoid dance rhythms. Butterworth's 'Loveliest of Trees' exemplifies the aesthetic and was a frequent point of motivic and textual allusion for later composers. Complete cycles tend to begin and end in this melancholic vein, turning to fast ('rollicking') songs for occasional respite in the middle. Texts specify a westward direction for the melancholic imagination, with concrete descriptions of and allusions to everyday rural places and locations—towns, hills, rivers—usually along the Severn Valley, especially in Shropshire and Gloucestershire. Intense significance is attached to the memory of or desire for these places; the feelings draw a musical response of intensive diatonicism, selective diatonic dissonance, and the schemata found in Parry's occasional choral compositions. After World War I, in the songs of Gurney and Finzi, Parry's originally public tone was transformed into an intimate, personal vision that was mainly reflective rather than dramatic or rhetorical. Complete songs, or diatonic passages from lengthy songs, seem to offer memories, brief glimpses, or fragments of an imagined greater diatonic continuity. Elgar's tendency to favour E flat major for referential utterances in this idiom is maintained, as is the stepwise bass motion in many cases and the reliance on successions of sixth chords, usually descending stepwise. The ii^7 open sonority with a melody line reaching up to degree 8 and falling away from it, prominent in *Blest Pair of Sirens* (see Ex. 1.2, bar 10 and later at the words 'O May We Soon Again Renew That Song') and also present in the drawing-room idiom and in Butterworth's 'Loveliest of Trees', was especially favoured as an expressive resource, often standing at the very beginning of emotionally intense songs. The account given here does not amount to a description of every song composed by any of these musicians—some had other options beyond intensive diatonicism—but it was a core nexus and a communicative code to which they often returned, and which retained integrity, referential status, and intense expressive significance.

New Paths around 1910, Taken and not Taken

All that said, a relatively varied palette of diatonic idioms is found as part of a new approach to song composition that emerged in the years before and after 1910, which also featured cyclic collections; a new interest in contemporary ruralist poetry; an orientation to western regions; melancholic, even morbid, sentiments; and folksong stylization and modality. Two Housman cycles, Vaughan Williams's *On Wenlock Edge* (composed and premiered in 1909; published in 1911) and Butterworth's *Six Songs from A Shropshire Lad* (pub. 1911) acquired near-canonical status in their reception over the next few decades through performance and recording and through compositional allusions in later songs by other composers. These cycles, along with Butterworth's *Bredon Hill and Other Songs* (published 1912), adopted techniques of French modernism (Debussy and Ravel) such as harmonic stasis and freely treated 'stacked-third' chords, used for the effect of their (diatonic) sonority rather than their harmonic functions. The diatonic 'scale' is thereby transformed into a 'pitch collection' with minimal hierarchical ordering of the pitch classes. Although diatonic dissonance is rather abundant in some of the songs of these collections, the schemata found in Parry's occasional choral works, throughout Elgar's music, in Vaughan Williams's early choral works, and in his songs to the texts of Victorian poets appear seldom. There is little intensive stepwise bass motion either: that was to return only later.

The Housman cycles of Vaughan Williams and Butterworth nevertheless set terms for mood and expressive tone that were often adopted in later collections of English song with a predominantly diatonic language. Reflective moods predominate, and slow or moderate tempi are preferred for the most ambitious songs, including often the first and last, these being interspersed with the odd 'rollicking' or ditty-like song. Narrative is only implicit; the poems were selected for some degree of coherence from literary sources that had little or no narrative dimension. Butterworth's opening cherry tree motive became a subject for intertextual allusion, spreading Housman's bitter irony through several musical genres and through songs that set contemporary ruralist poetry of other types. Direct allusion and near-quotation of passages from *On Wenlock Edge* are also found in later songs. When this happens at the very start of a Housman cycle, such as in Gurney's 'When Smoke Stood up from Ludlow' or in Ireland's 'The Lent Lily', or in the context of similar images in the songs' texts, the sense of a shared musical code extends beyond schemata and topics to particular melodic phrases, accompaniment figures and textures.[9] Gurney adopted the ensemble of string quartet and piano that Vaughan Williams chose for *On Wenlock Edge* shortly after studying composition with Vaughan Williams, in his Housman cycles *Ludlow and Teme* (published 1923) and *The Western Playland* (published 1926). Butterworth scored the first version of his *Love Blows as the Wind Blows* (composed in 1911–1913) for voice and string quartet without piano, as did Finzi for his first Hardy cycle, *By Footpath and Style* (1925).

The Housman cycles of Vaughan Williams and Butterworth rely heavily on diatonic collections, but they utilize a wide range of harmonic and melodic structures. In Vaughan Williams's 'Bredon Hill', the slow-moving, almost static, harmony of the instrumental introduction is built from stacked thirds and intensive diatonic dissonance which are now treated very differently from the similar local formations encountered in the choral music of Parry or his mentor S. S. Wesley. The dissonances are unresolved, and the harmonies are without functional meaning. The Mixolydian vocal melody, though, sounds like a folksong. 'Oh, When I Was in Love with You', another stylized folksong, begins in the Aeolian mode but drifts towards whole-tone pitch organization. Despite the lack of a single accidental in Butterworth's 'Is My Team Ploughing?' the song's tonic is unclear throughout: it simply inhabits a two-flat diatonic pitch collection. The two 'voices' that speak in the song have different diatonic vocabularies. One is harmonized with seventh chords that slowly descend in pitch,[10] and the other is harmonized with triads. By contrast, the folksong-like 'When I Was One and Twenty', which again completely lacks accidentals, has a two-sharp key signature but is consistently in E Dorian and has a kind of functional harmonic style. 'Look not in My Eyes' is different in turn, being broadly in major but introducing a flattened seventh degree intermittently as a modal effect. Despite the imitations of English folksong, the parallel fourths in Vaughan Williams's 'Bredon Hill', which represent the sound of church bells floating up from below the hill, closely recall passages from Ravel's *La vallée des cloches*, while Butterworth's setting of 'On the Idle Hill of Summer', is indebted to Debussy's *Pagodes*. Both sources provide models of nonfunctional harmony and harmonic stasis.

These cycles reveal a new musical style within English song, a new aesthetic, and a reorientation in terms of precursors and influence at a time of anti-German political sentiment and Franco-British *entente*. Nevertheless, this apparently pivotal moment can all-too easily be matched up with narratives about modernism in the arts around 1910 to argue, on nationalist terms, for a decisive shift away from 'German' musical idioms to 'English' ones. In fact, many of the new paths in compositional technique explored by Vaughan Williams and Butterworth around 1910 were largely rejected by their most prolific successors in English diatonic song. The chamber-music and orchestral compositions of Vaughan Williams and Howells explored in Chapter 3 may have built on this new approach for a decade or so, but, in their solo songs, Gurney, Ireland, and Finzi preferred the stepwise basses and contrapuntally orthodox diatonicism of Parry and Elgar to nonfunctional harmonies and consecutive root-position triads. Gurney's Housman cycles with string-quartet accompaniment often sound very much like Brahms, but seldom like Debussy or Ravel. After *By Footpath and Style* (1922), Finzi avoided the new pastoral style for his dozens of settings of Thomas Hardy's poetry of rural England.

Drawing-room Rapture and the Open ii[7]

The English diatonic tradition had many Victorian roots, and commercial music was among them. English art song did not wholly disdain the operatic vocal touches, sobs, and climactic high notes of the royalty ballad, all kept neatly within bounds and touched with sentimental piety. This was an alternative mode of diatonicism in English song, a recognizably different level of taste from the one originating in choral music into which composers who 'should have known better' could dip at times, as though they were indulging in a guilty pleasure. The central figure, though, was Roger Quilter, who made this mode his own and sustained it through much of his oeuvre. Quilter's intensively dissonant diatonicism relied on a characteristically sweet harmonic idiom based on circles of fifths and chords of the ninth with local chromatic touches, which shared more with popular idioms of the era than with Parry's reformed English diatonic manner.[11] An early example is 'Now Sleeps the Crimson Petal' Op. 3 No. 2 (published 1904). Quilter's style was later adapted by Ireland in some of his songs, and even Gurney was not entirely averse to it. There were areas of overlap with reformed diatonicism, especially in the process of expressive heightening for rapturous climaxes. English art songs from the 1900s that inhabit this stylistic borderland avoid contemporary pastoral poetry and allusions to western geographical regions. The texts are by Victorians such as Alfred Tennyson, Elizabeth Barrett Browning, Dante Gabriel Rossetti, and Robert Louis Stevenson. This was a transformed and polished drawing-room idiom, one that aspired to artistic status but did not forget its roots.

Early evidence of 'drawing-room rapture' can be found in a short instrumental composition by Elgar, *Chanson de Matin* Op. 15 No. 2 for violin and piano (probably composed around 1890 but published in 1899, later rescored for small orchestra). This piece prefigures the schematic patterns of later songs in this vein. The ii^7 open sonority with high 8 in the melody—a vocal-style 'top note'—occurs in the reprise of the main theme (Ex. 4.1(ii)), transforming the initial idea of the opening (Ex. 4.1(i)) into a more regular version of the Do–Re–Mi schema (but lacking the 'Do'; compare Ex. 2.15(iii)) with the open sonority over 'Re', albeit at a new *pp* dynamic level. In the string orchestra version, a dynamic swell at this moment in the accompanying parts underlines the expressive heightening. No chromatic alterations are used for this effect, which relies on diatonic dissonance, widening of the texture, melodic contour, and dynamics. The same process can be found in the second of Elgar's two short pieces for small orchestra entitled *Dream Children* Op. 43 (1902).

Ex. 4.1 Elgar, *Chanson de Matin* Op. 15 No. 2
(i)   bars 5–8

(ii)   bars 21–3

Elgar realized this process in more concretely vocal terms in 'Sabbath Morning at Sea', the third song from *Sea Pictures* Op. 37 (1899), a cycle with orchestral accompaniment, but again pointing the way to later English songs with piano accompaniment. Elgar's setting is ambivalently positioned between the English drawing room and Wagner's Bayreuth, mingling leitmotiv technique with intensive diatonicism that includes allusions to the opening of the *Meistersinger* Prelude (see Ex. 1.6(iii)). Elizabeth Barrett Browning's religious verses are given a grandiose treatment that conventional good taste might find breathless and overwrought. The opening orchestral phrase (Ex. 4.2) illustrates the line 'He shall assist me to look higher' with a sharply rising upper-voice melody against a diatonic, texturally hymn-like, succession of chords, suggesting eyes raised to the heavens somewhat in the fashion of William Holman Hunt's painting *The Awakening Conscience*. The stepwise descending inner part means that the chord spacing gradually 'opens' as the parts diverge, leading to an open ii^7 as the penultimate chord, a sonority that appears in several guises at later climaxes. The last of these, which dissolves the shifting tonality and fragmentary materials into a blaze of diatonic C major, brings together the 'look higher' motive with the equally diatonic allusions to the opening of the *Meistersinger* Prelude. The vocal part reaches its rapturous climax on a top G at the apotheosis version of 'look higher'. This moment signifies communion with the divine, and yet the style has distinctly vulgar origins, the diatonic phrase being repeated, after an initial 'windup' version, before the singer's top note is reached. The throbbing triplet chords that accompany much of the vocal setting exemplify what Plunket Greene identified as 'the main accompaniment of three-quarters of all British so-called "ballads"', which, he thought, 'seems to invite every fault in song'. 'It is the vade-mecum of the popular composer and the old, old friend of the

Ex. 4.2 Elgar, 'Sabbath Morning at Sea' (*Sea Pictures*, Op. 39), bars 1–3[1] (reduction)

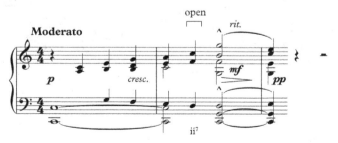

sloppy sentimentalist.' In its triplet form 'it is the only authentic ladder to heaven', and it adapts to the singer's self-regard: 'Does the tenor want to stay in 'Heaven' on that top A?—it is delighted to oblige'.[12] Elgar writes a pause in the score of 'Sabbath Morning at Sea' precisely at the climactic top G. Elgar did not purge his style of drawing-room elements, then, but he attempted to uplift them, 'assisting himself to look higher' by Wagnerizing middlebrow Victorian taste.

Another instance of expressive heightening around the open ii[7] is found in Vaughan Williams's 'Heart's Haven' from his Rossetti cycle *The House of Life* (1903). The opening bars of the melody (Ex. 4.3(i)) are transformed into a climactic version at the end of the setting of the first stanza (Ex. 4.3(ii)) with a top E (degree 8) over the open ii[7], a passage that relies on a rather dense application of diatonic schemata. This song maintains throbbing accompaniment chords throughout, and its level of taste is similar to that of 'Sabbath Morning at Sea'. At the climax (Ex. 4.3(ii) bars 22^3–23^2),

Ex. 4.3 Vaughan Williams, *The House of Life*. The House of Life. Words by Dante Gabriel Rossetti. Music by Ralph Vaughan Williams. Copyright © 1904 (Renewed) by Chester Music Limited trading as Edwin Ashdown. International Copyright Secured. All Rights Reserves. *Reprinted by permission of Hal Leonard Europe Ltd.*

(i) 'Heart's Haven', bars 3–5

Ex. 4.3 Continued

(ii) 'Heart's Haven', bars 19–25[1]

(iii) 'Silent Noon', bars 67–73[1]

there is even a five-note quotation of Elgar's melody at the climax of that song, also over an open ii^7. This style is not normally associated with the composer. Indeed, he largely laid it aside after *The House of Life*, with the possible exception of *Songs of Travel* (most songs composed during 1901–1904) and 'Easter' from *Five Mystical Songs*, where triplet accompaniment chords reappear. But *The House of Life* has touches of the Victorian drawing room throughout, as demonstrated, for instance, by the top note (again 8), pause, and repeated words at the end of 'Silent Noon' ('When twofold silence was the song [pause] the song of love').[13] The melody ends with a near-trite leap from a prolonged degree 5 down to 7 before closing on 1 (Ex. 4.3(iii)). This song's intensively diatonic E flat major does not call forth Parry-style schemata, although the key scheme (E flat major—G major—E flat major) is that of *Blest Pair of Sirens*, a plan that Vaughan Williams would later reprise on a grander scale and in full choral-orchestral style in *A Sea Symphony* (see Ex. 2.19(i)). The diatonic writing in this cycle is rather delicately poised between more and less reputable Victorian antecedents.

Another overlap of this kind is evident in a song composed a few years later by Quilter, 'My Life's Delight' Op. 12 No. 2 (1907, pub. 1908). Again the top 8 over an open ii^7 is the final climax of both stanza settings (Ex. 4.4(i) and (ii)). The second iteration of this phrase at the end of the second stanza widens the open sonority further for a superheightened version (Ex. 4.4(ii)). In each iteration, Quilter touches twice on an amalgam of the rising-fourth and plagal-tritone schemata within a descending chain of stepwise parallel-sixth chords. Quilter's favourite circle of fifths at the climax (bass motion 3–6–2–5–1) derives from an altogether different schematic world from that of Parry, Elgar, or Vaughan Williams, recalling popular song-writing practices. The breaking of the diatonicism by breathlessly tonicizing various keys within a single thematic sentence structure likewise points to a separate musical inheritance, indicating an incomplete rejection of Mendelssohn and thus a residue of pre-Parry, 'unreformed' Victorian taste. The 'heavenly light' described at the climax calls forth a sharply contrasted diatonic idiom from that of the pure, blazing, and massive E flat major with which Parry represented Milton's 'endless morn of light'.

John Ireland applied blended versions of intensive diatonicism in his music over a remarkably long period, at least from 1902 (*Elegiac Romance*) to 1958 (*Meditation on John Keble's Rogationtide Hymn*), over which time

SONGS OF PAIN AND BEAUTY 141

Ex. 4.4 Quilter, 'My Life's Delight' Op. 12 No. 2
(i)   bars 15⁴–21²

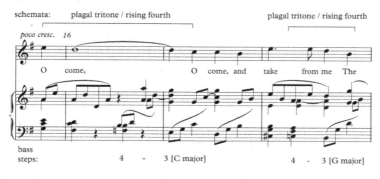

(ii)   bars 40–44²

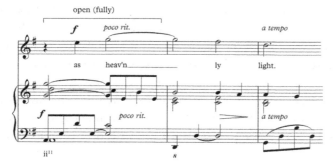

his approach changed remarkably little in style or genre. Ireland's solo songs do not amount to a sustained project in diatonic composition like Finzi's or even Gurney's. Many are not intensively diatonic at all, but others build on his own version of processional diatonicism along with Quilter's approach, with the same strong emphasis on circles of fifths with added ninths, although with the harmonic complexity taken a stage further. Processional diatonicism as a topic is found mainly in Ireland's sacred music, including that for organ (such as the two compositions mentioned above), which arose from Ireland's activities as a professional organist at London churches.[14] In his secular music, he moved on to modernist harmonic idioms with ample chromaticism. These were separate paths within his work; diatonicism was not a personal language through which almost everything was said, as was the case with Finzi, for instance. In Ireland's instrumental music, intensive diatonicism appears only intermittently, mainly in occasional works such as *These Things Shall Be* (1937) and *Epic March* (1942). (See the discussion in Chapter 5; Ex. 5.2 and 5.9.). Most instances are in E flat major, but in Ireland's pieces of this kind D flats usually appear quite early and prominently, a twist unique to him. Elgar is the primary model, often through an initial Do–Re–Mi in the bass or through allusions to the 'Church' theme from *The Apostles* and the 'Britain' motive from *Caractacus*.[15] Ireland's writing within this topic is not especially expansive and lacks the sprawling tendencies of Parry, Elgar, and Vaughan Williams. His melodies are often contained within four-bar phrases. Abundant harmonic decoration or substitution compensate for the rhythmic constriction.

Ireland drew on processional diatonicism in two songs composed in the second half of World War I, both in E flat major: 'Blow out You Bugles' to a text on war by Rupert Brooke (1918) and 'If There Were Dreams to Sell' by Thomas Lovell Beddoes (1918).[16] 'Blow out You Bugles' is poised between the new diatonic idioms recently developed by Vaughan Williams and those of Parry and Elgar, finally returning decisively to the latter. In E flat major, it begins with march rhythms, the regular crotchets of the bass descending stepwise. At the central climax of the song, however, the bugles blow out in parallel 5/3 triads with false relation effects and mediant-based harmonic shifts. This manner is not sustained, though. The song's conclusion conveys Brooke's lines about the spiritually redemptive nature of death in war—sentiments that today read as quite alarming—with a solemn, organ-like three-part accompaniment texture with octave doublings and

SONGS OF PAIN AND BEAUTY 143

7–6 suspensions in inner parts (Ex. 4.5). For the word 'Nobleness' (capital 'N') this could hardly be a more obvious compositional choice within the English tradition. In fact, by 1918 it was a cliché. The vocal part descends by a fourth on the word itself, leaping from one voice in the three-part texture to another, a trait commonly found in the practices of Parry, Elgar, and Finzi (the last-named described below). Here, however, transcendent values are not out of reach, as is so often the case in Finzi, but they appear to be directly available. The passage amounts to the conclusion and goal of the song, a resolution into tonal stability after the disturbing climax and a turn from representation of the material conflict of war to spiritual peace. The pause on the final rest directs the singer to leave a portentous silence before inviting the audience's applause. It is at first sight remarkable that Ireland could later have used a similar diatonic language for the Utopian, internationalist sentiments of his cantata *These Things Shall Be*

Ex. 4.5 Ireland, 'Blow Out, You Bugles', bars 46–52. © Copyright 1918 by Winthrop Rogers Ltd. Reproduced by permission of Boosey & Hawkes Music Publishers Ltd.

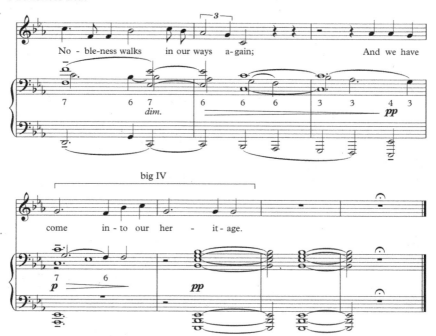

(1937; see Chapter 5). But these pieces share an ideological, even propagandistic, character, along with their grand idealism, even if the content of the messages differs. Ireland's way of writing in the diatonic idiom tends to be direct and unambiguous in its signals; it matches the text and 'expresses' it; and it did not change much through his entire adult life. It thus lends itself to such uses.

'If There Were Dreams to Sell' returns to the drawing-room mode. It is cast in four-bar phrases, neatly separated (Ex. 4.6). Ireland's harmonic progressions seldom move far from I–IV–V–I and its variants, albeit they

Ex. 4.6 Ireland, 'If There Were Dreams to Sell', bars 1–15. © Copyright 1918 by Winthrop Rogers Ltd. Reproduced by permission of Boosey & Hawkes Music Publishers Ltd.

are spiced up with extra diatonic dissonance and touches of modal mixture. Ireland alludes to the 'Britain' theme from Elgar's *Caractacus*, the original passage also presented in E flat major in the cantata (see Ex. 2.3). This leitmotiv is one of Elgar's diatonic melodies that is most easily adaptable to Ireland's idiom, as it is motivically repetitive and regular in phrase structure (it has a touch of the drawing-room itself). The closing melodic cadence has a pause on a high note and an ensuing dip below the tonic, just like Vaughan Williams's ballad-like moment in 'Silent Noon'.

Ireland's finest contributions to English diatonic song came a few years later with the bold decision to bring Housman 'indoors' in *The Land of Lost Content* (1921). In line with Vaughan Williams and Butterworth's approach, the songs of this collection are mainly moderate in tempo or slow and reflective, with a rumbustious one in the middle. The early allusions to two of Vaughan Williams's settings in the opening song, 'The Lent Lily', are reinforced by static or rocking harmonic effects, fixed-pitch collections instead of harmonic functions, and a folksong-like melody. But first impressions are deceptive, for three of the five remaining songs of the collection are in an expressively heightened—if not hysterical—post-Quilter idiom, contained within four-bar phrases and elaborated circle-of-fifths progressions full of ninth chords: 'Ladslove', 'The Vain Desire'—despite complex harmonic substitutions, still just in touch with diatonic models and popular origins—and 'Epilogue', with which the collection ends. There is no hint of folksong style in these later slow songs. 'Ladslove' is the closest to Elgar's style, starting the first vocal phrase with a bass Do–Re–Mi and recalling the 'Church' motive from *The Apostles* with the A flat major key and a fast-moving inner part doubled in octaves (Ex. 4.7). There is even a top-note 8 above an open ii^7 at the climax (bar 12). Within the musical Housman corpus this was a new tone, and a kind of 'crossover' relative to Quilter, who never set Housman.

The examples in this section record a convergence of separate diatonic streams from the Victorian inheritance and at times the emergence of a middle ground that reveals a remarkable blending of levels of taste. These were sensitive matters. Although the reform movement ostensibly shunned Victorian sentimentality and vocal display, in practice a relationship remained that even Parry might have admitted to being 'evolutionary'. Indeed, even in Gurney's and Finzi's later songs, top notes on the heightened ii^7 recur constantly as an expressive resource.

Ex. 4.7 Ireland, 'Ladslove', bars 2⁴–6. © Copyright 1921 Stainer & Bell Ltd, 23 Gruneisen Road, London N3 1DZ, www.stainer.co.uk. Reproduced by permission. All rights reserved.

'Loveliest of Trees' as Musical Memorial

Despite the prestige of Vaughan Williams's and Butterworth's Housman cycles, the diatonic idioms of Parry and of English choral and orchestral music before World War I poured back into English song in Gurney's works of the early 1920s (setting the poets of the 'Georgian Anthologies' of the 1910s) and in Finzi's works in the 1920s and 1930s (setting Thomas Hardy). It would hardly be an exaggeration to speak of a Parry revival in composition by two musicians trained as organists. This was not a public phenomenon, though, but a subtle matter of musical technique and semantics. In received critical opinion, after all, Parry's stock was by now at rock bottom, an extreme reaction following his death in 1918. The outward tone of English diatonic song was guided, rather, by the cult of Butterworth that emerged after World War I.

In his three sets of songs composed before World War I, Butterworth struck a note of tenderness and reflection that proved memorable, even iconic, for his successors. These were the original 'songs of pain and beauty'. He used fast tempi sparingly and avoided vigorous music in the first and last songs of his cycles. *Bredon Hill and Other Songs* is almost entirely quiet and highly atmospheric. 'Is My Team Ploughing', the final song from *Six Songs from 'A Shropshire Lad'*, closes in rapt stasis and without harmonic resolution, bringing the cycle to its conclusion, as it began, with an emphasis on soft sonorities without tonic or dominant harmonic functions or even a triad. Among Butterworth's memorably tender musical moments are the high E natural and D sharp that he asks the baritone voice to sing softly, almost as a whisper, in his setting of 'The Lads in Their Hundreds', on some of the most poignant words of the text. These aspects must have seemed still more significant after Butterworth became a casualty of World War I and was memorialized in public performances, especially his Orchestral Rhapsody *A Shropshire Lad* (premiere 1913), as he seemed to have lived out the fate of the Shropshire Lad described in the *Six Songs*. Housman's collection implies that this Lad's fate is to die overseas fighting for the British Empire. Butterworth's selection of poems and his manner of setting them is not so specific, although evidently the Lad is dead in the final song ('Is My Team Ploughing?').[17]

Butterworth's best-remembered song, indeed almost his epitaph, is the first one from *Six Songs*, 'Loveliest of Trees'. Motives from this song provided the sound of Butterworth's public memorialization in the Orchestral Rhapsody, which was performed during the BBC's Armistice Day broadcast in 1924.[18] The morbid tone of Housman's text, in which the 20-year-old Lad resolves to visit the woods to observe wild cherry trees in bloom since he may expect only 50 years of life remaining—an over-precocious sense of 'Et in Arcadia ego'—together with Butterworth's untimely death, helped to establish the theme of the transience of beauty in English diatonic song. The cherry tree motive that opens the song and the ii^7 sonority that follows it were key points of allusion for later song composers. Butterworth's diatonic writing is a strange amalgam, though. At the beginning of the song, after the cherry tree motive is presented, the ii^7 sonority is unfolded by means of a descending arpeggiation, the wider intervals in the lower parts opened out last and the sonority revealed by the depressed pedal. The influence of Debussy is evident, the descending arpeggio figures and stepwise motives recalling his piano prelude 'La fille aux cheveux de lin' (see especially Ex. 4.8(i), bars 8–9). The opening bars appear to have been modelled on the opening of 'Møte' from Grieg's *Haugtussa* Op. 67 (1895). Once the voice enters on the high B (Ex. 4.8(i)), the allusion to the ii^7 sonority is nevertheless unmistakable. In later English diatonic song, allusion to the cherry tree motive, or the use of the ii^7 open sonority as an opening gesture, is enough to signal that a 'song of pain and beauty' will follow in an expressive diatonic idiom. Thus, Butterworth subtly altered the field of meaning of the open ii^7, which could now be soft, tender, and melancholy as well as rapturous.

If it reoriented the emergent English tradition in some ways, then Butterworth's setting of 'Loveliest of Trees' maintained continuity in others.

148 ENGLISH DIATONIC MUSIC

Ex. 4.8 Butterworth, 'Loveliest of Trees' (*Six Songs from 'A Shropshire Lad'*)
(i) bars 1–9[1]

(ii) bars 16–19

Housman's word 'Eastertide' brings the long-deferred tonic arrival, with an abrupt transformation of mood and an emphatic climax with a processional manner for just two bars. Thick, heavily accented piano chords and the Meistersinger-tetrachord schema recall diatonic writing in choral and orchestral music by Parry, Elgar, and Vaughan Williams (Ex. 4.8(ii)). In the orchestral *A Shropshire Lad*, the materials of 'Loveliest of Trees' are adapted to produce a grander and more public manner that is more directly reminiscent of those choral and orchestral precedents. The initial ii^7 in its characteristic position is lost, as are the Debussy-like motives and textures, but not the Meistersinger tetrachord, its fanfare now scored for brass instruments and placed in E flat major (B + 12). Later in the *Rhapsody*, a harmonically stable, diatonic E flat major emerges as the main tonal centre, providing the key for the serene climax of the composition, in which both the 'Loveliest of Trees' motive and the 'Eastertide' fanfare return (G + 6–K + 2). This was Butterworth's public face for official memorialization. Butterworth's cherry-tree-themed compositions quickly entered the imaginations of English song composers, above all Gurney and Finzi, preoccupied, as they were, with the idea of transience.

Gurney's Traditionalism: The Open ii^7 Sets the Georgians

Most of Gurney's intensively diatonic songs, which record debts to both Parry and Butterworth, remained unpublished in his lifetime. They were among those uncovered and edited by Finzi, who may have favoured them given his own traditionalist and diatonic predilections, although they were probably in any case among the more polished documents within Gurney's chaotic *Nachlass*. These strophic settings record a certain general influence of what was heard at the time as English folksong, but they reveal little influence of French modernism in the fashion of Butterworth and Vaughan Williams around 1910. The same applies to Gurney's Housman cycles with the accompaniment of string quartet and piano, which were published during his lifetime. Although Gurney was well known to the professors at the Royal College of Music (he studied with Stanford before World War I and with Vaughan Williams after the war) and to a few advocates associated with the College, his was hardly a case of an institution promoting the legacy of its Director (Parry), not least because Gurney was too erratic a personality to be capable of sustained promotion. His music was heard at College concerts during World War I—'By a Bierside' and 'In Flanders', for instance, were done on 23 March 1917—and his poems were occasionally published in the College magazine.[19] But in practice the post-war Parry revival was a slow-burn and slow-release affair. Only after posthumous publication in the cases of both Gurney and Finzi and in the age of recording has its scope become evident.

Diatonicism was key to Gurney's distinctive expressive world. He was fluent in the idioms of the English tradition, which in some songs is polished and perfectly executed. Rich diatonic dissonance is found everywhere in his piano accompaniments, often based on rather conventional three- or four-part counterpoint concealed beneath figuration. Schemata reminiscent of Parry, Elgar, and the early Vaughan Williams are deployed at significant moments. The scores of some of his many folksong-like, strophic songs, such as 'Down by the Salley Gardens' and 'Walking Song', contain no accidentals at all. At other times he flattens the seventh, which is often the first and sometimes the only accidental to be introduced after a diatonic opening. In longer songs, however, his middle sections are often dramatic, with the harmony highly chromatic and the tonality unstable. Gurney could do a sentimental, drawing-room style as well employ syncopated accompaniments and cloying harmonies, as in 'Song of Silence' and 'The White Cascade'. He usually kept these styles separate, but they sometimes merged in yet another blend of levels of taste; the open ii^7, for instance, played a central role in his expressive world. He seldom adopted an openly processional rhythmic manner, although 'Beware! (Exile)' in E flat major, replete with the relevant schemata, shows that he could write orthodox processional diatonicism.[20] He showed little interest in whole-tone scales or nonfunctional harmony; when adopting a folksong-like manner, he is closer to Stanford and to Vaughan Williams's 'Linden Lea' than to Butterworth and Vaughan Williams in their Housman settings.[21]

One common type of Gurney song is a quadruple- or duple-metre strophic setting in a moderate tempo in major mode, with a running accompaniment slightly faster than the folksong-like vocal line. Gurney applies rich diatonic dissonance, especially secondary sevenths, maintains a good deal of stepwise motion in all parts, and tends to dwell on harmonies of predominant function such as IV, ii, and ii^7 for their sonority, over which the vocal line can float freely. Diatonic schemata are applied discreetly but expressively. Examples include 'Black Stichel', 'Dinny Hill', 'Walking Song', 'Ha'nacker Mill', 'The Ship', 'When Death to Either Shall Come', and 'The Cherry Trees'. In 'Black Stichel' the first line of each stanza ends with a rising-fourth schema, including even a pair of 7–6 suspensions in the manner of the opening bars of *Blest Pair of Sirens* (Ex. 4.9; note the lack of accidentals), although here emerging through a rippling piano texture typical of the solo song genre. In everyday speech, Gurney's manner might loosely be termed 'English pastoral music', but Gurney does not employ the new pastoral topic

Ex. 4.9 Gurney, 'Black Stichel', bars 1–7. 'A first volume of ten songs' by Ivor Gurney © Oxford University Press 1938. All rights reserved.

and did not venture into the less diatonic, post-Delius pastoral manner of Bridge, Warlock, Moeran, and Bax. Gurney's writing blends a somewhat old-fashioned aesthetic of folksong arrangement with a harmonic-contrapuntal language of intensive diatonic dissonance of nineteenth-century origin.

Gurney was no ideologist of cultural nationalism like Vaughan Williams, Butterworth, or Finzi, for whom varied activities such as composition, performance, dance, editing, field research, book collecting, and horticulture ran together as integrated life projects. Indeed, the different aspects of his life and art do not especially cohere. The significance of landscape to Gurney was shaped by localism rather than national sentiments and by personal experiences, including the physical experiences of walking long distances and of physical labour. At the same time, Gurney's musical realization of the sentiments of westward longing so prominent in the texts he chose to set drew deeply on a recent tradition of diatonicism in musical composition and on the conventions of folksong stylization, purely musical habits that lived in him vigorously. In this sense, his personal experience of place and landscape and his musical 'voice'—at least, his diatonic 'voice'—were unintegrated. Likewise, Gurney's creative activities as a poet and a composer ran along separate courses. As a poet he was concerned with his own everyday experiences, related directly in often irregular forms, forms of a kind that in music receded from his compositional style after World War I in line with his more consistent recourse to the musically amenable verses of the Georgian poets.[22] At times, Gurney the musician places portals, as it were, created from diatonic schemata (usually the ii^7 sonority), at the openings to his songs that mark out a boundary and announce that the listener will enter a conventionalized world on certain received terms, a world quite unlike that of most of his poetry. The melancholy atmosphere of many of Gurney's diatonic songs is only enhanced by the restrictions to which, specifically as a musician, he chose to adhere. The familiar topography and place names, the intensive diatonicism, and the schemata of the English tradition act as tight containers for intense feelings that for most late-nineteenth-century musical precursors would have been expressed through a far more extravagant harmonic language.

Disproportionate responses to texts relative to word-setting norms are characteristic of Gurney's approach. 'Western Sailors', which sets one of Gurney's own texts, uses the open ii^7 sonority 13 times in its approximately 150-second duration. The strophic form seems deliberately mechanical; both text and music are little less than excuses for this magical sign. Gurney tends to draw out sonorities such as this, or to return to them and reiterate them, as though searching in melancholy fashion for some significance that they seem to possess but that cannot be directly articulated. In this sense, his diatonic songs invite collective evaluation as a neo-Romantic collection of dispersed fragments from a single, greater, diatonic 'song' that he might 'soon again' wish to 'renew', but that, after the deaths of Butterworth (1916) and Parry (1918), has receded from his grasp.

Gurney's settings of Housman are unique in his oeuvre first in that they appear in cycles, not individual songs, and second on account of the piano and string quartet accompaniment. No doubt Gurney hoped these cycles would become companion pieces on concert programmes to Vaughan Williams's *On Wenlock Edge*, not least because there is no duplication of the texts that Vaughan Williams set in that cycle. The style is by and large dramatic, varied, harmonically fluid, and often Brahmsian in its melodic figures and textures. Gurney seldom used diatonicism for heightened expression when setting Housman. Gurney did set texts used by Butterworth, but in these cases he rather conspicuously reverses Butterworth's approach, as in 'Ludlow Fair' and 'When I Was One and Twenty'. There is one notable, and perhaps predictable, exception: 'Loveliest of Trees'. Gurney's lushly diatonic setting owes a good deal to Schumann, but the opening melodic phrase is essentially a re-composition of the opening of Butterworth's setting, with the 'Loveliest of Trees' motive all-pervasive. A solo violin enters on the top 8, like the voice in Butterworth's setting. Gurney sounds the notes of the ii^7 sonority simultaneously, although later he even replicates Butterworth's descending arpeggiation. The ii^7 returns as a ritornello-like gesture at the reprise of the opening and again near the end of the song before an instrumental coda.

The open ii^7 became the sonic symbol of Gurney's Gloucestershire and the Shropshire-Lad-like desire for it in his compositional persona. He had two distinctive ways of applying it in practice. On the one hand, there are songs in Gurney's strophic manner such as 'Western Sailors' that 'ruralize' and 'westernize' the rapture of the drawing room. The open ii^7 appears on words such as 'love', 'heart', and 'Severn', and the mood is relatively happy and idyllic. 'The Boat Is Chafing' begins on ii^7 in the piano and introduces the same harmony when the voice part first enters (Ex. 4.10). The text is again about 'western sailors'. 'Dinny Hill' is a tiny gem that begins as though it will be a song of Gurney's strophic type, but it turns out to have only one stanza, a delightfully witty effect. The text ends: 'And all the heart of my desire is now to be this day in Gloucestershire.' Gurney has the melody rise to

Ex. 4.10 Gurney, 'The Boat Is Chafing', bars 1–4. 'A second volume of ten songs' by Ivor Gurney © Oxford University Press 1938. All rights reserved.

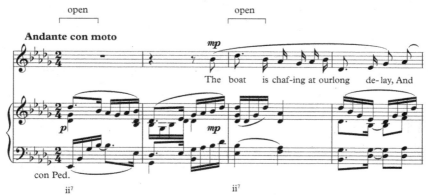

top 8 and an open ii^7 on the word 'heart'. A second approach was to use the ii^7 open sonority like a signature or signal at the start of a song, where it stands out and is minimally integrated with the rest of the piece. Non-tonic opening harmonies were a technique favoured by the early Romantics and especially beloved of Schumann, but the choice of the open ii^7 is an unmistakable allusion to the English diatonic tradition, and to Butterworth in particular. In this usage there is no textual cue; the ii^7 has simply spread into Gurney's setting of anything with a broadly Georgian tone. Two-sharp tonalities are favoured, resulting in a characteristic position for the pianist's right-hand fingers on the open fourth and fifth between d', g', and d".

One of Gurney's best-known songs, 'Severn Meadows', to his own text 'Only the Wanderer', begins in this way (Ex. 4.11.); the sonority later returns to introduce the second stanza like a tiny ritornello. The text was written while Gurney was serving in France during World War I and conveys his homesickness for Gloucestershire. However, the dream-world opened by the 'portal' of the ii^7 is, in a paradox typical of English diatonic song, the world of the

Ex. 4.11 Gurney, 'Severn Meadows', bars 1–5. 'Severn Meadows' by Ivor Gurney © Oxford University Press 1969. All rights reserved.

contemporary English Bach revival. The slow-moving vocal line 'wanders', while the right-hand part of the piano accompaniment meanders around it, following roughly the same contour, like the waters of the meadows. The bass line moves slowly but not stepwise; the metre is seldom clear. Gurney's model in 'Severn Meadows' is not processional diatonicism but, rather, organ improvisation and especially the chorale-prelude technique. The phrases of the slow melody are separated by long rests; the faster accompaniment figuration continues through those rests, often without cadencing harmonically at the end of the melody's phrases. Gurney was an accomplished organist and a devoted Bachian, who wrote four choral preludes on English hymn tunes around this time (as yet unpublished).[23] In this respect, he only continued a trend: Parry, Vaughan Williams, and Howells all composed chorale preludes for organ in these years, mainly on Victorian hymn tunes.[24] Gurney might have known something of the new pastoral idiom that was emerging at this time in the work of his friend and peer-mentor Howells, but, if he did, he made no concession to it in setting his own pastoral verses.

'An Epitaph', to a text by Walter de la Mare, begins with another soft ii^7 chord, and its text alludes to the 'West Country' and the beauty it hides, yet it is composed in a quite contrasted way (Ex. 4.12; another passage wholly lacking accidentals). Both vocal line and accompaniment are much more fluid and varied than those of 'Severn Meadows', while the rising-fourth schema returns in elaborate realizations (compare the same schema realization in Ex. 4.9). The song's closing bars change the mood, becoming starker and more reflective. If the opening alludes to the start of Butterworth's first Housman cycle, then the piano postlude refers to the end, the postlude of 'Is My Team Ploughing?'. At the same time, the feeling of an organ improvisation returns, and the final cadence is a plagal-tritone progression. 'The Scribe', to another text by de la Mare, again begins with an open ii^7 in a two-sharp context (Ex. 4.13), but otherwise the setting is again different in tone, drawing first on sweet, drawing-room harmonic clichés and later a stormy Wagnerian harmonic style.

For Gurney, then, the function of the open ii^7 sonority was variable. Sometimes it symbolizes Gloucestershire as an object of desire, and the River Severn in particular. At other times it is integrated into the musical setting of the text. At yet others, though, it seems to have no such meaning and stands apart from the rest of the song as a purely formal gesture of introduction or separation of the stanzas, as a personal signature, as a sign of the melancholy of Gurney's musical art, and as a substitute for a more conventional piano introduction. Gurney usually proceeds from the ii^7 to dominant harmony and then to tonic

Ex. 4.12 Gurney, 'An Epitaph', bars 1–10. 'A second volume of ten songs' by Ivor Gurney © Oxford University Press 1938. All rights reserved.

or some tonic substitute; the harmonic function of the chord is not eroded, and it does not become pure sonority. The use of this chord, then, was not a continuation of the modernist tendencies of Vaughan Williams's and Butterworth's Housman cycles; instead, allusions to Butterworth serve a wider symbolism of absence and loss conveyed through a traditional harmonic language.

Finzi's Traditionalism

More than any other composer, Gerald Finzi drew together the threads explored so far in this chapter. He wove in his own as well, once again

SONGS OF PAIN AND BEAUTY   157

Ex. 4.13 Gurney, 'The Scribe', bars 1–8. 'A second volume of ten songs' by Ivor Gurney © Oxford University Press 1938. All rights reserved.

derived from English diatonic practices. He developed a distinctive version of English diatonic music with his own conventionalized language and even his own version of the processional topic. Once he had established it in the late 1920s, Finzi's use of this language was ubiquitous in both his vocal and his instrumental music and could provide the setting for almost any kind of text, although it was especially suited for conveying feelings of fading glory, songs of 'innocence and experience', and serene moods touched by sorrow. Finzi's adoption of intensive diatonicism as a compositional voice matches his lifelong commitment to an idea and practice of English life and culture, including his choice of houses in rural locations in Gloucestershire, Wiltshire, and Hampshire. In particular, his relocation from Harrogate to Painswick above the Costwold escarpment in 1922 followed in the footsteps of William Morris and many arts-and-crafts practitioners, while giving him views across the Severn Valley to locations associated with his favourite poets and composers.[25] By temperament he was a collector, conservationist, and preservationist who performed, edited, and published unknown eighteenth-century English music and who cultivated many varieties of apple trees, some of them endangered, in his personal orchard.[26] As a composer, he restricted himself mainly to small ensembles and small-scale forms, attending especially to the crafting of exquisite detail. Finzi was especially receptive to the idea of English musical tradition. Around the time of his move to the Cotswolds, he wrote on the back of a sheet of paper, amongst notes that he was taking on 'English character', the initials 'RVW' three times and then the names Holst, Butterworth, Parry, Elgar, and Gurney.[27] In doing so, he identified a group of contemporary English composers—now a canon in Finzi's mind, if not yet in public performance or critical reception—whose music was steeped in diatonicism and whose homeland landscapes he could survey, almost in a single view, from close to his own (newly adopted) home.

Finzi admired Parry's music at a time when it was an unfashionable taste, and he fought to preserve and promote Parry's legacy in practical ways. He helped to catalogue and clear out Parry's daughter's collection of his manuscripts and distribute them to libraries; he advocated Parry's music through transcription and publication; and in 1948 he delivered a BBC Radio broadcast talk for the centenary of Parry's birth.[28] His compositional practice ran in parallel, giving Parry's idiom renewed life in newly composed music. In the mid-1920s Finzi moved away from the new pastoral style that Vaughan Williams and Howells had developed in the more recent past and returned to processional and hymn-like idioms. For Trevor Hold, Finzi's 'greatest debt' as a song composer was to Parry, not only for his 'Arnoldian "High Seriousness" towards song composition' and 'meticulous scansion and word-setting', but also for a 'contrapuntally based diatonic idiom' and 'that "nobilmente" strain which occurs so often in Finzi's music'.[29] Stephen Banfield agrees—'When it is diatonic Finzi's idiom seems to derive from Parry'—although he attributes some of the counterpoint to Finzi's study with R. O. Morris in the late 1920s.[30] Echoes of Parry's 'Jerusalem', which Finzi orchestrated for a performance at Leeds in 1922,[31] can often be heard in his music. *Blest Pair of Sirens* is predictably invoked throughout Finzi's 'Ceremonial Ode' *For St Cecilia* (1947), composed for a St Cecilia Festival at the Royal Albert Hall. Like Parry's Ode, it is a celebration of the art of music in the celebratory tone of the occasional choral commission.[32]

As his list of names suggests, Finzi was attuned to most earlier and current exponents of English diatonic music, in some cases well before their music was familiar in public performance. Butterworth's cherry tree motive is echoed in many places in his compositions as a symbol of beauty and transience.[33] Vaughan Williams's *A Pastoral Symphony* (1922) was a key point of reference for many of Finzi's compositions of the early 1920s, although less so thereafter. In turn, Finzi regarded Gurney as a tragic, neglected genius. He sought to bring Gurney's music to public attention by assembling a tribute for *Music & Letters* and by uncovering and editing the manuscripts of his songs and poems for publication.[34] The editing of Gurney's music in turn influenced Finzi as a composer. At times all these influences, along with texts that return to the pastoral themes of earlier English song, are brought together in a grand synthesis, guided by something of Parry's earnestness and feeling for musical ethics.[35] Finally, Finzi's conversational, sometimes recitative-like word setting and his fastidious scansion may owe something to Parry's son-in-law Harry Plunket Greene, the posthumous co-author with Finzi's teacher Edward Bairstow (1874–1946) of *Singing Learned from Speech* (1946), a work that continued Greene's campaign for a reformed English song. Plunket Greene's ideas were probably already well known to Bairstow by the time he was instructing Finzi at York Minster.[36]

Finzi's diatonic style is marked by even 'higher' dissonance than is usually found in Parry or Elgar: elevenths and thirteenths are frequently left unresolved or are resolved freely. Chromatic harmony is used sparingly as a means of heightened expression, save for piquant 'false relations' that recall English Renaissance polyphony. Stepwise motion is found abundantly in all voices in contrapuntal textures, not just the bass. Like Elgar, Ireland, and the early Vaughan Williams, Finzi favoured E flat major disproportionately for his passages of expressively heightened diatonicism. The post-Parry diatonic schemata of English music are applied knowingly in Finzi and, just as in Gurney, are often 'milked' for all they are worth. The elegiac *Romance* for string orchestra Op. 11 (1951), for instance, adopts a highly restricted idiom set in E flat major and almost entirely reliant on stepwise bass motion and harmonization by means of sixth chords, mainly 6/3s. A descending tetrachord in the bass is answered by a series of rising-fourth schemata in both the themes presented, and expressive emphasis passes to the continual reiterations of the rising-fourth schema and the alterations of detail in its realizations. Throughout his music, Finzi easily slipped into hymn-like or organ-style textures in three or four parts that move mainly stepwise with abundant suspensions, usually dominated by parallel sixth chords. The melodies that he works around these textures are often shaped by stepwise motion interspersed with leaps of fourths or fifths between harmony notes given by the accompaniment. This type of writing is found in Parry and especially in Elgar; the 'rising fourth' schema is just a special case of it. By contrast, once he had worked through the impact of Vaughan Williams's *Pastoral Symphony*, Finzi seldom adopted folksong stylization, modality, harmonic stasis, florid melodic lines, or irregular metre, instead favouring regular pulse articulation in at least one part, usually the stepwise bass, over long passages. Only his ongoing tolerance of consecutive fifths, often clearly highlighted, is shared with the new pastoral style; this much is certainly not a debt to Parry.

In fact, Finzi pushed regular stepwise bass motion much further than either Parry or Elgar, both of whom preferred to break it up after a while and avoid excessive uniformity.[37] In effect, Finzi devised his own processional style as a subtopic of post-Parry processional diatonicism, perhaps with a nod to Holst's ostinato style of processional music. Finzi's writing can often be modelled by the rule of the octave; he favoured complete octave motions in the stepwise bass or at least complete descending tetrachords and ascending pentachords. The regular, stepwise motion in his piano accompaniments often seems potentially endless, while a recitative-like, fragmentary, or conversational vocal part is hung around the greater continuity. There are three versions in different tempi: one version is stately or moderate in tempo and usually relies on a three-part texture, which may tend to hymn or chorale-prelude topics; one is lively with staccato accompaniment; and one is very slow and otherworldly, with a Holstian detachment.[38]

Finzi's melodic lines often bound upward somewhat in the manner of Parry and Elgar.[39] He liked to begin melodies with upward-leaping anacrusis figures. Finzi's biographer Diana McVeagh points to the opening phrase of his song 'Childhood among the Ferns', the very first notes of his Hardy cycle *Before and After Summer*, as a 'melodic figure ... crucial to his musical personality' (Ex. 4.14).[40] Whereas Gurney's opening ii[7] chords are soft and serene, usually opening a world of rapt contemplation or reflection, Finzi's opening phrase and extra-dissonant ii harmony (with eleventh and ninth) are impassioned. The anacrusis figure leaps up to the top B flat, which is followed by a sighing, descending figure of the cherry tree type. The shape is heightened by the hairpin dynamics and *tenuto* markings, giving a feeling of deep inhalation and exhalation: this is already 'song' before the human singer begins to sing. Instead of functioning as a predominant chord that leads to dominant and tonic, Finzi's ii harmony acquires a plagal function as it is converted into a 'big IV' in bar 2 with hymn-like texture and a rich 9–8 suspension. But just as often in Gurney, there is something disproportionate

SONGS OF PAIN AND BEAUTY   161

Ex. 4.14 Finzi, 'Childhood among the Ferns' (*Before and After Summer*), bars 1–3². © Copyright 1949 by Boosey & Co. Ltd. Reproduced by permission of Boosey & Hawkes Music Publishers Ltd.

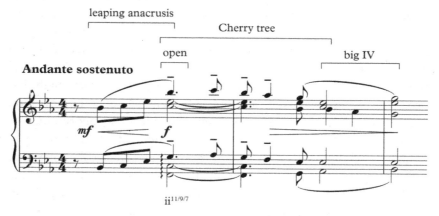

in this passage, by conventional expressive standards, that indicates a melancholic mode of diatonic writing. The intensity of Finzi's feelings for detail means that a great climax and release of tension can be compressed into two bars of intensive diatonicism and densely applied schemata.

Finzi's preferred poet for his solo songs with piano was Thomas Hardy, whose verses he set over forty times, leaving a further twenty planned settings unfinished. From these songs Finzi assembled four collections for publications of varying degrees of coherence: *By Footpath and Style* (published 1925), *A Young Man's Exhortation* (published 1933), *Earth and Air and Rain* (published 1936), and *Before and After Summer* (published 1949). Two more collections were assembled and published after his death by his family and friends: *I Said to Love* and *Till Earth Outwears* (both published 1958). Hardy's intractable poetry was seldom set by other composers of English diatonic music, but Finzi devoted himself to the task as a lifelong project. This move is not illogical at first glance, as Hardy shared with Housman a taste for irony and pessimism, a concern for nature and landscape often tinged with regret, and a western localism, albeit a somewhat more southerly west ('Wessex') than Housman's Shropshire. Critical opinion is split over whether Finzi does justice to Hardy. As Trevor Hold points out, the poet's wide range of subject matter, irony, multilayered ambiguity, and intellectualism must speak through Finzi's restricted musical vocabulary.[41] To some degree Finzi's music inevitably folds Hardy's poetry back into the English musical tradition that he prized, so that Hardy's sun 'breaks forth' to echoes of Parry and Butterworth and of Gurney's settings of the similarly ruralist but otherwise profoundly different Georgians. Hold complains that 'Four-part contrapuntal textures—the "SATB sound" so beloved by those English composers conceived in the organ loft—haunt almost every song, whatever the subject matter, whether relevant or not.'[42] This perspective captures something of the autonomy of the language of English diatonic music. When applied imaginatively, though, Finzi's tight musical system can result in moving, lyrical realizations of groups of texts. In the last two Hardy collections that he assembled, the diatonic topics of procession and hymn create cyclic connections across the collection, opportunities for textless piano 'commentaries' in epilogues, and moments of 'thematic transformation' in the Romantic sense, in which melodies change their meaning as their original rhythmic character, shaped around a particular line of the text, is altered to accommodate a hymn-like or processional passage in response to some textual irony or narrative development.

Finzi's First 'English' Synthesis: Pastoral and Commemoration

Finzi did not reach his characteristic idiom immediately. In the 1920s, his first English synthesis, mainly in vocal music with the accompaniment of string ensemble, was relatively broad in scope, encompassing the new pastoral topic as well as processional styles, the latter largely dirge-like. Finzi also blended the elegiac and the pastoral modes in his choices of literary themes and texts, and around his works in this vein he spun a web of allusions, both textual and musical, to English artists who died in World War I. The merging of the elegiac and the pastoral, especially in the pathos of soldiers killed abroad fighting for the British Empire, was already a theme of Victorian poetry—Housman was not the first on this scene—but in the 1920s it became an official, public mode of commemoration. In 1924, the emphasis of the BBC's Armistice Day broadcast programme moved to pastoral music and the work of poets and composers killed in the war, including *English Pastoral Impressions* by Finzi's school music teacher Ernest Farrar (1885–1918) and Butterworth's *A Shropshire Lad*. These pieces stood alongside more overtly commemorative pieces such as Sullivan's Overture *In Memoriam* and Elgar's 'For the Fallen'.[43] The young Finzi had attended the premiere of Vaughan Williams's *Pastoral Symphony* in 1922 and at least one further early performance conducted by the composer.[44] This was long before Vaughan Williams revealed the work's connections with his experiences during World War I, but Finzi evidently grasped this dimension of the composition because he worked its style, along with cadenza-like violin figures reminiscent of *The Lark Ascending*, into his compositions of this time, which are predominantly bleak, grief-stricken, ruminative and undramatic, with minimal discharge of emotion.

Finzi hoped to publish *A Severn Rhapsody* (1923) and *Requiem da Camera* (composed 1923–1924) together as 'English Rhapsodies and Elegies'.[45] Both the *Rhapsody* and the outer movements of the *Requiem* juxtapose and even blend the new pastoral and processional topics. Both develop subdued, lyrical, and elegiac moods with a tendency to grow to processional climaxes in the middle of movements, along with a heavy, trudging tread, unsteady metre, and anguished mood. Both call to mind the first movement of the *Pastoral Symphony* with stretches of free diatonic counterpoint, overlapping woodwind solos, triplet figures interspersed with crotchets and quavers, and predominantly conjunct melodic motion. These movements work Butterworth's cherry tree motive into their melodic lines, either overtly at the outset (*Requiem*) or gradually (*A Severn Rhapsody*). Both make paratextual allusions to British artists who died in the war: the choral *Requiem* is dedicated to the memory of Finzi's teacher Farrar, while the *Rhapsody* carries an epigraph from the late Rupert Brooke. The *Requiem*'s texts are all pastoral reflections on the war, by Thomas Hardy ('In the Time of "The Breaking of Nations"') and the Georgians John Masefield ('August 1914') and Wilfrid Wilson Gibson ('Lament'; 'We Who Are Left'). The music mainly underlines the pastoral aspects, except for a few moments at the end of the opening and closing movements, when 'The Last Post' emerges on woodwind instruments, growing out of the cherry tree motive through intertwining contrapuntal lines, and merging with improvisatory cow calls akin to the *ranz des vaches*. The bugle call, sounding, as it were, across a peaceful musical 'landscape', resonates with several other atmospheric passages in recent English music, including the concluding bars of Butterworth's *A Shropshire Lad*; the second movement of Vaughan Williams's *Pastoral Symphony*; and the closing moments of *Flos Campi* (discussed in Chapter 3).[46]

'Only the Wanderer' (1925), which sets the poem by Gurney that Gurney himself set to music under the title 'Severn Meadows', shares its material and style with the outer movements of the *Requiem* and the *Severn Rhapsody*. At the time, Gurney was hardly known either as a musician or as a poet outside a small circle of admirers connected with his time at the Royal College of Music, so his text takes its place within the tight network of personal associations in Finzi's compositions of this time. The song begins with the same modified version of Butterworth's cherry tree motive as does the *Requiem* (Ex. 4.15(i), bars 1–2¹). In the song, the cherry tree motive reappears at the end, bringing the piece to a close in F minor. But this is only the framing key of a 'double-tonic complex', for the rest of the song is mainly in E flat major with a processional stepwise bass and intensive diatonic dissonance. The settings of both of Gurney's two stanzas blend processional and pastoral topics, yet the nature of that combination differs significantly, amounting almost to a transformation. For the first stanza, the processional topic is more prominent, with a rhythmically regular stepwise bass, largely ascending. The first vocal phrase echoes the last phrase of Parry's 'Jerusalem' melody (bar 5); this allusion appears to be independent of the sentiments of the respective poems, although they share the word 'England's' at this point. For the second stanza the direction of bass motion changes from ascending to descending, as the texture, mode, and key change to reflect darker thoughts. For the final two lines of text, the balance of topics shifts to the new pastoral, with piping effects on a pentatonic scale with a mixture of duplet and triplet quavers (in the *Requiem* these figures are played by solo woodwind instruments in line with pastoral practice). The stepwise bass is still present but now has slowed largely to minim rate, giving an impression of more static harmony (Ex. 4.15(ii)). The song invites spatial metaphors, suggesting the contemplation of a wide, perhaps empty, landscape, not least on account of the markings 'placido' at the opening and 'tranquillo' for the setting of the last two lines of text, which refer to the 'Severn meadows'. In the ensuing piano epilogue, the Butterworth allusion is marked 'chiaro', as though the melody drifts across a landscape on the wind. Here Butterworth's melody is presented as a quotation, a wordless message spoken from afar, outside the setting of the poem's text.[47]

The anguished tone of Finzi's 'Oh Fair to See' (1929) could hardly have been predicted from an innocent reading of Christina Rossetti's text, which conveys only a childlike delight in the blossom and fruit of a cherry tree. Finzi's musical setting amounts to a strong compositional intervention that brings the text into the orbit of Housman and Butterworth, conferring 'pain' on Rossetti's 'beauty' (Ex. 4.16), just as he does on Traherne's 'wonder and glory'. Like 'Only the Wanderer', the song relies tonally on a double-tonic complex, beginning on a chord of C minor and ending on a chord of C major,

Ex. 4.15 Finzi, 'Only the Wanderer'. © Copyright 1966 by Boosey & Co. Ltd. Reproduced by permission of Boosey & Hawkes Music Publishers Ltd.
(i)   bars 1–5

(ii) bars 14–20

Ex. 4.16 Finzi, 'Oh Fair to See', bars 1–12. © Copyright 1966 by Boosey & Co. Ltd. Reproduced by permission of Boosey & Hawkes Music Publishers Ltd.

while the vocal part is set largely in a diatonic E flat major. That E flat major music relies on mainly four-part diatonic textures with much stepwise motion in all parts and rather free diatonic dissonance. In comparison with 'Only the Wanderer' there is less uniform pulse articulation by the bass, while the metre and phrase structure are much more regular. There is no hint of pastoral topic. A simplified version of Finzi's leaping anacrusis figure is central, initially setting the words of the title (bars 2^1–4^1), sometimes coordinated with the ii^7 harmony (bar 7, where the harmony is ii^9; bar 11). Finzi's peculiar voicing of these chords has his own kind of open sonority with abundant melodic doubling at the sixth. The final dissonant version is the most intense: a tragic outcry that requires a literal deep intake of breath by the singer before its upward leap and then dying fall.

In these compositions, all of them carrying both commemorative and pastoral associations in either text or music or both, Finzi sought a response to his intense, intuitive sense of English musical tradition. His solution was a sweeping synthesis that tended to combine everything at once. Much of this quiet music is almost overloaded with imprecise significance, contributing to its general air of foreboding. Processional and pastoral topics are blended in a way that is seldom attempted by anyone else. In the texts, poems of war and of pastoral contemplation are brought together. There is a dedication to Finzi's teacher Farrar, who as noted earlier died in World War I and who introduced him to Gurney's music. There are musical allusions to Parry, Elgar, Vaughan Williams, and, frequently, to Butterworth's cherry tree motive and a text by Gurney with very personal content. Maybe Finzi realized, however, that this approach was so intimate, understated, and privately coded that only a few people in the world could hope to appreciate it. In future vocal works he narrowed his range in some ways, especially in terms of musical topics and literary sources. But this greater focus went along with an increasingly flexible response to texts and a loosening of the monotony of mood of his first English synthesis.

Finzi's Later Hardy Cycles: Processional Diatonicism Revived

Finzi's first song cycle set to texts by Hardy, *By Footpath and Style* (1922), scored for string quartet and solo voice, inhabits the world of the *Requiem*, *Rhapsody* and 'Only the Wanderer'; it relies on the new pastoral topic and adopts a tone of lament or dirge. Occasional 'voices'—either literal or instrumental—sing sadly in a free melodic style against a static harmonic 'landscape'. Against this background, Finzi's later diatonic style, and the style of the later Hardy cycles in particular, amount to a deliberate choice to avoid pastoral topic and work with a different kind of diatonic syntax. In the later Hardy collections that Finzi selected for publication himself, intensively diatonic idioms are found in two distinct guises: first, wrapped up in tightly organized, ditty-like, or folksong-stylized strophic songs and, second, applied in more supple ways and integrated into through-composed, structurally complex songs for narrative effect.

The first type is represented by three songs, which are distributed in each of the three later Hardy sets that Finzi saw published in his lifetime: 'The Sigh' (*A Young Man's Exhortation*), 'To Lizbie Brown' (*Earth and Air and Rain*), and 'Amabel' (*Before and After Summer*). They stand out from their surroundings in each case and sound far more like one another than like anything else in these collections. All three texts are romantic reminiscences of individual women and express tender regret in different ways. All are varied strophic settings, somewhat folksong-like with relatively regular phrases. Intensive stepwise motion is found in most parts in the accompaniment, but the pacing of the bass notes is often quite varied. The vocal parts are lyrical but tend to stick around scale degree 5 and do not conclude decisively; the listener is left with the impression that further iterations of the stanzas could appear in endlessly varied guises. 'To Lizbie Brown' and 'Amabel' are in E flat major, although they do not especially recall the style of *Blest Pair of Sirens* or the responses to that work of Elgar and Vaughan Williams. Stephen Banfield places 'Amabel' in a group of E flat major compositions by Finzi that are marked by 'mellowness of sonority and figuration' and touch on romance and memory, linking them to Vaughan Williams's 'Silent Noon' (also in E flat), and the piano writing to the discrete folksong accompaniments of Cecil Sharp and Stanford.[48] Diatonic schemata that recall the practices of Parry and Elgar are scattered throughout the songs, but come and go with the strophic variation: rising fourth in 'The Sigh' and 'To Lizbie Brown', a climactic ii[7] open sonority in the latter at the words 'lost Lizbie Brown', and a plagal tritone at the climax of 'The Sigh'.

Finzi's approach to these texts is charming, but his success at, or interest in, text-setting is uneven, especially for 'Amabel'. In that song he does not capture Hardy's embittered irony, which dwells on the woman's lost beauty and conventionalized personality. Finzi responds to the form of the text—the setting being rhythmically impeccable as usual—but not the content, beyond the usual mingling of beauty and sorrow and a general tone of regret, conveyed through intensive diatonicism, a very stepwise bass and a three- or four-part texture throughout. As in Gurney, there is a sense here of the autonomy of English diatonic song as a musical phenomenon that is linked with a complex of literary images but not necessarily the subtleties of the individual text.

Finzi's second new type of intensive diatonic writing is found in his last two Hardy cycles, *Earth and Air and Rain* and *Before and After Summer*. In contrast to the 'ditties', the songs in which this writing occurs are diverse in material, tempo, rhythm, and key, predominantly fragmentary in form, and harmonically unstable. At times the music suddenly switches to a diatonic topic—processional or hymn-like or an amalgam of the two. The notational style of the score usually changes too, with stems pointing up and down on each staff to differentiate four contrapuntal parts, as in a music student's chorale-based harmony exercise. But the associations that a musician might bring to such sounds or notational practices are seldom directly reflected in Hardy's texts, which do not refer to processions, church services, uplifting spiritual experiences or festive occasions in the calendar of church, state, or educational institutions. In Finzi's settings, these passages offer dramatic contrast and pauses for tenderness or melancholy reflection: the dynamics are soft, and the atmosphere is rapt. Often the passages appear to offer fragmentary memories of the transcendence and eternity to which Hardy's disillusioned but impassioned poetry bids farewell.

'When I Set out for Lyonesse' *(Earth and Air and Rain)* describes a long journey on foot, represented by a 'walking bass' that begins with the descending stepwise tetrachord 8–7–6–5 (Ex. 4.17 (i)). The setting of the second stanza, which hints at an extraordinary personal experience at Lyonesse, gradually transforms the pacing rhythm into a hymn-like texture with big IVs and rising fourths, while changing mode to the tonic major

Ex. 4.17 Finzi, 'When I Set out for Lyonesse' *(Earth and Air and Rain)*.
© Copyright 1936 by Boosey & Co. Ltd. Reproduced by permission of Boosey & Hawkes Music Publishers Ltd.
(i)   bars 5^3–9

Ex. 4.17 Continued

(ii) bars 23–31

(Ex. 4.17(ii)). The regular pulse articulation passes from the bass to the dissonances in inner parts, which resolve stepwise in conventional fashion. The bass motion changes too to slower, rising pentachords 1–2–3–4–5, first in E major, then in B major. The first stanza is recalled in the rhythm of the melody, confirming that this is a transformation, not a complete contrast, although in its contour the melody fits its new topic, leaping from one contrapuntal voice to another in a fashion reminiscent of Parry. The passage of Hardy's text that this music sets has no religious connotations. The diatonic topic is simply Finzi's response to the revelation of a special experience and personal transformation that happened to the poet at Lyonesse.

'Channel Firing' (*Before and after Summer*) is a varied, through-composed setting of Hardy's bitter satire on contemporary politics and religion in which several supernatural voices speak in a dramatic exchange, but spiritual redemption goes awry. Diatonic idioms appear twice, precisely when the text refers, with irony and pathos, to eternity. On both occasions Finzi alludes to Elgar's music. This setting, like 'When I Set out for Lyonesse', begins with a pacing gesture, albeit a soft, slow one that accompanies the sounds of distant explosions. The skeletons in a southern English graveyard think the Last Judgement is at hand, but God intervenes to tell them that it is only the British Navy practising its gunnery in the English Channel. He does not approve of its bellicosity and considers calling off the apocalypse altogether (thus putting an end to eschatological illusions and leaving humans unalterably mortal). Finzi responds decisively with a sudden drop in dynamics, the direction 'con tendrezza', a stepwise descending bass line, an allusion to his favourite upward anacrusis shape, an open sonority on a secondary seventh chord, and a chorale-like texture with dense but conventionally resolved diatonic dissonances (Ex. 4.18). At 'rest eternal sorely need' he alludes to the 'Church' motive from Elgar's *The Apostles* (compare with Ex. 2.6). There are layers of irony here, for while the diatonic idiom functions as a memory of eternity, the eternity mentioned by Hardy's God is not redemption but annihilation. At the end of the song, the guns' roaring is said to be heard 'As far inland as Stourton Tower and Camelot and starlit Stonehenge', lines that Finzi sets with another sudden diatonic turn, a reduction in dynamics, widely spaced chords, a melodic allusion to Elgar's 'Nimrod' at the original pitch level,[49] and a performance direction to slow and die away as the bass descends stepwise over an octave from C to C. These historic and legendary places with spiritual associations—tokens of transcendence—recede before the noise of the machinery of war, but the recollection of their meaning is captured by the momentary turn to the lofty diatonic idiom.

'The too short time' (*Before and after Summer*) is very varied and fragmentary, tonally unstable (there is no key signature), metrically ambiguous (the bar lines are notated only in dotted form), with much recitative-like

Ex. 4.18 Finzi, 'Channel Firing' (*Before and after Summer*), bars 42–7. © Copyright 1949 by Boosey & Co. Ltd. Reproduced by permission of Boosey & Hawkes Music Publishers Ltd.

writing. The text describes falling leaves, one of which—like God and the skeletons in 'Channel Firing'—'speaks'. As it does so, Finzi switches to a diatonic topic for the leaf's recollection of the transient 'summer show' that it and its peers put on. Earlier in the song, a descending tetrachord in the lowest part—not really a 'bass' as the notes do not support separate harmonies—helped to portray the falling leaves. It is now transformed into the bass of a diatonic phrase, twice tracing the tetrachord F#–E–D–C# in Finzi's customary regular crotchets. The realization in the upper parts by means of sixth chords is hymn-like. The dissonances at quaver level— mainly the standard 7–6 suspensions—are conventionally resolved, while the vocal part leaps by fourth or fifth between notes of different stepwise-moving voices of the accompaniment (Ex. 4.19(i)). In the setting of the second stanza, this style recurs in a grander, Parry-like or Elgarian vein, as the 'day' now 'speaks' of the past summer, the bass again descending stepwise (Ex. 4.19(ii)). Each of these diatonic passages is only a bar or two in length, before the imaginary voice shrugs: 'Alas, not much!' At first sight of the score, the musical associations of the suddenly processional and hymn-like style at the words 'Now we have finished our summer show / Of what we knew the way to do' might appear simply incongruous. The topic's significance lies in its function as a momentary recollection of things eternal that passes across the through-composed setting like a memory through the mind even as it recognizes the transience of summer and of all things.

The final song of *Earth and Air and Rain*, 'Proud Songsters', changes mood and key for the setting of the poem's second and final stanza, introducing four-part harmony in a completely diatonic D major with abundant suspensions and passing notes, intensive stepwise motion in all parts, and chorale-like notation of stems (Ex. 4.20). At this point in the poem, the text turns from the first stanza's description of birdsong at dusk to a reflection on the recent origins of the young birds' bodies in 'particles of grain' and 'earth and air and rain'. The song concludes with a fragment of the B minor music of the lengthy opening piano introduction and the setting of the first stanza, thus framing the diatonic music in a manner similar to the double-tonic effects of 'Only the Wanderer' and 'Oh Fair to See'. But before that fragmentary close, the piano introduces a tiny one-and-a-half-bar fragment of processional topic, still in D major but without an especially hymn-like manner, of a kind unfamiliar from this song or from anything else in the collection. This is well-spaced three-part writing over an ascending bass pentachord, with wide leaps in the melody in the manner of Parry and Elgar. The coda of Elgar's Symphony No. 1 (Ex. 2.14(ii)) is recalled,[50] a passage also in D major with a melody at a similar pitch level and with a similar contour, again set against a stepwise ascending bass pentachord. Finzi's phrase is broken

Ex. 4.19 Finzi, 'The Too Short Time' (*Before and after Summer*). © Copyright 1949 by Boosey & Co. Ltd. Reproduced by permission of Boosey & Hawkes Music Publishers Ltd.

(i) bars 14–17

(ii) bars 29–32

SONGS OF PAIN AND BEAUTY 175

Ex. 4.20 Finzi, 'Proud Songsters' (*Earth and Air and Rain*), bars 30–40.
© Copyright 1936 by Boosey & Co. Ltd. Reproduced by permission of Boosey & Hawkes Music Publishers Ltd.

Ex. 4.20 Continued

off incomplete in its second bar; a comma sign is even marked in the score before a rest. This phrase is like a passing memory of a heightened moment, like a little apotheosis that got lost, or a quotation from something else, perhaps a much broader, grander melody, requiring a deep breath if sung, but here played softly by the piano and marked 'espress'.

There is nothing spiritual about Hardy's tender but disillusioned, materialist vision that might correspond with Finzi's 'churchy' style, and there is no processional dimension to the text at all, which is about birds. The diatonic topic functions as a contrast with the song's default style and reflects the change of mode in the text from lyrical and descriptive to intellectual, personal, and reflective. The procession, such as it is, is heard only in fragmentary form, as though from afar. Finally, there is an intertextual dimension to the key of D major for the second stanza, as it is shared with the first song of the collection, 'Summer Schemes', the text of which also refers to birdsong and with which the second stanza shares pentatonic melodic figures. 'Summer Schemes' has a sunny disposition, looking ahead to summer rather than back to it, although it contains questioning, reflective moments, the latter set in a chorale-like manner like that of the final stanza of 'Proud Songsters', with a melody line of a similar contour and pitch level to that of the piano epilogue. The fact that the closing words give the whole collection its title leaves the impression that the snatch of processional music for the piano is somehow a reflection of everything described in the earlier songs through the metaphor of the brief, passionate lives of the songbirds.

Finzi's songs, like his musical oeuvre as a whole, amount to a coherent traditionalist project, consistent with the way he chose to live his life, which reflects active choices about musical style, genre, and literary texts. Those choices meant a narrowing of expressive resources in some ways, for which the intense significance invested in diatonic idioms and their application compensated to a degree. Finzi initially mastered the pastoral style that was current in the early 1920s, but he eventually abandoned that diatonic topic for the main body of his solo songs, returning to the processional topic, three-and-four-part hymn-like writing, and some of Parry's schemata. Likewise the web of intertextual allusions and memorial dedications that characterize his early vocal works was loosened. In the later Hardy settings, the synthesis of English elements is less all-encompassing, but the use of diatonic topics within individual songs is often subtler and is integrated into complex narratives or dialogues. The mood of dazed grief found in his early vocal music changes to a pervasive melancholy.

Finzi's musical project is the most conspicuous case of musical traditionalism in English diatonic song, but similar concerns motivated the other composers discussed in this chapter. All sought a recognizable sound for English music in diatonic conventions, usually established, occasionally new, and all attempted syntheses of various sources in the hope of renewing and expanding that music. Despite the new approaches of Butterworth and Vaughan Williams in their Housman cycles, the legacy of Parry and the example of Elgar retained their central importance, not just for the available techniques and schemata of processional diatonicism but also for what amounted to an elevated style and indeed the idea that such a style was desirable in the solo-song genre. For Gurney and Finzi in particular, pre-war associations of intensive diatonicism with eternity and transcendent values informed complex settings as well as straightforward ones and shaped not just confident visions but expressions of loss, irony, and regret.

5

Tracts for the Times

English Diatonic Music at Peace and War, 1937–1953

In the mid-1930s, English diatonic music awoke from its pastoral contemplation and its elegiac thoughts of transience and turned outwards to face immediate crises at home and abroad. The next two decades witnessed industrial unrest, the abdication of King Edward VIII, the worsening political situation in Europe, World War II, and the subsequent fear of nuclear war. It was also an age of two coronations, those of 1937 and 1953, which provide the approximate *termini* for the survey undertaken in this chapter. These were national landmark occasions at which music by English composers featured prominently in long orchestral and liturgical programmes. During these years, music could be disseminated widely and rapidly through BBC broadcasts and on the soundtracks of films for cinema. Composers attempted to meet the crises that confronted their civilization with music that was public, visionary, and at times national, aiming above all to communicate with a wide audience and spread a message. They abandoned aestheticism for service and the advocacy of causes. To accomplish their tasks, they revived traditions: musical, literary, and intellectual. They drew texts from some of the perceived pinnacles of the English literary canon: Shakespeare, Wordsworth, Shelley, and the King James Bible. They reflected on high-minded ideals of humanism and spiritual transcendence; on the dignity and mission of the art of music itself; and on 'big words' with capital letters, such as Love, Music, Peace, and Courage. To realize these visions in musical terms, they drew on the idiom that they seem to have regarded as their musical correlate: processional diatonicism. First established by Parry and Elgar before World War I, the style was revived in its original grand, public mode, if sometimes updated for the era of broadcast and film. The subtopic 'unison hymn' was worked especially hard—for instance, in the trios of orchestral marches as well as in actual hymns for unison chorus—perhaps on account of its direct, unembellished manner, although the 'choral ode' subtopic appeared too in some of the more elaborate designs. In this way, composers unfolded redemptive visions of peace and national unity, executed commissions for state ceremonies, and even provided official wartime propaganda. The urgency of their mission of public communication meant that they often relied on direct and familiar symbolism in words and music and sometimes eclectic stylistic references. Ambiguity and allusiveness now appear to have been regarded, doubtless in the spirit of the time, as unaffordable luxuries.

'Is it (so to speak) the "Jerusalem" brand or the "Blest pair of sirens" brand that you want?' asked Vaughan Williams of Adrian Boult in September 1940.[1] He was writing in response to an invitation from Boult on behalf of the BBC and indirectly the Ministry of Information—the British government's wartime propaganda unit—for a patriotic song with orchestral accompaniment. His question reveals assumptions about the terms of any such composition. Despite Vaughan Williams's popular reputation, there was no question for him of reviving English folksong or Tudor polyphony to execute this task. His starting point was automatically Hubert Parry's post-Wagnerian and post-Victorian diatonic idioms, and he evidently assumed that Boult would understand that as well. Expressed in the terminology developed in this book, he was in effect asking Boult which of the two subtopics of processional diatonicism—unison hymn or choral ode— would be suitable. In the event, Vaughan Williams went for the '"Jerusalem" brand' in the unison hymn 'England, My England', although he later withdrew his 'offer' of the song to the BBC and asked for the return of all manuscript materials in protest against the corporation's banning of the music of the composer Alan Bush on account of his Communist politics.[2] Nevertheless, John Ireland fully exploited the "'Blest Pair of Sirens" brand' in his coronation cantata *These Things Shall Be* (1937), as did Gerad Finzi in his festival cantata *For St Cecilia: Ceremonial Ode* (1947) and his *Intimations of Immortality* (1950). This chapter examines the compositions of these genres—unison choral hymn and choral cantata—along with those of a third, the post-Elgar orchestral march. The chapter also discusses a single 'abstract' composition— Vaughan Williams's Symphony No. 5—which shares much of the tone and many of the diatonic conventions of compositions of the three main genres. Vaughan Williams therefore receives the lion's share of attention, but that reflects the range and subtlety of his application of diatonic conventions in this period.

At a technical level, the resurgence of diatonic conventions from the pre-World War I era is remarkable, as is the strong tendency to regularization of their application. The schemata from the opening bars of *Blest Pair of*

Sirens—Meistersinger tetrachord and rising fourth—returned in the music of this era after a long break. The Meistersinger tetrachord in its descending form opens choral compositions such as Finzi's *For St Cecilia* and Walton's *Coronation Te Deum* (1953) and marches such as Bax's *London Pageant* (1937; the same schema begins the trio as well), his *Coronation March* (1953), Walton's *Spitfire Prelude* (1943; twice—see discussion below), and Bliss's *Welcome the Queen* (1954). It provides the setting for the title words of Ireland's *These Things Shall Be*. The rising-fourth schema appears near the start of the grand melodies of Walton's coronation march *Crown Imperial* (1937), his film score *Went the Day Well?* (1943), his march for the television series *A History of the English-Speaking Peoples* (1959), and his *Spitfire Prelude*. It is prominent in the big processional tunes in Ireland's *These Things Shall Be* and his *Epic March* (1942), and it is heard in the title theme of Vaughan Williams's score for the film *49th Parallel* (1941). *Spitfire Prelude* and *For St Cecilia* follow the script established by *Blest Pair of Sirens*, the *Meistersinger* tetrachord and rising-fourth schemata appearing in their regular order (see Appendix B) at the very start of the compositions. The trio tune of *Crown Imperial* works along these lines too (see Ex. 1.8 and the discussion in Chapter 1). E flat major made a resurgence as the main key of heightened diatonic episodes in cantatas and big tunes such as those of *Went the Day Well?* and *Epic March*. Even Vaughan Williams at times reverted to this key for his passages of intensive diatonicism, returning to his practice of the 1910s after many years of avoiding the association. But it is not just the frequency and consistency of these allusions that is striking. The technical fluency with which composers realized and manipulated the diatonic conventions is also extraordinary, given the lack of any formal training in them or the existence of any labels such as they have been given in this book.

Coronations, Festivals, and Commissions

The coronations of George VI and Elizabeth II were the first to be broadcast and recorded. The 1937 ceremony was broadcast live by the BBC on radio and could be viewed later in the cinema, while the 1953 coronation was shown live on BBC television.[3] In 1937 the BBC broadcast a whole day of coronation programming. From a musical point of view, there are therefore two different aspects of these coronations to consider: the ceremonies themselves in Westminster Abbey, which were witnessed by only a few hundred people; and the broadcasts, publicity, and recordings that surrounded the ceremonies and the prestige that accrued to compositions commissioned for them.

For these coronations, the approach of the musical organizers—the organist of Westminster Abbey, the Master of the Kings Music, and the Archbishop of Canterbury—continued the concept established in 1902 by Sir Frederick Bridge.[4] The music for the service was a survey of English sacred choral music down through the centuries, consistent with a notion of the evolutionary development of English music. There were commissions from contemporary composers as well, which, by implication, would keep the tradition alive. In 1937 the orchestral programme that preceded the service was an international one, in line with the earlier coronations of 1902 and 1911, as a gesture of welcome to foreign guests, but in 1953 even this programme was entirely British. The organist, William McKie, reported that the committee 'decided that the programme should be all English'.[5] As at the earlier coronations, the musical programme was lengthy, and the occasion amounted to a grand celebration of English music. Both coronations were opportunities for the music profession to advertise itself and to reflect on musical tradition and extend it in an official and celebratory state occasion.

Whether even a musically informed listener at the ceremonies or the broadcasts would have discerned any meaningful pattern of style or development from the musical programmes is debatable. Most likely they would have experienced pockets of stylistic coherence within wider diversity and historical eclecticism. In 1937 they would have heard Walton's *Crown Imperial*, Elgar's *Imperial March*, Edward German's *Coronation March,* and the finale of Elgar's 'Enigma' Variations before the service, Parry's 'I Was Glad' at the opening of the service, and Elgar's Pomp and Circumstance Marches Nos. 1 and 4 after it. Aside from S. S. Wesley's 'Thou Wilt Keep Him in Perfect Peace', the diatonic tradition would have been less in evidence in the liturgical compositions and anthems by William Boyce, William Byrd, Orlando Gibbons, Handel, Henry Purcell, Christopher Tye, Edward Bairstow, Henry Walford Davies (1869–1941), and George Dyson (1883–1964). The slow movement of Arnold Bax's Third Symphony was an interesting choice in the orchestral programme, as it gestures initially to the new pastoral style, although any such impression would likely have been swamped within the lengthy programme of other pieces both British and Continental. There was plenty of post-Victorian English diatonicism on the 1953 programme, although little of it was new. Elgar's 'Nimrod' appeared for the first time, taking the central place in state and royal ceremonial that it retains to this day, along with Parry's 'Jerusalem', Holst's 'Jupiter', three of Elgar's *Pomp and Circumstance* marches, Ireland's *Epic March*, Walton's *Crown Imperial* and *Orb and Sceptre*, and Bax's *Coronation March*. There was also a nod in the modal and pastoral direction, this time with 'Greensleeves', Butterworth's *The Banks of Green Willow*, Vaughan Williams's motet 'O Taste and See', a short, lyrical setting that contains no accidentals at all, and Howells's 'Behold, O God Our Defender' (discussed in Chapter 6). Howells's composition was possibly the outstanding one of the 1953 coronation, exhibiting a completely different aesthetic from the rest of the music. The big choral commissions at these coronations were the *Te Deum* settings of Vaughan Williams (1937) and Walton (1953). Both are sectional and episodic in form and are filled with loud and splendid fanfares and martial idioms but end softly. Walton's setting has a Meistersinger tetrachord at its opening bars but does not take schematic allusions any further. Neither composition, however, is especially concerned with the elements of the diatonic tradition considered in this study, and certainly not in comparison with some of the other pieces the composers were writing in those years.

The choral works that did take forward the diatonic tradition were cantatas produced for festivals and other occasions: Vaughan Williams's *Dona Nobis Pacem* for the Huddersfield Festival of 1936, his *Serenade to Music* for Henry Wood's fiftieth anniversary jubilee concert of 5 October 1938, Ireland's *These Things Shall Be* for a coronation concert and BBC broadcast in 1937, Finzi's *For St Cecilia: Ceremonial Ode* for the St Cecilia Festival of 1947, and his *Intimations of Immortality* for the Three Choirs Festival of 1950. The Cheltenham Festival, despite its many commissions, did not generate much new music of the diatonic tradition other than the Finzi Cello Concerto (1955). The Festival of Britain appears not to have had a very coherent commissioning policy in music. The choral foundations of English cathedrals and Oxbridge chapels commissioned liturgical music of an intensively diatonic flavour during this period, but the tasks fell mainly to Herbert Howells, who was creating a new branch of the tradition of a different kind, as Chapter 6 will show.

The BBC's alliance with the Ministry of Information did not apparently generate any major commissions after Boult's approaches to Vaughan Williams and Ireland in late 1940. Film production was guided by Ministry of Information principles, but after *49th Parallel* (1941) did not attract its financial resources.[6] Vaughan Williams later responded to an invitation to write music for a morale-raising film entitled *Dim Little Island* (1949) produced for the Ministry's successor, the Central Office of Information.[7] He also wrote music for a short film entitled *The People's Land* (1943) to celebrate the fiftieth anniversary of the National Trust, another instance of music for a cause.

Orchestral Marches

The 1937 coronation came three years after Elgar's death, and the genre of the orchestral march that he initiated and that became identified with popular patriotic celebrations and state occasions appears to have been regarded as no longer his personal property. Not all of Elgar's marches follow the same model. Nevertheless Pomp and Circumstance No. 1, the most popular march, is rather formulaic in form and is available for imitation, as Elgar himself showed in No. 4 and to an extent in No. 5. Writing one of these marches appears, at first sight, to be a primarily technical exercise for a competent composer. A brilliant quick march is followed by a noble tune in unison-hymn manner, first softly in a register suitable for male voices, then in a loud 'all together' version. A reprise of the quick march follows, and then there is a second apotheosis of the hymn, now in the tonic key, before a brief closing reference to the quick march. In practice, however, only Elgar and Walton seem to have been able or willing to bring off this type of piece.

Walton's marches were successful acts of musical communication insofar as they reached a wide audience. He had no intellectual message to communicate with them, but he was highly adept at inferring the models for the diatonic conventions and applying them in new ways. His marches allude distinctly to Parry, Elgar, and early Vaughan Williams, updating their styles with crisp, lively rhythms, syncopations, and glittering orchestration for the quick marches that rivals Elgar's scoring. Walton shaped *Crown Imperial* around a gradual overall crescendo across the whole piece and introduced a part for organ. In both of his coronation marches, he expanded the percussion battery: bass drum, side drum, tenor drum, cymbals, glockenspiel, triangle, tubular bell, and gong for *Crown Imperial*; and timpani, cymbals, suspended cymbal, side drum, bass drum, and tambourine for *Orb and Sceptre*. Walton's coronation marches, then, are noisy pieces. Walton introduced slow, ceremonial fanfare passages too, in effect staging a coronation ceremony in sound for millions of listeners who did not attend the actual occasion.

Crown Imperial takes Elgar's Pomp and Circumstance March No. 5 (1930), the elder composer's most recent contribution, as its immediate model, a work produced only seven years earlier in an updated populist manner. Both marches are in C major with a unison-hymn trio in A flat major with similar melodic openings, followed by an apotheosis version and a final apotheosis in C major at the end of the piece. Both trio tunes begin with an almost-literal stepwise bass descent of an octave in A flat major from 8 to 1. Walton, however, transforms Elgar's fragmentary, tonally unstable theme into a riper, sweeping tune that is more akin to those of Pomp and Circumstance Marches Nos. 1 and 4 (see Ex. 1.8). The style is a rather subtle amalgam, however. The three-part texture, though no less Elgarian, points to Elgar's choral and orchestral works rather than his marches, while the rising-fourth schema near the start of Walton's tune is never found in Elgar's march-trio melodies and again suggests choral music, especially following the initial tetrachord descent, which leads to the often-repeated *Blest Pair of Sirens* sequence (Meistersinger tetrachord / rising fourth) in its regular order. Here Walton weaves together some threads of the English tradition that were usually separate.[8]

Walton's *Spitfire Prelude* (1942; Ex. 5.1) is perhaps the most handsome musical tribute of all in this era to Parry's *Blest Pair of Sirens*. Its opening pages pack in a dense succession of allusions to the post-Victorian English tradition and twice confirm the Meistersinger tetrachord / rising-fourth succession as a signature of 'English' style. The two realizations of this script are, however, quite contrasted in manner, reflecting the different subtopics of processional diatonicism. The bass of the opening section moves entirely stepwise, while upward-leaping melodies that cover inner-part suspensions unfold flamboyantly above it, evoking the opulent sound world of contemporary film music (Ex. 5.1(i). The topic at the opening is fanfare, and the schema is Meistersinger tetrachord (with chromaticization of the 6–5 step in bar 4). The rising-fourth schema is realized twice, though incompletely in each case and on the first occasion before the tetrachord has been completed (bars 4–5), the usual bass step 4–3 sounded here in the horns in an inner-part motion. The notes of the melodic figure are hidden in the first trombone part, but a leap up to 5 (from 1—thus actually a fifth rather than the usual fourth) is picked out by the first trumpet. In the second instance of the schema (bars 7–8), a 7–6 suspension sounds above a bass 4, preceded by a dotted-figure leap that recalls bar 1 of *Blest Pair of Sirens*. The final melodic 5 to complete the rising-fourth figure needs to be heard in the high covering violin notes in

Ex. 5.1 Walton, *Spitfire Prelude and Fugue*, Prelude (reduction). 'Prelude and Fugue ("The Spitfire")' by William Walton © Oxford University Press 1961. All rights reserved.

(i) bars 1–8

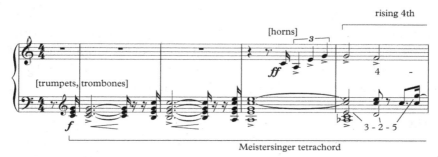

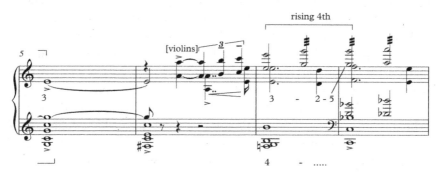

(ii) fig. 1, bar 1–fig 1, bar 5[1]

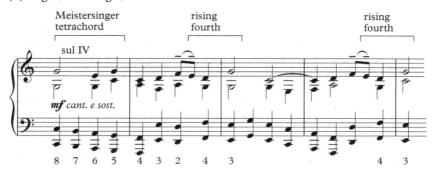

bar 8. Even though the bass does not proceed to the expected 3, the allusion is again audibly clear. The big march tune that follows is in Elgarian 'unison hymn' manner, presenting the same succession of schemata once again— Meistersinger tetrachord followed by two rising fourths—now, in contrast,

as unambiguously as could be wished (Ex. 5.1(ii)). After *Crown Imperial* (see Ex. 1.8), Walton evidently had this schematic succession in march-trio style well grooved. The contrasting realizations—allusive and embellished, then direct and clear—are appropriate to the subtopics here: choral ode and unison hymn, respectively. As if these allusions were not enough, between the two passages cited in Ex. 5.1 Walton precisely recalls the characteristic triplet figures and harmonic context at the climax of the first movement of Vaughan Williams's *A Sea Symphony* (compare *A Sea Symphony*, i, fig. F, bars 5–7; *Spitfire Prelude*, bars 12–15). The *Spitfire Prelude* thus re-creates English musical tradition, cramming diatonic references one upon another. The film *The First of the Few* (1942) from which this music arose was an official wartime production in harmony with Ministry of Information principles, although whether most of its viewers would have recognized Walton's virtuoso performance in evoking English musical tradition is doubtful.

A good point of comparison and contrast with Walton's approach is Ireland's *Epic March* (1942). It is not as technically brilliant as Walton's marches, but it does carry a message of sorts—or was meant to. It was written in response to an invitation from Adrian Boult, the BBC, and the Ministry of Information in November 1940, a few months after Boult had asked Vaughan Williams for his patriotic song. *Epic March* is prefaced with a definition of the word 'epic': 'Concerning some heroic action or series of actions and events of deep and lasting significance in the history of a nation or race.' The opening section indicates grim determination rather than patriotic celebration, while the trio tune is close to the manner of the big tune of Ireland's recent cantata *These Things Shall Be*, which expresses a Utopian vision of peace and friendship. Ireland evidently wanted to compose as an artist-intellectual, commenting on the present world situation through music. Some years later he said that *Epic March* was '*meant* to be anti-fascist music'.[9]

Boult told the composer that in offering the commission, he and the BBC had in mind Ireland's *London Overture* and the 'big broad tune in "These Things Shall Be". With a blend of the spirit and essence of these two—(in fact, wouldn't an adaptation, in measure, of the latter tune make a splendid trio in the March?)—the appeal is guaranteed straight away.'[10] But Ireland soon got stuck. He vacillated over the title, the music, and the commission itself.[11] He wrote to Boult on 3 June 1941:

> I have thought the matter over carefully, and it is certain that I cannot do anything on the lines of 'Pomp and Circumstance' No. 1. It is not what I feel

appropriate at the present time. That is to say, I personally cannot feel that kind of music as my own reaction to the position.... What I have in mind is stern and purposeful rather than jolly and complacent....[12]

He then submitted to Boult examples of the opening fanfare and the first theme to find out whether they would be suitable, and he offered to discontinue work on the march if they were not. In the end, Ireland did essentially follow Boult's original suggestion, adapting the tune from *These Things Shall Be* (discussed below in the section on 'Cantatas') 'in measure'. In doing so he reprised yet again the particular mode of processional diatonicism that he had easily dropped into throughout his career (discussed in Chapter 4). Here again are the key of E flat major; a tendency for textures to fall into three-part counterpoint; abundant 'open' sonorities on secondary seventh harmonies; various other schemata; and plenty of 7–6 suspensions or appoggiaturas in inner parts (Ex. 5.2). The 'Largamente' tempo marking diminishes the feeling of the unison-hymn subtopic that is customary for such trio tunes—the precedent again was the equivalent tune from *These Things Shall Be*—although Ireland does not avoid an allusion to the heavy succession of notes in the *Crown Imperial* trio in the seventh and eighth bars. The reprise of the tune at the end of *Epic March* loses the characteristic textures and schemata

Ex. 5.2 Ireland, *Epic March*, bar 95–102 (reduction). © Copyright 1942 by Hawkes & Son (London) Ltd. Reproduced by permission of Boosey & Hawkes Music Publishers Ltd.

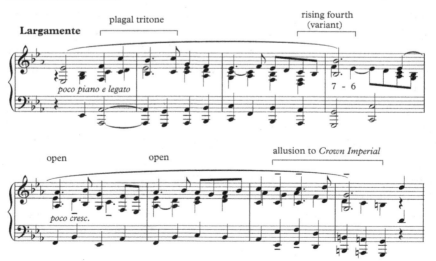

of processional diatonicism amidst a general apotheosis. Nevertheless, it is notable that Ireland's scruples about the genre did not extend to the topic of processional diatonicism itself as a mode of expression for antifascist music; like Vaughan Williams in his correspondence with Boult, he evidently regarded the legacy of Parry as part of the 'deal'. Only the manner of its realization was a matter for concern and reflection.

Still, this kind of work was not Ireland's *forte*. Likewise, neither Bax, with two coronation marches, *London Pageant* (1937) *and Coronation March* (1953), nor William Alwyn, with his *Festival March* for the 1951 Festival of Britain, could match Walton technically. Bax's marches are notable for the 'Irish' tone of the tunes of the trios, which replaces the processional hymn manner of Elgar, but the brilliant design and execution of such pieces was largely beyond either the interest or the capability of these composers.

Vaughan Williams's Unison Hymns

Vaughan Williams wrote ten actual unison hymns or 'songs' during World War II as a contribution to the war effort or as a commentary on the contemporary situation: 'A Hymn of Freedom' (1939), *Six Choral Songs to be Sung in Time of War* (1940), 'England, My England' (1941), 'A Call to the Free Nations' (1942), and 'The Airmen's Hymn' (1942). Another was arranged from his title music for the film *49th Parallel* as 'The New Commonwealth' (1943). The style of the unison hymn as Vaughan Williams practised it appears also in the main melody of his music for the film *Coastal Command* (1942) and at least twice in *Thanksgiving for Victory* (1944). These songs all attempt to stir their singers and listeners to rise to a cause and to action. The tone is sometimes patriotic, although more often the texts and music evoke a higher purpose or ideal such as freedom or peace. The songs are written for performance by amateur voices. They are rhythmically simple, avoid awkward intervals and were mostly published with accompanying Sol-fa notation. They range from propagandistic morale-raisers for government commission to an attempt in *Six Choral Songs* to elevate the genre into art. The latter is in effect a choral song cycle with a philosophical tone that attempts to transcend the quarrel of World War II and reassert universal humanist values. In this respect, the unison hymns furthered Vaughan Williams's vision of participative music-making, his belief that musical high culture rests on a great mass of amateur music making. They attempt to turn this grass-roots music-making to a higher purpose, just as Vaughan Williams did in his direction of amateur choirs. Vaughan Williams had been writing hymn tunes since his work on *The English Hymnal* (1906), but by the 1940s he no longer tried to build any on folk songs, as he did in that collection. Neither did he adopt the modal diatonicism of his earlier pastoral idiom. The unison hymns are consistent with Vaughan Williams's reformist ideas for English church music in that they avoid the intensive local chromaticism of some popular Victorian hymns; they usually modulate to and cadence in the dominant or the mediant key, and the *Six Choral Songs* often switch to or from more distantly related keys, but that is all.

Unison hymn as a subtopic of processional diatonicism was of course well established, even if it was never named as such. Not surprisingly, Vaughan Williams's main point of reference for writing in the genre of unison choral hymn was Parry's 'Jerusalem'. Holst's 'I Vow to Thee, My Country' must have been significant too because it was a hymn that Vaughan Williams, as editor of *Songs of Praise* (1925), was responsible for publishing. He selected those two hymns for the programme of a pageant at Dorking in 1938 that borrowed its title—'England's Pleasant Land'—from the text of 'Jerusalem'.[13] The communion song 'Wein und Brot' from Act I of *Parsifal* stood in the background, as it was little less than genre-defining (see Appendix A). But Vaughan Williams also drew on schematic patterns found in Victorian hymns. Here his main model was one of melodic shape. Two phrases—or at least components of melodic shape, as they are not always clearly separated—are presented, one (antecedent) rising, directly or indirectly, from degree 1 to 5 with the pattern 5–6–5 conspicuous, the second (consequent) descending, often stepwise, from degree 8 to 5. Modulation to the dominant may or may not occur in the consequent. Sometimes not all of these criteria will be met, and in practice there may be elaborations, omissions, or insertions; the patterns may be realized in a compact or a loose way, but the tune still recognizably belongs to the same family. Nevertheless, there is a clear sense of a regular order of first and second functional components. A few of Vaughan Williams's compositions gradually 'regularize' the schema within a teleological process leading to a climax or goal at which the regular order is given in full. Both 'Jerusalem' and 'I Vow to Thee, My Country' show some affinities with the model, although they do not follow it directly, and far less directly than Vaughan Williams usually did in the 1940s.

Vaughan Williams had adopted this 'Victorian hymn' schema earlier on occasion and in other types of pieces that sound little like unison hymns, most notably *Flos Campi* VI, where the two melodic phrases, each developed separately in octave/unison imitation, are the antecedent and consequent parts of the model, respectively (Ex. 3.10(ii)). It could be traced back, with a little latitude, to the unison hymn passages in the *Sea Symphony* ('Token of all brave captains'; 'A vast similitude interlocks all'), and it is found in the 'Cockney' music of the trio of the scherzo of the *London Symphony* (score letter N). But in the era between the coronations, the Victorian-hymn schema came to dominate Vaughan Williams's conception of 'tune', not just in his official wartime music such as the unison hymns, the *Coastal Command* theme, and *Thanksgiving for Victory* but even in some of his more ambitious art–music pieces, such as *Dona Nobis Pacem* and Symphony No. 5, especially at broad diatonic climaxes.

The melodic functions of the schema may be traced back through nineteenth-century hymns to the well-known Lutheran chorale 'Wachet auf', the subject for Bach's Cantata BWV 140. It is heard also at the opening of Mendelssohn's oratorio *Paulus* (1836). There is a much earlier precursor in the Gregorian chant 'O Sacrum Convivium', which Vaughan Williams would have known from the 'Liebesmahl' motive in *Parsifal*, the first phrase of 'Wein und Brot' and Elgar's *The Kingdom*. Indeed, he himself quoted the chant melody in 'Love Bade Me Welcome' from *Five Mystical Songs*. He would have found instances of the same patterns throughout the monumental Victorian collection *Hymns Ancient and Modern* (1861, 1875, 1904, 1906). Many of the hymns of this type in *Hymns Ancient and Modern* are in E flat major, where this type of tune sits well for amateur voices. (E flat major is also the overall key of Bach's cantata.)[14] Here some of the most acute sensitivities of the English musical revival are laid bare. For although certain hymns by musicians such as Monk (the editor), Ouseley, Wesley, and Stainer show these traits, the clearest translations of the 'Wachet auf'-type hymn tune into Victorian practice are those by John Bacchus Dykes. Although notorious for his chromaticism, Dykes strongly favoured the 'Victorian hymn' schema for his hymns and created memorable and popular tunes based on it. The Proprietors of *Hymns Ancient and Modern* had edited out some of Dykes's chromatic harmony for the 1904 edition, published only two years before publication of Vaughan Williams's own reformist *English Hymnal*. Many of Dykes's hymns are genuinely artistic compositions written in a vein that indicates he was conversant with European musical Romanticism. As such, they can be regarded as position statements about what a modern hymn can and should be. In true English reform-movement style, Vaughan

Williams, no less strong a musical personality, continued Dykes's approach but adapted it tellingly. In his compositions of the 1930s and 1940s, he effectively continued the Proprietors' policy by preserving Dykes's melodic tendencies but wiping out the harmonic blemishes. The two composers were not miles apart—Vaughan Williams wrote a tender tribute to Dykes with his hymn-prelude on 'Dominus regit me' (1936)—and Dykes favoured intensive diatonicism as well: he could hardly have composed on the 'Wachet auf' model had he not, although conspicuous chromatic detail sometimes crept into later phrases in his hymns.

Dykes's 'Holy, holy, holy' and 'Eternal Father, strong to save' (Ex. 5.3) are good examples of his realizations of the two melodic components of the schema.[15] (The allusions to plagal-tritone patterns in both of these hymns is further evidence of the Victorian roots of English diatonic music). Ironically, 'Eternal Father, strong to save' develops chromatic sequences in later phrases, including a chromatic rising scale in the melody that one would not normally expect to sing in a church. Sometimes Dykes developed rather elaborate compositions out of this schematic opening. 'Hark! Hark, my soul!',[16] for instance, is a four-part setting with complex rhythm and harmony, including triplet minims in inner parts sounding against duplet minims in outer parts, and chromatic details leading to the final cadence that recall Romantic piano pieces by Schubert, Mendelssohn, and Chopin.[17] Vaughan Williams's 'The Airmen's Hymn' (1942; Ex. 5.4), to words of the Earl of Lytton, shares the regular order of melodic functions in this type of hymn tune. However, the marcato direction for the pianist's or organist's right hand throughout the song and the firm, largely stepwise bass give it a processional, indeed march-like, character, which it preserves through changes of mood. There are no chromatic sequences, although there is a switch to G major, the mediant major key. (The E flat major / G major complex was of course well worn, being the main pairing of keys in *Blest Pair of Sirens*; Vaughan Williams had used it in 'Silent Noon' and in the opening section of 'The Explorers', the finale of *A Sea Symphony*.) With a treatment like this, Vaughan Williams in effect claimed the materials of the Victorian hymn schema for the English music revival, reversing Dykes's compositional approach to the same materials.

'A Hymn of Freedom' (1939) was probably Vaughan Williams's first wartime unison hymn. It clearly looks to 'Jerusalem' as a first model, being in D major and in triple metre, with a thick accompaniment texture, quite dense harmonic information, and busy inner parts. The rise and fall of Parry's opening ritornello and the melodic cadential figure at the end of each stanza

Ex. 5.3 John Bacchus Dykes, hymns
(i) 'Holy, Holy, Holy', bars 1–8

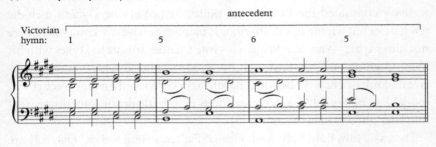

(ii) 'Eternal Father, Strong to Save', bars 1–4³

of 'Jerusalem' are echoed in the corresponding places in Vaughan Williams's hymn. Most striking, however, is the modulation to the mediant key (here F sharp minor) in the second phrase, the melody dropping a fifth from degree 7 to 4 in the same fashion as Parry at the same point in his tune (Ex. 5.5). That

Ex. 5.4 Vaughan Williams, 'The Airmen's Hymn', bars 4–11. 'The Airmen's Hymn' words by 2nd Earl of Lytton, music by Ralph Vaughan Williams © Oxford University Press 1942. All rights reserved.

figure and its mediant harmony may be regarded as a schema termed here '*Liebesmahl* mediant fifth drop', as they recall Wagner's adaptation of the 'O Sacrum Convivium' melody in the 'Liebesmahl' motive in *Parsifal*, and are especially redolent of the 'Wein und Brot' version sung at the communion climax of Act I (see Appendix A), where it sets the word *Mitleid* (compassion). The text by G. W. Briggs, a canon of Worcester Cathedral, is quite humble, pleading to God for forgiveness of sins, dreading that 'pride and vengeance rule our heart', describing war as 'man's sacrifice and shame', and imagining a future of peace and freedom for all peoples. The same cannot be said for W. E. Henley's poem 'England, My England', which Vaughan Williams appears to have selected himself in response to Boult's approach the following year on behalf of the Ministry of Information. England's eyes shine 'As the Lord were walking near, / Whispering terrible things and dear'. Nevertheless Vaughan Williams responded with the same formula: D major,

Ex. 5.5 Vaughan Williams 'A Hymn of Freedom', bars 7–10. © Oxford University Press. All rights reserved.

triple metre, a largely stepwise bass in regular crotchets and a rising melody in the ritornello. The setting is more martial, though, with the fanfares described in the text outlined in the melody. The Victorian hymn schema is a presence but is split between the ritornello (1 rising to 5) and the first phrase of the vocal melody (descent from 8). This song has a refrain, which directly echoes 'Jerusalem' in the cadential melodic phrase and, especially, in the descending minor third 8–6 for the word 'England'—exactly the same as in 'Jerusalem'—although the word is repeated here rather crudely, almost like a football chant (Ex. 5.6). The composition of these two hymns occurred, respectively, before and after the defeat of the French armies and the British Expeditionary Force in May 1940 and the Dunkirk evacuation.

The *Six Choral Songs*, commissioned by the BBC in 1939 for performance at the Proms of 1940, elaborate the sentiments of 'A Hymn to Freedom' rather than 'England, My England'. In the event, that premier never occurred because the Proms season was cancelled. The texts by Shelley were selected jointly by Vaughan Williams and his future wife Ursula Wood. She entitled each text 'A

Ex. 5.6 Vaughan Williams, 'England, My England', bars 24–31. 'England, My England' by Ralph Vaughan Williams, words by W. E. Henley (1849–1903) © Oxford University Press 1941. All rights reserved.

Song of . . . ', the subjects being, respectively, 'Courage', 'Liberty', 'Healing', 'Victory', 'Pity, Peace, and Love', and 'the New Age'. This succession of capitalized abstract nouns presented Shelley as an idealist thinker and a philosopher of humanist ideals. Inevitably, the choice of Shelley, and especially the text of No. IV, 'A Song of Victory', taken from *Prometheus Unbound* ('To suffer woes which Hope thinks infinite . . .), invoked the spirit of Hubert Parry. Parry's cantata *Prometheus Unbound* (1880) was a radical response to a Three Choirs Festival commission in its time, although it was remembered more by name than in performance or in musical idiom. Vaughan Williams's settings are elaborate, highly crafted versions of the unison hymn genre. To be sure, the tunes stick mainly to even note values, with few difficult leaps, and Sol-fa notation is given in the score. But the composition as a whole amounts to an attempt to raise the genre of the unison hymn to an art form, indeed a kind of song cycle, with varied tempo, metre, and dynamics, ambitious tonal shifts, and loose ternary or varied strophic forms. Teleological processes run through some of the 'songs', leading to transformation and climax by the end instead of mere repetition of stanzas; II, IV, and VI, for instance, move from tonic minor to major, ending more positively than they began. On the other hand, some songs end inconclusively: the conclusions of II and III remain provisional because the melody ends softly on degree 5 instead of descending to 1. There is evidence throughout of Vaughan Williams's taste for the fading vision (explored in Chapter 3).

The *Six Songs* eschew patriotism for a broader humanistic idealism. In particular, the sentiments of V ('A Song of Pity, Peace and Love') echo Vaughan Williams's transcendental tastes from his Whitman period before World War I as well as the tone of *Dona Nobis Pacem* with its long succession of capitalized abstract nouns ('Night', 'Heaven', 'Mother', 'Poets', 'Nature or God, or Love, or Pleasure', 'Sympathy', 'Pity, Peace and Love'). These 'big words' are in effect 'gods' of the human spirit that exist without doctrinal religion but that allow and invite a reinvigorated musical style of elevation, which Vaughan Williams duly rolls out, especially in the orchestral version of the *Six Songs*, recalling within a tiny frame some of his grandest music.

Debts to 'Jerusalem' are in relatively little evidence in the *Six Choral Songs*. Its cadential melodic phrase appears yet again for the end of each couplet in I, which perhaps helps to define the genre at the outset of the cycle, but thereafter such direct connections are difficult to hear. On the other hand, the Victorian-hymn schema is in evidence in I (opening phrase based around 1–5–6–5); II (climax at the turn to tonic major near the end with 5–6–5); II (introductory accompaniment passage as antecedent, first phrase of the melody as consequent as in 'England, My England'); V (the two parts in the regular order, first loosely, then ending with a more compact and recognizable version); and VI (relative to C major within an overall A Aeolian context). The 'big IV' schema effects the climax of II in a radiant passage of alternating tonic and elaborated subdominant harmonies with 9–8 suspensions, including one on the word 'Hope'. The passage as a whole strongly recalls the secondary theme of the first movement of Symphony No. 5, especially given the dotted rhythms that surround the big IV itself. Echoes of the Symphony continue in III with further elaborated subdominant harmonies alternating with tonic harmony in plagal progressions.

The centrepiece of the cycle and the expressive climax is undoubtedly V, 'A Song of Pity, Peace and Love', which returns for once to Vaughan Williams's pre-World War I processional style. The key is E flat major, the bass motion is almost entirely stepwise, and the bass line is rhythmically flexible, sometimes tied across bar lines, and not at all concerned with regular pulse articulation in march style. The 'Song' begins with the bass slipping down almost a complete octave, before ascending stepwise once again, the familiar order of stepwise bass motion established at the opening of *Blest Pair of Sirens*. The key and the throbbing triplet accompaniment look back to the style of 'Easter' from the *Five Mystical Songs*, and, ultimately, the communion song 'Wein und Brot' from *Parsifal*, which is not inappropriate given the sentiments of this 'Song of Pity, Peace and Love'.

A strong teleological process is at work in the Song, effecting a regularization of Victorian-hymn components at the climax. The phrase structure is initially very free and supple, the tonic chord even being displaced from the cadence-like tonic arrivals of the melody in the manner of a choral-prelude setting. The schema consequent 8–7–6–5 does not immediately follow the antecedent 1–5–6–5, appearing only at the end of a long opening paragraph. The Song ends with a heightened reprise of its opening materials, marked

Ex. 5.7 Vaughan Williams, 'A Song of Pity, Peace and Love' (*Six Songs to Be Sung in Time of War*), bars. 42–49[1]. 'A Song of Pity, Peace and Love' from 'Six Choral Songs to Be Sung in Time of War' by Ralph Vaughan Williams © Oxford University Press 1940. All rights reserved.

'Largamente' (Ex. 5.7). The materials are transformed into a compact, regular version that is closer to the schema model. This passage has the sound of a 'final chorus' in an earlier English cantata, such as the concluding patriotic hymns in Elgar's *The Banner of St George* and *Caractacus*; one could almost hear an organ entering here even in the version with piano. The passage could also be compared with the heightened, chorus-style versions of Elgar's unison-hymn-style tunes in Pomp and Circumstance No. 1, Symphony No. 1 (motto theme), and Enigma Variation XIV (see the discussion in Chapter 2). The two parts of the Victorian hymn schema are now presented much more tightly as antecedent and consequent phrases. The bass descent is completed to 1 and indeed continued for nearly two octaves, after which it ascends again stepwise, not only continuing the regular order of motions in the bass, but providing consistent contrary motion against the tune, which moves in exactly the opposite directions. In this sense too, the reprise is regularized, even though the rhythmic flexibility of the bass is preserved.

As is typical of Vaughan Williams, the vision unfolded in 'A Song of Pity, Peace and Love' is not the end of the 'composition' in the sense of the complete song cycle. Song VI ('A Song of the New Age') functions not unlike one of his symphonic 'epilogues' or the closing-off effects in his pastoral compositions, which leave the vision as a recollected ideal, not as present reality. Despite imagining 'A brighter Hellas' and 'Another Athens', the poet complains 'Oh, cease! Must hate and death return?' and even ends 'The world is weary of the past, / Oh, might it die or rest at last!' These are the final lines of the cycle, which hardly provide it with a rousing conclusion, and Vaughan Williams's music ends softly, turning to major quietly on 'die' to recall the vision. As such, the *Six Choral Songs* are a genuine Vaughan Williams art–music composition, with parallels in his major orchestral and choral works. From the composer's perspective, the choral unison hymn communicates to and through the people, spreading the word of great literature and high idealism with a popular touch.

The fact that *Six Choral Songs* was not even premiered at the Proms as planned because of unexpected defeat in war—an outcome that made the warnings against hubris of his early-war hymn texts look themselves hubristic—underlines the difficulties of this kind of approach to musical communication. Film music was more effective in practice, and for the rest of the war years Vaughan Williams turned in that direction for his more elaborate contributions. The next time he anticipated a positive outcome of the war, however, he was correct. *A Song of Thanksgiving* was written in 1944 in readiness for victory celebrations and for broadcast. It avoids subtle effects and is full of fanfare and vigorous processional gestures. The text is a bizarre compilation of Shakespeare, Isaiah, the Apocrypha, and Kipling (*Puck of Pook's Hill*), although it is a little less eclectic than the text of *Dona Nobis Pacem*. The opening fanfare outlines the antecedent element of the Victorian hymn schema, while the two passages in unison-hymn style ('And thou shalt be called "Sought Out"' and 'Land of Our Birth' for children's voices), both begin with the consequent element. Vaughan Williams's final unison-hymn composition was 'The New Commonwealth', which reprises a different set of schemata: big IV and rising fourth, the latter hardly found in Vaughan Williams's music since *A Sea Symphony*.

Cantatas

The choral festival commission was an obvious opportunity for communication. The occasion of the festival premiere was grand, traditional, and, for the amateur chorus members, participative. For forward-thinking musicians at least since the time of Parry, it had carried an ethos of spiritual ideals without religious doctrine. Parry led the way with his reformed choral works such as *Prometheus Unbound*, *Blest Pair of Sirens* and his ethical cantatas of the 1900s, while Vaughan Williams had contributed with *Toward the Unknown Region* and *A Sea Symphony*. Parry had told him to 'write choral music like an Englishman and a democrat', and composers now continued this principle for new, troubled times.

Two 'peace cantatas' stand out from the late 1930s: Vaughan Williams's *Dona Nobis Pacem*, premiered at the Huddersfield Festival in 1936, and Ireland's *These Things Shall Be*, broadcast by the BBC within its coronation programme in 1937, one day after the coronation itself. These compositions directly addressed the deteriorating European political situation with idealistic visions of peace and international harmony, including texts that quoted or alluded to the words of Isaiah. Both manipulated their texts strongly for the sake of a message; these are not 'settings' of texts that attempt to 'illustrate' them; the original text is a vehicle for a contemporary message that serves a cause beyond music. The *Times*' review called Vaughan Williams's cantata a 'tract for the time'. The work contained a 'message for to-day', which was 'the splendour and radiance of peace'.[18] Both works kept their messages simple and direct, and both relied heavily on musical conventions inherited from the nineteenth century, including diatonic conventions. In this way, they summoned the resources of their musical and cultural inheritance to spread a vision of the future. Both works have a moment of reversal of fortune (*peripeteia*) at which they suddenly find strength and hope. At this point the texts have the rhetorical repetition of the word 'nation' to indicate universalism and international solidarity. Both cantatas end with questions as to what the future will hold, asking for a practical response from the listeners.

Dona Nobis Pacem is a six-movement cantata with an eclectic and fragmentary text assembled from the Latin Mass, the Bible, Walt Whitman, and a parliamentary speech of the Victorian radical John Bright. Vaughan Williams revived or updated a setting of Whitman's 'Dirge for Two Veterans' that he had begun some twenty-five years earlier, before World War I and not long after *A Sea Symphony*. He also set Whitman's 'Beat! Beat! Drums!'. *Dona Nobis Pacem* is religious in much of its text and in its musical tone; its mood is at times devout, at others ecstatic. The great choral mass settings of the nineteenth century are evoked, especially the 'Dona Nobis Pacem' movement from Beethoven's *Missa Solemnis*, which Beethoven called a 'prayer for inner and outer peace'. Beethoven's urgent and anxious lament-style music for solo soprano for the very words 'Dona nobis pacem' and his martial music for brass instruments and timpani anticipate closely the tone of Vaughan Williams's two opening movements. Verdi's *Requiem* is also a point of reference, especially for the mood of terror and apocalypse in movements I and II. More generally, the explicitly redemptive role of intensive diatonicism in the cantata places it in a nineteenth-century tradition, which the otherwise syncretic text brings to focus with absolute clarity.

An example of the last point appears immediately in the first movement, an imploring setting of the 'Agnus Dei' text from the Latin Mass for solo soprano and chorus, initially laden with chromaticism and dissonance. Choral cries of fear follow on the single word 'dona' on a descending semitone motive that is a musical cliché for anxiety. The prayer for peace is granted by an interlude of purely diatonic peace and serenity before the music of the opening returns to conclude the movement gloomily. The movement thus presents a bold contrast of opposites and a complete transformation of mood that draws on traditional melodic and harmonic resources and does not trouble with any pretence of subtlety. In 1947 the composer remembered himself as a young man being for a moment 'properly shocked by the frank sentimentalism and sensationalism' of Verdi's *Requiem*. 'I remember being particularly horrified at the drop of a semitone on the word "Dona". Was this not the purest "village organist"?'[19] By 1936 he himself had no scruples in adopting this convention wholesale.

In 'Dirge for Two Veterans', the traditional signals are packed together in another moment of transformation as the funeral procession that dominates the movement gives way to a spiritual vision of universals and communion of souls, the living and the dead. Vaughan Williams responds to Whitman's 'big words' that cluster in the text at this point—'light', 'music', 'heart', 'love'—with part-song textures, soft trumpet calls, and diatonic counterpoint for strings with an image of ascent in the first violin part (Ex. 5.8(i)). The placing of this musical image in the interruption between settings of the words 'my veterans' (soloist) and 'My heart' (chorus) means that it seems to stand for the transcendence of death and for spiritual peace. In its musical style it anticipates the closing pages of Vaughan Williams's Fifth Symphony. With the imitation of distant trumpet calls and the diatonic counterpoint, the orchestra comments in almost Wagnerian fashion during the pause between vocal passages. As usual in Vaughan Williams's music, the ideal vision passes, and the music of the funeral procession returns to conclude the movement.

It is in the fifth movement (untitled) that *Dona Nobis Pacem* becomes most obviously a 'tract for the times', as fragments of texts of diverse origin are pieced together to further a new message for the present. From here to the end of the cantata, Beethoven's Ninth Symphony is the main precedent: there are recollections of the opening movement and its outcries of anxiety, phases of recitative for a solo baritone voice, and a fragmentary structure, all answered by a complete change of mood leading to choral rejoicing and a diatonic 'big tune'. Bright's words on the casualties of the Crimean War ('The Angel of Death has been abroad throughout the land') is replaced at the start of the sixth movement—the moment of reversal of fortune for the whole cantata—with words speaking of 'peace' from Daniel and Haggai. The sixth and final movement begins with one of Vaughan Williams's big set-piece round-singing-style episodes with octave/unison entries over a long tonic pedal. The key is E flat major, a return for the standard key for processional diatonicism in the English tradition before World War I, which Vaughan Williams had since neglected. The 'Victorian hymn' schema is outlined, mostly clearly in the orchestral introduction (Ex. 5.8(ii)). The text from Isaiah, 'Nation shall not lift up sword against nation / Neither shall they learn war any more', serves the peace movement of the 1930s, but it also roots the cantata in the English Old Testament oratorio tradition, linking prophet and people. The entry of the organ at this point underlines the genre: this is a 'choral festival' moment. The music now finds strength and hope, turning celebratory and diatonic, with text from the Gospel of St Luke ('Glory to

202 ENGLISH DIATONIC MUSIC

Ex. 5.8 Vaughan Williams, *Dona Nobis Pacem* (reductions) Vocal score: 'Dona Nobis Pacem' by Ralph Vaughan Williams © Oxford University Press 1936. All rights reserved. Full score: 'Dona Nobis Pacem' by Ralph Vaughan Williams © Oxford University Press 1936, 1971. All rights reserved.

(i)   IV ('Dirge for Two Veterans') fig. 27 bar 1–fig. 28 bar 2

Ex. 5.8 Continued

(ii) VI, fig. 34 bar 11–fig. 34 bar 23

God in the highest') and recollections of the 'Gloria' from Beethoven's *Missa Solemnis*. But as is usual in Vaughan Williams, the conclusion of the cantata is more questioning, with a return to the prayer-like music of the diatonic interlude of the first movement.

Ireland's *These Things Shall Be* shares many of the concerns and techniques of *Dona Nobis Pacem*. Premiered one day after Walton's *Crown Imperial*, it manifests a parallel resurgence of processional diatonicism, although its revival is that of the idealistic tone of pre-World War I choral works rather than Elgar's orchestral marches. If the big processional-diatonic episode at the heart of the cantata, setting the words 'Nation with nation', is not actually an allusion to *Dona Nobis Pacem*, then the text at least is surely an allusion to Isaiah, and the two cantatas are an instance of convergent musical responses. Ireland claimed that the work was 'an expression of British national feeling at the present time'.[20] By selecting lines from John Addington Symonds's Utopian poem 'A Vista' (1880), Ireland fashioned the textual underlay for an ultra-dramatic musical design in the manner of a nineteenth-century symphonic poem or programme symphony, with alternating of moods of anxiety, grim struggle, and grand diatonic redemption. The cantata portrays mental struggle and questions humanity's future. The whole-tone motive for 'Say, heart, what will the future bring?' is answered by splendid, assertive diatonic climaxes, resulting in an unsteady, overwrought, at times almost hysterical, effect that is not found in Symonds's poem. Ireland's setting places the big moment of reversal of fortune in such a way as to emphasize international political cooperation: again, sentiments that are not really conveyed by the sense of Symonds's unabridged poem. And whereas the poem definitely answers the question ('These things shall be.' 'They are no dream'), as does the title of the cantata, the music and the manner of setting the text leave things more doubtful. The final pages equivocate, and it is unclear how real the vision is supposed to be or whether it is left to the listeners to try to realize it.

These Things Shall Be is highly intertextual in its musical vocabulary. The main key is E flat major; there are outbursts of ecstatic counterpoint in 'choral-ode' manner, a Meistersinger tetrachord to set the very words 'These Things Shall Be' and an inverted tetrachord that follows the model of Elgar's 'Sabbath Morning at Sea' in tracing an ascending, modulating sequence. Parry-style 7–6 suspensions in the inner parts of choral textures are common. *These Things Shall Be* softly quotes the 'Internationale' (at the time a worker's hymn and the anthem of the Soviet Union), although Ireland replaced the melody after the initial broadcast performance.[21] Just before that moment occurs an allusion to the final elegiac reprise of the 'Spirit of Delight' motto theme from the finale of Elgar's Symphony No. 2.

The grand central section after the 'reversal' is a ripe and grandiose set-piece of English processional diatonicism, marked 'very broad and stately'. It appears that Ireland regarded this topic as the obvious vehicle for his Utopian vision, for he did not stint on it, apparently confident of its appeal, to put it in Milton's terms, to the listener's 'high-raised phantasy'. In vocal style, the passage lies somewhere between hymn and aria. After the orchestral presentation on strings (Ex. 5.9), the baritone soloist sings Symonds's stanza beginning 'Nation with Nation'. Ireland's intimate understanding of the idiom is evident in the pure diatonicism (one accidental in 19 bars in Ex. 5.9); intensive diatonic dissonance; stepwise bass motion; three-part contrapuntal texture with pairs of parts often moving in parallel sixths or tenths; dense application of open sonorities on secondary sevenths (ii^7, vi^7, iii^7, vii^7); the rising-fourth schema near the beginning of the tune, here complete with initial melodic 3 and a 'Blest Pair' 7–6 suspension (177^3–178^2); the rising-fourth variant that substitutes for a cadence in the manner of Elgar's 'Nimrod'; and an allusion to the 'Church' theme from Elgar's *The Apostles*. (Compare Ex. 5.9 bars 187–90 with Ex. 2.6, first four bars; compare also Ireland's earlier allusion in 'Ladslove' in Ex. 4.7.) Like 'Nimrod', 'Nation with Nation' is in a slow, triple metre with a tendency to duple groupings. 'Unto you that fear His Name' from Elgar's *The Kingdom* is also recalled, another piece in F major and triple metre with a *bel canto*-style solo vocal line. As shown in Chapter 4, Ireland had never been especially fastidious about differentiating his ways of diatonic writing from conventional Victorian tastes (see the discussion of his songs in Chapter 4). In 'Nation with Nation' the combination of sobbing vocal melody and pious sentiments again returns to the world of the Victorian drawing room.

Having long avoided the limelight and confined himself to solo songs and pieces for small instrumental ensembles, after World War II Gerald Finzi embarked on a more public career with a series of orchestral and choral works in answer to commissions from festival boards. The Three Choirs Festival premiered *Lo, the Full, Final Sacrifice* (1947), *Clarinet Concerto* (1949), and *Intimations of Immortality (Ode)* (1950), while the St Cecilia Festival—a charitable event in aid of musicians and their families—saw the first performance of *For St Cecilia: A Festival Ode* (1947). Perhaps through the influence of his friend Vaughan Williams, with whom he shared many interests, Finzi was able, in his choral works, to bring his vision of English musical tradition and of the legacy of Hubert Parry in particular to public attention. Although the underlying moods of *For St Cecilia* and *Intimations of Immortality* are opposite, both are 'odes' both textually and musically, the sound of the choral-ode subtopic being prominent. They call for the same forces: tenor soloist, chorus, and orchestra. Finzi's familiar processional elements (see Chapter 4) are all present, but they sit alongside allusions to Walton's music, especially in fast or

Ex. 5.9 Ireland, *These Things Shall Be*, bars 176–194 (reduction). © Copyright 1937 by Hawkes & Son (London) Ltd. Reproduced by permission of Boosey & Hawkes Music Publishers Ltd.

celebratory passages, in which Walton's *Belshazzar's Feast* (1931) is a rather immediate presence.

Between the premieres of these two cantatas, Finzi, a scholar of Parry's music and life, gave a 20-minute BBC broadcast on the centenary of Parry's birth on 27 February 1948 to introduce a Third Programme concert. He highlighted the choral, rather than the instrumental, works, admitting that they were mixed in quality, but that *Blest Pair of Sirens* was outstanding. Despite the well-informed perspectives that Finzi was able to bring, this was in effect a national broadcast of received wisdom within the English musical revival about Parry's status and his musical achievement, now made available to the general public. In his correspondence with Edward Blunden about the text of *For St Cecilia*, Finzi mentioned two of Parry's choral works based on texts of Robert Bridges: *Invocation to Music*, which has a theme similar to Finzi's *For St Cecilia*, and *A Song of Darkness and Light*.[22] The premiere of *For St Cecilia* might well be compared with the occasion half a century earlier when *Blest Pair of Sirens* was performed at the ceremonial laying of a foundation stone for a new building at the Royal College of Music by Prince Albert, later King Edward VII. The art and profession of music were again celebrated, with touches of the grand metaphysical vision, now in the Royal Albert Hall only a few metres from the College and in the same style of building in the 'Albertopolis' complex, by means of music of, at times, a remarkably similar style.

Finzi intervened in the composition of Blunden's text, guiding it in the directions of which he approved, and his music likewise guides the agreed-to text, somewhat neutralizing Blunden's efforts at humour. He was certainly in tune with the final hymn to St Cecilia's dream that 'bears the world along', and he set it in the manner of the choral-ode subtopic. It was St Cecilia who 'threw the palace open; and the throne / Blazed forth dominion of infinities'. By contrast, Blunden's nod to the eighteenth-century Augustan manner of Pope and Dryden is not really acknowledged in Finzi's setting, despite his interests in minor eighteenth-century English musicians. His emendations to the text resulted, by accident or design, in loss of the terms 'Britain' and 'Briton' (the latter a reference to Handel); only 'England' remains. The list of English musicians who followed St Cecilia includes John Merbecke, Byrd, John Dowland, Purcell, and Handel; Finzi replaced Arne and Wesley in Blunden's original with Dowland and Purcell, losing historical continuity in favour of an emphasis on the 'golden age'.[23]

Finzi's musical points of reference are not, however, the Tudor and Jacobean eras but Parry's choral style, Holst's processional manner, Elgar (moments from *Gerontius* and *The Apostles*), and Vaughan Williams's *Tallis Fantasia*.[24] Allusions to *Blest Pair of Sirens* are found throughout Finzi's own Ode, as Stephen Banfield has shown.[25] *For St Cecilia* has a three-flat key signature and ends in E flat major; the first choral entry with the main theme is also in E flat major. The succession of schemata at the opening (Ex. 5.10)

Ex. 5.10 Finzi, *For St Cecilia: Ceremonial Ode*, bars 1–9 (reduction). © Copyright 1948 by Boosey & Co. Ltd. Reproduced by permission of Boosey & Hawkes Music Publishers Ltd.

is standard, following the model of *Blest Pair of Sirens*, but the realization is somewhat oblique, in the fashion of chorale-ode-type passages in English diatonic music, despite the march and fanfare topics. The work is tonally eccentric in that it begins in A flat major. A stepwise descent in the lowest part in the texture proceeds all the way from degree 8 to degree 2, with a strong flavour of Meistersinger tetrachord in bars 1–2. The first 7–6 suspension figure of the rising-fourth schema is hinted at in bar 3 (C and B flat over the bass D flat), but the schema is not realized until bars 6–7, now in E flat major. The 3–2–5 figure is disguised within inner-part motions, but the pair of 7–6 suspensions over the bass 4–3 leaves no doubt about the family to which this progression belongs. The following bars (bars 8–9) turn to a more sweeping processional style in a three-part texture, reminiscent of both

Parry and Elgar. The rising-fourth schema is more obviously present now in the melody (bar 8), even if the bass A flat comes a little late for the first 7–6 suspension. In comparison with, for instance, the *Romance* for string orchestra (discussed in Chapter 4), the topical and schematic allusions of *For St Cecilia* are rather convoluted, in keeping with the public and ecstatic mood of the Ode genre.

The most memorable diatonic passages in *For St Cecilia* are in fact intimate, fragmentary ones for the tenor soloist with soft accompaniment, which recall passages from Finzi's Hardy settings (discussion at length in Chapter 4). At the rapt moment that introduces St Cecilia ('But where in all the saintly company'; fig. 10), marked *pp* sostenuto, 'molto meno mosso' and 'espress.', a more intimate Elgarian style appears, reminiscent of Elgar's *Wand of Youth* suites and 'Nimrod'. The recitative-like setting of this passage of the text quickly passes like a tiny allusion to a different world, recalling similar passages in 'The Too Short Time' and other Hardy settings. At its best, Finzi's fluid handling of his language in response to textual detail is brilliant, as always, though it can be breathless. In fact, *For St Cecilia* sounds forced and 'stiff' at times in a way that seldom afflicts Finzi in his Hardy settings.[26]

Finzi's second choral ode, *Intimations of Immortality*, is a remarkable concept. Wordsworth's ode is full of lines that have entered everyday English speech, but they are not obviously suited to musical realization. When *Intimations of Immortality* was performed for the second time at the Three Choirs Festival in 1951, the *Times* review brought up Parry, 'who first attempted the setting of metaphysical poetry in the form of a choral cantata'.[27] The critic might have pursued the link through Platonism. Milton's ode 'At a Solemn Musick', after all, alludes to the music of the spheres, which, according to Pythagorean doctrine, earthly humans in their material form can no longer hear. Yet, according to Milton, they may look ahead to a new 'attunement' with heaven as a result of the effect of music that sounds to their ears and its text. Wordsworth's premise that 'Our birth is but a sleep and a forgetting', updates the Platonic doctrine of *anamnesis*. Traces of Platonism in fact ran through English choral music of the era. Vaughan Williams had quoted Plato in the epigraph to *Sancta Civitas,* and in *Serenade to Music* he had set Shakespeare's lines on the music of the spheres from *The Merchant of Venice*. Elgar, Holst, and Howells favoured more general metaphysical interests. With the 1950 Three Choirs Festival, including a performance of Holst's *Hymn of Jesus* and the premiere of Howells's *Hymnus Paradisi*, Finzi's new cantata contributed to a festival of grand choral mysticism.[28] At the very opening, it appears that Finzi, like a poet beginning by appealing to the muses, tackles the challenge of Wordsworth's great ode by summoning the shades of his English precursors in mystical choral works. After the initial horn call, standing for immortality (itself a convention of English diatonic music, associated with eternity, resurrection, and apocalypse, discussed in Chapter 6 as 'deep call'), the following dissonant chords point directly to the opening of Vaughan Williams's *Sancta Civitas* and the widespread chords on string instruments to the opening of Elgar's *The Apostles*. The opening lines of the texts of those two compositions—'The spirit of the Lord is upon me' and 'I was in the spirit'—means that a coincidence is unlikely. A few bars later, the dissolution of Finzi's melody into clangourous bell-ringing effects again recalls the opening pages of *Sancta Civitas* and a later passage in the orchestral introduction seems to be an allusion to the 'Angel of the Agony' motive in Elgar's *Gerontius*.

Intimations of Immortality sounds a prevailing note of sadness that is largely absent from the other compositions considered in this chapter, which aspire to grand thoughts in their direct communication. The glory of the poet's former vision, after all, is irrecoverable. As such, Wordsworth's ode offers much opportunity for 'songs of pain and beauty', and to this extent Finzi's setting is an exteriorization of his solo song project. His compositional technique could handle such ambivalent moods; the fragmentary diatonicism for 'The Pansy at my feet', for instance, is in the style of his Hardy settings. Diana McVeagh hears 'melancholy mixed with grandeur' and notes the climaxes that 'die away slowly in overlapping imitations, a metaphor for "trailing clouds of glory"', both reactions pointing to an Elgarian sensibility.[29] Finzi recalls Vaughan Williams too in his preoccupation with eternity and the fading of the vision. However, there is no greeting from the celestial city here, with choirs of angels singing in round or processional bell ringing, only the 'eternal Silence'.

Finzi's keen awareness of, and debts to, established English diatonic practices is instantly evident in his setting of the opening lines of Wordsworth's long poem (Ex. 5.11). Finzi introduces a diatonic processional theme in the orchestral introduction: one of his steady plodding tunes, the bass moving stepwise in regular crotchets. In the introduction, it begins in a single-flat region (D minor with C naturals), a version that reappears for 'There was a time when meadow, grove, and stream, / The earth, and every common sight, / To me did seem': lines that occupy just four bars of Finzi's music. But the very next words—'Apparelled in celestial light, / The glory and the freshness of a dream'—seem to trigger, as it were, in the fastidious Finzi a musical response of 'choral ode'. After one transitional bar, the key of the processional music switches to a three-flat region and continues in the almost inevitable E flat major, now with choral voices joining the soloist in ecstatic counterpoint. The correspondence between key, texture, and sentiment is not exact: the ensuing choral climax occurs in B flat major, not E flat, before the ecstasy dies away and single-flat music returns. But this passage is nevertheless a remarkable example of Finzi's familiarity with the conventions, tonal, textual, and intellectual, of the diatonic tradition and his reliance on them to communicate, here by vividly realizing a textual detail. That said, this is hardly popular communication. Despite the ode genre, grand forces, and public occasion, there is something here of the aesthetic of a solo song that would normally be applied to a short lyric. Finzi could perhaps have expected members of the audience

Ex. 5.11 Finzi, *Intimations of Immortality*, fig. 4 bar 1–fig. 4 bar 11 (reductions). © Copyright 1950 by Boosey & Co. Ltd. Reproduced by permission of Boosey & Hawkes Music Publishers Ltd.

Ex. 5.11 Continued

at the Three Choirs Festival to have had some awareness of these references. Nevertheless, at these moments Finzi's music is a rather personal affair, aiming for the heights in a deliberately constrained language, and conducting a dialogue from afar with the music of Parry and Elgar.[30]

Vaughan Williams's Symphony No. 5

Vaughan Williams's Symphony No. 5 is without doubt a centrepiece of English diatonic music. Its critical reception has treated it as an almost religious experience in music and has attributed to it qualities of serenity, peace, and benediction. With hindsight, it stands out within Vaughan Williams's symphonic corpus, which otherwise, after the Pastoral Symphony, did not especially rely on diatonic conventions. The contrast with the violent and noisy Fourth (1934) and Sixth (1947) is extreme, even though the Fifth, alone among the composer's nine symphonies, was premiered and partly composed in wartime. The bleak or ambiguous signals of several of the composer's major works of the 1930s, such as the Piano Concerto (1931) and the one-act opera *Riders to the Sea* (1936), appear to be softened in the Fifth. The vision of peace is most apparent in the closing pages of the finale, and it is plausible to hear this passage as a celestial ascent in accordance with Vaughan Williams's interest in the musical representation of eternity and in light of the thematic connections of the Symphony with the music for his long-running Bunyan opera project, *The Pilgrim's Progress*, which was premiered eight years later in 1951.[31] One commentator has even called the Fifth a 'Symphony of the Celestial City'.[32] Alternatively, it might be said that, in the closing bars, Vaughan Williams sang the 'undisturbèd song of pure concent' that music, according to Milton, discloses to the 'high-raised phantasie'. He did so as the goal and culmination of a much longer, more ambitious, and more dramatic design than Hubert Parry attempted in his musical setting of 'At a Solemn Musick'.

The Fifth has the character of a deliberate position statement, a concise, articulate utterance for broad public reception. This is another composition with a message for its times, even though, owing to the lack of a text or programme, interpretation of that message is not straightforward. But the knowledge developed in this chapter of Vaughan Williams's contemporaneous activities and compositions can help. The Fifth aligns with the 'causes' that Vaughan Williams advocated doggedly in his everyday life in the years of its composition and with the music that he sometimes composed to support them. During World War II, Vaughan Williams espoused the policy of the newly established Federal Union, which called for a supranational body to control European defence policy.[33] The Symphony, begun in 1938, only two years after the premiere of *Dona Nobis Pacem* and in the year of the Munich agreement, returns to the themes of the cantata in a sometimes similar musical language. It also echoes the *Six Songs to Be Sung in Time of War* and draws on music that Vaughan Williams composed for a pageant to warn against suburban encroachment on the countryside. It transfers the tone of his music for these causes into the prestigious genre of the abstract Symphony. The hymn-like textures and melodic shapes that pervade the symphony emerge from the hymn writing and editing that were of course another cause that Vaughan Williams had pursued at various stages in his life, resulting in *The English Hymnal* (1906) and *Songs of Praise* (1925). Heard against the background of the conventions of English diatonic music, the Fifth stands out, furthermore, as an expression of the English Bach revival, another everyday concern of Vaughan Williams in his direction of amateur choruses.

Directly after its premiere, the Fifth was greeted as a summation of the composer's life's work. Viewed from the perspective of English diatonic music, the idea of a summation is a half-truth. To be sure, Vaughan Williams's subsequent major compositions—of which there were surprisingly many, despite his 75 years at the time of the Fifth's premiere—did not draw so deeply on diatonic conventions. In the Fifth, he used a broad selection of those conventions intensively and resourcefully, sometimes even blending them to create new, yet seemingly familiar, effects. Moreover, in the Fifth the conventions are drawn into a sophisticated symphonic 'plot' spanning all four movements. Vaughan Williams was successful in his handling of form in the Fifth, finding ways to accommodate his idiosyncratic musical language within a traditional symphonic framework in a way that he never surpassed or arguably even equalled, before or after. And by drawing together the English diatonic tradition and the genre of the abstract symphony, which since Beethoven had carried associations of grand idealism and humanism, and not least by adopting the key of the finale of Beethoven's Ninth Symphony, D major (also the key of his *Missa Solemnis* and much of Bach's Mass in B Minor, two of the pinnacles of choral-orchestral music), Vaughan Williams pursued revived classicism and channelled the English tradition into the Western historical mainstream. On the other hand, any idea that the Fifth is a summation of the whole English diatonic tradition is misleading insofar as it did not end with this work; the Fifth was far from the last inventive application of diatonic conventions or aesthetics. As we will see in Chapter 6, other composers, especially Howells and Tippett, continued its application in new and original directions in the later 1940s and the early 1950s and even beyond.

The symphonic character of the Fifth reflects a wider resurgence of interest in the genre of the symphony in mid-twentieth-century Britain; the dedication to Sibelius pinpoints the main model for British symphonies of that era.[34] Generative processes in the fashion of Sibelius are apparent from the outset: the first movement ('Preludio') begins indefinitely, before melodic fragments 'evolve' through a succession of variant versions, presumably in line with Vaughan Williams's understanding of the history of English folksong, gradually forming themselves into more complex shapes.[35] The redemptive plot typical of the symphony since Beethoven is broadly upheld by the Fifth. The tonal instability of 'Preludio' is finally replaced by the stable D major of the finale's coda. The serene ending of the Fifth in D major is more positive and less ambiguous than most of Vaughan Williams's symphonic endings and, of course, based on the evidence of Chapter 3, most of the endings of his major compositions in the pastoral style as well. At first glance, with this conclusion the teleological process of the post-Beethoven symphony appears to be completed successfully, the experience of eternity held fast.[36] However, as the following analysis will show, the symphony also records significant losses to set against its tonally stable ending, and in its manipulation of diatonic conventions, fading visions of eternity are no less characteristic of the Fifth, if perhaps less rhetorically underlined, than of earlier compositions Vaughan Williams based around a diatonic language.

Over its forty-minute time frame, the Fifth is one of the most consistently, even unremittingly, diatonic compositions of the English tradition. In particular, it is a symphony of grand diatonic climaxes: the secondary theme of 'Preludio', especially the version in the reprise; the three lament-like passages in the slow third movement ('Romanza'); and the grand processional and fanfare music of the finale ('Passacaglia'). The coda of 'Passacaglia' consists of forty-two bars in 4/4 metre at *moderato* tempo without a single accidental. But long stretches of less elevated music in the symphony are also largely diatonic, including much of the second movement ('Scherzo'), the passacaglia-style sections of the finale, and the early stages of 'Preludio'. In 'Passacaglia', the modal tendencies of the first three movements are replaced by a 'tonal' D major with leading notes, although dominant chords are still treated with circumspection and authentic cadences are avoided.[37] Vaughan Williams's favoured diatonic conventions are foregrounded, although cliché is avoided by tendencies to incompleteness and displacement (the complete version of a schema being avoided at a rhetorical climax or a moment of harmonic completion). Chromaticism is occasionally present, but as an antithetical force of the most obvious kind. The descending semitone motive, for instance, which left little room for ambiguity in the first movement of *Dona Nobis Pacem*, reappears as a destabilizing motive in the development section of the Fifth Symphony's 'Preludio'.

Relative to the post-Victorian tradition of English diatonic music as a whole, the Fifth largely adheres to the composer's favoured stylistic options and preferences. Aside from a processional, celebratory phase of music in 'Passacaglia'—a relatively brief episode—idioms and schemata associated with Parry and Elgar are neglected, in line with Vaughan Williams's stylistic changes around the start of World War I. In contrast with many other major compositions of this period, there are no Meistersinger tetrachords or rising-fourth schemata and there is no hint of either *Blest Pair of Sirens* or 'Jerusalem'. Instead, with folksong-like variants, round-singing effects, and hymn-like tunes and harmonic progressions, Vaughan Williams filled out his classical symphonic form with materials that could stand for a diatonic vernacular, the singing of the people. There is a measured return to some elements of the new pastoral topic: modality; melodic variants; direct switching between diatonic collections in the first two movements; piping effects on woodwind instruments in the last two movements; the intertwining of gapped-scale melodies in 'Romanza'; folksong stylization throughout 'Preludio' and in the trio-like central section of 'Scherzo'; and overall a taste for serenity. The passacaglia dance topic is something new, though: Vaughan Williams had used ostinato repetition as the basis for a movement but had not attempted a passacaglia of such a scale or complexity. Nevertheless, the choice of genre for the finale is another facet of Vaughan Williams's tried-and-trusted technique of repeating an entire melody at the unison or octave and adding further contrapuntal lines around it.

The related technique of imitative counterpoint at the unison or octave permeates the Fifth in all diatonic contexts. By implication, the historical practice of popular round-singing is everywhere the background from which the Symphony emerges, as a first evolutionary step in musical structure after pure (solo) folksong. Never before had Vaughan Williams spread this technique so extensively through a composition and through so many different tempi, moods, and materials, including fast music without an obviously vocal idiom. Example 5.12 shows only a selection of these passages, which dominate 'Preludio' in particular. Imitation of vocal-style writing appears throughout the symphony too. Some textures are hymn-like and some recall *a capella* vocal polyphony, but often there is an ambiguous blend of the two textures, especially in the last two movements. Resemblances to hymn tunes such as 'Lasst uns erfreuen', 'The First Nowell' (pointed out by the composer himself perhaps with some irony), and Vaughan Williams's own 'Sine Nomine' have been observed.[38] However, just as significant as these is the 'Victorian hymn' schema familiar from Vaughan Williams's unison hymns and from the redemptive final sections of *Flos Campi* and *Dona Nobis*

Pacem. It appears at heightened diatonic moments in the first, third, and fourth movements. Perhaps the most audibly prominent of all the diatonic conventions is the 'big IV', which is heard at the start of the secondary theme of 'Preludio' and, more obliquely, in the heightened passages in 'Romanza'. The grand, hymn-like, plagal progression associated with this schema, more than any of the other diatonic effects in the Symphony, surely stands for transcendence in some sense and perhaps for the 'big words' with capital letters found in *Dona Nobis Pacem* and the *Six Choral Songs*. (Certainly this was the case already in II, 'A Song of Liberty', from the *Six Choral Songs*.) Nevertheless, a definitive presentation of the big IV that is both confident in character and harmonically stable is not heard in the Fifth.

The first of the big IVs, the one that begins 'Preludio''s secondary theme, emerges from an evolutionary thematic process within the primary-theme section that assembles melody from fragments and variants. The process leads at first to a series of round-singing-style passages of octave or unison imitation (see Ex. 5.12(i), (ii) and (iii) for three such passages). After the lengthy opening paragraph dies away, the underlying dotted rhythm of the movement's opening horn calls resumes, and the secondary theme is sounded against it, giving the impression of a coherent thematic statement of measured melody and homophonic accompaniment at last emerging from the background of diverse, fragmentary motivic materials and the impression of semi-improvised collective singing. The texture is homophonic, diatonic, and broadly hymn-like; the melody follows the notes of the 'Alleluia' figures from 'Sine Nomine'.[39] An initial 5–6–5 melodic shape appears over the 9–8 suspension of the big IV, and the melody later moves from 8 down to 5 again, although the Victorian-hymn schema is only distantly evoked on this occasion. Plagal harmony dominates this passage. As the bass rises up the major scale, the harmonies that alternate with the tonic are elaborated subdominants, reversing the customary default harmonization of the bass 2 in such passages in Western art music, as formalized in the rule of the octave, which would have vii^6 or V$^4_2$ in that position. That default is the harmonization heard in the 'Do–Re–Mi' schema, which is often found in Elgar's diatonic passages and at the climax of the introduction to 'The Explorers' in Vaughan Williams's own *Sea Symphony* (passages discussed in Chapter 2).

Tonally, a sudden switch occurs at the start of the secondary theme to a four-sharp diatonic collection (here clearly implying E major), a 'bright' tonal effect in contrast to the single-sharp and three-flat diatonic regions of the primary-theme area. The glimpse of heaven, however, is soon eclipsed.

Ex. 5.12 Vaughan Williams, Symphony No. 5, instances of imitation at the octave or unison. 'Symphony No. 5' by Ralph Vaughan Williams © Oxford University Press 1946. All rights reserved.

(i)   Preludio, fig. 1 bar 1–fig. 1 bar 6 (Violin, Viola, and Cello parts)

(ii) Preludio, fig. 3 bar 8–fig. 3 bar 9 (Violin I and Violin II parts)

(iii) Preludio, fig. 4 bar 1–fig. 4 bar 4 (Violin II and Viola parts)

(iv) Preludio, fig. 6a bar 17–fig. 6a bar 18 (Violin and Viola parts)

Ex. 5.12 Continued

(v)   Preludio, fig. 10 bars 5–fig. 10 bar 7 (Flute parts)

(vi) Scherzo, fig. 2 bar 5–fig. 2 bar 7 (Clarinet and Bassoon parts)

(vii) Romanza, fig. 4 bar 13–fig. 4 bar 16 (Oboe and Cor anglais parts)

(viii) Passacaglia, fig. 4 bar 7–fig. 4 bar 13 (Clarinet and Trombone parts)

The secondary theme's continuation moves back to single-sharp territory, and its conclusion is indecisive, the third of the tonic triad omitted and the seventh lowered so that E minor is implied at the cadence: a 'collapse' into the local tonic minor. The recapitulation version of the secondary theme is ultra-ecstatic and almost vulgar: a note that Vaughan Williams very seldom struck. The scoring is brassy and fanfare-like with 'open' fourths and fifths in the wind parts; the diatonic dissonances are heightened by first-violin leaps into the highest possible register, somewhat in the 'feature-film' manner of Walton's *Spitfire Prelude* (Ex. 5.1(i)). Yet this passage is even more tonally unstable than in the exposition, beginning in B flat major but soon turning to G major and then G minor before ending on G without a third. A subdued coda follows, resuming the tonal ambiguity of the movement's opening. The attempted heaven-storming apotheosis of the secondary theme is therefore abortive, and the vision once again fades.

'Romanza' likewise tests out the big IV schema, searching for apotheosis time and again with high violin notes, full textures, and great diatonic 'waves', although it never realizes the schema as directly as the secondary theme of 'Preludio'. Vaughan Williams's own reference to the tune 'The First Nowell' is partly misleading here, even reductive, relative to his own music, as the straightforward plagal harmonies of that Victorian Christmas hymn are never sounded against the 8–7–6–5 melody in 'Romanza' until the very soft, benediction-like versions heard in the final bars, complete with 9–8 suspension (Ex. 5.13). Likewise, the similarity to the composer's own setting of the chorale 'Lasst uns erfreuen' in *The English Hymnal* does not extend to the literal big IV with 9–8 suspension that he applied thirty-five years earlier to the chorale (Ex. 5.14) until that very final moment in

Ex. 5.13 Vaughan Williams, Symphony No. 5, Romanza, fig. 11, bar 16–fig. 11 bar 18 (reduction). 'Symphony No. 5' by Ralph Vaughan Williams © Oxford University Press 1946. All rights reserved.

Ex. 5.14 Vaughan Williams, harmonization of 'Lasst uns erfreuen' ('Ye Watchers and Ye Holy Ones'), *The English Hymnal*, 519, bars 4^3–6^2. LASST UNS ERFREUEN arr. Ralph Vaughan Williams (1872–1958) from The English Hymnal. Reproduced by permission of Oxford University Press. All rights reserved.

the final bars. The movement's conclusion is reminiscent of similar soft and rapt big IV moments in the slow movements of *A Sea Symphony* and *A London Symphony*. By contrast, the many 'attempts' at more grandiose big IV moments in its three great diatonic orchestral waves are instead of the incomplete type found in *The Lark Ascending* and *Flos Campi*. Each of these instances of the incomplete schema must be heard relative to C major, but after a suggestion of an 'F major as IV' on a strong metrical beat, the overall A Aeolian tonality continually reasserts itself. The C major harmony of the implied plagal progression is never actually sounded. 'Romanza' in this way remains a lament full of 'deep breaths' and great 'sighs' rather than fulfilment. The tonal scheme of the movement directly parallels that of 'A Song of the New Age': A Aeolian with implied plagal progressions relative to C major, but turning to A major for the conclusion. A crucial difference lies in the fact that the 'Song' fully realizes its C major plagal progressions, whereas 'Romanza' does not.

'Romanza', no less than 'Preludio', is fluid and evolving: literal restatement is uncommon; variants abound; diatonic waves are progressively greater; sections are seldom defined by cadences. Although the three waves are the expressive centre of the Symphony, each a discharge of emotion that is carefully prepared—even 'staged'—by the preceding and intervening sections, in their structures they are ambiguous. The textures are something of a hybrid of contrapuntal polyphony and homophonic hymn. Individual harmonies are sometimes difficult to discern, given the free treatment of dissonance. The very first melodic phrase of the first diatonic wave resembles the complete Victorian-hymn schema (Ex. 5.15), although the antecedent component soon falls away in later iterations. The straight 8-7-6-5 in its 'Lasst uns erfreuen' or 'First Nowell' version does not appear in any of the later climaxes, where the complete melodic unit is, rather, a more extended

Ex. 5.15 Vaughan Williams, Symphony No. 5, Romanza, fig. 1, bar 1–fig. 1, bar 9 (Violin I part). 'Symphony No. 5' by Ralph Vaughan Williams © Oxford University Press 1946. All rights reserved.

stepwise descent to 3. In this way, the diatonic climaxes of 'Romanza' allude obliquely to diatonic schemata—several, in fact, at once—but do not realize them completely. By the end of the movement, the evaluation of gains and losses is not straightforward: the lament has turned outward and has found some collective, ritual form; yet the big IV schema and the 8–7–6–5 descent are fully realized only in a muted, detached manner at the very end.

'Passacaglia' steps out of the world of the earlier movements to some extent: the big IV schema is now absent; modality is avoided, and leading notes are present; the dance topic of the passacaglia theme and the strenuous processional version into which it develops foreground physical motion and human community rather than contemplation or heavenly visions. On the other hand, the movement continues and intensifies the Symphony's tendencies to octave and unison repetition, while the recurring melody of the dance evokes eternity in a new way. 'Passacaglia', moreover, continues the teleological processes of the rest of the Symphony and effects two phases of transformation. The first phase is the gradual crescendo and gaining of orchestral force over the first half of the movement, as the dance tune turns into a grand, celebratory procession with fanfare and a stepwise bass that regularly articulates the pulse. There is even a burlesque on the opening passacaglia tune in the manner of the apprentices' march from Act III of (and the Prelude to) *Die Meistersinger* and the 'Citizen' theme in Elgar's *Cockaigne*. It is as though the complete range of human society, extending from the noble to the humble, is included in the universal celebration. There is something here of Vaughan Williams's celestial processions from his pastoral compositions such as *The Shepherds of the Delectable Mountains* and the *Pastoral Symphony* (first movement; see Chapter 3), although this passage approaches Elgar's processional style more closely than Vaughan Williams usually did, with distant recollections of 'Enigma' Variation XIV.

This first transformation is not the final one, however. The processional music does not reappear in the second half of the movement. Although in its location within the movement it resembles a secondary theme, it is in fact already in the tonic key. The great crescendo therefore does not function as a sonata-form 'exposition' but has the monotonal structure of a recapitulation. At the end of the processional passage, the metre changes to common time and the passacaglia topic (in triple metre) never returns. Less than half of this movement is therefore in the metre and topic specified by its title. The monotonal, repetitious dance music of the opening, which could be deemed a 'first eternity', is superseded. By the end of the development-like middle section of the movement, materials from 'Preludio' return and the tempo of 'Preludio' then remains in place to the end of the movement, along with the 4/4 metre, although the mood, texture, and melodic materials are altered for the coda: the Symphony's final and decisive transformation.

The passacaglia theme itself (Ex. 5.16(i)) attracts two countersubjects, as they might be termed, which fit with it in counterpoint. Initially, they are played in direct succession in the first violin part (Ex. 5.16(ii)). These countersubjects recur frequently throughout the movement (see, for instance, Ex. 5.12(viii)). Just as in *Flos Campi* Section VI, also in D major, the countersubjects fulfil the Victorian-hymn schema's antecedent and consequent functions, the first rising from 1 to 5 and touching on 6, and the second falling stepwise from 8 to 5. Both end by descending stepwise to the tonic note, in another image of fulfilment and eternity. In the coda, a crucial permutation is made in these contrapuntal materials: the passacaglia melody itself recedes, and the countersubjects lead in their regular order (Victorian hymn antecedent / consequent). They are then repeated—always without intervallic transposition, thus at the octave or unison—in full on different

Ex. 5.16 Vaughan Williams, Symphony No. 5, Passascaglia, contrapuntal ingredients. 'Symphony No. 5' by Ralph Vaughan Williams © Oxford University Press 1946. All rights reserved.

(i) Passacaglia theme, bars 1–8^1 (Cello part)

(ii) Countersubjects I and II, bars 8–21 (Violin I part)

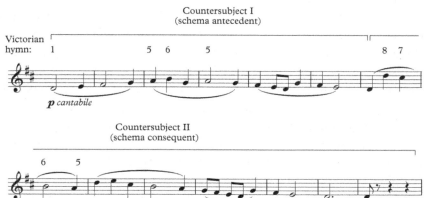

instruments with various contrapuntal elaborations in other parts in the manner of chorale-prelude writing. The latter genre is also recalled in the lack of authentic cadences to accompany the final tonic notes of the countersubject melodies: the other contrapuntal voices just continue on their way. The passacaglia melody itself appears only once in this coda, near the end, at a stage when the process of final motivic liquidation is already well underway, the countersubject melodies having been smoothed out into rising and falling scales of mainly even note values. The passacaglia melody is adapted to the quadruple metre, and almost nothing of the dance is left in it: the topic has turned altogether vocal in manner, with pastoral touches from woodwind instruments. The finale's topical transformation from dance to chorale prelude has been missed in the symphony's critical reception, perhaps on account of the coda's other direct and powerful signals, such as the imitation of multi-part vocal polyphony, images of celestial ascent, the plagal harmonic conclusion, and broad texture with strings split into 11 parts. The tone of this coda was in fact nothing new for Vaughan Williams, who had sounded it already in *Flos Campi* Section VI, in the 'hymn prelude' on 'Eventide' (1936), and, briefly, in the image of spiritual ascent and communion in 'Dirge for Two Veterans'. In analogy with that moment, the coda of the Fifth Symphony has the tone of music for 'big words'. Such words are unstated in the score, although they have certainly ben supplied in the work's critical reception.

In an essay entitled 'Some Thoughts on Beethoven's Choral Symphony', written concurrently with work on the Fifth Symphony in 1939 and 1940,[40] Vaughan Williams compared the approach to the divine in the choral works of Beethoven and of his 'beloved' Bach. Bach's theology was 'anthropomorphic' and did not seek the 'Supreme Being beyond the stars' but regarded God 'as the 'friend of souls', the Great King, the Bridegroom'. 'Beethoven when he looks into eternity sees clearer and further than Bach; but Bach when he thinks of his very human deity has the richer and warmer consciousness.'[41] Vaughan Williams was presumably thinking of Beethoven's unresolved diminished seventh chord and the sopranos' top G for 'Über Sternen muss er wohnen'. In this essay Vaughan Williams expressed—as ever—his personal preference for Bach, and he was evidently in tune with Bach's reliance on tradition and convention in spiritual matters. In his general compositional practice, Vaughn Williams's head ruled his heart in certain ways, as was evident in the always-fading visions of eternity documented in Chapter 3. In Symphony No. 5 he came closer to the Bachian end of the spectrum than usual, gathering the vernacular idioms of folksongs and hymn tunes that he found about himself in English musical life and infusing them into the genre of the abstract symphony. To be sure, Vaughn Williams by no means lost sight of the more contemplative, detached perspective of the 'intellectual' age of Beethoven down to his own present. Yet, the Symphony's decisive plot twist, as it were, is the replacement of the dance topic in 'Passacaglia' with chorale prelude. Contrapuntal materials and procedures remain consistent, but the original passacaglia's unison and octave repetitions of its materials are replaced by chorale-prelude-style unison and octave repetitions of those same materials, along with, of course, the instrumental imitation of vocal polyphony. In its topic and schemata, the coda recalls the hymn-prelude on 'Eventide' most strongly: a neo-Bachian treatment of materials drawn from Victorian popular sacred music. In this light, the ultimate evolutionary process of the Fifth—beyond even its gradual structuring of 'raw' folksong-like motives into images of round singing—is the transformation of stylized community-owned tunes (the two countersubjects in their Victorian-hymn format) into elaborate, highly crafted art music of spiritual aspiration.

Unlike most of the other compositions considered in this chapter, Vaughan Williams's Symphony No. 5 is an abstract work that does not carry a textual message. It was not composed for a commission, a celebration, or a festival, or even specifically for broadcast. But it shares much of the tone of Vaughan Williams's compositions for 'causes', along with the general 'outward turn' of this era—the tone of grand idealism, the urge for direct communication, the particular theme of 'peace', and the resurgence of diatonic conventions. In this sense it sounds like another 'tract for the times', one that adopts the teleological processes and the redemptive plot outline of the post-Beethoven symphonic tradition but fills the complex forms of the symphonic genre with what the composer understood as the materials of everyday community music-making.

6

The New Ecstasy

Howells and Tippett

At the same time that the mainstream of English diatonic music was turning outward and was directly engaging the public, two major personal projects in diatonic composition were emerging in the work of Herbert Howells and Michael Tippett, which took it in quite different directions. They again spanned the period from the late 1930s to the mid-1950s, but they did not present themselves as 'tracts for the times', being more aesthetically and spiritually conceived, renewing and intensifying the ecstatic tendencies of English diatonic music. Both contributions were serious artistic endeavours, more coherent and sustained than the mixture of cantatas, occasional works, unison hymns, and a symphony considered in Chapter 5. Both projects ended at about the same time in the mid-1950s, after which both composers moved largely in other directions, with only a handful of 'throwbacks' to come before their much later deaths in 1983 and 1998, respectively. Both composers developed distinctive personal styles within the diatonic language and pursued divergent paths in terms of purposes, genres, and the instrumental and vocal forces for which they wrote. Neither composer indulged in the conspicuous Parry allusions that were abundantly documented in Chapter 5, aside from some relatively oblique recollections in Howells. Instead, it was Vaughan Williams—who was personally well acquainted and professionally involved with both composers—whose music was a concrete presence and influence for both, especially as regards modality. These composers responded directly to the leading figure of the immediately preceding generation rather than Parry the 'grandfather'. The closing scene of Tippett's *The Midsummer Marriage* in particular is close to Vaughan Williams's practice in its choice of topical vocabulary—its selection from the stock of available diatonic conventions—and in their association with the idea of eternity. Vaughan Williams's death in 1958 may not have actually caused the termination of these projects, which by then were petering out anyway, but it certainly marked the end of an era.

The ecstasy of Howells's and Tippett's diatonic music reflects their shared religious temperaments, though neither was an adherent of any doctrine and in all probability neither believed in God in the conventional sense. Howells turned to the Anglican liturgical tradition, giving the evening canticles in particular an intimate, personal touch, whereas Tippett's imagery was pagan. Nevertheless, in both cases their music was informed by the psychology of religious experience, in Tippett's case guided by his readings in Jungian theory, and in both cases it is lushly sensual at times, with a strong feeling of eroticism at moments of glorious relaxation and abundance, which both composers unashamedly drew out by means of repetition. Even in the mid-twentieth century, then, the heaven-storming aspect of the Romantic legacy in music and its taste for apotheosis and transcendence in musical climaxes were still very much present, though now with an English diatonic accent. Moreover, both composers remained deeply concerned with 'song' in an ideal as well as a literal sense, just as Parry had been in setting the words of Milton's 'At a Solemn Musick'. For Howells this higher lyricism was connected with the medieval music revival, for Tippett with folksong and with opera and its history. Both, however, mixed this metaphor with another: in Howells's case celestial light, and in Tippett's, dance, resulting in distinctive patterns of interference.

Howells's New Style

Howells's diatonic music of the 1940s and 1950s was a broad synthesis of different aspects of the English diatonic tradition, as well as the opening of a new chapter in English sacred music. Howells's work emerged through two distinct but interrelated streams. At this time he composed abundantly for the Anglican liturgy, creating what became the backbone of the post-war repertory of Anglican choral music, especially in his settings of the evening canticles, of which Howells produced sixteen that were premiered from 1945 onwards. With these pieces, a few anthems, and a Te Deum, Howells effectively created the modern sound of Anglican choral evensong, a service that had been broadcast weekly on BBC Radio from the 1920s and was already a national institution. He was in great demand for the rest of his life from major churches in Britain and eventually the United States, which vied with one another to commission Howells's compositions. Howells met the commissions reliably, newly comfortable in a functional role and serving these institutions with well-crafted music for their everyday use, always paying attention to the acoustics of the buildings for which he was writing. At the midpoint of Howells's long career and after some troubles in the middle, both musical and personal, he had finally found his metier. The Howells style in Anglican choral music can be heard first in the four anthems of 1941 ('O Pray for the Peace of Jerusalem', 'We Have Heard with Our Ears', 'Like as the Hart', and 'Let God Arise') and then in the Te Deum and Jubilate 'Collegium Regale' for King's College Cambridge (1944); the Magnificat and Nunc Dimittis setting 'Collegium Regale' again for King's (1945) and the setting for Gloucester (1946); the motets 'Where Wast Thou?' (1948), 'King of Glory' (1949), 'God Is Gone Up' (1950), and 'The House of the Mind' (1954); the Magnificat and Nunc Dimittis settings for New College, Oxford (1949), Worcester (1951), and St Paul's (1951); and the Office of the Holy Communion 'Collegium Regale' (1956), which in part recycles material from the earlier King's settings. The texts of these pieces are in English, even when the titles are in Latin.[1] After the mid-1950s, Howells continued to write sacred music, but he developed a more austere style, which today is seldom heard in performance.

The second of Howells's two streams concerns fewer, but generally much bigger, highly dramatic choral-orchestral works that premiered at the Three Choirs Festival with texts mainly in Latin: *Hymnus Paradisi* (1951 but composed from 1938 and drawing on material from the early 1930s), *Missa Sabrinensis* (1954), and, a little later than the period covered here, *Stabat Mater* (1965). Howells's coronation motet 'Behold, O God, Our Defender' (1953), though much shorter, can also be counted in this stream. These works explore extreme and contrasted states of consciousness ranging from deep depression to ecstatic elation and employing the resources of diatonicism to convey the overmastering experience of celestial light. This was the vision of eternity for Howells ('lux perpetua') in diatonicism. At first glance similar to Milton's vision as realized by Parry, and occasionally reminiscent of the closing bars of Parry's *Blest Pair of Sirens* (setting the words 'eternal morn of light'), Howell's vision is in fact much more visceral, a musical analogy for blinding light, in which tonal harmonic function is disturbed and undifferentiated diatonic sonority obtrudes, as though consciousness is overwhelmed by a mystical experience of unity. In this second stream of composition, eternity for Howells became something 'other' like the 'numinous' in the psychology of religious experience as described a few years earlier by Rudolph Otto.[2] Howells's biographer Christopher Palmer indeed wrote of the 'luminous-numinous' in Howells, and also placed his characteristic harmony somewhere between 'consonance enhanced' and 'dissonance tamed'.[3] Such effects appear in the liturgical compositions too—the first stream—and there is overlap in effect, style, and diatonic conventions between the two streams, but they appear in the anthems and canticles in more modest and allusive guises, or simply as a light-touch sweetness.

Until Howells initiated his new project, Anglican choral music had been rather peripheral to English diatonic music. Although Parry had drawn on the Anglican choral tradition, he had done so selectively. Unlike his teacher Samuel Sebastian Wesley, he generally avoided liturgical composition, instead diverting Wesley's compositional approach through other channels. Howells's teacher Charles Stanford had made a major contribution to the Anglican musical repertory, including many settings of the evening canticles, but Stanford had not undertaken the stylistic purge of Mendelssohnian elements that was the starting point for Parry and almost everything that came after him in English diatonic music. Stanford's approach can still be heard in the canticle settings of George Dyson in the interwar period. But despite Stanford's description of Howells as 'my son in music' and Howells's undoubted respect for his teacher's professionalism, Stanford's music was not the starting point for Howells's new style. In the meantime, William Henry Harris (1883–1973) had anticipated aspects of it, especially in his still well-known motet 'Faire Is the Heaven' (1925), a piece rich in diatonic dissonance that recalls the idiom of Parry's recent *Songs of Farewell* (1918). Edgar Bainton's (1880–1956) 'And I Saw a New Heaven and a New Earth' (1928), another piece that has survived in performance, is in a similar vein. Harris and Bainton were hardly as prolific as Howells, however, and did not build on these efforts successfully. In comparison to these composers, Howells was more technically fluent and speedier in composition and drew more widely than they did on almost all dimensions of the English diatonic tradition. The idiom that resulted struck a new and unsuspected note in Anglican choral music, and one that today can too easily be taken for granted or even regarded as complacent. Adjectives that have been well used to describe Howells's later church music include sensuous, ecstatic, melancholy, intimate, and spiritual, although it is also conventionally majestic at times. The very familiarity of the 'Howells sound', his embrace of the Anglican liturgy, his copious productivity in canticles, his highly professional response to commissions, and his delivery of relatively easily performable work on time can obscure the originality of his artistic and spiritual vision.

Musical ecstasy in Howells's liturgical music can be heard most obviously in the Allegri-style, high-treble lines soaring over wide choral textures.[4] Sometimes the organ omits the notes of the treble line to enhance this effect, picking out only the alto part as its own top line for a while. Such passages tend not to be isolated moments but gather together in a series of dynamic 'waves' arising from melodic variants that hold the exalted state for a sustained period, usually against slow harmonic motion, rather scrupulously avoiding dominant harmony except occasionally at the end of sections for half cadences. The diatonic pastoral style of Vaughan Williams and Howells himself is an obvious precedent for this type of writing. Howells, as was always the case in his compositional career, was interested in 'mood' and in how it could be created, sustained, and modified. He sometimes switches between diatonic collections for different sections to make a cumulative effect, changing the mood but sustaining the intensity of the diatonicism. Musical ecstasy may also arise from the abundant and simultaneous diatonic dissonances that result in stacks of thirds and even seconds—phenomena at the brink of 'tone clusters'—creating interference in the sense-making of a listener relative to traditional triadic and seventh-chord harmony.

The grand, *largamente* conclusion of the Collegium Regale Te Deum (Ex. 6.1) shows most of these traits. The treble line stays around e♭" and tests out the shape f"–e♭" in four variant phrases. At one point, six of the seven notes of the three-flat diatonic collection are sounding against each other (bar 199), including a cluster of three notes separated by major seconds; this is at one level the outcome of stepwise motion in the parts, but the tempo is so leisurely that the listener also hears the moment as total diatonic sonority. The extract concludes a lengthy passage of lyrical, exalted, almost entirely three-flat diatonicism, which in turn concludes a piece composed of lengthy diatonic sections juxtaposed in palindromic form—three-flat, six-flat, four-flat, six-flat, three-flat—each sustaining a different but no less exalted mood. In the Collegium Regale Nunc Dimittis, the sombre, two-flat opening gives way to a sudden, radiant ascent to a high g" in the treble part and a switch to a one-flat diatonic collection with pentatonic tendencies (Ex. 6.2). Conventional wisdom and practice would warn against repeating this effect for fear of overworking it, but Howells does so immediately, with a similar melodic and harmonic approach and a similar falling figure after the climax, leaving an impression of waves of exalted sighs. The Sanctus movement of *Hymnus Paradisi* contains a passage that sounds like ritual bell-tolling or a procession, in which harmonic function is partly implied

Ex. 6.1 Howells, Te Deum (Collegium Regale), bars 190–203 (reduction). Te Deum (Collegium Regale) Liturgical Text and Music by Herbert Howells. Copyright © 1945 (Renewed) by Novello & Company Limited. International Copyright Secured. All Rights Reserved. *Reprinted by permission of Hal Leonard Europe Ltd.*

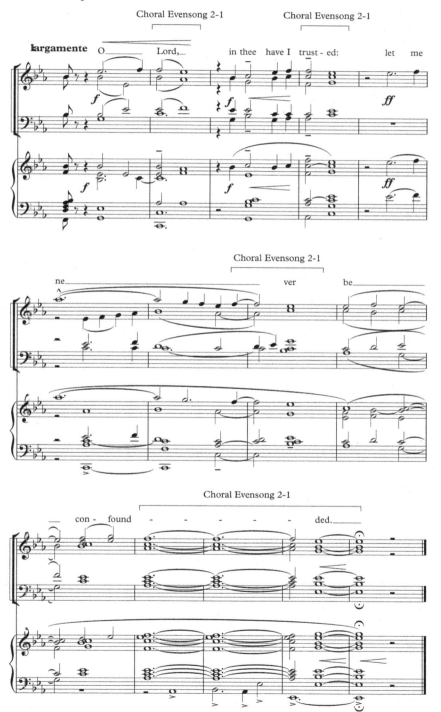

Ex. 6.2 Howells, Nunc Dimittis (Collegium Regale), bars 26–34. Collegium Regale 1945 Magnificat and Nunc Dimittis Liturgical Text and Music by Herbert Howells. Copyright © 1945 (Renewed) by Novello & Company Limited. International Copyright Secured. All Rights Reserved. *Reprinted by permission of Hal Leonard Europe Ltd.*

but largely overridden by the density of the tone clusters (Ex. 6.3). There is some sense of appoggiatura function in the 'snap' rhythms, which would indicate a consonance/dissonance distinction, and a stepwise descending bass line suggests harmonic changes, but there is little clear sense of whether the various harmonic functions (relative to E major) are tonic, subdominant, or dominant. The music inhabits a harmonically static condition within the four-sharp pitch collection, underlined by the elaborate range of dynamic and accent markings, leaving a sense of undifferentiated exaltation.

At times, as at the opening of the same 'Santcus', Howells favoured a combination of melodic syncopation, melisma, and pentatonicism and the three-part doubling of melodies for women's voices, which was already established—not least in Vaughan Williams—as a musical code for ecstatic experience.[5] His choral music is full of false relations at the seventh degree and alternations of major and minor thirds that sound like blue notes (the B♭s and B♮ in Ex. 6.2, for instance), but these are often harmonized in ways that, ironically, recall Delius. Howells pursued this approach thoroughly in *Hymnus Paradisi*, and it gives the notorious anthem 'Like as the Hart'

Ex. 6.3 Howells, *Hymnus Paradisi*, IV, 'Sanctus', fig. 36 + 5–fig 36 + 8. *Hymnus Paradisi*. Music by Herbert Howells. Copyright © 1938 (Renewed) by Novello & Company Limited. International Copyright Secured. All Rights Reserved. *Reprinted by permission of Hal Leonard Europe Ltd.*

(1941) its languishing, sensual qualities. It also appears in the canticles, especially in the Nunc Dimittis settings, including Collegium Regale (at 'For mine eyes . . .') and at the opening of the St Paul's Nunc Dimittis. Another Delian trait is Howells's penchant for florid pentatonic melody and harmonic stasis as a release of harmonic tensions arising from leading notes and tritones. This technique was vital for the powerful climaxes in Howells's major choral-orchestral works *Hymnus Paradisi* and *Missa Sabrinensis* and contributed to ecstatic release in his canticle settings and anthems too. The process occurs twice in Ex. 6.2 (the second to third bars of the extract and the sixth to seventh).[6]

Certain phases in the sung liturgy offered Howells opportunities for ecstatic passages that he took regularly. He developed a strong line in ending sections with broad, cumulative power: the first of these is perhaps the one in the anthem 'We Have Heard with Our Ears' (1941); the next is that of the Collegium Regale *Te Deum*, and then many of the 'Gloria' sections in the canticles. (In line with Western liturgical practice, the 'Gloria Patri' text is appended to the texts of both the Magnificat and the Nunc Dimittis; Howells often used the same or very similar music for these two passages.) By contrast, the earlier stages of many of the canticle settings are pervaded by more intimate, melancholy feelings, though still verging on the ecstatic. This is especially the case in the Nunc Dimittis settings, at or around the words 'To be a light to lighten the Gentiles' (as in Ex. 6.2), words that resonate with Howells's interest in the musical representation of celestial light. The allusion to eternity at the end of the Magnificat text ('Abraham and his seed forever') also elicits a range of effects, including, in the Winchester canticles, the complete three-flat diatonic collection sounding together for 'forever'. Howells was alert to the intimate nature of the canticle texts and often avoided the customary assertive opening for the Magnificat,[7] holding back strength for the Gloria Patri and bringing out the inward aspect of Mary's glorious vision of the future.

Howells's English Traditions: Medievalism, Vaughan Williams, and Parry

Howells has sometimes been linked with Anglo-Catholicism,[8] and he certainly shared something of the aesthetic of the Oxford Movement, including a taste for the Middle Ages, the sights and sounds of the medieval church, and an urge to revive them in the present. In his notes on medieval cathedrals, he imagines the New Jerusalem come down to earth in the 'pearly gates, priceless jewels, streets of pure gold and transparent glass (Rev XXI)'.[9] Howells responded to medieval Latin literature, which he knew from the research and translations of Helen Waddell. He set the Stabat Mater text in his last major composition at the age of 73, which had almost been waiting for him, resuming the theme of extreme spiritual experience that he had explored throughout the second half of his career. In his writing on plainchant, he noted the 'lack of the major-minorish nature of which most modern tunes are full' and the lack of leading notes.[10] Reflection on this music amounted to a kind of revelation, in which 'a new Heaven and a new Earth would flood my imagination and I w[ou]ld be ready to re-act to the ancient plainsong of the western Church'. In an all-embracing vision of musical unity—and eternity—the Tudors would finally 'make sense' to him, and he would be 'ready' to hear Vaughan Williams's *Tallis Fantasia* and to understand it as an answer to the questions raised by the modes and plainchant. The trombone melody at the outset of Holst's *Hymn of Jesus* would arouse in his imagination a 'panorama' of the medieval world, and he would see Alcuin, Bede, St Ambrose, Pope Gregory, Alfred the Great, and Charlemagne. Moreover, he would realize that they 'were linked up spiritually with our own Holst and Vaughan Williams'.[11]

However extravagant the connection between Vaughan Williams, Holst, and Pope Gregory may be, it indicates something of the holistic vision of transhistorical musical unity that came to Howells when his imagination was 'flooded'. It was not entirely without substance either, as witnessed by the organum effects at the opening of Vaughan Williams's *Tallis Fantasia* or the quotation of 'O Sacrum Convivium' in 'Love Bade Me Welcome'. In fact, the irregular metrical organization and florid vocal lines that were so characteristic of Vaughan Williams's pastoral idiom already indicated an affinity with plainchant and organum—rather more so than with English folksong—and Howells perhaps realized this affinity only belatedly. Unsurprisingly, then, the core of Howells's stylistic synthesis of English diatonic tradition was the modal-diatonic style that he and Vaughan Williams had already developed in the 1910s and early 1920s. (It could not have escaped Howells that in *Sancta Civitas* Vaughan Williams had used this idiom to set the words from Revelation that he quoted in his thoughts on medieval cathedrals.) The modality, avoidance of dominant harmony and leading notes, slow harmonic motion or even harmonic stasis, and paratactic formal approaches, such as variant writing, were sustained in his new style, with new effects of scoring and texture allowed by the chorus-and-organ format and by specific church acoustics.

236   ENGLISH DIATONIC MUSIC

The opening of the Collegium Regale Nunc Dimittis (Ex. 6.4) presents 15 bars of purely diatonic harmony and melody, the solo tenor melody resembling plainchant: the melody line begins, ends, and centres on a single note (b♭) moving in largely even note values, with mainly stepwise melodic motion interspersed with small leaps. There is little feeling of metre, the

Ex. 6.4 Howells, Nunc Dimittis (Collegium Regale), bars 1–15. Collegium Regale 1945 Magnificat and Nunc Dimittis Liturgical Text and Music by Herbert Howells. Copyright © 1945 (Renewed) by Novello & Company Limited. International Copyright Secured. All Rights Reserved. *Reprinted by permission of Hal Leonard Europe Ltd.*

notated metre changing frequently. The opening of the preceding Magnificat proceeds along similar lines, the eventual doubling of the melody line in 6/4 chords in the choir's female voices sounding a little like organum. This was again Howells's approach in the later canticle settings that to this day are his most frequently performed, those for Gloucester (1946) and St Paul's (1951), which are set mainly in 3/2 metre and in moderate or slow tempi, the accompaniment largely eschewing use of the organ pedals.

Howells did not favour intensive stepwise bass motion as such. Although secondary sevenths are sometimes found in the richer, climactic passages of diatonicism, he mainly steered clear of the schemata of Parry. The 7–6 suspensions in inner parts, so characteristic of the Parry idiom and its extensive legacy in English diatonic music—found abundantly at this time in Finzi, for instance—are seldom present in Howells's sacred music. Howells's main connection with Parry lies in the closing bars of *Blest Pair of Sirens* (Ex. 6.5) rather than its opening, which influenced almost everyone else in English diatonic music. Howells was in tune, after all, with the 'endless morn of light' that these bars celebrated. In *Blest Pair of Sirens*, Parry brought back his instrumental opening as a kind of closing ritornello, but with vocal parts present, to cap the closing fugue. Now even the B natural chromatic passing note of bar 2 is absent, and the diatonicism is pure. The harmonic emphasis is on the subdominant, the final cadence of the work plagal. The IV–I progression with the 1–2–3 figure in the upper line alludes to the closing bars of the Prelude to *Die Meistersinger* and of Wagner's opera as a whole. While the orchestra delivers the rising fourth schema, the highest soprano line in the choral parts picks up an inner part in that schema, which brings out a melodic 2–1 figure over first-inversion tonic harmony (fifth bar of the extract). The parallels with the closing bars of Howells's Collegium Regale *Te Deum*, also in E flat major with a massive texture, are obvious (Ex. 6.1). Parry's soprano phrase is almost quoted in Howells's setting of 'in thee have I trusted', and the melodic 2–1 is at the same pitch level as Parry's (f″ and e♭″). The organ part sounds Parry's final 1–2–3 figure and elaborates his plagal cadence, although Howells's soprano part sticks to the 2–1. In this light, one might even hear a reprise of the style of Wesley here, especially in the close diatonic dissonance already noted near the end of Howells's setting, which recalls the taste for piquant effects in Wesley's 'Amen' passages. Still, Howells' characteristic close dissonances for the representation of celestial light contrast with Parry's preferences for open sonorities and dissonances of the seventh and wider intervals. Moreover, the glaring consecutive fifths between alto and treble parts in bar 191 could

Ex. 6.5 Parry, *Blest Pair of Sirens*, fig. H + 30–fig. H + 38

not have been permitted on Parry's terms, let alone Wesley's; they point instead to the legacy of Vaughan Williams and Holst, and before them Debussy. Nevertheless, within the world of English diatonic music, the Te Deum works its way from a Walton-like opening—the allusion is to the recent *Crown Imperial*—to a massive, revelatory, Parry-like conclusion.

Howells's interest in the end of *Blest Pair of Sirens* rather than the beginning is confirmed by the finale of *Hymnus Paradisi*, 'Holy Is the True Light', which links celestial light, eternity, and E flat major. The key of E flat major does not feature prominently in earlier movements, while the finale begins in E flat minor: not at all a common pairing with E flat major in English diatonic music, despite the latter's ubiquity. Thus, the final and greatest climax of this work again has the quality of a revelation, recalling once more the closing bars of *Blest Pair of Sirens* in its reiteration of the pitches e♭" and f" in the soprano part ('Rejoice with gladness evermore'; Ex. 6.6). As is so often the case in Howells, the schemata found at the opening of *Blest Pair of Sirens*,

Ex. 6.6 Howells, *Hymnus Paradisi*, VI, 'Holy Is the True Light', fig. 71 + 4–fig. 72 + 1. *Hymnus Paradisi*. Music by Herbert Howells. Copyright © 1938 (Renewed) by Novello & Company Limited. International Copyright Secured. All Rights Reserved. *Reprinted by permission of Hal Leonard Europe Ltd.*

Ex. 6.6 Continued

Meistersinger tetrachord and rising fourth, which featured so abundantly in public-facing music of the diatonic tradition at this time, are not in evidence at all; rather, the 2–1 figure dominates this climax.

These comparisons point to a new schema that emerges in Howells's sacred music: the 2–1 appoggiatura in the treble part over tonic or subdominant harmony, or even a combination of these or substitutes for one or both. The numbers 2 and 1 refer here to scale degrees, not intervals above the bass. The figure appears at climaxes and has a grand, ecstatic effect, but also—as an appoggiatura—a yearning quality: a typical 'mixed mood' of the kind Howells favoured. Howells may not have invented this sound-image: aside from the inner part at the beginning and end of *Blest Pair of Sirens*, the 2–1 proliferates in Harris's 'Faire is the Heaven' (1925), especially in the closing bars. There are other grand appoggiaturas too in Howells in a tonic harmonic context: 4–3 over tonic harmony and likewise 6–5, but the 2–1 is the most common and the most tellingly placed. Although the distinction cannot be pushed too far, there are broadly two lines in this schema, just as in Howells's diatonic project as a whole, which could be termed the 'Choral Evensong 2–1'—as it is heard so often in the repertory performed at major Anglican churches at that service and contributes to its atmosphere—and the '*elato* 2–1', which occurs at euphoric climaxes marked '*elato*' in Howells's major choral-orchestral works. In the latter case, the 2–1 is usually combined with vigorous, fanfare-like, rising pentatonic figures in the orchestra that leap up ecstatically to 5–6.

The 6 is treated as being consonant within tonic harmony: a shorthand for 'pentatoncism' and an indication of momentary harmonic stasis and lack of direction. Textures are extreme, with chorus parts and most orchestral instruments packed tightly in a high register—the metaphor of blinding light from above is an inescapable analogy—and just a few strong low notes (including liberal use of the bass drum) briefly punctuating. These *elato* passages are not exactly joyful as such, but they amount to submission to overpowering force. They are also somehow redolent of grief, and thus they are a mixture of agony and ecstasy, in line with sentiments in the medieval Latin poetry that interested Howells. In both versions, but especially in the second, adjacent notes in the diatonic scale or even independent triads in close position may be stacked, the music maintaining only a tenuous connection with harmonic function and the distinction of consonance and dissonance. The 2–1s themselves tend to cluster in variant versions: a single one is seldom found in isolation. At the end of the Collegium Regale Te Deum (Ex. 6.1), the 2–1 figure, usually as an appoggiatura, is given four times in the treble part in different guises, always with diatonic harmony that contributes other dissonances too but avoids any hint of a dominant chord. In *Hymnus Paradisi*, the 2–1 in its euphoric version occurs at the greatest climaxes of the central Sanctus (Ex. 6.7) and the finale (Ex. 6.6). In Howells's day, the soaring top lines carrying the melodic 2–1 figure would have been sung by boy trebles in the liturgical music and by women in the choral-orchestral pieces, so the two versions distinguished here may have had subtly different sonorities in performance.

On only one occasion did Howells's project in diatonic music overlap with the repertory of official and occasional works explored in Chapter 5: the 1953 coronation motet 'Behold, O God Our Defender', which was used as the introit at the service.[12] This short piece, however, sharply contrasts with almost all other coronation commissions of the era. There is no celebratory tone, no Elgarian march or unison hymn topic, and no Meistersinger tetrachord / rising-fourth pairing. Instead the motet is an extreme experience that could easily be called numinous, moving from a sombre opening to a visionary climax and back, and suggesting in its closing bars a funeral procession. The central vision is an instance of consciousness-flooding in Howells, much like a blinding light from above, as a 2–1 figure moves from a low to a high octave and the diatonic collection switches from four-sharp to white-note diatonicism and back. In Howells's original version with orchestral accompaniment, the rising trumpet figures at this moment recall the passage in Wagner's *Parsifal* when the grail begins to glow red. With this piece, Howells's imagination seems to have been

Ex. 6.7 Howells, *Hymnus Paradisi*, IV, 'Sanctus', fig. 42 + 3–fig. 42 + 5. *Hymnus Paradisi*. Music by Herbert Howells. Copyright © 1938 (Renewed) by Novello & Company Limited. International Copyright Secured. All Rights Reserved. *Reprinted by permission of Hal Leonard Europe Ltd.*

captured by the thought of Westminster Abbey and the high vaults of its medieval architecture, a glimpse of the New Jerusalem, rather than the institution of the British monarchy or the occasion of the coronation.

Howells renewed the tradition of English diatonic music and gave it life within the Anglican church so that it became an everyday reality in performance, intimately familiar to generations of choristers, choral scholars, organists, and worshippers. Howells's interest in mysticism was not new in the tradition, nor even was his sensuality (Vaughan Williams's 'Love Bade Me Welcome' and *Flos Campi* had anticipated that), although he took them further and blended pleasure and pain, agony and ecstasy. Howells's conception of recent English musical tradition had to do with the revelation of something even grander: a vision of the origin of all Western music in Gregorian chant and the diatonic modes. His music too tends to be a gradual revelation through ecstasy, being often on the brink of dissolving harmonic function and logic. Howells, uniquely in the tradition, was more interested in grand endings than in grand beginnings and in working his way to them. At times Howells wrote music of extreme experience, a point that can easily be obscured by his apparently conventional persona and professional behaviours.

Tippett's Diatonicism

Tippett's compositional involvement with intensive diatonicism was the longest of any English composer, stretching nearly sixty years from the String Quartet No. 1 (1936–1937) to *The Rose Lake* (1991–1993; premiere 1995). Unlike Howells, Tippett did not apply intensively diatonic idioms in sacred music, and he worked it into a wider range of genres. The main compositions of this kind—also those most favoured in reception and performance down to today—are the *Concerto for Double String Orchestra* (1938–1939); the opera *The Midsummer Marriage* (1946–1952; premiere 1955), in particular the *Ritual Dances* from that opera, which premiered in 1953, two years before the full opera, and have since functioned in performance and recording as a separate orchestral composition; the *Fantasia Concertante on a Theme of Corelli* (1953); and the Piano Concerto (1953–55). Also relevant are passages from String Quartet No. 2 (1941–1942), Symphonies Nos. 1 and 2 (1944–1945, 1956–1957) and the Triple Concerto (1978–1979). The core of Tippett's work in diatonicism was *The Midsummer Marriage*, as much for its ambitious design and intellectual conception as for its compositional influence or even frequency of performance in the seventy years since its premiere. This was a grand opera, composed with an awareness of operatic theory and tradition, that also drew deeply on intensive diatonicism and invested in the idiom for radiant climaxes and imagery of transformation and transcendence. Tippett's musical aesthetic and approach to composition changed decisively in the late 1950s, and thereafter he did not invest so heavily in intensive diatonicism, although it did occasionally reappear in later works for moments of heightened expression in the old, familiar ways, even as it coexisted with more heterogenous materials. Before that change of style, it must be said that—despite the tone and concerns of much of the academic literature on Tippett—he adopted the diatonic tradition rather wholeheartedly. Even if some of his musical fingerprints were his own, his selection and application of conventions owed everything to recent English musical tradition, and to Vaughan Williams in particular.[13]

Tippett's intensive diatonic writing nevertheless developed within a more neoclassical aesthetic than the rest of the English diatonic tradition, with influences from seventeenth- century idioms, Beethoven, and Stravinsky mingling, along with 'jazzy' syncopations derived from cakewalk and ragtime,[14] and blue notes that also sound a little like 'English' false relations. He favoured three- or four-movement abstract instrumental cycles such as symphony, concerto, string quartet, and piano sonata, and he preferred clear phrase structures to the sprawling choral writing and metrically irregular passages of many other composers of the tradition. Processional diatonicism is largely absent from Tippett's work, as are schemata associated with Parry and Elgar, whereas familiar traits of Vaughan Williams's music, such as modality, folksong quotation or stylization, parallel 5/3 triads, false-relation effects, chorale-prelude textures, and stylized birdsong for solo violin are commonly found. Tippett's lively dance rhythms and lithe, strenuous instrumental polyphony were also new to the tradition, as was his 'crunchy' delivery of 4–3 inner-voice appoggiaturas ('snaps'), especially in harness with syncopations. In dance-like passages and elsewhere, Tippett, like Howells, did not avoid repetition, even, or especially, at heightened, ecstatic moments that are harmonically static and homophonic. The interval of the perfect fourth gives a characteristic sonority for Tippett in both melodic succession and harmonic structures, especially parallel dyads. Fast figuration, often based on these dyads, may function as 'rustle', like a 'sound surface', against which 'foreground' instruments make lyrical utterances, as in the 'Prelude' and 'Transformation' of the *Ritual Dances* or in the final pages of the finale of the *Concerto for Double String Orchestra*. In the latter, motoric rhythms turn into alternating-note figuration like the 'forest murmurs' in Wagner's *Siegfried*. Yet the physical vigour of Tippett's idiom does not finally override the primary metaphor of song—in the case of the *Concerto*, stylized folksong as the climax of the work—which is shared with the rest of the diatonic tradition. Example 6.8 shows Tippett's lively rhythms, syncopations, static harmony, repetitions, parallel 5/3s, and modally flavoured flat sevenths.

In *The Midsummer Marriage* and in other compositions by Tippett of the 1950s, intensive diatonicism serves dynamic processes of generation, transition, and transformation. This was a new function for English diatonic music, which reflects Tippett's interest in Jungian theory and its concept of 'individuation', the inner journey to psychological wholeness. Intensive diatonicism is now associated with natural cycles, sex, daybreak, and generation or regeneration from nature, although the old association with eternity remains in place too. The musical correlates include generative processes growing from silence or soft rustling into grand, vigorous climaxes, indicating wholeness and abundance; an emphasis on the intervals of the perfect fourth and the major second; and dance rhythms, especially fleet and lively. There is often, too, a 'magical' sonority and special scoring—for instance, celesta, flute, and harp—featuring high notes and bell-like sounds (Ex. 6.9). Given its later adoption by several composers after Tippett—described below in Conclusion and Legacy—this complex amounts to the final topic to emerge in English diatonic music, which may be termed 'magic wood', as that is the site of personal transformation in Act II of *The Midsummer Marriage*. The Prelude from the *Ritual Dances*, while not illustrating an actual sunrise on stage—that comes instead at the very beginning and end of the opera to different music—is in effect an ecstatic musical sunrise that recalls the sunrise music in Ravel's *Daphnis et Chloé*. Its radiant C major climax (fig. 148), despite a 'Lydian' raised fourth in the horns and a spattering of notes from outside the diatonic collection in the very high first flute part, is clearly intensively diatonic relative to the norms of mid-twentieth-century Western art music. The 'Transformation' music from the *Ritual Dances*, which occurs between each dance in Act II, begins with magical sounds associated with the strange temple shown at the back of the operatic stage set (Ex. 6.9), using free dissonance within the diatonic collections. This music is supposed to represent the mediation of conscious and unconscious realms of the psyche: the prerequisite for psychological wholeness. The Transformation music effects a change of diatonic collection from E flat major (three-flat diatonicism) to C major (white-note diatonicism; see the end of the fourth bar of the extract). Once C major is reached, clarity of figuration and vigorous dance energy emerge, especially in the parallel-fourth figures for trumpets.

In addition to such direct shifts between collections, a technique he shared with Howells, Tippett sometimes blends different diatonic collections in different instrumental groups, or he lets one emerge gradually while others recede. The presence of multiple diatonic layers means that his music sometimes has a recognizably diatonic sound without being confined to a single diatonic collection at a given moment. At the opening of the Prelude to the *Ritual Dances*, the magical sonority includes harp figuration drawn from a one-sharp diatonic collection and flute figuration drawn largely from a four-sharp collection. Trumpet and trombone outline a C sharp minor triad, adding a further layer that could belong to a three- or four-sharp collection. In a different context Tippett himself admitted using a '"layers of sound" technique' in the *Fantasia Concertante on a Theme of Corelli*, linking it with Stravinsky.[15]

Tippett liked to shift decisively between collections too, but his way of executing such shifts was unique: use of the raised fourth to move the conceptual major-mode diatonic collection 'sharpwards', as it were, around the circle of fifths. Tippett probably thought of this effect in terms of 'brightening', following the ideas of Vincent d'Indy.[16] The opening of the Piano Concerto is a big crescendo over several minutes of changing but locally static diatonic collections; it begins with tinkling magical music and generative melodic processes, with many fourths in the left-hand figuration and parallel-fourth right-hand dyads (Ex. 6.10). Although the key signature has four flats, the only D sounded is a D natural, and the right hand pushes further 'sharpwards' with its A natural near the end of the very first bar. By bar 4 the right hand reaches the next stage in the 'bright' direction with an E natural (its collection is now one-flat diatonic), while the left hand 'follows' a little behind with a D natural instead of its former D flats. The sunrise-like climax a few pages later pauses for big harmonic steps within five-flat (fig. 6), three-flat (fig. 7) and four-flat (fig. 8) diatonic collections, the latter presumably intended as the goal of the generative process, as it matches the diatonic collection indicated by the key signature. Another instance of the sharpward drift is found in Ex. 6.8.

Ex. 6.8 Tippett, *Concerto for Double String Orchestra*, first movement, fig. 3 + 10–fig. 4. Reproduced by permission of Schott Music Ltd. All rights reserved.

THE NEW ECSTASY 247

Some aspects of this style had precursors in English diatonic music. There was already a loose generative complex around melodic figures based on ascending fourths and seconds. The complex centred on collections of three or four pitch classes, thus it was 'not yet' diatonic in the generative process, at best 'tetratonic', like a 'first music' of nature. The opening cadenza of Vaughan Williams's *The Lark Ascending* is of this type (see the discussion in Chapter 3); it gradually broadens into pentatonicism before the composition

Ex. 6.9 Tippett, *The Midsummer Marriage*, 'Transformation' (*Ritual Dances*), fig. 152–fig. 152 + 6. Reproduced by permission of Schott Music Ltd. All rights reserved.

Ex. 6.9 Continued

moves on in its generative process to folksong, folk dance, and hints of sacred music. The metaphor behind the complex is of rising motion—that of the lark or the sun—not just of the bird's song. Melodic figures of this type appear in Vaughan Williams's music at all levels and were absorbed into his general melodic vocabulary. That is to some extent true of Tippett too: for instance, all three movements of the *Concerto for Double String Orchestra* begin with this type of melodic gesture, as does the second movement of the Piano Sonata No. 1. Sometimes Tippett adopted the solo violin figuration too, and in these cases he comes so close to Vaughan Williams that 'lark ascending' has in effect become a topic.

A second topic, which could be termed 'deep call', suggests a direct summons that comes from beyond even the earthly natural world, evoking a transcendent spiritual dimension, a call from eternity, possibly resurrection, apocalypse, the onset of mystical vision, or its recollection. In this form, the rising melodic figure resembles a fanfare more than birdsong, flight, or natural rustling; it is sounded softly but distinctly, sometimes in a solo instrument, either without accompaniment or against a very soft, sparse, atmospheric accompaniment. A single line rises through the scale degrees

Ex. 6.10 Tippett, Piano Concerto, first movement, bars 1–5. Reproduced by permission of Schott Music Ltd. All rights reserved.

5-1-2-5—or some close variant of this pattern that features ascending intervals of the perfect fourth and major second—in moderate, even note values. There is little sense of articulation of pulse, and we find little audible indication of metre. The figure appears especially at the opening of compositions or movements. It is found at the opening of Part II of Elgar's *The Dream of Gerontius* (Ex. 6.11(i)), indicating the soul's awakening to a spiritual realm without time or space; at the outset of the introduction (and in the Epilogue) of Vaughan Williams's *A London Symphony* (Ex. 6.11(ii)), before the Westminster Chimes announce a transition into everyday time (this instance is closer to the 'nature' end of the spectrum than Elgar's); at the opening of 'Holy is the True Light', the final movement of Howells's *Hymnus Paradisi*; at the opening of the *Sanctus* from Howells's Collegium

Regale Communion Service; and at the opening of Finzi's *Intimations of Immortality*. In the last case, the melody likely signifies 'immortality' and later sets the words 'our birth is but a sleep and a forgetting'. 'Deep call' can also be heard elsewhere in Vaughan Williams's music: in the offstage trumpet summons to Pilgrim before he plunges into the river in *The Shepherds of the Delectable Mountains* (Ex. 3.9); at the end of the E flat natural trumpet solo in the second movement of the *Pastoral Symphony* (Ex. 6.11(iii)); and at the crucial, redemptive moment in 'Dirge for Two Veterans' from *Dona nobis pacem* (Ex. 5.8(i)). In this guise as 'deep call', one can count the sunrise music from *The Midsummer Marriage* (Ex. 6.11(iv)), which follows and precedes words in the libretto about eternity. The music here sounds scale degrees 1 and 2 concurrently and 5 separately. The slow versions at the outset of the slow movements of Tippett's Piano Sonata No.1 and the *Concerto for Double String Orchestra*, both of which precede the Scottish folksong 'Ca' the Yowes', belong to the same melodic family, although they lack the obvious mystical or apocalyptic associations of the other examples.

Tippett's relation to English diatonic tradition was itself a kind of transformation: the preservation of some stylistic traits and conventions and something of the aesthetic associated with them, blended with other streams of influence. Tippett's concern had much to do with finding an individual voice in relation to relatively strong recent traditions, both English and, more generally, Western. Cultivating and broadening a faltering tradition in the manner of Vaughan Williams or establishing music as an ethical medium beyond entertainment or bad taste in the manner of Parry were no longer priorities for Tippett. Tippett was scrupulously concerned not to reject anything absolutely—on his Jungian terms that would have amounted to 'shadow projection'—but to recognize the strong and weak points of everything he encountered and build all his musical experiences into a synthesis.

Tippett and Vaughan Williams

Tippett's attitude toward and relationship with Vaughan Williams, both personal and musical, were of critical importance for his diatonic musical idiom. Vaughan Williams was in effect the leader of English music in Tippett's formative years. Some of the literature on Tippett can leave the impression that he rejected Vaughan Williams and his music, but that was hardly the case. According to his biographer, Ian Kemp, who must have had it from Tippett's

Ex. 6.11 The topic 'deep call' in English diatonic music
(i) Elgar, *The Dream of Gerontius*, Part II, bars 1–4

(ii) Vaughan Williams, *A London Symphony*, first movement, bars 1–3 (reduction). © Copyright Stainer & Bell Ltd, 23 Gruneisen Road, London N3 1DZ, www.stainer.co.uk. Reproduced by permission. All rights reserved.

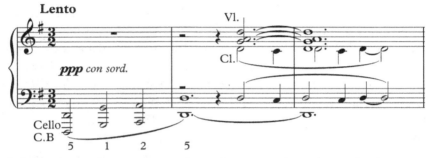

(iii) Vaughan Williams, *A Pastoral Symphony*, second movement, fig. G + 3–fig. G + 6, E flat natural trumpet part. © 1990 by Joan Ursula Vaughan Williams All rights for the UK, Republic of Ireland, Canada, Australia, New Zealand, Israel, Jamaica, and South Africa administered by Faber Music Ltd. Reproduced by kind permission of the publishers. *A Pastoral Symphony*. Music by Ralph Vaughan Williams. Copyright © (Renewed) by Ralph Vaughan Williams. International Copyright Secured. All Rights Reserved. *Reprinted by permission of Hal Leonard Europe Ltd.*

(iv) Tippett, *The Midsummer Marriage*, Act III, Scene 9, fig. 484 + 1–fig. 485 + 4. Reproduced by permission of Schott Music Ltd. All rights reserved.

mouth, he approved of Vaughan Williams's new compositional paths of the 1930s—by which time he had moved on from his strongly pastoral phase.[17] Tippett liked the opening pages of the *Tallis Fantasia*, but not the entrance of the solo viola or the music thereafter, which is in a pastoral idiom. He also liked the opening pages of the *Pastoral Symphony* but found the work as a whole tedious. He disliked the 'heartiness' of the scherzos of the *London Symphony* and the *Pastoral Symphony*. Nevertheless 'in general VW was a warm and fatherly figure',[18] and the two men developed a rapport. Tippett put on *The Shepherds of the Delectable Mountains* in 1927 with amateur performers at a time when the work was still quite new, and the composer attended the performance.[19] Vaughan Williams supported Tippett at his trial as a conscientious objector in 1943, describing his works as 'a distinct national asset';[20] and in 1956 he invited him to join the committee of the newly founded Ralph Vaughan Williams Trust, on which Tippett served for twenty-two years.[21] The two men worked together on saving the BBC's Third Programme in 1958, and, also in that year, Vaughan Williams attended the rehearsals and premiere of Tippett's Symphony No. 2, a work for which he expressed admiration in a private communication.[22] He, his wife Ursula, the composer, and the conductor Adrian Boult were photographed sitting together, Vaughan Williams at Tippett's side, as Boult consulted the composer on interpretation of the score.

Tippett and Vaughan Williams disagreed about Tippett's pacifism and conscientious objection and exchanged letters on the subject in which they preached at each other as though from soap boxes.[23] But this very fact indicates a degree of mutual respect and toleration of differences. Vaughan Williams must have been impressed by Tippett's work with amateur music groups, such as the local madrigal choir at Oxted and local opera productions, his conducting of cooperative choirs, and his role as director of music at Morley College beginning in 1940, a post that Vaughan Williams's close friend Holst had once held. In this activity Vaughan Williams would have recognized something of the approach to English musical renewal in which he believed and that he had attempted to pursue himself. In January 1944, Tippett invited Vaughan Williams to the premiere of his oratorio *A Child of Our Time*, his comments on the work pointing to an understanding of Vaughan Williams's attitudes and their overlap with his own: 'I think it[']s a work you will like—even the spirituals, I was going to say, are somehow brought within the tradition.'[24] The two composers also shared an intellectual background in Victorian evolutionist thought, in Tippett's case via James Frazer's historical anthropology and its wide subsequent influence. In

1970, Tippett praised 'what [Vaughan Williams] had accomplished both for himself and for us'. Speaking on a BBC television Omnibus programme on Vaughan Williams, he explained: 'I think now through him, as well as others, but through him especially we were made free.'[25] Read in one way, these sentiments make the elder composer into a redeemer. Tippett remained friends with Vaughan Williams's wife Ursula for decades, and, a few years after Vaughan Williams's death, he even proposed marriage to her.[26] It seems clear that, for Tippett, Vaughan Williams was the dominant figure of English music, overshadowing Parry and Elgar. Coming to terms with his work and legacy was a significant task conceptually and musically, and in Tippett's music of the 1940s and 1950s, that meant accepting much of what diatonicism meant for Vaughan Williams and working with it.

Concerto for Double String Orchestra

Tippett's *Concerto for Double String Orchestra* is at first sight quite neo-classical in layout, a conventional three-movement cycle of sonata allegro, ternary slow movement, and sonata-rondo finale. Many years after its composition, Tippett pointed to Beethoven as the model for the succession of movements in the instrumental cycle. In particular, he traced the 'song–fugue–song layout' of the second movement to the Andante of Beethoven's String Quartet in F minor, Op. 95.[27] He also identified the concerti grossi of Handel as an influence on the work's scoring. The ritornello-like gestures and motoric rhythms in the fast outer movements indicate a general 'Baroque concerto' aesthetic, though also a modern, neoclassical one. In fact, the scoring for double string orchestra is not that of a Baroque concerto grosso, and if anything it points to Vaughan Williams's *Tallis Fantasia*, especially when a solo violin is heard in the slow movement. Tippett admitted 'I attached myself partly to a special English tradition—that of the Elgar *Introduction and Allegro* and Vaughan Williams's *Fantasia on a Theme of* [sic] *Thomas Tallis*, both of which intermingle the intimacy of the solo string writing with the rich sonority of the full-string ensemble.'[28] This 'special English tradition'—the phrase itself indicating a convergence with Vaughan Williams's thinking—had been continued already in many compositions by Elgar and Vaughan Williams themselves and by composers such as Parry, Bridge, Warlock, Howells, Finzi, Bliss, and Britten. Few of them, however, had adopted such intensive diatonicism as Tippett in his *Concerto*.[29]

Tippett seems to have aimed for a continuous flow of energy in the outer movements. In the first movement, this effect is achieved partly through the contrapuntal textures. Counterpoint was a touchstone for self-consciously modern music of the interwar years, a neoclassical taste that stood against 'harmony', conceived, at least, as a sentimental, late-Romantic phenomenon. For Tippett something of this stance may have come through the private lessons he took with R. O. Morris. In composition, it was represented by Hindemith and by the compositional reception of the theory of 'linear counterpoint' of Ernst Kurth, as it was understood at the time. In 1958 Tippett wrote an essay on Hindemith's *Ludus Tonalis*, in which he discerned, amongst other things, a 'strong sense of tradition'.[30] Tippett's tendency to move the diatonic collection gradually 'sharpwards' is already present in the *Concerto*; this too plays into an anti-Romantic agenda, negating what Tippett, in a letter to his friend Francesca Allinson about English folksong, called 'German Schwermut'.[31] After all, the tendency to favour flatward modulation had been a defining characteristic of German Romantic music from Schubert onwards. The constant urge for 'freshness' and 'brightness' means that the *Concerto*'s diatonicism is unstable and fluid in its pitch collections.

Nevertheless, there are times when the 'flow' abates momentarily and the texture turns relatively homophonic, and these moments are easily perceived as 'ecstatic' (Ex. 6.8). Although the sound is on first hearing quite unlike that of Howells, there are some similarities. The harmony is static, the melody has a minor seventh degree and syncopations, it suggests a gapped scale, and it is doubled with parallel 5/3s. This is a momentary glimpse of a syncopated and harmonically static dance of joy, with a feeling of relaxation and enjoyment of existence rather than striving for attainment. The perceived metre changes too, groups of three minims temporarily replacing groups of two. Therefore, this passage briefly stands outside the temporality of the rest of the movement, before the ritornello reasserts the default.[32]

The *Concerto* lacks topical references to processional diatonicism or the new pastoral style, although it does employ modality throughout as well as folksong, both literal ('Ca' the Yowes' in the second movement,) and stylized (the coda of the finale). As noted above, at the start of all three movements, there are clear allusions to Vaughan Williams's melodic vocabulary by means of rising figures with perfect fourths and major seconds. However, Vaughan Williams's pastoral style avoids dominant harmony and the raised leading notes, which do not appear to have troubled Tippett, as well as rhythmic

Ex. 6.12 Tippett, *Concerto for Double String Orchestra*, third movement, fig. 45 + 3–fig. 45 + 7. Reproduced by permission of Schott Music Ltd. All rights reserved.

'snaps' of the kind found in the coda of the finale, figures historically associated with Scottish folksong rather than English.[33]

In fact, the coda of the finale, if it recalls any antecedents, is a little reminiscent of the coda of the finale of Mendelssohn's 'Scottish' Symphony, one of the few pieces in the standard repertory that introduces a new theme—also with a certain folksong-like tone—at the end of its finale. Like Mendelssohn's coda, Tippett's simulates the entry of a chorus with instrumental means. This is a heightened, lyrical, and ultra-diatonic passage with a largely pentatonic melody. It is prepared by something like an instrumental intake of breath. The string sonority of the final bars is strange (Ex. 6.12): as the music slows down on a tonic chord, a 'cow call' figure on scale degrees 6, 5, and 3 leads to a dyadic ending with only the pitch classes C and E sounded. This conclusion might suggest Grieg or Sibelius more than anything in the English tradition. It feels strenuous, sinewy, and 'outdoor', and is surely meant to signify 'joy' along with the whole of the coda, and even the whole finale. Ultimately, however, the coda is indubitably 'song', no less than the slow movement, despite the *Concerto*'s dance elements.

The Midsummer Marriage

The Midsummer Marriage is a central work in Tippett's compositional career, bringing together his intellectual interests in anthropology, symbolism, and Jungian thought and his diatonic musical language. Its magical sound and sonority influenced a number of other pieces, including Tippett's own (Piano Concerto, *Fantasia Concertante on at Theme of Corelli*, Symphony No. 2). The pagan imagery of Tippett's libretto, which includes the celebration of sex, the praise of the rising sun, and the fire dance described by James George Frazer in *The Golden Bough* contrast with the more frequently Christian imagery of English diatonic music to that point. The emphasis on the body and sex as the path to this eternity was new; in 'At a Solemn Musick', after all, Milton called the body a 'dead thing' which sacred vocal music, to its glory, was able to 'pierce', and there is little in the tradition to contradict that. Still, the opera's intellectual concerns were still about eternity and transcendence, and intensive diatonicism had always signified these things in the English tradition.

Diatonicism plays a key role in the ritual quality that Tippett hoped would percolate through the opera and almost become part of the action, blending with it seamlessly. His essay on the opera is infused with Frazerian evolutionary thinking that links sophisticated literary practices to earlier, 'primitive' rituals. He complained that 'Western music, at least since the convention of opera, moved quite away from the stubborn, primitive, hieratic element, as did all the sister arts'.[34] Tippett wrote of 'the transcendent or religious experience' on the stage, which it seems to have been his aim to bring back, and of the 'special music' that can present 'the poetic, theatrical moment which is out of time'.[35] There are passages of intensive diatonicism throughout the opera at moments of ecstasy. Some of these are in numbers for solo voices, such as Mark's aria in Act I and Madame Sosostris's in Act III.[36] But it is mainly the set-piece or 'ritual' parts of the opera, which are either purely orchestral or mainly choral-orchestral, that are significant for their intensive diatonicism. The *Ritual Dances* are in effect a separate orchestral piece, which shares little music with the sung portions of the opera and which was premiered two years before the opera was staged. The Prelude, Transformation music, and the first three dances occur in the largely nonvocal Act II to accompany on-stage ritual actions by dancers. The culminating Fire Dance occurs in Act III, along with the reprise of Transformation and the Prelude, which is directly followed by another passage of intensive diatonicism in the final scene of the opera. This Act III phase does include singing and limited plot actions, although little solo singing, thus mainly conveying collective experience.

The diatonic semantics of these sections is quite ramified, deriving from nineteenth-century musical Romanticism as well as from the English diatonic tradition. The Prelude's Ravel-like sunrise is an obvious allusion on account of the rich scoring, the gradual crescendo, the birdsong-like figures, and the rising trumpet figure that cuts through the texture at the climax. None of the three occurrences of the music in the opera, however—at the opening of Act II, later in Act II just before the first three ritual dances, as the lovers Mark and Jennifer kiss and enter the magic wood, and in Act III at the climax of the Fire Dance and the symbolic union of Mark and Jennifer—coincides with either of the opera's two dawn scenes. The magic wood is indicated by a passage scored for horns, which continues a venerable Romantic tradition. The horns' texture, though, is chorale-like and sounds like the music for a ritual procession as much as a sunrise, even if such a procession does not occur onstage during any of its iterations any more than a sunrise. The fast woodwind figuration changes its meaning between iterations. In Act II it suggests twittering birdsong or rustling branches, but in Act III it stands for the flickering of the flames of the kindled fires, and as such it recalls the 'magic fire' music from Act III of Wagner's *Die Walküre*, which Tippett mentioned in his essay on the opera as an instance of what music can do on an empty stage.[37] Transformation begins with the music for celesta and flutes that is associated with the temple and the 'Ancients' within it;[38] the 1–2–5 figure also suggests 'deep call'—here a call from the unconscious—and its generative possibilities. As the trees of the wood onstage begin to move (in the Act II iteration), the diatonic collection changes from three-flat to white-note. This is a typical nineteenth-century 'sound sheet', indicating nature. There is little sense of a consonance/dissonance distinction in either collection; rapid 'surface' motion makes general diatonic 'rustling' in a relatively static harmonic context.

The music of the final scene of *The Midsummer Marriage* is heard in performance much less often than the *Ritual Dances*, but it is here that Tippett draws most deeply on established conventions of English diatonic music. In some ways, this scene is little less than a tribute to Vaughan Williams, a point that may have been obscured by the general belief amongst music historians that Vaughan Williams's life and work were dominated by folksong and Tudor influences. Tippett's topical vocabulary in the finale is close to that favoured by Vaughan Williams, with references to round-singing, chorale prelude, deep call, and lark song on solo violins. The generation of musical idioms associated with the church (chorale prelude), first from nature (bird song) and then through the first human musical structure of canon at the unison, is very much in line with the evolutionary thinking of Vaughan Williams and has clear precedents in *The Lark Ascending*, the *London Symphony*, and

Symphony No. 5. Tippett surely had this passage in mind when, near the start of his essay on the opera, he alluded to the moment in Schiller's *Wilhelm Tell* when the author asks for the actors to leave the stage and sunrise to be represented with lighting. He believed this direction had never been followed because it could not be, but with music available, he thought, that possibility would change.[39] In his musical solution to this dramatic problem, he piled on allusions to recent English diatonic music. The moment of sunrise is met with a deep-call figure that specifically recalls another such figure and another musical sunrise: the opening of Vaughan Williams's *London Symphony* (compare Ex. 6.11(ii) and (iv)). Dawn breaks to the sound of not one musical lark but four, represented by four solo violins (Ex. 6.13). Their melodic figures are mainly tetratonic, like those of Vaughan Williams's lark, and they undertake a kind of avian round-singing with their canon at the unison. This was an eccentric topical blend that even Vaughan Williams never attempted. (The same kind of melody appears earlier in Mark's aria in Act I in which the text includes the actual phrase 'the lark ascending'.) Moreover, the birdsong is only one stage in a generative process that leads to a culminating allusion to sacred music,[40] just as in Vaughan Williams's conception in *The Lark Ascending* (see Chapter 2). In the remarkable passage that follows, three of Vaughan Williams's diatonic conventions are combined. As the four larks continue with their twittering, a much slower, hymn-like melody in long, even note values creeps in, thus turning the overall topic into chorale prelude. In the pauses between phrases of this melody—another chorale-like trait—Mark and Jennifer sing offstage with deep-call-style melismata. (Ex. 6.14 shows only the hymn melody on flute and the soloists' calls, omitting the rest of the busy texture.) The chorale-prelude texture returns in a grand apotheosis in the closing chorus to end the opera.[41]

The closing scene of *The Midsummer Marriage* was neither the first nor the last occasion on which Tippett activated this group of topics. In *A Child of Our Time* he had substituted spirituals for chorales. He used the chorale-prelude topic in the 'Intrada' from the *Suite for the Birthday of Prince Charles* (1948), using the hymn tune 'Crimond,' which had been sung at the wedding of Princess Elizabeth and Philip Mountbatten. This was combined with an opening deep-call figure, imitation of pealing bells, broad, diatonic open sonorities, and echoes of the finale of Vaughan Williams's Fifth Symphony, also in D major.[42] And fifteen years after *The Midsummer Marriage*, he brought the same elements redolent of Vaughan Williams into his *Shires Suite* (1970) for the Leicestershire Youth Orchestra, including canons in

Ex. 6.13 Tippett, *The Midsummer Marriage*, Act III, Scene 9, fig. 498–fig. 498 + 9. Reproduced by permission of Schott Music Ltd. All rights reserved.

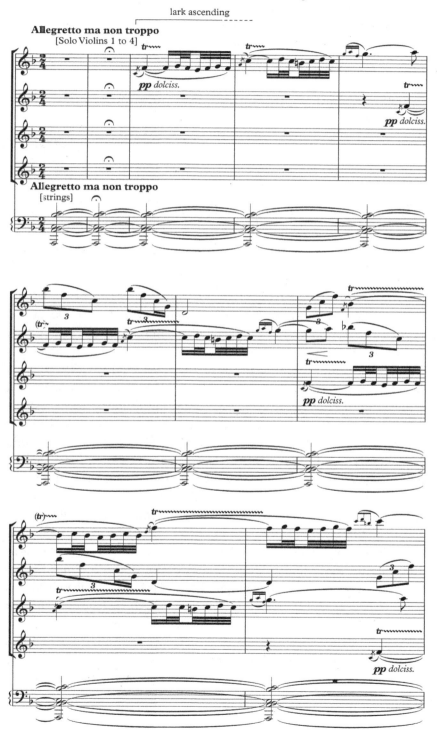

Ex. 6.14 Tippett, *The Midsummer Marriage*, Act III, Scene 9, fig. 501 + 2– fig. 504 + 2 (flute and solo voice parts only). Reproduced by permission of Schott Music Ltd. All rights reserved.

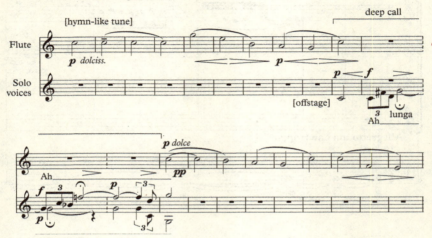

all the choral movements, with 'Sumer is icumen in' in the first; ascending-fourth fanfares; and a chorale-prelude-like ending for Byrd's canon 'Non nobis Domine'.[43] Vaughan Williams's own work at the time of the opera's composition, a time when the two men knew one another well, suggests a degree of convergence between them in the 1950s. Vaughan Williams had only deepened his concern with hymn tunes and chorale-prelude textures since the coda of the finale of his Symphony No. 5, for instance, in *Fantasia (Quasi Variazione) on the 'Old 104th' Psalm Tune* (1949), effectively a second Piano Concerto with chorus and orchestra; a setting of the 'Old 100th' for chorus, congregation, orchestra, and organ for the coronation of Elizabeth II in 1953; *Prelude on an Old Carol Tune* (1953) for small orchestra; and *Two Organ Preludes founded on Welsh Folk Songs* (1956). Vaughan Williams was not attempting anything as big in conception as the Fifth at this time, or as radiantly diatonic; in many respects, he was content to pursue his concerns with amateur music making. From this perspective Tippett continued something of the grand tone of Vaughan Williams's Fifth that Vaughan Williams himself had left behind but moved it into the Royal Opera House and put the diatonic conventions into the mouths of professional singers.

Vaughan Williams's music of course remained Christian in its sources and imagery in a way that *The Midsummer Marriage* did not. From this perspective, the chorale prelude at the end of the opera sits uneasily with its otherwise pagan imagery. Moreover, the chorale prelude represented a particular Protestant, bourgeois form of Christian worship. Vaughan Williams praised Bach as 'the great bourgeois'; his Bach was a working town musician from a family of town musicians who was in touch with the everyday piety of the townsfolk, their familiar domestic activities, and their songs of praise. These, in Vaughan Williams's view, he elaborated in extraordinary ways to make works of musical greatness. As noted in Chapter 5, Vaughan Williams confessed his instinctive sympathy with this approach in his essay on Beethoven's Ninth Symphony: Bach's approach to the divine via everyday forms was more congenial to him than Beethoven's more abstract and philosophical one. It appears that Tippett's natural eclecticism and desire for synthesis of influences overrode criteria of intellectual consistency when it came to the opera's final scene. Once again, in line with English tradition overall, he steered the diatonic music of transcendence back from the dance that had dominated the other set-pieces of the opera to song, and, furthermore, an ideal 'song' in the form of a wordless hymn that sounds against the literal singing of the characters on stage.

Fantasia Concertante on a Theme of Corelli

Fantasia Concertante on a Theme of Corelli, like *Concerto for Double String Orchestra*, is scored for a nonstandard string orchestra in a way that points to Baroque music. Nevertheless, the three-part division of the string ensemble recalls the Vaughan Williams *Tallis Fantasia* more than it does anything by Corelli or any other Baroque composer; groups labelled in the score 'Concerto Grosso' and 'Concertino' are supplemented by a 'Concerto Terzo', producing another double-string-orchestra composition, this time with soloists as well, just as in the Vaughan Williams work. The opening pages of the *Fantasia* are however modelled quite closely on Corelli, and the schemata are those of the eighteenth century, especially the descending bass tetrachord in minor, or 'Phrygian tetrachord'. Despite the stepwise bass, this schema does not appear in English processional diatonicism, which favours the major mode, and the central fugue likewise does not obviously draw on any of the diatonic conventions. All this changes, however, with the 'alla pastorale' section, an expansive outpouring of lyrical violin melody and one of the most luxuriant heightened passages of the whole English diatonic tradition. After the dramatic climax of the fugue that precedes it, this is a total transformation of mood, a release of tension, and a discovery of a secret, radiant inner world. Once revealed, the music dwells in this state, enjoying its richness and repeating its climaxes and sonorities.

It is unclear what the 'alla pastorale' has to do with the Corelli materials presented earlier in the *Fantasia* or why it 'belongs' to the work at all in any thematic or even general stylistic sense.[44] Its topics and schemata are those of the English diatonic tradition; Corelli's Phrygian tetrachords are shunned for its duration. First comes a passage of lark song for two solo violins in canon at the octave (Ex. 6.15). The F major key and 6/8 metre are the same as the parallel passage in the final scene of *The Midsummer Marriage*; in fact, the 'alla pastorale' could almost be a continuation of that music, albeit with only a lark duet instead of a quartet.[45] It is as though the Corelli business of the rest of the work is set aside to indulge a spinoff from the opera, which by the time of the *Fantasia*'s premiere had been composed but awaited performance. The energy of the lark music is discharged by means of a big IV marked *espressivo* with a dynamic swell in all parts, making a great 'sigh' and a feeling of relaxation. This passage approaches and even exceeds in lushness the big IVs in Vaughan Williams's *The Lark Ascending, Flos Campi, Serenade to Music,* and the 'Preludio' of Symphony No. 5 (see Exx. 3.13(iii), 3.8, and 5.13).

Between the big, sustained moments on tonic and subdominant harmonies, the alla pastorale even sounds echoes of Elgar and Parry. Elgar's *Introduction and Allegro* (a piece scored for a genuine concerto grosso ensemble) can be heard in a four-note melodic figure presented in a descending sequence similar to Elgar's, although with Tippett's characteristic doublings in perfect fourths. Tippett seldom evoked processional diatonicism in anything like the Parry manner, but it does appear fleetingly here, just after what the composer called 'the grandest climax of all' (fig. 45).[46] An ascending stepwise bass is harmonized with 7–6 suspensions and is given a broad string texture in the customary key of E flat major. This sounds like a momentary interpolation of music of a quite different diatonic idiom: rich, grand, and processional.

Overall, the *Fantasia* does not really come off as a musical composition. If it aspires to be a neoclassical work that updates and transforms the Baroque idiom of Corelli, then that agenda is simply set aside for the alla pastorale, which in its tone and mood comes to dominate the work.[47] The ensuing return to the Corelli materials to complete the composition in a lively fashion is anticlimactic after this powerful 'transformation'.

Ex. 6.15 Tippett, *Fantasia Concertante on a Theme of Corelli*, fig. 79–fig. 79 + 3. Reproduced by permission of Schott Music Ltd. All rights reserved.

Conclusion and Legacy

Howells and Tippett approached composition in the 1940s and 1950s with a keen awareness of the immediate English musical past and a sense of tradition. Their work continued the phenomenon of English diatonic music and remained invested in its broad concerns. At its outset, Parry's setting of Milton's 'At a Solemn Musick' had associated intensive diatonicism with ideal song and with eternity. Those associations remained in place for Elgar, Vaughan Williams, Gurney, Finzi, and Ireland. Howells and Tippett took them up, renewing the tradition for the mid-twentieth century, with a new interest in ecstasy and its expression through music. Many of the topics and schemata that had been established over the preceding sixty years were preserved, along with much of their established meaning. The status of intensive diatonicism as semiotically marked—a special musical idiom, set aside from perceived norms of the musical language—remained in place; this was a prerequisite for the expressive world in which these composers moved until the mid-1950s. With intensive diatonicism, Howells and Tippett, like their forebears, aimed to take listeners out of their everyday responses to music and make them feel or imagine some alternative state of elevation or exaltation. The idiom was conceived, from beginning to end, as a 'special music', as Tippett put it, 'out of time'.

By the late 1950s, the big projects in English diatonic music were complete, but through the later twentieth century its idioms could still be heard in abundance alongside other stylistic currents, as musical composition in Britain became increasingly eclectic. The accompanied choral music of Edmund Rubbra (1901–1986), including *The Morning Watch* (1941), *Song of the Soul* (1952), *Inscape* (1965), *Veni Creator Spiritus* (1966), and *Natum Maria Virgine* (1968), is deeply connected with the tradition of English diatonic music. Rubbra was a pupil of Holst and a devout Catholic with a taste for Bach and for chorales, whose choice of texts—St John of the Cross, Henry Vaughan, John Donne, and Gerard Manley Hopkins—and the idioms in which he set them reveal shared concerns with Elgar, Vaughan Williams, and Howells.[48] The main inheritor of Howells's choral mantle was John Rutter (1945–). On musical terms, however, Rutter could be described as a 'low-church' figure who pursued a synthesis of the choral tradition with jazz and popular-music idioms and did not work with the sprawling, plainchant-like lines of Howells or evoke a medieval atmosphere or eroticism. Rutter's ethos was something of a revival of the spirit of popular Victorian religion with which Parry and his successors had decisively broken. That said, on the rare occasions when Howells himself broke his ban on leading notes and dominant harmonies and tidied up his phrases into regular groups of bars, he anticipated Rutter, for instance, in the opening pages of his motet 'God Is Gone Up' (1950).

In the 1940s, Benjamin Britten (1913–1976) engaged with the history of English music, including diatonicism, folksong, Christmas carols, plainchant, and genres for amateur use in compositions, such as *A Ceremony of Carols* (1942) and the festival cantata *Rejoice in the Lamb* (1943), and in arrangements of John Gay's *The Beggar's Opera* (1948) and of British folksongs.[49] There was clearly some convergence with Tippett's direction of travel, although Britten's diatonicism was not as sustained in his compositional activity overall, and its semantics were rather different, given Britten's strong personal interest in the idea of innocence under threat. That sensibility hardly featured elsewhere in English diatonic music either before Britten or in his time. Britten did not pursue the ecstatic possibilities of intensive diatonicism as Howells and Tippett did; instead his diatonic passages tends to be drawn into dramatic schemes and musical antitheses. Britten's technical polish worked against the sprawling tendencies of most other musicians in the tradition, and his legacy for later British composition lay in other areas.

In orchestral music, Tippett was regarded as a leader in British composition by the late 1950s, and elements of his style were widely adopted. The two main influences were the *Concerto for Double String Orchestra* and the *Ritual Dances*. The legacy of the *Concerto* can be heard in compositions such as Elizabeth Maconchy's (1907–1994) Symphony for Double String Orchestra (1953), William Mathias's (1934–1992) Divertimento for String Orchestra (1958), and, much later, John McCabe's (1939–2015) *Pilgrim* (1998) for double string orchestra. *Pilgrim* also recalls the *Fantasia Concertante on a Theme of Corelli*; its last climax reiterates the melodic figure from the big IV progression of the 'alla pastorale'. The *Ritual Dances* were even more influential than the *Concerto*, especially the characteristic sonorities and figuration of 'Transformation', with its scoring for celesta and woodwind. In later British compositions, those instruments are often joined by the harp, which plays a major role in the 'Prelude' and elsewhere in Tippett's *Ritual Dances*. The enchantment of the topic 'magic wood' as it is termed here drew Mathias in the third movement of Symphony No. 1 (1966); in the opening pages of Concerto for Harp and Orchestra (1970); at the opening of the first of his *Celtic Dances* (1972); and in *Laudi* (1973). It can be heard in places in all seven symphonies by McCabe, at the opening of *The Chagall Windows* (1974), and in *Concerto for Orchestra* (1982). The third movement of the Mathias Symphony is an interesting conception that recalls the processional music and climax of the Introduction from the *Ritual Dances*, along with Tippett's characteristic 'brightening' modulations, plus studied allusions to the coda of the finale of Vaughan Williams's Symphony No. 5. For Mathias there was evidently no conflict between these influences in what is a highly tradition-conscious synthesis. The movement sets out on a spiritual journey of transcendence by means of conventions handed down from composers of the last two generations.

Tippett himself returned to intensive diatonicism—as well as to pastoralism—in his final major composition, an orchestral piece entitled *The Rose Lake: A Song without Words for Orchestra* (1995). The piece takes as its subject Lake Retba in Senegal, where the algal waters shine pink in bright sunlight. The work alternates vigorous sections led by percussion with passages of serene lyricism, each beginning with strong signals of intensive diatonicism. The first of these passages, in which, according to the composer's programmatic score markings, 'the lake begins to sing', is in E flat major. In a note for the first recording of *The Rose Lake*, Tippett explained 'the idea that took shape gradually was that some kind of lyric utterance would burgeon within the design, initially polarized against a sharper, more pungent element, but ultimately reach a climactic stage where song reigned supreme'.[50] Tippett's sound world might have moved on from Parry's in his setting of Milton's 'At a Solemn Musick' over a century earlier, but the association of intensive diatonicism with elevated, ideal song remained with him to the end.

Glossary of Conventions of English Diatonic Music

Schemata

2–1: Found in choral music, especially that of Howells. The scale degree pattern 2–1 in a soaring treble part occurs over tonic or subdominant harmony or a combination of the two or a substitute. Often reiterated in different guises. The 'Choral Evensong 2–1' is found in Howells's liturgical works for chorus and organ, whereas the '*elato* 2–1'; is found in his choral-orchestral compositions at euphoric climaxes in connection with the marking *elato*, usually with leaping pentatonic figures in orchestral strings.

Big IV: A grand and ecstatic or in some way portentous subdominant chord with 9–8 appoggiatura or suspension (occasionally 7–6). The IV is usually followed by I, making a grand plagal progression, although sometimes another harmony such as vi substitutes for I in a more elusive version.

Do–Re–Mi: Venerable schema dating back at least to the eighteenth century. In English diatonic music, it is used in the version with the rising 1–2–3 in the bass rather than the treble. The uppermost voice in the texture will usually proceed 8–7, although it may not return to 8 as was customary in the eighteenth century, instead descending to 5, with Handelian echoes. Typically found at the opening of themes or sections.

Liebesmahl mediant fifth drop: A descending melodic leap from degree 7 to degree 3 in a major-key melody, with mediant harmony (iii) or even a cadence in the mediant key. Redolent of Wagner's *Parsifal*; can be heard in the 'Liebesmahl' music at the opening of the Prelude; during the communion ceremony in Act I; and in the ensuing communion song 'Wein und Brot', which appears to have been a model for many instances of unison hymn in English diatonic music (see Appendix A). In Parry's 'Jerusalem', the fifth drop occurs on the word 'England's'.

Meistersinger tetrachord: The most common schema for opening phrases of themes or movements. Stepwise bass motion 8–7–6–5 takes place beneath a sustained tonic chord or at least minimal harmonic activity; typically the texture is thick and massive, and the bass is doubled in octaves. Derives from the opening of the Prelude to Wagner's *Die Meistersinger von Nürnberg* and the opening of Parry's *Blest Pair of Sirens*.

Open sonority: The harmonization of a bass scale step (usually 2, sometimes 6) with a diatonic minor seventh chord, or sometimes with a 6/3 chord with a strong emphasis on an appoggiatura or suspended seventh. The spacing of the voices will leave 'gaps' in the upper parts, the smallest intervals being fourths; the interval above the bass will usually be at least an octave and often a tenth.

Plagal tritone: A realization of the bass 4–3 step with 5/3 and 6/3 chords and 'churchy' ascending passing-note motions in one or two inner parts. A diatonic half-diminished seventh chord with an augmented fourth results as a 'passing harmony'. Often found in Victorian hymn settings and at plagal 'Amen' cadences.

Victorian hymn: A melodic schema. Its two components are defined by melodic shape, often, though not always, clearly separated as phrases. The first (antecedent) rises, directly or indirectly, from degree 1 to degree 5 with the pattern 5–6–5 conspicuous; the second (consequent) descends, often stepwise, from 8 to 5. Modulation to the dominant may occur in the consequent. Origins lie in the chant 'O sacrum convivium', the Lutheran chorale 'Wachet auf', and in many Victorian hymns.

Rising fourth: A rather complex but very recognizable schema based around a characteristic realization of the bass 4–3 step. The uppermost part typically rises by the interval of a fourth from 2 to 5, often preceded by 3 (thus 3–2–5), 3–2 being the resolution of a 7–6 suspension, literal or implied. Often, as in the classic case near the opening of Parry's *Blest Pair of Sirens*, there is a pair of 7–6 suspensions, the second occurring in an inner part once the melody has leapt up to 5. Occasionally, the rising fourth leap may be inverted to a falling fifth. The schema typically functions as a second or 'later' event in a phrase or theme (it is not harmonically suited to the role of opening a theme). Thus, it has something of the function of a 'riposte' in the galant style. Antecedents are found in Victorian sacred music.

Topics

Choral ode: A subtopic of processional diatonicism. Typified by a contrapuntal choral texture of an elevated and ecstatic mood with grand rising melodic figures, ample diatonic dissonance, and a text of praise or expansive sentiments, usually on a metaphysical subject. Schemata tend to be realized obliquely, with much embellishment, similar to 'figurative' language, in contrast to the other subtopic, unison hymn.

Chorale prelude: A complete hymn tune or hymn-like tune sounded in long note values, while other parts freely add contrapuntal embellishments in faster note values. A Bachian allusion. Sometimes found in organ music (as in Bach) but may be a textural allusion in orchestral compositions. Often the tonic note at the end of a phrase in the main melody is, characteristically, not harmonized with the tonic chord, and the embellishing parts continue. One of Vaughan Williams's modes of diatonic contrapuntal writing that rely on reiteration of a melody at the unison or octave levels.

Deep call: Soft, fanfare-like rising figure, foregrounding fourths, fifths, and whole-tone steps (e.g., 5–1–2–5). Presented as though from afar; sparse, static accompaniment or none at all. Redolent of eternal things, a call from 'beyond', resurrection or apocalypse. Sometimes linked also with earthly sunrise. The first instance is found at the opening of Part II of Elgar's *The Dream of Gerontius*.

Lark ascending: Rhythmically free, cadenza-like passages for one or more solo violins with soft, static accompaniment of strings. Strongly ascending motions, especially based on 'tetratomic' collections, that is, subsets of the diatonic collection with four pitch-class elements, thus 'pre-pentatonic', an original music of 'nature'. Imitation of both the ascending flight of the lark and its song. Associations with dawn and with human spiritual aspirations. Original instance heard at the opening of Vaughan Williams's *The Lark Ascending*.

Magic wood: Soft, harmonically static passage typically scored for celesta, harp, and 'murmuring' high woodwind. Sometimes 'dancing' figures in parallel fourths. Derives from Tippett's *Ritual Dances* and Act II of his opera *The Midsummer Marriage*. Allusions are found in orchestral music of the later twentieth century, which lie largely outside the scope of this book.

Processional diatonicism: By far the most common and characteristic diatonic topic in English music after 1887. Defined by stepwise bass motion within a conspicuously diatonic, major mode harmonic context and an uplifting mood. The diatonicism will be 'intensive', that is, standing out relative to the standard harmonic style of nineteenth-century tonal music. By default a public mode. The bass motion may articulate the pulse, thus tending to march-like rhythms and 'walking bass', or it may be merely step*wise* in its motion. Intensive use of diatonic dissonance (multiple suspensions, appoggiaturas, etc.) is typical, although not definitive. Associated with a set of schemata gathered from nineteenth-century sources and presented in synthesis in Hubert Parry's *Blest Pair of Sirens* (1887), which defined the topic and stamped it with Miltonic associations of spiritual elevation.

New pastoral: One component of a broader, novel overall approach to pastoral music in the 1910s. Free, unmeasured, quasi-improvisatory melodic lines, often for wordless voice or solo instrument, suggestive of plainchant; mixture of duplet and triplet quavers. Often freely intertwining melodic lines and chamber-music textures. Modal, pentatonic or 'gapped-scale' collections; consecutive fifths and parallel root-position triads; strong avoidance of leading-note function and dominant harmonic function. Occasional imitation of cow calls, shepherds' piping, or stylized folksong. In contrast to traditional pastoral topic, dance rhythms, compound duple metre, and the doubling of melodic lines in thirds are not central.

Round singing: A tune presented in imitation or canon by different instruments or voices at the same pitch level or under octave transposition. One of Vaughan Williams's modes of diatonic contrapuntal writing that rely on reiteration of a melody at the unison or octave levels. Scoring may be purely instrumental, the 'singing' thus metaphorical. On an evolutionary account of music history, this texture may connote a first level of musical structure after 'pure' solo folksong. Round singing was regarded historically as a peculiarly English musical practice by historians of the late Victorian and Edwardian periods.

Unison hymn: A subtopic of processional diatonicism. Either a regular marching bass beneath a simple, mainly stepwise melody of even note values, or a throbbing accompaniment of repeated triplet chords to a more fluid melody. Intensive diatonic dissonance is less characteristic of this subtopic than of choral ode, and schemata will be realized more directly. Both types of unison hymn tunes may allude to 'Wein und Brot', the communion song from Act I of Wagner's *Parsifal* (see Appendix A). Texts or contexts are idealistic and may be patriotic and populist. The tune may be instrumental, without voices, but if so it will imply a vocal setting and may acquire a text later.

Motives

Inverted tetrachord: The rising line 3–4–5–6 in major as a discrete melodic motive in the highest voice, usually in the context of a massive texture and processional topic. In its usual and 'regular' position, it functions as a follow-up to the default Meistersinger tetrachord, a descending figure presented by the bass.

Cherry tree: Melodic motive roughly of the form 8 (long)–7–6–4–5 in imitation of the opening vocal phrase of George Butterworth's 'Loveliest of Trees'. Usually a deliberate intertextual allusion. Elegiac associations with the transience of beauty and life. May memorialize Butterworth or others who suffered untimely deaths, especially in war.

Keys

A♭ major: The key of Elgar's *The Apostles* (largely) and Symphony No. 1 and, overall, of Wagner's *Parsifal*. Occasionally used after Elgar with direct allusion to *The Apostles*.

E♭ major: By far the most common key for processional diatonicism. Not associated with the other diatonic topics. Derives from Parry, *Blest Pair of Sirens* and probably from 'Wein und Brot', the communion hymn from Wagner's *Parsifal* (see Appendix A). Sometimes G major appears alongside it, in line with Parry's main secondary key in *Blest Pair of Sirens*.

D major: Associations both stirring/patriotic and spiritual (peace, attainment of a spiritual goal or the heavenly city). Elgar, *The Dream of Gerontius*, conclusion of both parts; Pomp and Circumstance March No. 1 and First Symphony, third movement; Parry, 'Jerusalem'; Vaughan Williams, *Flos Campi*, Section VI, Symphony No. 5. The key of spiritual monuments of Western art music, especially choral, for example, Bach, 'Gloria', 'Sanctus' and 'Dona Nobis Pacem' from Mass in B minor, Beethoven, *Missa Solemnis*, Symphony No. 9, finale; Wagner, 'Good Friday Music' from *Parsifal* and the triumphant statement of the 'Parsifal' motive near the end of Act III.

APPENDIX A

The Grail Knights' Communion Hymn 'Wein und Brot' from *Parsifal* Act I as 'Begetter' of English Diatonic Music

APPENDIX B

'Regular Orders' of English Diatonic Conventions

Stepwise Bass Motion Descending / Ascending

Within the context of the topic 'processional diatonicism'. Canonical examples include the opening of the Communion hymn 'Wein und Brot' from Wagner's *Parsifal* (see Appendix A) and the opening of Parry's *Blest Pair of Sirens*. This order usually indicates a lofty or spiritual tone.

Meistersinger Tetrachord / Rising Fourth

This pairing is found at the opening of Parry's *Blest Pair of Sirens* and is the most common schematic script in English diatonic music. The pacing of the concatenation may vary: tight and loose versions are possible, spanning only a few bars or many bars.

Meistersinger Tetrachord / Inverted Tetrachord

Found at the opening of the Prelude to Wagner's *Die Meistersinger*. The first component is often found without the second in English diatonic music, so when they are presented together there may be a notable sense of completeness or of direct Wagnerian allusion.

Do-Re-Mi / Plagal Tritone

This succession reverses the usual order of stepwise bass motion, as it begins with rising motion before briefly descending at the second schema, although these models are often obscured. Favoured by Elgar, for example, 'Enigma' Variations, Symphony No. 1, motto theme.

Victorian Hymn Antecedent / Consequent

Favourite arrangement of Vaughan Williams, dominating his concept of 'tune' in the second half of his career. The two components may be presented and extended separately (still in the 'regular order') before being brought together (*Flos Campi*, VI). They may be presented in loose, elaborated versions (still in the regular order), which are then tightened into a closer association ('A Song of Pity, Peace and Love'), with a more hymn-like effect. Alternatively, they may be presented as 'countersubjects' to another melody, before later assuming their regular order as first and second components as the outcome of a teleological process (Symphony No. 5, 'Passacaglia').

Notes

Introduction

1. See, for instance, Robert O. Gjerdingen, *Music in the Galant Style* (New York: Oxford University Press, 2007); Job IJzerman, *Harmony, Counterpoint, Partimento: A New Method Inspired by Old Masters* (New York: Oxford University Press, 2018); Giorgio Sanguinetti, *The Art of Partimento: History, Theory and Practice* (New York: Oxford University Press, 2012).
2. For instance, Wye Jamison Allanbrook, *Rhythmic Gesture in Mozart: 'Le nozze di Figaro' and 'Don Giovanni'* (Chicago: University of Chicago Press, 1983); Leonard G. Ratner, *Classic Music: Express, Form and Style* (New York: Schirmer, 1980); V. Kofi Agawu, *Playing with Signs: A Semiotic Interpretation of Classic Music* (Princeton, NJ: Princeton University Press, 1991); and more recently for an overview, Dauta Mirka (ed.), *The Oxford Handbook of Topic Theory* (New York: Oxford University Press, 2014).
3. This book describes the repertory as 'English' rather than 'British', although the two concepts are complexly intertwined. The musicians described themselves and their music as English for the most part. The self-styled English music revival contributed to the first phase of English cultural nationalism, which arrived late on the European scene at the end of the nineteenth century, long after British nationalism. Krishan Kumar, *The Making of English National Identity* (Cambridge: Cambridge University Press, 2003), Chapter 7 ('The Moment of Englishness').
4. Maconchy probably came closest to the style in *Proud Thames*, an overture for the coronation year of 1953, but diatonic music was not her main interest.
5. Bennett Zon, *Evolution and Victorian Musical Culture* (Cambridge: Cambridge University Press, 2017); Jeremy Dibble, 'Parry as Historiographer', *Nineteenth-Century British Music Studies I*, ed. Bennett Zon (Aldershot: Ashgate, 1999), 37–51; Jeremy Dibble, 'Parry, Stanford and Vaughan Williams: The Creation of Tradition', in *Ralph Vaughan Williams in Perspective*, ed. Lewis Foreman (London: Albion Press, 1998), 25–47.
6. This thinking is in line with Jay Winter, *Sites of Memory, Sites of Mourning: the Great War in European Cultural History* (Cambridge: Cambridge University Press, 1998).
7. On Parry. see especially Jeremy Dibble, *C. Hubert H. Parry: His Life and Music* (Oxford: Clarendon Press, 1992).
8. Christopher Palmer, *Herbert Howells: A Study* (Borough Green, Sevenoaks: Novello, 1978); 14.
9. Frank Howes, *The English Musical Renaissance* (London: Secker & Warburg, 1966), 24–25, 262.
10. Ralph Vaughan Williams, *National Music and Other Essays* (Oxford: Oxford University Press, 1962; 2nd ed., 1987).
11. David Manning (ed.), *Vaughan Williams on Music* (New York: Oxford University Press, 2008); Hugh Cobbe (ed.), *Letters of Ralph Vaughan Williams 1895–1958* (New York: Oxford University Press, 2008).
12. Meirion Hughes and Robert Stradling, *The English Musical Renaissance 1840–1940: Constructing a National Music*, 2nd ed. (Manchester: Manchester University Press, 2001), 76, 77, 79, 99.
13. Ibid., 82.
14. Alain Frogley, 'Rewriting the Renaissance: History, Imperialism and British Music since 1840', *Music & Letters* 84/2 (2003), 241–57 (pp. 249–51).

Chapter 1

1. The term 'topic' was made familiar by Ratner in *Classic Music*. My understanding of processional diatonicism overlaps with what James Brooks Kuykendall calls the 'English ceremonial style', but the two are not identical. Kuykendall places the orchestral march genre centrally, in particular the hymn-like trios of the marches of Elgar and, especially, Walton. Walton's importance partly reflects Kuykendall's interest in the afterlife of the style in mainstream film and television in the late twentieth century. See *The English Ceremonial Style Circa 1887–1937 and Its Aftermath* (PhD dissertation: Cornell University, 2005), Chapter 3, 83–170.

2. Anthony D. Smith, *Chosen Peoples: Sacred Sources of National Identity* (New York: Oxford University Press, 2003); *The Cultural Foundations of Nations: Hierarchy, Covenant, and Republic* (Oxford: Blackwell, 2008), Chapter 5 ('Covenantal Nations'), 107–34.
3. Jeremy Dibble, *C. Hubert H. Parry* (New York: Oxford University Press, 1992), 283.
4. For a recent view of this work, see Phyllis Weliver, 'The Parrys and *Prometheus Unbound*: Actualizing Liberalism', in *Music and Victorian Liberalism: Composing the Liberal Subject*, ed. Sarah Collins (Cambridge: Cambridge University Press, 2019), 151–79.
5. Charles Villiers Stanford, *Pages from an Unwritten Diary* (London: Edward Arnold, 1914), 310; cited in Stephen Banfield and Nicholas Temperley, 'The Legacy of Sebastian Wesley', in *Music and the Wesleys*, ed. Stephen Banfield and Nicholas Temperley (Urbana: University of Illinois Press, 2010), 200–29 (p. 219).
6. Ralph Vaughan Williams, 'Religious Folk Songs', lecture at Pokesdown Technical School, Bournemouth (1902), cited in Michael Kennedy, *The Works of Ralph Vaughan Williams*, 2nd ed. (Oxford: Oxford University Press, 1980), 33.
7. Ralph Vaughan Williams, Preface to *The English Hymnal* (London: Oxford University Press, 1906), xi; cited in Manning, *Vaughan Williams on Music*, 31–37 (p. 32).
8. Julian Onderdonck, 'Folksong Arrangements, Hymn Tunes and Church Music', in *The Cambridge Companion to Vaughan Williams*, ed. Alain Frogley and Aidan J. Thomson (Cambridge: Cambridge University Press, 2013), 136–56 (pp. 146–48). For a nuanced account of the sentimentality debate amongst Victorian musicians, see William J. Gatens, *Victorian Cathedral Music in Theory and Practice* (Cambridge: Cambridge University Press, 1986), 74–81.
9. Hughes and Stradling, *The English Musical Renaissance*, 3–8.
10. Gatens, *Victorian Cathedral Music*, 35.
11. Remark by Howells in 'Music in Worship', transcript of a discussion between Howells, Alec Robertson, and Erik Routley recorded on 28 January 1960. Royal College of Music, Howells Archive, Box C. Cited in Sophie Cleobury, *The Style and Development of Herbert Howells's Evening Canticle Settings* (MPhil dissertation, University of Birmingham, 2007), 7–8.
12. Jeremy Dibble, 'Parry as Historiographer', in *Nineteenth-Century British Music Studies* vol. 1, ed. Bennett Zon (Aldershot: Ashgate, 1999), 37–51; Bennett Zon, *Music and Metaphor in Nineteenth-Century British Musicology* (Aldershot: Ashgate, 2000), 151–64.
13. Vaughan Williams, 'National Music', in *National Music and Other Essays*, 2nd ed. (Oxford: Oxford University Press 1987), n. 60.
14. Letter from Elgar to Parry. 27 May 1903, cited in Jeremy Dibble, 'Parry and Elgar: a New Perspective', *Musical Times* 125 (No. 1701) (1984), 639–43 (p. 641); Ralph Vaughan Williams, 'A Musical Autobiography', in *National Music and Other Essays*, 177–94 (p. 180); 'Vaughan Williams's Talk on Parry and Stanford, 1957', given as a Composers Concourse lecture on Composers and Teachers, in *Heirs and Rebels: Letters Written to Each Other and Occasional Writings on Music by Ralph Vaughan Williams and Gustav Holst*, ed. Ursula Vaughan Williams and Imogen Holst (London: Oxford University Press, 1959), 97.
15. Adaptation of a BBC broadcast talk on Parry by Gerald Finzi from 1948, cited in Diana McVeagh, *Gerald Finzi: His Life and Music* (Woodbridge: Boydell, 2005), 165; Herbert Howells, 'Hubert Parry' (text of the Crees Lecture, delivered at the Royal College of Music on 7 October 1968), in Christopher Palmer, *Herbert Howells (1892–1983): A Celebration* 2nd ed. (London: Thames Publishing, 1996), 276–83 (p. 280).
16. 'Hubert Parry', in Palmer, *A Celebration*, 278.
17. Dibble, *C. Hubert H. Parry*, 16.
18. Ibid., 32–33.
19. Ibid., 43
20. Ibid., 11–12, 24–27, 38; also Jeremy Dibble, 'Hubert Parry and English Diatonic Dissonance', *British Music Society Journal* 5 (1983), 58–71; (pp. 64–65).
21. Dibble, 'Hubert Parry and English Diatonic Dissonance', 59. For performance statistics, see Stephen Banfield and Nicholas Temperley, 'The Legacy of Sebastian Wesley', in *Music and the Wesleys*, ed. Stephen Banfield and Nicholas Temperley (Urbana: University of Illinois Press, 2010), 216–29.
22. Dibble, *C. Hubert H. Parry*, 257; Dibble, 'Hubert Parry and English Diatonic Dissonance', 68.
23. See Samuel Wesley, *12 Voluntaries for the Organ* (1805–1816), in which most of the solemn passages have extensive slow stepwise bass motion, always marked 'Diapasons'. See also the organ introduction to Samuel Sebastian Wesley's anthem 'O Lord, Thou Art My God', quoted in Peter Horton, *Samuel Sebastian Wesley: A Life* (Oxford: Oxford University Press, 2004), 94.

Further links with the past are found in the 'Romanesca' schema in Ex. 1.1, bars 16–17 and in the allusion to the 'Prinner schema in bars 9–15. See Gjerdingen, *Music in the Galant Style*, 25–43, 45–60.
24. Dibble, *C. Hubert H. Parry*, 57–68.
25. Ralph Vaughan Williams, 'What Have We Learned from Elgar?', in *National Music and Other Essays*, 248–55 (p. 253).
26. Hughes and Stradling, *The English Musical Renaissance*, 9.
27. Frederick Ouseley, 'Church Music' paper read at the Manchester Church Congress 14 October 1863 [Ob Tenbury e.3 (2)], 31–32; 'Modern English Music' in Emil Naumann, *The History of Music* vol. 2, trans, F. Praeger, ed. F. A. G. Ouseley (London: Cassell, 1888), 1274–314 (p. 1239); both cited in Rosemary Golding, *Music and Academia in Victorian Britain* (Farnham: Ashgate, 2013), 75.
28. J. A. Fuller Maitland, *English Music in the XIXth Century* (New York and London: E. P. Dutton & Co.; Grant Richards, 1902), 78, 92, 194.
29. Hughes and Stradling, *The English Musical Renaissance*, 55.
30. Banfield and Temperley, 'The Legacy of Sebastian Wesley', 219–20; Peter Horton, 'The Highest Point up to That Time Reached by the Combination of Hebrew and Christian Sentiment in Music', in *Nineteenth-Century British Music Studies*, Vol. 3, ed. Peter Horton and Bennett Zon (Aldershot: Ashgate, 2003), 119–34 (pp. 119–20).
31. Dibble, *C. Hubert H. Parry*, 257.
32. Bennett Zon, 'From Great Man to Fittest Survivor: Reputation, Recapitulation and Survival in Victorian Concepts of Wagner's Genius', *Musicæ Scientæ*, 13/2 (September 2009), 415–45 (p. 421).
33. C. Hubert H. Parry, *The Evolution of the Art of Music* (New York: Greenwood Press, 1896), 427; cited in Zon, 'From Great Man to Fittest Survivor', 421.
34. Dibble, *C. Hubert H. Parry*, Chapter 5 ('Dannreuther'), 97–127; Jeremy Dibble, 'Edward Dannreuther and the Orme Square Phenomenon', in *Music and British Culture, 1785–1914: Essays in Honour of Cyril Ehrlich*, ed. Christina Bashford and Leanne Langley (Oxford: Oxford University Press, 2000), 275–98.
35. Parry's diary, unidentified date, August 1876, 16 May 1877; cited in Dibble, *C. Hubert H. Parry*, 141, 146.
36. Parry, *Evolution*, 424; cited in Zon, 'From Great Man to Fittest Survivor', 431.
37. Charlies Villiers Stanford, *Interludes, Records and Reflections* (London: John Murray, 1922), 145–46.
38. Charles Villiers Stanford, *Musical Composition* (New York: Macmillan, 1911), 45.
39. Ibid., 46.
40. On chromaticism and the influence of Spohr on Victorian cathedral music, see Gatens, *Victorian Cathedral Music*, 106, 142–44, 170–71, 177.
41. Ibid., 113.
42. Jeremy Dibble, 'Parry's *Guenever*: Trauma and Catharsis', in *King Arthur in Music*, ed. Richard Barber (Cambridge: D. S. Brewer, 2002), 35–50; Peter Atkinson, *Regeneration and Re-enchantment: British Music and Wagnerism, 1880–1920* (PhD dissertation, University of Birmingham, 2017), Chapter 1 ('Parry's *Guenever*').
43. Diary, Shulbrede Priory. On 30 May Parry recorded: 'In evening to Die Meistersinger. I went with extreme anticipation of delight, and was far more delighted than my utmost expectation could rise to. I think I never enjoyed any performance in my life so much.' For more of Parry's Wagner experiences around this time, see Dibble, *C. Hubert H. Parry*, 198–99.
44. Arthur Groos, 'Constructing Nuremberg: Typological and Proleptic Communities in *Die Meistersinger*', *19th-Century Music* 16/1 (1992), 18–34 (pp. 26–32).
45. Dibble, *C. Hubert H. Parry*, 283.
46. On Elgar's 'chivalrous rhetoric', see Matthew Riley, *Edward Elgar and the Nostalgic Imagination* (Cambridge: Cambridge University Press, 2007), 57–58. To be sure, these idioms appear elsewhere in Parry's music and at times echo King Mark's lament from Act II of *Tristan und Isolde*.
47. Herbert Howells, 'Concerto for String Orchestra (i)' (programme note for a performance of April 4 1974), reproduced in Palmer, *A Celebration*, 402–3 (p. 403); cited in Stephen Banfield, 'Elgar's Counterpoint: Three of a Kind', *Musical Times* 140 (1999), 29–37 (p. 37).
48. *The Apostles*, Part II/6 'At the Sepulchre', and *The Kingdom*, Part II, 'At the Beautiful Gate', opening bars. Dibble, 'Hubert Parry and English Diatonic Dissonance', 69; Dibble, 'Parry and Elgar', 643.

49. Dibble, 'Parry's *Guenever*', 46.
50. Kuykendall's account of 'rules' for the bass lines of '"big tune" moments of English ceremonial music' (regular motion, faster than the melody, stepwise, usually descending, but sometimes leaping up by a seventh) largely overlap with the understanding of processional diatonicism developed here, except for the fact that regular articulation of pulse is not always found in the broader processional topic. Kuykendall's focus tends to be on marches, with the trios of Elgar's Pomp and Circumstance marches exemplary. *The English Ceremonial Style*, 133, 129.
51. Gjerdingen, *Music in the Galant Style*, 77–89. The Do–Re–Mi can occur in two forms, which are related by invertible counterpoint in the outer parts. One part moves 1–2–3, the other 8–7–8. The version with 1–2–3 in the treble is not especially characteristic of English diatonic idioms of this era. The version with 1–2–3 in the bass will typically continue the treble descent from 7 rather than returning to 8.
52. This is sometimes called a 'lamento' or 'passacaglia' bass, although these concepts tend to include chromatic versions. William E. Caplin, 'Topics and Formal Functions: The Case of the Lament', in *The Oxford Handbook of Topic Theory*, ed. Danuta Mirka (New York: Oxford University Press, 2014), 415–52.
53. Examples include the theme from Edward German's *Coronation March* and Vaughan Williams's *Toward the Unknown Region* and 'Easter' from *Five Mystical Songs* (see Ex. 2.17 and 2.20(ii)).
54. Gjerdingen, *Music in the Galant Style*; Giorgio Sanguinetti, *The Art of Partimento: History, Theory, and Practice* (New York: Oxford University Press, 2012).
55. Job IJzerman, *Harmony, Counterpoint, Partimento: A New Method Inspired by Old Masters* (New York: Oxford University Press, 2018), 78–98.
56. Gjerdingen, *Music in the Galant Style*, 167.
57. See Gjerdingen on, for instance 'Romanesca' and 'Prinner' in *Music in the Galant Style*, 25–60.
58. Dibble, *C. Hubert H. Parry*, 26.
59. Brian Newbould, 'Elgar and Academicism 2: Practice beyond Theory', *Musical Times* 146 (2005), 25–41 (pp. 31–32).
60. Vaughan Williams, 'A Musical Autobiography', 186.
61. Simon Gunn, *The Public Culture of the Victorian Middle Class: Ritual and Authority and the English Industrial City* (Manchester: Manchester University Press, 2000), Chapter 7, 'The Rites of Civic Culture', 163–86 (p. 168).
62. W. H. Reed, *Elgar* (London: Dent, 1939), 87; Jerrold Northrop Moore, *Edward Elgar: A Creative Life* (New York: Oxford University Press, 1984), 465.
63. Gunn, *Public Culture*, 164–78.
64. Ben Roberts, 'Entertaining the Community: The Evolution of Civic Ritual and Public Celebration, 1860–1953', *Urban History* 8/31 (2016), 1–20 (pp. 6–9).
65. Ibid., 9–10. See also Brad Beaven, *Visions of Empire: Patriotism, Popular Culture and the City 1870–1939* (Manchester: Manchester University Press, 2012), 81–86.
66. Dibble, *C. Hubert H. Parry*, 258–59.
67. Ibid., 485.
68. Dibble, 'Hubert Parry and English Diatonic Dissonance', 68.
69. See Symphony No. 2, iv, F + 8; Symphony No. 3, iv, opening; Symphony No. 4, ii, opening, iv, H + 11.
70. Dibble, *C. Hubert H. Parry*, 218–19.
71. See the extracts from Parry's diary cited in Dibble, 'Parry and Elgar', 640–41.
72. On *Gerontius*, see diary 6 June 1903, cited in Dibble, *C. Hubert H. Parry*, 391. According to Herbert Howells—to whom Parry had related the story—Parry once invited Elgar to sign the visitors' book at the Royal College of Music. Elgar scrawled his name across a blank page in such a high-handed fashion that 'as soon as his back was turned, Parry tore the page right out of the book'. Conversation with Richard Walker and Robert Spearing, 1 April 1971, in Palmer, *A Celebration*, 351.
73. David Wright, 'Sir Frederick Bridge and the Musical Furtherance of the 1902 Imperial Project', *Europe, Empire and Spectacle in Nineteenth-Century British Music*, ed. Rachel Cowgill and Julian Rushton (Aldershot: Ashgate, 2006), 115–29, (p. 121).
74. Frederick Bridge, *A Westminster Pilgrim* (London: Novello, 1918), 182, cited in Matthias Range, *Music and Ceremonial at British Coronations: From James I to Elizabeth II* (Cambridge: Cambridge University Press, 2012), 227. David Wright, 'Sir Frederick Bridge', 129.
75. Jeffrey Richards, *Imperialism and Music: Britain 1876–1953* (Manchester: Manchester University Press, 2001), 101–7; Wright, 'Sir Frederick Bridge', 118, 129.

76. Parry, Diary, 9 August 1902; cited in Dibble, *C. Hubert H. Parry*, 387. For more details, see Kuykendall, *The English Ceremonial Style*, 192–99; and Range, *Music and Ceremonial*, 233. The impression given by David Cannadine in his well-known essay on the history of English royal ceremony that the musical performances of this era were slick and professional in comparison with the slovenliness of earlier practices is not true in every respect, even though Bridge evidently improved the standards overall. See David Cannadine, 'The Context, Performance and Meaning of Ritual: The British Monarchy and the "Invention of Tradition", c. 1820–1977', in *The Invention of Tradition*, ed. Eric Hobsbawm and Terrence Ranger (Cambridge: Cambridge University Press, 1983), 101–64 (pp. 130–31).
77. Richards, *Imperialism and Music*, 114, 119.
78. Bernard Benoliel, *Parry before Jerusalem: Studies of His Life and Music with Excerpts from His Published Writings* (Aldershot: Ashgate, 1997), 46–49; Michael Allis, *Parry's Creative Process* (Aldershot: Ashgate, 2003), 142–46; Dibble, *C. Hubert H. Parry*, 277–78.
79. For instance, *Scenes from the Bavarian Highlands* and the first 'dream interlude' from *Falstaff*.
80. Gerald Newman, *The Rise of English Nationalism: A Cultural History, 1720–1830* (New York: St. Martin's Press, 1997).
81. Some details can be found in Allis, *Parry's Creative Process*, 142–44.
82. Compare GB Lcm 4168 f.2–v.2 (Royal College of Music) with the published score from A + 5.
83. GB Lcm 4168 f. 9; GB Lcm 4170, v.6.

Chapter 2

1. Dibble, 'Parry and Elgar', 641.
2. Edward Elgar, *A Future for English Music and Other Lectures*, ed. Percy M. Young (London: Denis Dobson, 1968), 49.
3. Vaughan Williams, *National Music and Other Essays*, 6, 12, 40.
4. Ernest Newman, 'Elgar: Some Aspects of the Man and His Music', *Sunday Times*, 25 February 1934; cited in *An Elgar Companion*, ed. Christopher Redwood (Ashbourne: Sequoia and Moorland, 1984), 155.
5. See especially Mark Freeman, '"Splendid Display; Pompous Spectacle": Historical Pageants in Twentieth-Century Britain', *Social History*, 38/4 (2013), 423–55 (p. 424); for a lengthy analysis of the Edwardian pageant craze, see Ayako Yoshino, *Pageant Fever: Local History and Consumerism in Edwardian England* (Tokyo: Waseda University Press, 2011); and Deborah Sugg Ryan, '"Pageantitis": Frank Lascelles' 1907 Oxford Historical Pageant, Visual Spectacle and Popular Memory', *Visual Culture in Britain*, 8/2 (2007), 63–82.
6. Freeman, '"Splendid Display; Pompous Spectacle"', 427. Deborah S. Ryan, 'Staging the Imperial City: the Pageant of London, 1911', in *Imperial Cities: Landscape, Display and Identity*, ed. Felix Driver and David Gilbert (Manchester: Manchester University Press, 1999), 117–35 (p. 124).
7. Cited in Ryan, 'Staging the Imperial City', 126.
8. Nalini Ghuman, 'Elgar and the British Raj: Can the Mughals March?', in *Edward Elgar and His World*, ed. Byron Adams (Princeton, NJ: Princeton University Press, 2007), 249–85; Deborah Heckert, 'Working the Crowd: Elgar, Class and Reformulations of Popular Culture at the Turn of the Twentieth Century', in *Edward Elgar and His World*, ed. Byron Adams, 287–315; Moore, *Creative Life*, 627–32; Richards, *Imperialism and Music*, 65–67.
9. Bernard Porter, 'Elgar and Empire: Music, Nationalism, and the War', in *Oh, My Horses! Elgar and the Great War*, ed. Lewis Foreman (Rickmansworth: Elgar Editions, 2001), 133–73 (pp. 153–54).
10. Moore, *Creative Life*, 768–69. See also Lewis Foreman, 'A Voice in the Desert: Elgar's War Music', in Foreman, *Oh, My Horses! Elgar and the Great War*, 263–85 (pp. 279–84); Nalini Ghuman, "An Imperial Leitmotif: *Elgar's Pageant of Empire*," in *Exhibiting the Empire: Cultures of Display and the British Empire*, ed. John AcAleer and John MacKenzie (Manchester: Manchester University Press, 2016), 220–56; Richards, *Imperialism and Music*, 194–208.
11. Richards, *Imperialism and Music*, 195.
12. Aidan Thomson finds Elgar's techniques proto-cinematic: 'Elgar and the City: the *Cockaigne* Overture and Contributions of Modernity', *Musical Quarterly*, 96/2 (2013), 219–62 (pp. 236–39).
13. Moore, *Creative Life*, 342; Thomson, 'Elgar and the City', 219.
14. Elgar himself, however, claimed that his model was Delibe's *Sylvia*. See Moore, *Creative Life*, 345.
15. The repeated four-note stepwise figure on the approach and the entry of the organ at the apotheosis of Bax's 'big tune' are clear references to the parallel moment in *Cockaigne*.

16. Tom Hulme, '"A Nation of Town Criers": Civic Publicity and Historical Pageantry in Interwar Britain', *Urban History* 44/2 (2017), 270–92.
17. Peter Atkinson discerns a related complex around the tonal pairing of the keys of C major and E flat major and the idea of community in some of the compositions discussed here, notably *Caractacus*, *Cockaigne* and *The Kingdom*. Atkinson, *British Music and Wagnerism*, Chapter 2.
18. For a summary of these themes, see Matthew Riley and Anthony D. Smith, *Nation and Classical Music: From Handel to Copland* (Woodbridge: Boydell, 2016).
19. The names of themes are taken from the analysis by *Yorkshire Post* music critic Herbert Thomson, who was at least guided by Elgar. *Caractacus. A Cantata. The Words Written for Music by H.A. Acworth, C.I.E. The Music by Edward Elgar (Op. 35). Book of Words with Analytical Notes by Herbert Thompson*. Novello's Series of the Words of Oratorios, Cantatas, &c. (London: Novello, n.d. [?1900]).
20. Herbert Thomson (see note 19 above), heard in the final version 'a certain touch of Philistinism', and wondered whether Elgar intended sarcasm. Julian Rushton, 'Musicking Caractacus', in *Music and Performance Culture in Nineteenth-Century Britain*, ed. Bennett Zon (Farnham: Ashgate, 2012), 221–40 (p. 232).
21. Julian Rushton, *Elgar: 'Enigma' Variations* (Cambridge: Cambridge University Press, 1999), 46.
22. Ibid.
23. Rushton, 'Musicking Caractacus', 233.
24. At its opening appearance, Jaeger labelled the idea in his score extract 'Christ's peace' and in his text 'Christ's presence and Christ's peace'; in relation to 'Be Merciful' he called it 'the Christ idea'. He did not connect its shape with the 'rising' theme of the text at this point. A. J. Jaeger, *The Dream of Gerontius: Analytical and Descriptive Notes* (Sevenoaks: Novello, 1974), 8, 10.
25. See Banfield, 'Elgar's Counterpoint', 34.
26. In this case, a landscape of rustling sounds in the orchestra, harmonic stasis, and a four-part women's chorus provides the backdrop for recollection of the opening of Section I—a soprano soloist representing the Angel Gabriel speaking to Jesus in the mountains before dawn—with the effect of a flashback memory.
27. See, for instance, the grand statement of 'Church' during the Prelude to Part II of *The Apostles* (fig. 142); the ecstatic statement of 'Apostles' in bars 7–9 of the Prelude to *The Kingdom*; the central climaxes of 'The Sun Goeth Down' from *The Kingdom*; also *The Apostles* fig. 214 + 2 and *The Kingdom* fig. 95 + 5.
28. Aidan Thomson views the tonal disjunction as a sign of conflict of individual freedom and the modern metropolis. 'Elgar and the City', 247–52. For Peter Atkinson the tonality of *Cockaigne* is part of an inter-opus association of C major and E flat major in Elgar's oeuvre, which is Wagnerian in its practice of associative tonality and specifically in the significance of these keys in relation to the Prelude to *Die Meistersinger* and the idea of community. See *British Music and Wagnerism*, Chapter 2.
29. Some famous examples of the 'Amen' progression (with root position tonic harmony rather than first inversion) include the harmonization of the first phrase of 'Wachet auf' at the opening of Mendelssohn's *Paulus* and the closing plagal progression at the end of his *Meeresstille und glückliche Fahrt*.
30. Gjerdingen, *Music in the Galant Style*, Chapter 3, 45–60.
31. See Matthew Riley, 'Heroic Melancholy: Elgar's Inflected Diatonicism', in *Elgar Studies*, ed. J. P. E. Harper-Scott and Julian Rushton (Cambridge: Cambridge University Press, 2007), 284–307 (pp. 287–90).
32. Ibid., 294–96.
33. James Hepokoski calls these versions 'weaker' and 'stronger', hearing the former as potentially 'modal' and given to 'decay', and the latter potentially more cadentially directed. 'Gaudery, Romance and the "Welsh Tune": Introduction and Allegro, Op. 47', in *Elgar Studies*, ed. J. P. E. Harper-Scott and Julian Rushton (Cambridge: Cambridge University Press, 2007), 135–71 (pp. 147–54).
34. On this type of effect in Elgar, see Matthew Riley, 'Rustling Reeds and Lofty Pines: Elgar and the Music of Nature', *19th-Century Music*, 26/2 (2002), 155–77.
35. Newbould, 'Elgar and Academicism 2', 37. Hepokoski notes that the second version of the tune in the *Introduction* with its 'striding pulses' is the basis for the apotheosis version with its '"English-imperial"-Handelian striding basses'. See 'Gaudery, Romance, and the "Welsh Tune"', 151, 164.
36. A possible antecedent for this succession is found in the slow aria 'Ombra mai fù' from Handel's *Serse*.

37. David W. Bebbington, *Evangelicalism in Modern Britain: A History from the 1730s to the 1980s* (London: Routledge, 1993). Elgar's affinities with the evangelical movement appear clearly in the conversion 'scenes' in *Scenes from the Saga of King Olaf* (1896) and *The Kingdom* (1906).
38. The opening of the 'Enigma' theme may be indebted to the first three bars of Corelli's 'Christmas' Concerto Op. 6 No. 8, also in G minor with a similar texture and outer voices at the same pitch levels.
39. Julian Rushton, *Elgar: 'Enigma' Variations* (Cambridge: Cambridge University Press, 1999), 16, 56.
40. Vaughan Williams, 'A Musical Autobiography', 180.
41. Howells, 'Hubert Parry', 276.
42. Ralph Vaughan Williams, 'The Teaching of Parry and Stanford', in *Vaughan Williams on Music*, ed. David Manning(New York: Oxford University Press, 2008), 315–22 (p. 315). This text was originally a BBC Third Programme broadcast.
43. Ralph Vaughan Williams, 'Sir Hubert Parry', in Manning (ed.), *Vaughan Williams on Music*, 295–96 (p. 296); originally published as a tribute to Parry on his death in the Royal College of Music publication *The Music Student* 11/3 (1918), 79.
44. VaughanWilliams, 'Sir Hubert Parry', 295.
45. Vaughan Williams, 'The Teaching of Parry and Stanford', 316.
46. Dibble, *C. Hubert H. Parry*, 227.
47. Stephen Town, '"Full of Fresh Thoughts": Vaughan Williams, Whitman and the Genesis of *A Sea Symphony*', in *Vaughan Williams Essays*, ed. Byron Adams and Robin Wells (Aldershot: Ashgate, 2003), 73–101 (pp. 75–77).
48. Vaughan Williams, 'A Musical Autobiography', 182.
49. Vaughan Williams, 'The Teaching of Parry and Stanford', 316.
50. Vaughan Williams, 'A Musical Autobiography', 180.
51. Vaughan Williams, 'The Teaching of Parry and Stanford', 315.
52. Vaughan Williams, 'A Musical Autobiography', 180.
53. Vaughan Williams, 'The Teaching of Parry and Stanford', 317–18.
54. Ralph Vaughan Williams, 'What Have We Learned from Elgar?' [1934], in Vaughan Williams, *National Music and Other Essays*, 248–55 (p. 252).
55. Vaughan Williams, 'A Musical Autobiography', 188.
56. Vaughan Williams, 'What Have We Learned from Elgar?', 252–53.
57. Vaughan Williams, 'National Music', 41-2.
58. Vaughan Williams, 'What Have We Learned from Elgar?', 252.
59. Vaughan Williams, 'National Music', 42; 'What Have We Learned from Elgar?', 252.
60. Vaughan Williams, 'What Have We Learned from Elgar?', 252.
61. Jeremy Crump, 'The Identity of English Music: The Reception of Elgar 1898–1935', in *Englishness: Politics and Culture 1880–1920*, ed. Robert Colls and Philip Dodd (Beckenham: Croom Helm, 1986), 164–90.
62. Vaughan Williams, 'A Musical Autobiography', 180.
63. Vaughan Williams, 'What Have We Learned from Elgar?', 252.
64. Ibid., 253.
65. Kennedy, *The Works of Ralph Vaughan Williams*, 79, 85, 114, 132, 183, 281. For discussion of the 'ceremonial style' of the hymn, see Kuykendall, *The English Ceremonial Style*, 205–6. Relative to the reformist agenda of the *English Hymnal*, it may be significant that 'Sine Nomine' replaces a setting of the same text by the Victorian composer Joseph Barnby. The cries of 'Alleluya!' unmistakably recall Elgar's setting of that word in *Gerontius*.
66. Kennedy, *The Works of Ralph Vaughan Williams*, 114.
67. Dibble, 'The Creation of Tradition', 43–46.
68. Eric Saylor, 'Political Visions, National Identities, and the Sea Itself: Stanford and Vaughan Williams in 1910', in *The Sea in the British Musical Imagination*, ed. Eric Saylor and Christopher M. Scheer (Woodbridge: Boydell, 2015), 205–24 (pp. 208–16).
69. Kennedy, *The Works of Ralph Vaughan Williams*. 131. See also Dibble, 'The Creation of Tradition', 46; Charles Edward McGuire, 'Vaughan Williams and the English Music Festival: 1910', in *Vaughan Williams Essays*, ed. Byron Adams and Robin Wells (Aldershot: Ashgate, 2003), 235–68 (p. 240).
70. In Neo-Riemannian theory, these triads would be said to be related as 'hexatonic poles', an association with special properties and associations. David Manning discusses this opening along with other applications of Neo-Riemannian theory to Vaughan Williams's music. Manning,

Harmony, Tonality and Structure in Vaughan Williams's Music (PhD dissertation, University of Bristol, 2003), 97. On hexatonic poles, see Richard Cohn, 'Uncanny Resemblances: Tonal Signification in the Freudian Age', *Journal of the American Musicological Society* 57/2 (2004), 285-324.

71. Vaughan Williams, 'What Have We Learned from Elgar?', 17.
72. See also the processional passage at 'A vast similitude interlocks all' in the second movement and 'Silent Noon' from *The House of Life*.
73. Stephen Town argues for the influences of the passages or works of Parry, Stanford, Elgar and Delius, with varying degrees of persuasiveness. '"Full of Fresh Thoughts": Vaughan Williams, Whitman and the Genesis of *A Sea Symphony*'", in *Vaughan Williams Essays*, ed. Byron Adams and Robin Wells(Aldershot: Ashgate, 2003), 73-101.

Chapter 3

1. This picture is broadly consistent with that developed by Eric Saylor, who argues for two phases of English pastoral music, the second being much better defined and coherent than the rather nebulous first. However, given its emphasis on diatonicism, this chapter draws a distinction between competing schools even during the second phase. Eric Saylor, *English Pastoral Music: From Arcadia to Utopia, 1900-1955* (Urbana: University of Illinois Press, 2017), 5.
2. 'Autobiographical Notes' (a conversation with Christopher Palmer), in Palmer, *Herbert Howells: A Study*, 11-17 (p. 12).
3. On the history of the pastoral topic in art-music composition, see Raymond Monelle, *The Musical Topic: Hunt, Military and Pastoral* (Bloomington: Indiana University Press, 2006), Chapters 14 and 15 (pp. 229-71).
4. Herbert Howells, 'Vaughan Williams's "Pastoral" Symphony', *Music & Letters* 3/2 (1922), 122-32 (124, 125).
5. An exception is the opening of Part II of *The Dream of Gerontius*, a passage that may have influenced Vaughan Williams.
6. Monelle, *The Musical Topic*, 270, 271.
7. Ibid., 271, 273.
8. Ibid., 268.
9. Stradling and Hughes, *The English Musical Renaissance*, 82.
10. Howells, 'Vaughan Williams's "Pastoral" Symphony', 125.
11. This is a matter of degree. Michael Vaillancourt has noted many of these features in the Pastoral Symphony but maintains that the work still manifests 'symphonic dualism', albeit in a novel guise. See 'Modal and Thematic Coherence inn Vaughan Williams's *Pastoral Symphony*', *Music Review* 52 (1991), 1-22.
12. Su-Yin Mak, 'Schubert's Sonata Forms and the Poetics of the Lyric', *Journal of Musicology* 23/2 (2006), 263-306.
13. Herbert Howells, unpublished note on Violin Sonata No. 1, reproduced in Palmer, *A Celebration*, 448.
14. David Maw, '"I Am a 'Modern' in This, but a Britisher Too": Howells and the Phantasy', in *The Music of Herbert Howells*, ed. Phillip A. Cooke and David Maw (Woodbridge: Boydell, 2013), 185-221 (pp. 187-212).
15. Howells, 'Vaughan Williams's "Pastoral" Symphony', 123. See Paul Spicer, *Herbert Howells* (Bridgend: Seren, 1998), 40-41.
16. Cited in Saylor, *English Pastoral Music*, 104.
17. Edward F. Rimbault, *The Rounds, Catches, and Canons of England; A Collection of Specimens of the Sixteenth, Seventeenth, and Eighteenth Centuries Adapted to Modern Use* (London: Cramer, Wood & Company, date unknown, *c.* 1870), vii.
18. William Barclay Squire, 'Round', in *Grove's Dictionary of Music and Musicians*, ed. J.A. Fuller Maitland, Vol. IV (London: Macmillan, 1908), 165-66 (p. 165).
19. W. S. Rockstro, 'Sumer is icumen in,' in *Grove's Dictionary of Music and Musicians*, ed. J.A. Fuller Maitland, Vol. IV (London: Macmillan, 1908), 747-54 (p. 753).
20. Howells, 'Vaughan Williams's "Pastoral" Symphony', 129, 130.
21. The Roman numeral annotations show the on-beat appoggiatura dissonances, but in fact both ninth and seventh dissonances appear within each minim of subdominant harmony.
22. Daniel M. Grimley, 'Landscape and Distance: Vaughan Williams and the Symphonic Pastoral', in *British Music and Modernism 1895-1960*, ed. Matthew Riley (Farnham: Ashgate: 2010), 147-74 (pp. 172-73).

23. Ibid., 172.
24. Francesca Brittan, 'On Microscopic Hearing: Fairy Magic, Natural Science and the *Scherzo fantastique*', *Journal of the American Musicological Society* 64/3 (2011), 527–746.
25. In *Sancta Civitas* there is no big 'set piece' of octave/unison counterpoint as in *Flos Campi*, although there are many instances of the tendency, such as at 'Let us be Glad' (fig. 6); 'For in one Hour' (fig. 29 seventh bar), 'And the voice of the harpers' (fig. 32, fifth bar), 'no more in thee' (fig. 34); 'Heaven and Earth are full of thy glory' (fig. 51, second bar).
26. The most significant contributions are those of Wilfrid Mellers, *Vaughan Williams and the Vision of Albion* (London: Pimlico, 1991 [1989]), Chapter 459–76; George Revill, 'The Lark Ascending: Vaughan Williams's Monument to a Radical Pastoral', *Landscape Research* 16/2 (1991), 25–30; David Manning, *Harmony, Tonality and Structure in Vaughan Williams's Music* (DPhil diss., University of Wales, Cardiff, 2003).
27. Mellers, *Vaughan Williams and the Vision of Albion*, 59.
28. Meredith alludes to a greater and more abstract 'song' that the lark awakens in human beings and in the final words of the long poem, states that the 'fancy sings' after the lark is lost in the sky. This is surely resonant with Milton's 'high-raised phantasie' that can recall the everlasting 'song' of praise that all creatures once made to God.
29. Both the processual dimension and the indefiniteness are pointed out in the Marxist account of the composition by George Revill, 'Vaughan Williams's Monument to a Radical Pastoral'.
30. James Hepokoski, *Sibelius: Symphony No. 5* (Cambridge: Cambridge University Press, 23–26.
31. Ibid., 26–27.
32. David Manning notes the replacement of C sharp by C natural in advance of the final cadenza, although his discussion is mainly concerned with competing 'pitch centres' (E and D) rather than with alternative pitch-class collections. Manning, *Harmony, Tonality and Structure in Vaughan Williams's Music*, 59, 66.
33. Mellers, *Vaughan Williams and the Vision of Albion*, 62.
34. Saylor, *English Pastoral Music*, 5.
35. Even Robert Stradling, in an essay that describes the Anglicization of Delius, admits this point. 'On Shearing the Black Sheep in Spring: The Repatriation of Frederick Delius', in *Music and the Politics of Culture*, ed. Christopher Norris (London: Lawrence & Wishart, 1989), 69–105 (pp. 90, 103 n. 43). See also Jeremy Dibble, *The Music of Frederick Delius: Style, Form and Ethos* (Woodbridge: Boydell, 2021), 291–92.
36. See also Warlock, *An Old Song* (1917), No. 2, from *Folk-Song Preludes* (1918) and *Serenade for Strings* (1923). Warlock arranged Delius's *In a Summer Garden* for piano.
37. For details, see Stradling, 'On Shearing the Black Sheep in Spring', 69–72.
38. On the organ entry, see Daniel M. Grimley, 'Music, Ice and the "Geometry of Fear": The Landscapes of Vaughan Williams's Sinfonia Antartica', *Musical Quarterly* 91(1–2) (2008), 116–50 (pp. 136–41).
39. This is the impression left at times by Hughes and Stradling, *The English Musical Renaissance*, 74–101.
40. Cited in Palmer, *A Celebration*, 431.
41. For an account of the incident, see Spicer, *Herbert Howells*, 80–81.

Chapter 4

1. Eleanor Rawling, 'Walking into Clarity: the Dynamics of Self and Place in the Poetry of Ivor Gurney', *GeoHumanities* 2/2 (2016), 509–22; Ceri Owen, 'Making an English Voice: Performing National Identity during the English Musical Renaissance', *Twentieth-Century Music* 13/1 (2016), 77–107 (pp. 97–104); see also Daniel M. Grimley, *Delius and the Sound of Place* (Cambridge: Cambridge University Press, 2018), although the subject is mainly orchestral music.
2. Harry Plunket Greene, *Interpretation in Song* (New York: Macmillan, 1912).
3. In the view of Trevor Hold, *Parry to Finzi: Twenty English Song Composers* (Woodbridge: Boydell, 2002), Parry's songs 'almost single-handedly established an art-song tradition, laying down, for better or worse, its ground rules and patterns: the poets to set; the method for setting English words; its scope; and its special English "sensibility"', 17–18. For the specifically diatonic tradition considered in the present study, the critically important 'patterns', in the sense of harmonic/contrapuntal schemata, derive rather from Parry's occasional choral works.
4. On Plunket Greene's ideas on English singing and voice, see Owen, 'Making an English Voice', 87–97.

5. Ralph Vaughan Williams, 'Gervase Elwes', in Manning, *Vaughan Williams on Music*, 57–59 (p. 59). See Owen, 'Making an English Voice', 98.
6. Howes, *The English Musical Renaissance*, especially Chapter XII; 'Holst and Vaughan Williams: Emancipation', 230–45 and Chapter XIII, 'The Nationalists', 246–63.
7. The Victorian drawing-room or 'royalty' ballad is the foil for Banfield's argument about the emergence of 'sensibility', although he too admits its tenacity. *Sensibility and English Song: Critical Studies of the Early Twentieth Century* (Cambridge: Cambridge University Press, 1985), Chapter 1, 1–14.
8. See Pamela Blevins, *Ivor Gurney and Marion Scott: Song of Pain and Beauty* (Woodbridge: Boydell, 2008), 104.
9. Compare Gurney's 'When Smoke Stood up from Ludlow' with Vaughan Williams's 'On Wenlock Edge' and 'Bredon Hill'; Gurney's 'In Flanders' with Vaughan Williams's 'Clun'; Ireland's 'The Lent Lily' with Vaughan Williams's 'Bredon Hill' and 'Is My Team Ploughing'; and Finzi's 'In the Time of the "Breaking of Nations" ("Only a Man Harrowing Clods")' with Vaughan Williams's 'Is My Team Ploughing'.
10. At one point, this passage s identical note-for-note to a passage from Grieg's String Quartet. Banfield, *Sensibility and English Song*, 147.
11. Quilter's interest in the ballad repertory and his stylistic roots therein have been noted, but a clear demonstration of them has not been attempted beyond melodic details. Valerie Langfield, *Roger Quilter: His Life and Music* (Woodbridge: Boydell, 2002), 111–113; Trevor Hold, *Parry to Finzi: Twenty English Song Composers* (Woodbridge: Boydell, 2002), 137–39.
12. Plunket Greene, *Interpretation in Song*, 54, 53, 54, 55, 56. Greene added: 'No doorstep on a winter's night is complete without it. It has discovered more orphans than the combined force of the Metropolitan police; it has saved more children's lives than the whole of the Country Holiday Fund' (p. 54).
13. Hold calls out Quilter on the very same technique—'the cliché repetition of the final lines'—in his song 'June'. 'This is, in fact, the ballad itself, no more, no less.' *Parry to Finzi*, 138–39. Banfield notices the ballad origins of 'Heart's Haven'; *Sensibility and English Song*, 81.
14. Fiona Richards points out that 'there is little sign of musical development from early to late pieces [of Ireland's church music]'. *The Music of John Ireland* (Aldershot: Ashgate, 2000), 204.
15. For the 'Church' theme, the anthem 'Greater Love Hath No Man' (1912), the song 'Ladslove', and the cantata *These Things Shall Be*; for the 'Britain' theme, the song 'If There Were Dreams to Sell' and the 'Elegy' from the *Downland Suite*.
16. Another song in this style is 'O Happy Land' (1941), the melody of which is very similar to that of 'Blow Out, You Bugles'. The mood of this piece is similar to that in Ireland's 'occasional' war-time pieces. Richards, *The Music of John Ireland*, 197.
17. At various stages of composition and planning, Butterworth appears to have been considering a longer, perhaps more obviously narrative cycle. His eventual selection and order were influenced by the first of all Housman songs cycles, Arthur Somervell's *A Shropshire Lad* (1904), which coaxes a tragic narrative out of a selection of Housman's verses. Hold, *Parry to Finzi*, 236. Banfield, *Sensibility and English Song*, 52.
18. Rachel Cowgill, 'Canonizing Remembrance: Music for Armistice Day at the BBC, 1922–7', *First World War Studies* 2/1 (2011), 75–107 (p. 79).
19. Blevins, *Song of Pain and Beauty*, 104–5.
20. Ivor Gurney Collection, Gloucestershire Archives D10500/1/M/2/27/3. Dated February 1921.
21. On Gurney's conservative musical language, see Hold, *Parry to Finzi*, 269–72.
22. Banfield, *Sensibility and English Song*, 195.
23. Ivor Gurney Collection, Gloucestershire Archives, D10500/1/M/5.
24. Parry had recently produced two books of chorale preludes (1912, 1916) and a book of chorale fantasias (1915), most of his tunes being English hymns, while Gurney's peer-mentor Herbert Howells had published three 'Psalm Preludes' (1916). Ralph Vaughan Williams brought out *Three Hymn Preludes Founded on Welsh Hymn Tunes* in 1920. Banfield, *Sensibility and English Song*, 188–89.
25. Stephen Banfield, *Gerald Finzi: An English Composer*, 2nd ed. (London: Faber, 2008), 60–62.
26. Banfield, *Sensibility and English Song*, 276.
27. Diana McVeagh, *Gerald Finzi: His Life and Music* (Woodbridge: Boydell, 2005), 19.
28. Banfield, *Gerald Finzi*, 400–403; McVeagh, *Gerald Finzi*, 164–66.
29. Hold, *Parry to Finzi*, 395.
30. Banfield, *Sensibility and English Song*, 280.

31. McVeagh, *Gerald Finzi*, 22.
32. Banfield, *Gerald Finzi*, 346–49.
33. McVeagh, *Gerald Finzi*, 60.
34. Banfield, *Gerald Finzi*, 393–96.
35. Hold, *Parry to Finzi*, 395.
36. Banfield, *Gerald Finzi*, 34.
37. Diana McVeagh finds 'stiffness' in harmonic pacing in some of Finzi's efforts. See *Gerald Finzi*, 160, 262.
38. Examples of the first type include *A Severn Rhapsody*, all four movements from the topically uniform *Requiem da Camera*, *Nocturne: New Year's Music*, *Eclogue*, *Elegy* for Violin and Piano, 'Intrada' and 'Rhapsody' from *Dies Natalis*, the main theme of *Intimations of Immortality*, and the theme of the Cello Concerto's second movement. On the second type, see Hold, *Parry to Finzi*, 396. Examples include 'Introit', 'Aria' from *Farewell to Arms*, and 'The Salutation' from *Dies Natalis*. Examples of the third type include 'O Mistress Mine' and 'The Rapture' from *Dies Natalis*. Examples of the last type include 'The Comet at Yell'ham' and 'At a Lunar Eclipse'.
39. Hold, *Parry to Finzi*, 398.
40. Banfield, *Sensibility and English Song*, 294; McVeagh, *Gerald Finzi*, 10.
41. Hold, *Parry to Finzi*, 403–404, 414. Stephen Banfield's assessment is much more positive. *Sensibility and English Song*, 275–87
42. Hold, *Parry to Finzi*, 400.
43. Cowgill, 'Canonizing Remembrance', 79.
44. Diana McVeagh, *Gerald Finzi: His Life and Music* (Woodbridge: Boydell, 2005), 25.
45. Stephen Banfield, *Gerald Finzi: An English Composer* (London: Faber, 1998), 79.
46. The opening and closing orchestral passages from the third movement of the *Requiem*, which sets Hardy's lines 'Only a man harrowing clods / . . . With an old horse' alludes to a motive from the instrumental refrain from Vaughan Williams's setting of Housman's morbid poem 'Is My Team Ploughing?' from *On Wenlock Edge*.
47. Finzi also uses the marking 'chiaro' for the piano's imitation of distant gun blasts in 'Channel Firing' from *Before and After Summer*, which is clearly intended to be heard as a sound carrying across a wide landscape from afar.
48. Banfield, *Gerald Finzi*, 242, 244. Stanford's Irish folksong settings may be a precedent for the choice of E flat, or even 'Grandeur' from *A Sheaf of Songs from Leinster*, Op. 140 (1914), which also has a three-flat key signature and Finzi-like sudden accelerations in durational values in the vocal line. Again pointed out by Banfield, *Sensibility and English Song*, 35.
49. For another 'Nimrod' allusion, see Ex. 4.16, bars 9–10.
50. Noticed also by Banfield, *Gerald Finzi*, 214.

Chapter 5

1. Vaughan Williams, letter to Adrian Boult, about 4 September 1940, cited in Cobbe, *Letters of Ralph Vaughan Williams*, 304.
2. Vaughan Williams, letter to the BBC Director General, 9 March 1941, cited in Cobbe, *Letters of Ralph Vaughan Williams*, 314.
3. Range, *Music and Ceremonial at British Coronations*, 31.
4. Ibid., 244.
5. Typed document by William McKie in the Westminster Abbey Library, cited in ibid., 258.
6. Jeffrey Richards, 'Vaughan Williams and British Wartime Cinema', in *Vaughan Williams Studies*, ed. Alain Frogley (Cambridge: Cambridge University Press, 1996), 139–65 (p. 147).
7. Ibid., 162.
8. The trio of *Orb and Sceptre* also begins with a stepwise descent of almost an octave, but the schematic realization differs.
9. Letter to Nancy Bush, 20 June 1942; cited in Richards, *The Music of John Ireland*, 198. Ireland underlined the antifascist meaning in his correspondence with Alan and Nancy Bush. Alan Bush, who had been Ireland's student, was a Communist. Kate Guthrie, 'Propaganda Music in Second World War Britain: John Ireland's "Epic March"', *Journal of the Royal Musical Association* 139/1 (2014), 137–75 (pp. 165, 167).
10. Adrian Boult, letter to John Ireland, 28 November 1940; cited in Richards, *The Music of John Ireland*, 198.
11. Kate Guthrie, 'Propaganda Music in Second World War Britain: John Ireland's "Epic March"'. *Journal of the Royal Musical Association* 139/1 (2014), 153–67.

286 NOTES

12. Ireland, letter to Adrian Boult, 3 June 1941, cited in Foreman, 'John Ireland and the BBC', in *The John Ireland Companion*, ed. Lewis Foreman (Woodbridge: Boydell, 2011), 79–115 (pp. 95–96).
13. Saylor, *English Pastoral Music*, 132.
14. E flat major is also the overall key of Bach's Cantata BWV 140, 'Wachet auf, ruft uns die Stimme'.
15. 'Nicaea', No. 160 and 'Melita', No. 370 in the 1875 edition.
16. 'Vox Angelica', No. 223 in the 1875 edition.
17. See also Dykes, 'Jesus, Lover of my soul' (Hollingside, No. 193); Dykes, 'Sweet flowerlets of the martyr band' ('Salvate Flores', No. 68); Stainer, 'Hail, gladdening light' ('Sebaste', No. 18); Stainer, 'My God, I love Thee' (St Francis, No. 106); James Watson, 'Fair waived the golden corn' (Holyrood, No. 339); many more could be cited.
18. 'Huddersfield Choral Society. Dr. Vaughan Williams's new work', *The Times*, London, 3 October 1936, p. 10. Cited in Scott Hochstetler, '*Dona Nobis Pacem*: Vaughan Williams's Federalist Manifesto', *The Choral Journal* 49/12 (2009), 42–52 (p. 50). Hochstettler, however, exaggerates in calling the work a 'Federalist manifesto', since, as he documents, the founding of the Federal Union in Britain took place only in late 1938 and Vaughan Williams's references to it and to its cause—placing the defence policy of member states in the hands of an international body—date at the earliest from October 1939.
19. Vaughan Williams, 'A Musical Autobiography', 183.
20. Cited in Lewis Foreman, 'John Ireland in the Concert Hall: Orchestral and Choral-Orchestra Music', in *The John Ireland Companion,* ed. Lewis Foreman (Woodbridge: Boydell, 2011), 193–218 (p. 209).
21. Richards, *The Music of John Ireland*, 188.
22. McVeagh, *Gerald Finzi*, 157.
23. For the textual alterations, see ibid., 162–63. On the relationship with Blunden see also Banfield, *Gerald Finzi*, 342–53.
24. McVeagh, *Gerald Finzi*, 159–60.
25. Banfield, *Gerald Finzi*, 346–49.
26. This quality of his music is noted by Diana McVeagh, *Gerald Finzi*, 160.
27. Cited in McVeagh, *Gerald Finzi*, 191.
28. Ibid., 187.
29. Ibid., 188.
30. For further perspectives on *Intimations of Immortality*, see Banfield, *Gerald Finzi*, 369–388; McVeagh, *Gerald Finzi*, 86–192.
31. The connections are documented by Hugh Ottaway, 'Vaughan Williams's Symphony in D and "The Pilgrim's Progress": A Comparative Note', *Musical Times* 94/1328 (October 1953), 456–58.
32. Kennedy, *The Works of Ralph Vaughan Williams*, 283. This was not really the tone of Ottoway's original article about the association, which treated the Symphony as a separate—and perhaps more successful—work. Ottaway, 'Vaughan Williams's Symphony in D'.
33. Scott Hochstettler, '*Dona Nobis Pacem*: Vaughan Williams's Federalist Manifesto.' *The Choral Journal* 49/12 (2009), 45–46.
34. Peter Franklin, 'Sibelius in Britain', in *The Cambridge Companion to Sibelius*, ed. Daniel M. Grimley (Cambridge: Cambridge University Press, 2004), 182–95. See also J. P. E. Harper-Scott, '"Our True North": Walton's First Symphony, Sibelianism, and the Nationalization of Modernism in England, *Music &Letters* 89/4 (2008), 562–89; and David Stern, '"One Thought Grows out of Another": Sibelius's Influence on Ralph Vaughan Williams's Fifth Symphony', *Sibelius in the Old and New Worlds: Aspects of his Music, its Interpretation, and Reception*, ed. Timothy L. Jackson, Veijo Murtomäki, Colin Davis, and Timo Virtanen (Frankfurt am Main: Lang, 2010), 383–400.
35. Murray Dineen, 'Vaughan Williams's Fifth Symphony: Ideology and Aural Tradition', in *Vaughan Williams Essays*, ed. Byron Adams and Robin Wells (Aldershot: Ashgate, 2003), 17–27; David Stern, 'One Theme Grows out of Another: Sibelius's Influence on Ralph Vaughan Williams's Fifth Symphony', in *Sibelius in the Old and New World: Aspects of his Music, its Interpretation, and Reception*, ed. Timothy L. Jackson, Veijo Murtomäki, Colin Davis, and Timo Virtanen (Frankfurt am Main: Peter Lang, 2010), 383–400 (pp. 388–91).
36. The tonal resolution at the end of the symphony and its likely meaning are discussed by Mellers, *Vaughan Williams and the Vision of Albion*, 176–86 and by Arnold Whittall, 'Symphony in D Major: Models and Mutations', in *Vaughan Williams Studies*, ed. Alain Frogley (Cambridge: Cambridge University Press, 1996), 187–212.
37. Mellers, *Vaughan Williams and the Vision of Albion*, 183.

38. Frank Howes, *The Music of Ralph Vaughan Williams* (London: Oxford University Press, 1954), 48; Kennedy, *The Works of Ralph Vaughan Williams*, 282.
39. Kennedy, *The Works of Ralph Vaughan Williams*, 281. Vaughan Williams borrowed this figure in turn from the setting of the same word in Elgar's *The Dream of Gerontius*.
40. Whittall points out the relevance of this essay. 'Symphony in D Major', 209.
41. Ralph Vaughan Williams, 'Some Thoughts on Beethoven's Choral Symphony', in *National Music and Other Essays*, 2nd ed. (Oxford: Oxford University Press, 1987), 83–120 (p. 90).

Chapter 6

1. For an account of Howells's turn to the new style in choral music, see Phillip A. Cooke, 'A "Wholly New Chapter" in Service Music: *Collegium Regale* and the *Gloucester Service*', in *The Music of Herbert Howells*, ed. Phillip A. Cooke and David Maw (Woodbridge: Boydell, 2013), 86–99.
2. Rudolph Otto, *The Idea of the Holy*, trans. John W. Harvey (London: Oxford University Press, 1924 [1917]).
3. Palmer, *A Celebration*, 147. See also Jonathan Clinch, '"Beauty Springeth out of Naught": Interpreting the Church Music of Herbert Howells', *British Postgraduate Musicology* 11 (2011), 1–12 (p. 8).
4. The treble line at 'As it was in the beginning' in the 'Gloria' passages from the Gloucester Magnificat and Nunc Dimittis are much admired in this regard. Spicer, *Herbert Howells*, 137; Cooke, 'A "Wholly New Chapter"', 97.
5. On melisma and ecstasy in Howells, see Paul Spicer, 'Howells's Use of the Melisma: Word Setting in his Songs and Choral Music', in Cooke and Maw, *The Music of Herbert Howells*, 100–15.
6. Phillip Cooke points out Howells's blending of pleasure and pain, agony and ecstasy in this kind of writing: 'the harsh dissonances of the tritone and minor second are bitter flavours, but it is precisely this bitterness that makes us realise how sweet the sweetness of Howells's resolutions can be'. Cooke, 'A "Wholly New Chapter"', 96.
7. On the sleeve notes for Argo RG 507, Howells recalled 'a promise (mine) that, if I made the setting [Collegium Regale] of the *Magnificat*, the mighty should be put down from their seat without a brute force that would deny this canticle's feminine association. Equally, that in the *Nunc Dimittis*, the tenor's domination should characterize the gentle Simeon. Only the "Gloria" should raise its voice. The given promise dictated style, mood and scope.' Palmer, *A Celebration*, 400.
8. Palmer, *A Celebration*, 211; see also Clinch, '"Beauty Springeth out of Naught"', 10–11; Cooke, 'A "Wholly New Chapter"', 94–95.
9. Palmer, *A Celebration*, 145.
10. Undated notes, cited in ibid., 145.
11. Ibid., 148.
12. David Maw takes this piece as an illustration of the essential paradox of Howells's life and music. 'Introduction: Paradox of an Establishment Composer', in Cooke and Maw (eds.), *The Music of Herbert Howells*, 1–7 (pp. 1–2).
13. As Oliver Neighbour puts it in a study of their relationship, 'It is hard to believe that Vaughan Williams's example had no bearing on the warm diatonicism that formed the basis of numerous episodes in Tippett's works and at a further remove suffused his whole style'. 'Ralph, Adeline, and Ursula Vaughan Williams: Some Facts and Speculation (with a Note about Tippett)', *Music & Letters* 89/3 (2008), 337–45 (p. 344). For further discussion of Tippett's relationship to English tradition, see David Clarke, '"Only Half Rebelling": Tonal Strategies, Folksong and "Englishness" in Tippett's Concerto for Double String Orchestra', in *Tippett Studies*, ed. David Clarke (Cambridge: Cambridge University Press, 1999), 1–26; Christopher Mark, 'Tippett and the English Traditions', in *The Cambridge Companion to Michael Tippett*, ed. Nicholas Jones and Kenneth Gloag (Cambridge: Cambridge University Press 2013), 25–47.
14. For instance, in the finale of the First Piano Sonata; the 'cakewalk' rhythm is noted by Ian Kemp, *Tippett: The Composer and His Music* (London: Eulenburg and Da Capo, 1984), 137.
15. Tippett, letter to Richard Howgill, 9 May 1958, in Thomas Schuttenhelm (ed.), *Selected Letters of Michael Tippett* (London: Faber, 2005), 19; cited in Thomas Schuttenhelm, *The Orchestral Music of Michael Tippett* (Cambridge: Cambridge University Press, 2014), 122.
16. Kemp, *Tippett*, 89–90.
17. Ibid., 136.
18. Ibid., 44.
19. Ibid., 19.

20. Ursula Vaughan Williams, *RVW: A Biography of Ralph Vaughan Williams* (London: Oxford University Press, 1964), 254–55.
21. Kemp, *Tippett*, 55.
22. Neighbour, 'Ralph, Adeline and Ursula Vaughan Williams', 343; Kennedy, *The Works of Ralph Vaughan Williams*, 390.
23. Vaughan Williams, letter to Tippett, 17 December 1941; Tippett, letter to Vaughan Williams, January 1944; Cobbe, *Letters of Ralph Vaughan Williams*, 329–30, 368–69.
24. Tippett, letter to Vaughan Williams, January 1944; Cobbe, *Letters of RalphVaughan Williams*, 368.
25. Cited in Neighbour, 'Ralph, Adeline and Ursula Vaughan Williams', 344.
26. Ibid., 343.
27. Meirion Bowen (ed.), *Tippett on Music* (Oxford: Clarendon Press, 1995), 92.
28. Ibid., 92.
29. Kemp, *Tippett*, 138.
30. Bowen, *Tippett on Music*, 78.
31. Michael Tippett, *Those Twentieth-Century Blues: An Autobiography* (London: Hutchinson, 1991), 128; cited in Clarke, 'Only Half Rebelling', 10.
32. See also the passages at fig. 2 + 10 and fig. 5 + 4.
33. At the time he was composing the *Concerto*, Tippett was in touch with his friends Francesca Allinson, who was in the later stages of writing a book on the Irish influence of English folksong, and Jeffrey Mark, who had studied Scottish and Northumbrian folk music. Allinson's book—which was never published on account of her untimely death in 1945—would have challenged Cecil Sharpe's arguments about the purity of English folksongs. In the secondary literature on Tippett, Sharpe and Vaughan Williams appear to be conflated, and his connections with Allinson and Mark are viewed as a sign of Tippett distancing himself from Vaughan Williams. But Vaughan Williams's view of English folksong was not that of Sharpe, even if he admired and supported Sharpe's project. Vaughan Williams was interested in English folksong as an evolutionary phenomenon and accepted that it was changeable and variant-based. On the ambiguous influence of Jeffrey Mark on the *Concerto*, see Schuttenhelm, *Orchestral Music of Michael Tippett*, 40–41. On Allinson's project and Tippett's reactions to it, see Kemp, *Tippett*, 69–70; Clarke, 'Only Half Rebelling', 3–30.
34. Michael Tippett, 'The Midsummer Marriage', in Bowen, *Tippett on Music*, 185–208 (p. 188).
35. Ibid.
36. Mark, 'Tippett and the English Traditions', 32–36.
37. Tippett, 'The Midsummer Marriage', 186.
38. Kemp, *Tippett*, 240.
39. Tippett, 'The Midsummer Marriage', 185.
40. The melody of the hymn at this point is mainly inaudible on the commercial recording of *The Midsummer Marriage* conducted by Colin Davis (LP Philips 6703.027 (1971), CD reissue Lyrita SRCD2217, 1995). The flute and horn parts that present the melody are marked *p* and 'un poco solo', and 'dolciss.', whereas the other instruments are marked *pp*. The hymn tune must have been audible at some point in the opera's performance history, as it was noticed by Kemp and by Arnold Whittall, who even remarked on the chorale-prelude topic. Kemp, *Tippett*, 277; Whittall, *The Music of Britten and Tippett*, 2nd ed. (Cambridge: Cambridge University Press, 1990), 140.
41. A few pages earlier, during the Fire Dance there is an ecstatic canon at the octave for Mark and Jennifer, as they sing the praise of fertility. The melodic vocal style here differs from Vaughan Williams's round-singing passages, being more Purcellian than Vaughan Williams ever was or wanted to be.
42. Meirion Bowen notes the chorale-prelude topic in the 'Intrada'. *Michael Tippett* (London: Robson Books Ltd., 1997), 63.
43. Ibid., 67–68.
44. Meirion Bowen suggests the finale of Corelli's Christmas Concerto, but this allusion seems relatively distant. Ibid., 158.
45. The 6/8 metre is, however, difficult to discern in most performances. The composer said that the 'alla pastorale' was 'in characteristic siciliano rhythm'. 'The Score', in Bowen, *Tippett on Music*, 259–68 (p. 264). Bowen notes that the rhythm is easily lost in slow performances. *Michael Tippett*, 158.
46. Tippett, 'The Score' in Bowen, in Bowen, *Tippett on Music*, 265.

47. Anthony Pople, who tries to make sense of the Corelli Fantasia through the teaching methods of R. O. Morris, breaks off his analysis quite early in the piece and never gets as far as the 'alla pastorale'. 'From Pastiche to Free Composition: R. O. Morris, Tippett, and the Development of Pitch Resources in the *Fantasia Concertante on a Theme of Corelli*', in David Clarke (ed.), *Tippett Studies* (Cambridge: Cambridge University Press, 1999), 27–57.
48. On Rubbra's choral music, see Ralph Scott Grover, *The Music of Edmund Rubbra* (Aldershot: Scolar Press, 1993), Chapter 9 ('The Choral Music'), 382–508; Stephen Town, *An Imperishable Heritage: British Choral Music from Parry to Dyson: A Study of Selected Works* (Farnham: Ashgate, 2021), Chapter 9 ('Symphony No. 9, Sinfonia Sacra') by Edmund Rubbra', 217–46 and Chapter 10 ('*The Morning Watch*, Op. 55 by Edmund Rubbra'), 247–61.
49. See Heather Wiebe, *Britten's Unquiet Pasts: Sound and Memory in Postwar Reconstruction* (Cambridge: Cambridge University Press, 2012), 11, 16–24, 42.
50. Tippett, quoted by Meirion Bowen, on the liner notes to the recording of *The Rose Lake*. *The Rose Lake* and *The Vision of St Augustine*, Conifer Records Ltd (BMG) 75605 51304 2 (1997), 5; cited in Mark, 'Tippett and the English Traditions', 45.

Bibliography

Acworth, H. A., and Thomson, Herbert. *Caractacus. A Cantata. The Words Written for Music by H. A. Acworth, C.I.E. The Music by Edward Elgar (Op. 35). Book of Words with Analytical Notes by Herbert Thompson.* Novello's Series of the Words of Oratorios, Cantatas, &c. London: Novello, n.d. [?1900].

Adams, Byron. 'Musical Cenotaph: Howells's *Hymnus paradisi* and Sites of Mourning'. In *The Music of Herbert Howells*, ed. Phillip A. Cooke and David Maw, 285–308. Woodbridge: Boydell, 2013.

Adams, Byron. (ed.). *Edward Elgar and His World*. Princeton, NJ: Princeton University Press, 2007.

Adams, Byron and Wells, Robin (eds.). *Vaughan Williams Essays*. Aldershot: Ashgate, 2003.

Agawu, V. Kofi. *Playing with Signs: A Semiotic Interpretation of Classic Music*. Princeton, NJ: Princeton University Press, 1991.

Allanbrook, Wye Jamison. *Rhythmic Gesture in Mozart: 'Le nozze di Figaro' and 'Don Giovanni'*. Chicago: University of Chicago Press, 1983.

Allis, Michael. *British Music and Literary Context: Artistic Connections in the Long Nineteenth Century*. Woodbridge: Boydell, 2021.

Allis, Michael. *Parry's Creative Process*. Aldershot: Ashgate, 2003.

Allis, Michael and Watt, Paul (eds.). *The Symphonic Poem in Britain*. Woodbridge: Boydell, 2020.

Atkinson, Peter. *Regeneration and Re-enchantment: British Music and Wagnerism, 1880-1920.* PhD dissertation, University of Birmingham, 2017.

Banfield, Stephen. *Sensibility and English Song: Critical Studies of the Early Twentieth Century*. Cambridge: Cambridge University Press, 1985.

Banfield, Stephen. 'Elgar's Counterpoint: Three of a Kind'. *Musical Times* 140 (1999): 29–37.

Banfield, Stephen. *Gerald Finzi: An English Composer*. 2nd ed. London: Faber, 2008.

Banfield, Stephen and Temperley, Nicholas. 'The Legacy of Sebastian Wesley'. In *Music and the Wesleys*, ed. Stephen Banfield and Nicholas Temperley, 216–29. Urbana, Chicago and Springfield: University of Illinois Press, 2010.

Beaven, Brad. *Visions of Empire: Patriotism, Popular Culture and the City 1870-1939*. Manchester: Manchester University Press, 2012.

Bebbington, David W. *Evangelicalism in Modern Britain: A History from the 1730s to the 1980s.* London: Routledge, 1993.

Benoliel, Bernard. *Parry before Jerusalem: Studies of his Life and Music with Excerpts from his Published Writings*. Aldershot: Ashgate, 1997.

Bixby, Philip. *'The Landscape Is Empty': The Lateness of Pastoral Conventions in the Music of Frank Bridge, Gustav Holst, and Ralph Vaughan Williams, 1910-1930*. Master of Fine Arts dissertation. University of California, Irvine. 2019.

Blevins, Pamela. *Ivor Gurney and Marion Scott: Song of Pain and Beauty*. Woodbridge: Boydell, 2008.

Bowen, Meirion (ed.). *Tippett on Music*. Oxford: Clarendon Press, 1995.

Bridge, Frederick. *A Westminster Pilgrim*. London: Novello, 1918.

Brittan, Francesca. 'On Microscopic Hearing: Fairy Magic, Natural Science and the *Scherzo fantastique*'. *Journal of the American Musicological Society* 64/3 (2011): 527–746.

Cannadine, David. 'The Context, Performance and Meaning of Ritual: The British Monarchy and the "Invention of Tradition", c. 1820-1977'. In *The Invention of Tradition*, ed. Eric Hobsbawm and Terrence Ranger, 101–64. Cambridge: Cambridge University Press, 1983.

Caplin, William E. *Classical Form: A Theory of Formal Functions for the Instrumental Music of Haydn, Mozart and Beethoven*. New York: Oxford University Press, 1998.
Caplin, William E. 'Topics and Formal Functions: The Case of the Lament'. In *The Oxford Handbook of Topic Theory*, ed. Danuta Mirka, 415–52. New York: Oxford University Press, 2014.
Clarke, David. '"Only Half Rebelling": Tonal Strategies, Folksong and "Englishness" in Tippett's Concerto for Double String Orchestra'. In *Tippett Studies*, ed. David Clarke, 1–26. Cambridge: Cambridge University Press, 1999.
Clarke, David. *The Music and Thought of Michael Tippett: Modern Times and Metaphysics*. Cambridge: Cambridge University Press, 2001.
Cleobury, Sophie. *The Style and Development of Herbert Howells' Evening Canticle Settings*. MPhil dissertation, University of Birmingham, 2007.
Clinch, Jonathan. '"Beauty Springeth out of Naught": Interpreting the Church Music of Herbert Howells'. *British Postgraduate Musicology* 11 (2011): 1–12.
Clinch, Jonathan. 'Tunes all the Way? Romantic Modernism and the Piano Concertos of Herbert Howells'. In *The Music of Herbert Howells*, ed. Phillip A. Cooke and David Maw, 170–84. Woodbridge: Boydell, 2013.
Cobbe, Hugh (ed.). *Letters of Ralph Vaughan Williams 1895–1958*. New York: Oxford University Press, 2008.
Cohn, Richard. 'Uncanny Resemblances: Tonal Signification in the Freudian Age'. *Journal of the American Musicological Society* 57/2 (2004): 285–324.
Collins, Sarah. 'Nationalisms, Modernisms and Masculinities: Strategies of Displacement in Vaughan Williams's Reading of Walt Whitman'. *Nineteenth-Century Music Review* 14 (2017): 65–91.
Collins, Sarah (ed.). *Music and Victorian Liberalism: Composing the Liberal Subject*. Cambridge: Cambridge University Press, 2019.
Colls, Robert. *Identity of England*. Oxford: Oxford University Press, 2002.
Cooke, Phillip A. 'A "Wholly New Chapter" in Service Music: *Collegium regale* and the *Gloucester Service*'. In *The Music of Herbert Howells*, ed. Phillip A. Cooke and David Maw, 86–99. Woodbridge: Boydell, 2013.
Cowgill, Rachel, and Rushton, Julian (eds.). *Europe, Empire and Spectacle in Nineteenth-Century British Music*. Farnham: Ashgate, 2006.
Cowgill, Rachel, and Rushton, Julian. 'Canonizing Remembrance: Music for Armistice Day at the BBC, 1922–7'. *First World War Studies* 2/1 (2011): 75–107.
Crump, Jeremy. 'The Identity of English Music: The Reception of Elgar 1898–1935'. In *Englishness: Politics and Culture 1880–1920*, ed. Robert Colls and Philip Dodd, 164–90. Beckenham: Croom Helm, 1986.
Dibble, Jeremy. 'Hubert Parry and English Diatonic Dissonance'. *British Music Society Journal* 5 (1983): 58–71.
Dibble, Jeremy. 'Parry and Elgar: A New Perspective'. *Musical Times* 125 (1984): 639–43.
Dibble, Jeremy. *C. Hubert H. Parry: His Life and Music*. Oxford: Clarendon Press, 1992.
Dibble, Jeremy. 'Parry, Stanford, and Vaughan Williams: The Creation of Tradition'. In *Ralph Vaughan Williams in Perspective*, ed. Lewis Foreman, 25–47. London: Albion Press, 1998.
Dibble, Jeremy. 'Parry as Historiographer'. In *Nineteenth-Century British Music Studies* vol. 1, ed. Bennett Zon, 37–51. Aldershot: Ashgate, 1999.
Dibble, Jeremy. 'Edward Dannreuther and the Orme Square Phenomenon'. In *Music and British Culture, 1785–1914: Essays in Honour of Cyril Ehrlich*, ed. Christina Bashford and Leanne Langley, 275–98. Oxford: Oxford University Press, 2000.
Dibble, Jeremy. *Charles Villiers Stanford: Man and Musician*. Oxford: Oxford University Press, 2002.
Dibble, Jeremy. 'Parry's *Guenever*: Trauma and Catharsis'. In *King Arthur in Music*, ed. Richard Barber, 35–50. Cambridge: D. S. Brewer, 2002.
Dibble, Jeremy. *The Music of Frederick Delius: Style, Form and Ethos*. Woodbridge: Boydell, 2021.

Dineen, Murray. 'Vaughan Williams's Fifth Symphony: Ideology and Aural Tradition'. In *Vaughan Williams Essays*, ed. Byron Adams and Robin Wells, 17–27. Aldershot: Ashgate, 2003.
Elgar, Edward. *A Future for English Music and Other Lectures*, ed. Percy M. Young. London: Denis Dobson, 1968.
Evans, Peter. *The Music of Benjamin Britten*. 2nd ed. Oxford: Clarendon, 1996.
Foreman, Lewis (ed.). *From Parry to Britten: British Music in Letters 1900–1945*. London: Batsford, 1987.
Foreman, Lewis. 'A Voice in the Desert: Elgar's War Music'. In *Oh, My Horses! Elgar and the Great War*, ed. Lewis Foreman, 263–85. Rickmansworth: Elgar Editions, 2001.
Foreman, Lewis. 'John Ireland in the Concert Hall: Orchestral and Choral-Orchestral Music'. In *The John Ireland Companion*, ed. Lewis Foreman, 193–218. Woodbridge: Boydell, 2011.
Franklin, Peter. 'Sibelius in Britain'. In *The Cambridge Companion to Sibelius*, ed. Daniel M. Grimley, 182–195. Cambridge: Cambridge University Press, 2004.
Freeman, Mark. '"Splendid Display; Pompous Spectacle": Historical Pageants in Twentieth-Century Britain'. *Social History*, 38/4 (2013): 423–55.
Frogley, Alain (ed.). *Vaughan Williams Studies*. Cambridge: Cambridge University Press, 1996.
Frogley, Alain. *Vaughan Williams's Ninth Symphony*. Oxford: Oxford University Press, 2001.
Frogley, Alain. 'Rewriting the Renaissance: History, Imperialism and British Music Since 1840'. *Music & Letters* 84/2 (2003): 241–257.
Frogley, Alain and Thomson, Aidan J. (eds.). *The Cambridge Companion to Vaughan Williams*. Cambridge: Cambridge University Press, 2013.
Fuller Maitland, J. A. *English Music in the XIXth Century*. New York: E. P. Dutton; Grant Richards, 1902.
Gatens, William J. *Victorian Cathedral Music in Theory and Practice*. Cambridge: Cambridge University Press, 1986.
Ghuman, Nalini. 'Elgar and the British Raj: Can the Mughals March?' In *Edward Elgar and His World*, ed. Byron Adams, 249–85. Princeton, NJ: Princeton University Press, 2007.
Ghuman, Nalini. 'Elgar's *Pageant of Empire*, 1924: An Imperial Leitmotif'. In *Exhibiting the Empire: Cultures of Display and the British Empire*, ed. John McAleer and John MacKenzie, 220–56. Manchester: Manchester University Press, 2016.
Gjerdingen, Robert O. *Music in the Galant Style*. New York: Oxford University Press, 2007.
Gloag, Kenneth, and Jones, Nicholas (eds.). *The Cambridge Companion to Michael Tippett*. Cambridge: Cambridge University Press, 2013.
Golding, Rosemary. *Music and Academia in Victorian Britain*. Farnham: Ashgate, 2013.
Goldmark, Daniel. 'Music, Film and Vaughan Williams'. In *Vaughan Williams Essays*, ed. Byron Adams and Robin Wells, 207–33. Aldershot: Ashgate, 2003.
Greene, Harry Plunket. *Interpretation in Song*. New York: Macmillan, 1912.
Grimley, Daniel M. and Rushton, Julian (eds.). *The Cambridge Companion to Elgar*. Cambridge: Cambridge University Press, 2005.
Grimley, Daniel M. 'Music, Ice and the "Geometry of Fear": The Landscapes of Vaughan Williams's *Sinfonia Antartica*'. *Musical Quarterly* 91/1–2 (2008): 116–50.
Grimley, Daniel M. 'Landscape and Distance: Vaughan Williams and the Symphonic Pastoral'. In *British Music and Modernism 1895–1960*, ed. Matthew Riley, 147–74. Farnham: Ashgate: 2010.
Grimley, Daniel M. *Delius and the Sound of Place*. Cambridge: Cambridge University Press, 2018.
Groos, Arthur. 'Constructing Nuremberg: Typological and Proleptic Communities in *Die Meistersinger*'. *19th-Century Music* 16/1 (1992): 18–34.
Grover, Ralph Scott. *The Music of Edmund Rubbra*. Aldershot: Scolar Press, 1993.
Gunn, Simon. *The Public Culture of the Victorian Middle Class: Ritual and Authority and the English Industrial City*. Manchester: Manchester University Press, 2000.
Guthrie, Kate. 'Propaganda Music in Second World War Britain: John Ireland's "Epic March"'. *Journal of the Royal Musical Association* 139/1 (2014): 137–75.

Harper-Scott, J. P. E. '"Our True North": Walton's First Symphony, Sibelianism, and the Nationalization of Modernism in England'. *Music & Letters* 89/4 (2008): 562–89.
Heckert, Deborah. 'Working the Crowd: Elgar, Class and Reformulations of Popular Culture at the Turn of the Twentieth Century'. In *Edward Elgar and His World*, ed. Byron Adams, 287–315. Princeton, NJ: Princeton University Press, 2007.
Hepokoski, James. *Sibelius: Symphony No. 5*. Cambridge: Cambridge University Press, 1993.
Hepokoski, James. 'Gaudery, Romance and the "Welsh Tune": Introduction and Allegro, Op. 47'. In *Elgar Studies*, ed. J. P. E. Harper-Scott and Julian Rushton, 135–71. Cambridge: Cambridge University Press, 2007.
Hochstettler, Scott. '*Dona Nobis Pacem*: Vaughan Williams's Federalist Manifesto'. *The Choral Journal* 49/12 (2009): 42–52.
Hold, Trevor. *Parry to Finzi: Twenty English Song Composers*. Woodbridge: Boydell, 2002.
Horton, Peter. '"The Highest Point up to That Time Reached by the Combination of Hebrew and Christian Sentiment in Music"'. In *Nineteenth-Century British Music Studies* 3, ed. Peter Horton and Bennett Zon, 119-34. Aldershot: Ashgate, 2003.
Horton, Peter. *Samuel Sebastian Wesley: A Life*. Oxford: Oxford University Press, 2004.
Howells, Herbert. 'Vaughan Williams's "Pastoral" Symphony'. *Music & Letters* 3/2 (1922): 122–32.
Howes, Frank. *The Music of Ralph Vaughan Williams*. London: Oxford University Press, 1954.
Howes, Frank. *The English Musical Renaissance*. London: Secker & Warburg, 1966.
Hughes, Meirion, and Stradling, Robert. *The English Musical Renaissance 1840–1940: Constructing a National Music* 2nd edn. Manchester: Manchester University Press, 2001.
Hulme, Tom. '"A Nation of Town Criers": Civic Publicity and Historical Pageantry in Interwar Britain'. *Urban History* 44/2 (2017): 270–92.
IJzerman, Job. *Harmony, Counterpoint, Partimento: A New Method Inspired by Old Masters*. New York: Oxford University Press, 2018.
Jaeger, A. J. *The Dream of Gerontius: Analytical and Descriptive Notes*. Sevenoaks: Novello, 1974.
Kemp, Ian. *Tippett: The Composer and his Music*. London: Eulenburg and Da Capo, 1984.
Kennedy, Kate. 'Ambivalent Englishness: Ivor Gurney's Song Cycle Ludlow and Teme'. *First World War Studies* 2/1 (2011): 41-64.
Kennedy, Michael. *The Works of Ralph Vaughan Williams*. 2nd ed. Oxford: Oxford University Press, 1980.
Kumar, Krishan. *The Making of English National Identity*. Cambridge: Cambridge University Press, 2003.
Kuykendall, James Brooks. *The English Ceremonial Style Circa 1887–1937 and Its Aftermath*. PhD dissertation: Cornell University, 2005.
Langfield, Valerie. *Roger Quilter: His Life and Music*. Woodbridge: Boydell, 2002.
Mak, Su-Yin. 'Schubert's Sonata Forms and the Poetics of the Lyric'. *Journal of Musicology* 23/2 (2006): 263–306.
Manning, David. *Harmony, Tonality and Structure in Vaughan Williams's Music*. PhD dissertation, University of Bristol, 2003.
Manning, David. (ed.). *Vaughan Williams on Music*. New York: Oxford University Press, 2008.
Mark, Christopher. 'Tippett and the English Traditions'. In *The Cambridge Companion to Michael Tippett*, ed. Kenneth Gloag and Nicholas Jones, 25–47. Cambridge: Cambridge University Press 2013.
Martin, David. 'The Sound of England'. In *Nationalism and Ethnosymbolism: History, Culture and Ethnicity in the Formation of Nations*, ed. Steven Grosby and Athena S. Leoussi, 68–83. Edinburgh: Edinburgh University Press, 2007.
Maw, David. 'Introduction: Paradox of an Establishment Composer'. In *The Music of Herbert Howells*, ed. Phillip A. Cooke and David Maw, 1–7. Woodbridge: Boydell, 2013.
Maw, David. '"I Am a 'Modern' in This, but a Britisher Too": Howells and the Phantasy'. In *The Music of Herbert Howells*, ed. Phillip A. Cooke and David Maw, 185–221. Woodbridge: Boydell, 2013.

McGuire, Charles Edward. *Elgar's Oratorios: The Creation of an Epic Narrative*. Aldershot: Ashgate, 2002.
McGuire, Charles Edward. 'Vaughan Williams and the English Music Festival: 1910'. In *Vaughan Williams Essays*, ed. Byron Adams and Robin Wells, 235–68. Aldershot: Ashgate, 2003.
McVeagh, Diana. *Gerald Finzi: His Life and Music*. Woodbridge: Boydell, 2005.
Mellers, Wilfrid. *Vaughan Williams and the Vision of Albion*. 2nd ed. London: Pimlico, 1991.
Monelle, Raymond. *The Musical Topic: Hunt, Military and Pastoral*. Bloomington: Indiana University Press, 2006.
Moore, Jerrold Northrop. *Edward Elgar: A Creative Life*. New York: Oxford University Press, 1984.
Neighbour, Oliver. 'Ralph, Adeline and Ursula Vaughan Williams: Some Facts and Speculation (with a Note about Tippett)'. *Music & Letters* 89/3 (2008): 337–45.
Newbould, Brian. 'Elgar and Academicism 1: The Untutored Genius'. *Musical Times* 146 (2005): 71–84.
Newbould, Brian. 'Elgar and Academicism 2: Practice beyond Theory'. *Musical Times* 146 (2005): 25–41.
Newman, Gerald. *The Rise of English Nationalism: A Cultural History, 1720-1830*. New York: St. Martin's Press, 1997.
Onderdonk, Julian. 'Hymn Tunes from Folk-Songs: Vaughan Williams and English Hymnody'. In *Vaughan Williams Essays*, ed. Byron Adams and Robin Wells, 103–28. Aldershot: Ashgate, 2003.
Onderdonk, Julian. 'Folksong Arrangements, Hymn Tunes and Church Music'. *The Cambridge Companion to Vaughan Williams*, ed. Alain Frogley and Aidan J. Thomson, 136–56. Cambridge: Cambridge University Press, 2013.
Ottaway, Hugh. 'Vaughan Williams's Symphony in D and "The Pilgrim's Progress": A Comparative Note'. *Musical Times* 94 (October 1953): 456–58.
Otto, Rudolph. *The Idea of the Holy*. Trans. John W. Harvey. Oxford: Oxford University Press, 1924.
Owen, Ceri. *Vaughan Williams, Song, and the Idea of 'Englishness'*. PhD thesis. Oxford University, 2014.
Owen, Ceri. 'Making an English Voice: Performing National Identity during the English Musical Renaissance'. *Twentieth-Century Music* 13/1 (2016): 77–107.
Owen, Ceri. 'On Singing and Listening in Vaughan Williams's Early Songs'. *19th-Century Music* 40/3 (2017): 257–82.
Palmer, Christopher. *Herbert Howells: A Study*. Borough Green: Novello, 1978.
Palmer, Christopher. *Herbert Howells (1892-1983): A Celebration*. 2nd ed. London: Thames Publishing, 1996.
Parry, C. Hubert H. *Studies of Great Composers*. London: G. Routledge and Sons, 1887.
Parry, C. Hubert H. *The Evolution of the Art of Music*. New York: Greenwood Press, 1896.
Parry, C. Hubert H. *Johann Sebastian Bach*. London: G. P. Putnam's Songs, 1910.
Pople, Anthony. 'From Pastiche to Free Composition: R. O. Morris, Tippett, and the Development of Pitch Resources in the *Fantasia Concertante on a Theme of Corelli*'. In *Tippett Studies*, ed. David Clarke, 27–57. Cambridge: Cambridge University Press, 1999.
Porter, Bernard. 'Elgar and Empire: Music, Nationalism and the War'. In *Oh, My Horses! Elgar and the Great War*, ed. Lewis Foreman, 133–73. Rickmansworth: Elgar Editions, 2001.
Range, Matthias. *Music and Ceremonial at British Coronations*. Cambridge: Cambridge University Press, 2012.
Ratner, Leonard G. *Classic Music: Expression, Form and Style*. New York: Schirmer, 1980.
Rawling, Eleanor. 'Walking into Clarity: the Dynamics of Self and Place in the Poetry of Ivor Gurney'. *GeoHumanities* 2/2 (2016): 509–22.
Redwood, Christopher (ed.). *An Elgar Companion*. Ashbourne: Sequoia and Moorland, 1984.
Reed, W. H. *Elgar*. London: Dent, 1939.
Revill, George. 'The Lark Ascending: Vaughan Williams's Monument to a Radical Pastoral'. *Landscape Research* 16/2 (1991): 25–30.

Richards, Fiona. *The Music of John Ireland*. Aldershot: Ashgate, 2000.
Richards, Jeffrey. 'Vaughan Williams and British Wartime Cinema'. In *Vaughan Williams Studies*, ed. Alain Frogley, 139–65. Cambridge: Cambridge University Press, 1996.
Richards, Jeffrey. *Films and British National Identity: From Dickens to Dad's Army*. Manchester and New York: Manchester University Press, 1997.
Richards, Jeffrey. *Imperialism and Music: Britain 1876–1953*. Manchester: Manchester University Press, 2001.
Riley, Matthew. 'Rustling Reeds and Lofty Pines: Elgar and the Music of Nature'. *19th-Century Music* 26/2 (2002): 155–77.
Riley, Matthew. *Edward Elgar and the Nostalgic Imagination*. Cambridge: Cambridge University Press, 2007.
Riley, Matthew. 'Heroic Melancholy: Elgar's Inflected Diatonicism'. In *Elgar Studies*, ed. J. P. E. Harper-Scott and Julian Rushton, 284–307. Cambridge: Cambridge University Press, 2007.
Riley, Matthew. *British Music and Modernism, 1895–1960*. Farnham: Ashgate, 2010.
Riley, Matthew. 'Liberal Critics and Modern Music in the Post-Victorian Age'. In *British Music and Modernism, 1895–1960*, ed. Matthew Riley, 13–30. Farnham: Ashgate, 2010.
Riley, Matthew and Anthony D. Smith, *Nation and Classical Music: From Handel to Copland*. Woodbridge: Boydell, 2016.
Rimbault, Edward F. *The Rounds, Catches, and Canons of England; a Collection of Specimens of the Sixteenth, Seventeenth, and Eighteenth Centuries Adapted to Modern Use*. London: Cramer, Wood & Company, date unknown, c. 1870.
Roberts, Ben. 'Entertaining the Community: The Evolution of Civic Ritual and Public Celebration, 1860–1953'. *Urban History* 8/31 (2016): 1–20.
Rockstro, W. S. 'Sumer is icumen in'. In *Grove's Dictionary of Music and Musicians*, ed. J.A. Fuller Maitland, Vol. IV, 747–54. London: Macmillan, 1908.
Rodmell, Paul. *Charles Villiers Stanford*. Aldershot: Ashgate, 2002.
Rupprecht, Philip. *Britten's Musical Language*. Cambridge: Cambridge University Press, 2001.
Rupprecht, Philip (ed.). *Rethinking Britten*. New York: Oxford University Press, 2013.
Rushton, Julian. *Elgar: 'Enigma' Variations*. Cambridge: Cambridge University Press, 1999.
Rushton, Julian. 'Musicking *Caractacus*'. In *Music and Performance Culture in Nineteenth-Century Britain: Essays in Honour of Nicholas Temperley*, ed. Bennett Zon (ed.), 221-40. Farnham: Ashgate, 2012.
Ryan, Deborah S. 'Staging the Imperial City: The Pageant of London, 1911'. In *Imperial Cities: Landscape, Display and Identity*, ed. Felix Driver and David Gilbert, 117–35. Manchester: Manchester University Press, 1999.
Ryan, Deborah S. '"Pageantitis": Frank Lascelles' 1907 Oxford Historical Pageant, Visual Spectacle and Popular Memory'. *Visual Culture in Britain*, 8/ 2 (2007): 63–82.
Sanguinetti, Giorgio. *The Art of Partimento: History, Theory, and Practice*. New York: Oxford University Press, 2012.
Savage, Roger. *Masques, Mayings and Music-Dramas: Vaughan Williams and the Early Twentieth-Century Stage*. Woodbridge: Boydell, 2014.
Savage, Roger. *The Pre-History of 'The Midsummer Marriage': Narratives and Speculations*. London: Routledge, 2020.
Saylor, Eric. '"It's Not Lambkins Frisking At All": English Pastoral Music and the Great War'. *Musical Quarterly* 91/1–2 (2008): 39–59.
Saylor, Eric and Scheer, Christopher M. (eds.). *The Sea in the British Musical Imagination*, Woodbridge: Boydell, 2015.
Saylor, Eric and Scheer, Christopher M. 'Political Visions, National Identities, and the Sea Itself: Stanford and Vaughan Williams in 1910'. In *The Sea in the British Musical Imagination*, ed. Eric Saylor and Christopher M. Scheer, 205–224. Woodbridge: Boydell, 2015.
Saylor, Eric and Scheer, Christopher M. *English Pastoral Music: From Arcadia to Utopia, 1900–1955*. Urbana: University of Illinois Press, 2017.

Scheer, Christopher. 'For the Sake of the Union: The Nation in Stanford's Fourth Irish Rhapsody'. In *Europe, Empire and Spectacle in Nineteenth-Century British Music*, ed. Rachel Cowgill and Julian Rushton, 159–70. Farnham: Ashgate, 2006.

Scheer, Christopher. 'A Direct and Intimate Realization: Holst and Formalism in the 1920s'. In *British Music and Modernism, 1895–1960*, ed. Matthew Riley, 109–24. Farnham: Ashgate, 2010.

Schuttenhelm, Thomas, ed. *Selected Letters of Michael Tippett*. London: Faber, 2005.

Schuttenhelm, Thomas. *The Orchestral Music of Michael Tippett*. Cambridge: Cambridge University Press, 2014.

Smith, Anthony D. *Chosen Peoples: Sacred Sources of National Identity*. New York: Oxford University Press, 2003.

Smith, Anthony D. *The Cultural Foundations of Nations: Hierarchy, Covenant, and Republic*. Oxford: Blackwell, 2008.

Soden, Oliver. *Michael Tippett: The Biography*. London: Weidenfeldt & Nicholson, 2019.

Spicer, Paul. *Herbert Howells*. Bridgend: Seren, 1998.

Spicer, Paul. 'Howells's Use of the Melisma: Word Setting in his Songs and Choral Music'. In *The Music of Herbert Howells*, ed. Phillip A. Cooke and David Maw, 100–15. Woodbridge: Boydell, 2013.

Squire, William Barclay. 'Round'. In *Grove's Dictionary of Music and Musicians*, ed. J.A. Fuller Maitland, Vol. IV, 165–66. London: Macmillan, 1908.

Stanford, Charles Villiers. *Musical Composition*. New York: Macmillan, 1911.

Stanford, Charles Villiers. *Pages from an Unwritten Diary*. London: Edward Arnold, 1914.

Stanford, Charles Villiers. *Interludes, Records and Reflections*. London: John Murray, 1922.

Stern, David. '"One Thought Grows out of Another": Sibelius's Influence on Ralph Vaughan Williams's Fifth Symphony'. In *Sibelius in the Old and New Worlds: Aspects of his Music, Its Interpretation, and Reception*, ed. Timothy L. Jackson, Veijo Murtomäki, Colin Davis, and Timo Virtanen, 383–400. Frankfurt am Main: Lang, 2010.

Stradling, Robert. 'On Shearing the Black Sheep in Spring: The Repatriation of Frederick Delius'. In *Music and the Politics of Culture*, ed. Christopher Norris, 69–105. London: Lawrence & Wishart, 1989.

Stradling, Robert. 'England's Glory: Sensibilities of Place in English Music, 1900–1950'. In *The Place of Music*, ed. Andrew Leyshon, David Matless and George Revill, 176–96. New York: Guilford Press, 1998.

Thomson, Aidan J. 'Elgar and Chivalry'. *19th-Century Music* 28/3 (2005): 254–75.

Thomson, Aidan J. 'Elgar and the City: The *Cockaigne* Overture and Contributions of Modernity'. *Musical Quarterly* 96/2 (2013): 219–62.

Tippett, Michael. *Those Twentieth-Century Blues: An Autobiography*. London: Hutchinson, 1991.

Town, Stephen. '"Full of Fresh Thoughts": Vaughan Williams, Whitman and the Genesis of *A Sea Symphony*'. In *Vaughan Williams Essays*, ed. Byron Adams and Robin Wells, 73–101. Aldershot: Ashgate, 2003.

Town, Stephen. *An Imperishable Heritage: British Choral Music from Parry to Dyson: A Study of Selected Works*. Farnham: Ashgate, 2021.

Vaillancourt, Michael. 'Modal and Thematic Coherence in Vaughan Williams's *Pastoral Symphony*'. *Music Review* 52 (1991): 1–22.

Vaughan Williams, Ralph. 'Preface' to *The English Hymnal*. London: Oxford University Press, 1906.

Vaughan Williams, Ralph. *National Music and Other Essays*. 2nd ed. Oxford: Oxford University Press, 1987.

Vaughan Williams, Ralph and Holst, Gustav. *Heirs and Rebels: Letters Written to Each Other and Occasional Writings on Music by Ralph Vaughan Williams and Gustav Holst*. Ed. Ursula Vaughan Williams and Imogen Holst. London: Oxford University Press, 1959.

Vaughan Williams, Ursula. *Ralph Vaughan Williams: A Biography*. London: Oxford University Press, 1964.

Weliver, Phyllis. 'The Parrys and *Prometheus Unbound*: Actualizing Liberalism'. *Music and Victorian Liberalism: Composing the Liberal Subject*, ed. Sarah Collins, 151–79. Cambridge: Cambridge University Press, 2019.

Whittall, Arnold. *The Music of Britten and Tippett: Studies in Themes and Techniques*. 2nd ed. Cambridge: Cambridge University Press, 1990.

Whittall, Arnold. 'Symphony in D Major: Models and Mutations'. In *Vaughan Williams Studies*, ed. Alain Frogley, 187–212. Cambridge: Cambridge University Press, 1996.

Whittall, Arnold. *British Music after Britten*. Woodbridge: Boydell, 2022.

Wiebe, Heather. *Britten's Unquiet Pasts: Sound and Memory in Postwar Reconstruction*. Cambridge: Cambridge University Press, 2012.

Winter, Jay. *Sites of Memory, Sites of Mourning: The Great War in European Cultural History*. Cambridge: Cambridge University Press, 1998.

Wright, David. 'Sir Frederick Bridge and the Musical Furtherance of the 1902 Imperial Project'. In *Europe, Empire and Spectacle in Nineteenth-Century British Music*, ed. Rachel Cowgill and Julian Rushton, 115–29. Aldershot: Ashgate, 2006.

Yoshino, Ayako. *Pageant Fever: Local History and Consumerism in Edwardian England*. Tokyo: Waseda University Press, 2011.

Zon, Bennett. *Music and Metaphor in Nineteenth-Century British Musicology*. Aldershot: Ashgate, 2000.

Zon, Bennett. 'From Great Man to Fittest Survivor: Reputation, Recapitulation and Survival in Victorian Concepts of Wagner's Genius'. *Musicæ Scientæ*, 13/2 (September 2009): 415–45.

Zon, Bennett (ed.). *Music and Performance Culture in Nineteenth-Century Britain: Essays in Honour of Nicholas Temperley*. Farnham: Ashgate, 2012.

Zon, Bennett. *Evolution and Victorian Musical Culture*. Cambridge: Cambridge University Press, 2017.

Index

For the benefit of digital users, indexed terms that span two pages (e.g., 52–53) may, on occasion, appear on only one of those pages.

Bach, Johann Sebastian, 4–5, 8–9, 53–55, 75, 107, 154–55, 190–91, 213–14, 224–25, 260–61, 264
Barnby, Joseph, 14–15
Bax, Sir Arnold, 37–38, 40, 51, 125–26, 150–51, 179–80, 181–82, 188
Beethoven, Ludwig van, 9, 22–23, 25, 57, 75, 90, 200, 201–3, 214–15, 224–25, 243–44, 253, 260–61
Bliss, Sir Arthur, 37–38, 179–80, 253
Bridge, Sir Frederick, 41–42, 89, 181
Britten, Benjamin, 253, 264–65
Butterworth, George, 47, 127–28, 129–30, 131–35, 145, 146–50, 151–54, 155–59, 161–67, 177, 181–82

Debussy, Claude, 94–95, 98–99, 124–25, 132–33, 134–35, 147–49, 237–38
Delius, Frederick, 6–7, 91–92, 124–26, 150–51, 233–34
Dykes, John Bacchus, 14–15, 107, 190–91

Elgar, Sir Edward, 2, 4, 5–6, 11–12, 13–14, 17–19, 24–25, 27–28, 29–33, 36–45, 46–75, 77–82, 86–87, 90, 98, 109–11, 116–17, 127–28, 129–33, 134–35, 136–45, 147–49, 150, 156–58, 159–61, 162–63, 166–68, 171–76, 177, 178–79, 181–82, 183–86, 188, 190–91, 197–98, 203–5, 207–12, 215–16, 217, 222, 241–42, 243–44, 248–50, 252–53, 262, 263–64
Apostles, The, 47, 58–63, 70–72, 80–82, 86, 87, 109–11, 140–42, 145, 171, 204–5, 207–10
Caractacus, 13–14, 41, 47–48, 53–58, 60–61, 63–64, 140–42, 144–45, 198
Chanson de Matin, 136
Cockaigne, 50–51, 63–66, 78, 222
Crown of India, The, 48–49, 53–55
Dream of Gerontius The, 38–39, 41, 58–62, 77–78, 86, 109–11, 207–10, 248–50
'Enigma' Variations, 29–31, 36–37, 41, 57, 58, 63–66, 72–75, 77–78, 87, 171, 181–82, 197–98, 204–5, 209, 222

Empire March, 48, 49–50, 51–53
Grania and Diarmud, 51–53
Imperial March, 40, 41, 48, 49–50, 51–53, 181–82
Introduction and Allegro, 63–64, 68–70, 253, 262
Kingdom, The, 58–61, 63
'Land of Hope and Glory', 5–6, 31, 40–41, 42–43, 48, 49–50, 86
Music Makers, The, 23–26, 31, 57
Organ Sonata, 36–37, 64–66
Pomp and Circumstance Marches, 13–14, 31, 40–41, 42–43, 48, 51–53, 78, 181–82, 183, 184, 186–87, 197–98
Sea Pictures, 31–33, 78, 80–82, 86, 137–40, 204
Symphony No. 1 31, 70–72, 197–98
Symphony No. 2 51–53, 63–64, 204
Evolutionism, 4–5, 16–18, 20–23, 25–26, 46, 76–77, 82, 89, 96–98, 105–7, 118–22, 123, 145, 181, 216–17, 224–25, 252–53, 256, 257–58

Finzi, Gerald, 2, 6–7, 11–12, 17, 18–19, 36–38, 91, 109–11, 127–32, 133–35, 140–44, 145, 146, 147–49, 151–52, 156–77, 179–80, 182, 205–12, 237–38, 248–50, 254, 263–64
Before and After Summer, 160–62, 167–69, 171–73
By Footpath and Style, 133–35, 161–62, 167
Earth and Air and Rain, 161–62, 167–71, 173–77
For St Cecilia, 158, 179–80, 182, 205–9
Intimations of Immortality, 109–11, 179, 182, 205–6, 209–12, 248–50
'Oh Fair to See', 164–66, 173–76
'Only the Wanderer', 154–55, 163–66, 171–76
Requiem da Camera, 163–64, 167
Romance for String Orchestra, 159–60, 207–9
Severn Rhapsody, A, 163–64

Gurney Ivor, 2, 6–7, 8–9, 11–12, 91, 103–4, 127–36, 140–42, 145, 146, 147–58, 163–64, 166–67, 168, 177, 263–64

INDEX

Holst, Gustav, 7–8, 36–38, 160, 181–82, 189, 207–10, 234–35, 237–38, 252–53, 264
Howells, Herbert
  Fantasy String Quartet, 92–93, 94
  Hymnus paradisi, 104, 109–11, 125–26, 209–10, 228–29, 230–34, 238–41
  Magnificat and nunc dimittis (Collegium regale), 227–28, 236–37
  Piano Quartet, 92–93, 99–101, 103–4
  Rhapsodic Quintet, 92–93, 98–101, 104
  Te Deum (Collegium regale), 227–28, 230–33, 234, 237–38

Ireland, John, 2, 11–12, 29–31, 36–38, 47, 129–30, 133–36, 142–45, 159–60, 179–80, 181–83, 186–88, 199–200, 203–5, 207–9
  'Blow Out, You Bugles', 142–44
  Epic March, 179–80, 181–82, 186–88
  Greater Love Hath No Man, 47
  'If There Were Dreams to Sell', 142–44
  'Ladslove', 145
  These Things Shall Be, 29–31, 140–44, 179–80, 182, 186, 187–88, 199–200, 203–5

Maconchy, Elizabeth, 2, 265–66
Mathias, William, 265–66
McCabe, John, 265–66

Parry, Sir Charles Hubert Hastings, 1, 4, 5–6, 7–9, 11–45, 46–53, 64–66, 72, 75–80, 82–84, 86–87, 89, 90, 91, 94–95, 98, 107, 109–11, 116–17, 123, 127–44, 145, 146, 147–50, 152, 154–55, 156–60, 161–62, 163–64, 166–68, 169–76, 177, 179, 181–82, 183, 184–86, 187–88, 189, 191–96, 199, 204, 205–13, 215–16, 226, 227, 228–29, 237–38, 243–44, 250, 253, 262, 263–64, 266
  Blest Pair of Sirens, 1, 5–7, 9–10, 11–12, 13–14, 17–19, 20–23, 25–38, 40–41, 42–44, 45, 47–48, 51, 55, 63–64, 70, 75, 77, 80–82, 83–84, 86, 87, 89, 104, 131–32, 138–40, 150–51, 158, 167–68, 179–80, 184–86, 191, 196–97, 199, 204–5, 206–9, 228–29, 237–41
  'Bridal March' (*The Birds*), 18–19, 41
  Chorale Preludes, 36–37, 107, 154–55
  De Profundis, 18–19
  Glories of our Blood and State, The, 18–19, 75
  I Was Glad, 11–12, 13–14, 40–43, 44, 83–84, 109–11, 181–82
  Jerusalem, 5–6, 11–12, 36–37, 40–41, 42–43, 47–48, 49–50, 70–72, 78–79, 86, 179, 181–82, 189–94, 215–16

  Prometheus Unbound, 20, 25–26, 194–96, 199
  Songs of Farewell, 40–41, 109–11, 229
  Symphony No. 3 ('English'), 43–45
  Three Chorale Fantasias, 36–37, 107

Quilter, Roger, 2, 129–31, 135–36, 140–42, 145

Ravel, Maurice, 94–95, 98–99, 132–33, 134–35, 244–45, 256–57
Rubbra, Edmund, 109–11, 264
Rutter, Sir John, 264

Sentimentality, 15–16, 76–77, 131, 135–36, 137–38, 145, 150, 200, 254
Stainer, John, 25, 29–31, 36–37, 41–42, 66, 190–91
Stanford, Sir Charles Villiers, 12, 14–15, 18–19, 24–25, 41–42, 75–77, 130–31, 149, 150, 167–68, 229

Tippett, Sir Michael, 1, 2, 9–10, 214, 226, 227, 243–66
  Concerto for Double String Orchestra, 243–44, 247–50, 253–55, 261–62, 265–66
  Fantasia Concertante on a Theme of Corelli, 243, 245, 255–56, 261–62, 265–66
  Midsummer Marriage, The, 1, 9–10, 226, 243, 244–45, 248–50, 255–61, 262
  Piano Concerto, 243, 246, 255–56
  Ritual Dances, 243–45, 256–58, 265–66
  Rose Lake, The, 266

Vaughan Williams, Ralph, 2, 3–4, 5–9, 11–12, 14–19, 20, 29–31, 36–38, 42–43, 45, 46–47, 58–60, 75–89, 90–93, 94, 96–101, 104–26, 129–31, 132–35, 138–45, 146, 147–50, 151–53, 154–56, 158–60, 162–63, 166–68, 177, 179–80, 181–83, 184–86, 187–203, 205–6, 207–10, 212–25, 226, 230, 233–35, 237–38, 242–44, 247–48, 253, 254–55, 257–62, 263–64, 265–66
  Dona nobis pacem, 182, 189–90, 196, 198–204, 213–14, 215, 216–17, 248–50
  English Hymnal, The, 15, 79–80, 188–89, 190–91, 213–14, 220–21
  Fantasia on a Theme by Thomas Tallis, 91, 123–24, 207–9, 234–35, 250–52, 253, 261–62
  Five Mystical Songs, 58–60, 79–80, 87, 89, 92–93, 104–5, 116–17, 138–40, 190–91, 196–97, 235, 242–43
  Flos Campi, 90, 92–93, 104, 108–9, 113–16, 123, 125–26, 163, 189–90, 216–17, 220–21, 223–24, 242–43, 262

Four Hymns, 92–93, 104
House of Life, The, 79–80, 104, 138–40
In the Fen Country, 79–80
Lark Ascending, The, 3–4, 90–93, 104, 108–9, 116–25, 220–21, 247–48, 257–58, 262
Linden Lea, 105–7, 150
London Symphony, A, 108–9, 189–90, 220–21, 248–52, 257–58
On Wenlock Edge, 92–93, 130–31, 132–34, 152–53, 155
Pastoral Symphony, A, 90, 92–93, 94, 97–98, 99–101, 113–15, 116, 123–24, 125–26, 158–60, 162–63, 164–66, 177, 248–52
Sancta civitas, 104–5, 109–11, 153–54, 209–10, 235
Sea Symphony, A, 29–31, 37–38, 58–60, 75–76, 77–78, 79–80, 82–87, 109, 114–15, 138–40, 184–86, 189–90, 191, 198–99, 200, 217, 220–21
Serenade to Music, 109, 182, 209–10, 262
Shepherds of the Delectable Mountains, The, 90, 92–93, 104, 109–14, 115, 123, 194–96, 222
Sinfonia Antartica, 125–26
Six Songs to be Sung in Time of War, 5–6, 188–89, 194–99, 216–17
Songs of Travel, 79–80, 130–31, 138–40
Symphony No. 5 3–4, 108–9, 125–26, 179, 190–91, 196, 212–25, 257–60, 262, 265–66
Three Preludes Founded on Welsh Hymn Tunes, 107
Toward the Unknown Region, 75–76, 79–83, 84, 87, 199

Wagner, Richard, 4–6, 8–9, 12, 13–14, 15–16, 17, 22–27, 31–33, 38–39, 41–43, 47–48, 51, 55, 60–61, 70–72, 75, 90, 92–93, 137–38, 155, 179, 191–94, 201, 237–38, 241–42, 243–44, 256–57
Die Meistersinger von Nürnberg, 13–14, 23–27, 31–33, 37–38, 51, 80–82, 87, 137–38, 222, 237–38
Götterdämmerung, 23
Parsifal, 5–6, 13–14, 23–24, 25–26, 27–28, 42–43, 70–72, 82–83, 87, 189, 190–94, 196–97, 241–42
Siegfried, 24, 243–44
Siegfried Idyll, 25
Tristan und Isolde, 15–16, 24, 25
Walton, Sir William, 2, 11–12, 19–20, 35–36, 37–38, 40, 179–80, 181–82, 183–86, 188, 203–4, 205–6, 217–20, 237–38
Crown Imperial, 13–14, 29–31, 35–36, 179–80, 181–82, 183–86, 187–88, 203–4, 237–38
Spitfire Prelude and Fugue, 179–80, 184–86, 217–20
Wesley, Samuel Sebastian, 2, 13–15, 19–22, 33–35, 36–37, 41–42, 66, 70–72, 76, 79–80, 134, 181–82, 190–91, 207, 229, 237–38